The Art of Being In-between

The Art of Being In-between

NATIVE INTERMEDIARIES, INDIAN IDENTITY, AND LOCAL RULE IN COLONIAL OAXACA

YANNA YANNAKAKIS

Duke University Press | Durham and London | 2008

© 2008 Duke University Press

All rights reserved

Printed in the United States of
America on acid-free paper ∞

Designed by Heather Hensley

Typeset in Warnock Pro by
Keystone Typesetting, Inc.

Library of Congress Cataloging-
in-Publication Data appear on the
last printed page of this book.

For Aiden

and Marianna,

my fellow travelers

and storytellers

Contents

Preface

The adage "many Mexicos,"[1] which recognizes the nation's wide-ranging regional differences, could be modified to apply to the southern Mexican state of Oaxaca. Oaxaca's indigenous groups speak fifteen languages,[2] the most of any state in Mexico. The "many Oaxacas" of one of Mexico's poorest states typify the puzzle of Mexican nationhood and its colonial antecedent: How can a state—colonial or modern—govern a territory characterized by such a plurality of ethnic groups?

The Sierra Norte of Oaxaca encompasses the region from the top of the Sierra Madre north of Oaxaca City to the coastal plains of the Gulf of Mexico, an area far removed from the bustling commercial activity of the Valley of Oaxaca. From the top of the first range of mountains to the Zapotec Rincón (corner), seemingly unending chains of lush slopes and valleys unfold toward the horizon and Veracruz. The dwellings, churches, and municipal plazas of the region's indigenous communities cluster in pockets and saddles two-thirds of the way up the mountains. The cultivated land, where Serranos grow coffee, corn, beans, bananas, and mangoes, stretches across the mountains' shoulders, and intermittently down toward gorges and valleys whose steep grades obscure the view of the rushing water that cuts through them.

Here, at first glance, one finds a fabled "land that time forgot." Indeed, the people of Oaxaca's central valleys consider the people of the Sierra Norte to be traditional to a fault in their lifeways and worldview. The sierra is a repository of "tradition" and "Indian custom" in the imagination of the valley citizenry, much the way that the state of Oaxaca stands in for an authentic and nostalgic "Indian" Mexico in the eyes of the thousands of visitors who stream into Oaxaca City from Mexico City and other "modern" urban centers to purchase handicrafts in colorful regional markets and experience the Day of the Dead or Holy Week in their most folkloric guises. This problematic juxtaposition between a "modern" Mexico and a "traditional," "Indian" Mexico is a central tension in Mexican national identity, a tension that has become more pronounced in the last two decades and has situated "Indian" regions like Chiapas and Oaxaca at the heart of contentious national debates and conflictive cultural processes.

The flawed nature of the "modern" versus "traditional" construct, based on a discredited model of cultural evolution, should not discourage us, however, from noting historical continuities in Oaxaca's indigenous communities. As a whole, in the face of pressures imposed by colonialism and nation building, Oaxaca's indigenous communities have protected their territory from Spanish and mestizo incursion, and preserved their religious practices and political autonomy to a degree largely unparalleled by other indigenous groups in Mexico, with the exception perhaps of the Maya of Chiapas and Yucatan.

The remote location and physical geography of the Sierra Norte make the autonomy of its indigenous communities appear particularly pronounced. Native autonomy has a long legal genealogy, and has persisted more in some regions than in others. During the colonial period, the Crown recognized the independence of the *pueblos de indios* (semiautonomous, self-governing communities) of the República de Indios throughout New Spain in electing their own municipal governments, in the ownership of land, and in the practice of local customs. Today, indigenous landholding in the Sierra Norte is remarkably persistent. Almost all land is indigenous owned. The boundaries of some territorial parcels persist unchanged from the colonial period. Further, indigenous communities in Oaxaca continue to elect their own officials in their own manner, in some cases through community consensus. They continue their traditions of communal labor (*tequio*) for public works and during harvests of maize. Although Spanish is the national language, most sierra communities conduct official business in Zapotec, Mixe, or Chinantec, the languages of the region. Many communities even operate on their own clock, refusing to recognize daylight saving time.

The autonomy of sierra communities is closely tied to the state and national government's disinterest in the region, explainable in part by the poverty of its people, the lack of profitable natural resources, and diffuse political resistance. At first glance, this attitude of neglect and forgetting seems reciprocal: as much as national and state officials seem to have forgotten the sierra, the people of the sierra seem equally content to forget the Mexican government. The sierra's native peoples speak of federal and state officials in pejorative terms, as infrequent and opportunistic interlopers in regional affairs. On closer observation, however, sierra communities have a tighter relationship with government officials than they acknowledge, thanks to the political and bureaucratic work of elite intermediary figures.

Throughout Latin America, state officials and national elites have relied on native leaders to broker fraught relationships with native communities. National histories of Latin American nation-states have tended to characterize Indian-state relations in two general modes: antagonism (including violent repression and marginalization) and co-optation (including cultural assimilation).[3] *Caciques* and *gamonales*—local strongmen who rule through a combination of violence and material concessions, and use their connections with the state for personal gain—cut the archetypal figure of the native intermediary. Scholarship on *caciquismo* and *gamonalismo* has contributed immensely to our understanding of the staying power of authoritarian rule and the interpenetration of violence and political legitimacy in places like Mexico and Peru.[4]

However, the antagonism and co-optation brokered by caciques and gamonales has overshadowed an entire register of subtler forms of native brokerage and cultural mediation during both the national and colonial periods. Through political engagement and cultural struggle, native brokers and representatives of the state have co-constructed a symbolic order that has shaped native culture and identity, on one hand, and national identity and the state, on the other.[5] In Mexico, for every cacique, there are many native municipal secretaries, priest's assistants, and go-betweens who through their face-to-face interactions and written negotiations with civil and Church officials keep the nation-state running in a way that avoids selling out the cultural and political aspirations of local people but maintains enough of a relationship with the state to satisfy national pretensions to unity and territorial control.

During the 1990s and the first decade of the twenty-first century—the era of "democratization" that followed two decades of Latin American "authoritarianism"—the brokerage of native intermediaries has provided a foundation for a new kind of relationship between indigenous peoples and nation-states. For example, the governments of Mexico, Colombia, Ecuador, and Bolivia declared their nations officially "pluriethnic" in an effort to make room in the body politic for politically and culturally semiautonomous indigenous communities.[6] Two native intermediary figures in particular have been recognized for their struggles and negotiations with their respective states: in 1992, Rigoberta Menchú Tum became the first indigenous woman of Latin America to win the Nobel Peace Prize, and in 2006, the people of Bolivia elected Evo Morales as their first indigenous president. In February 2007, Menchú announced her own historic bid for Guatemala's presidency. These two figures and others like them have become potent agents—and controversial symbols—of a new Latin America.[7]

In the Sierra Norte of Oaxaca, native intermediary figures come from prominent families in native communities, and most are men, although women have also played an active and vocal role in community political life. In some cases, the status of native intermediaries derives from their economic resources, and in others it comes from respect for political service rendered by themselves or their forebears. Their education also distinguishes them. Training as teachers, engineers, and accountants requires time away from the sierra in urban centers where they learn their way around state bureaucracies and institutions.

The role of native intermediaries requires them to spend significant time and energy in transit between the sierra and the statehouse in Oaxaca City, in taking care of "business" (*trámites*) and "managing papers" (*manejando papeles*). The issues at stake in their work vary, but they all have bearing on the daily lives of the people in their communities. For example, evangelical Protestantism made inroads in much of the sierra during the 1980s. By the 1990s, some communities appeared on the verge of dissolution as the recent converts refused to provide their labor, resources, or moral support for *tequio*, the cargo system (a system in which the community elects representatives into a hierarchy of civil and religious offices), or the innumerable religious fiestas. In one such community, when tensions finally reached a boiling point, the municipal authorities expelled the converts, arguing that their refusal to participate in key elements of community life disqualified them from living in its boundaries.[8] The municipal officials grounded their case against the converts in the legal rhetoric of *costumbre* (custom), which grants indigenous communities a degree of autonomy in the oversight of community affairs. The state responded that the article of the Mexican Constitution that protects freedom of religion should override costumbre in this particular case.

In the meantime, a flurry of legal activity occurred behind the scenes as the community's intermediaries—some of whom were based in Oaxaca City, and others of whom were based in the community—traveled between the community and the statehouse, attempting to broker a compromise and protect the municipal president from federal agents who were rumored to be en route to the sierra. Due in large part to their efforts, the president avoided a jail term. The tradeoff was that the community had to accept the presence of the Protestants, whether they participated in community life or not. Costumbre was compromised in the interests of preserving a degree of community autonomy, symbolized by the president's freedom.

As this politico-cultural negotiation makes clear, the indigenous communities of the sierra have an important relationship with the Mexican government, characterized by a pronounced tension between indigenous autonomy in local matters and dependence on the state for conflict resolution. This relationship could not exist without the native intermediaries who according to their own admission knew "the ways of the Indians and the ways of the city." They are alphabetically, bureaucratically, and legally bicultural, bilingual, and literate. In particular, their facility with the discourses of "costumbre," "community," and "Indian"—all of which are colonial in their origins—provides them with a legal and cultural terrain on which to negotiate the boundaries between community autonomy and state intervention. Indeed, a colonial framework largely defines the political culture of the sierra. If we are to understand the workings of the Mexican nation-state, we must examine how native intermediaries brokered the tensions between native autonomy and state power, and "periphery" and "center" over the *longue durée*. The place to start is the colonial period.

This book examines the intersection of two historical processes that account for Spanish, and more broadly, European colonial power: political expropriation and control, and cultural encounter and change. Too often they have been treated as distinct phenomena and as one-way processes: domination and acculturation imposed by "European colonizers" on "colonized natives." More recently, scholars have encouraged us to think in terms of the cultural convergences produced by colonialism.[9] Although this approach takes into account discrepancies in power, the focus on "colonial consciousness" and the realm of the symbolic at times either obscures colonialism's coerciveness and violence or portrays that violence in such a totalizing way as to leave little room for subaltern agency.[10]

This book resolves the tension in studies of colonialism between hegemony and violence, on the one hand, and subaltern agency and institutional power, on the other. It does so through an integration of the concerns of cultural and social history: a close examination of the workings of symbolic power strongly grounded in an analysis of local social relations. I argue that native intermediaries, through their participation in overlapping social networks and their deployment of a range of communicative skills—alphabetic literacy, bicultural performance, and Spanish discourses of fealty and local custom—produced a colonial hegemony: a common symbolic framework through which native peoples and Spanish officials struggled over forms of local rule and the meaning of Indian identity. Yet the values and symbols that natives and Spaniards came to share had divergent implications and, given the proper circumstances, could ignite conflict and violence. So while native intermediaries won the grudging consent of Spain's native subjects and secured a political legitimacy for themselves, the hegemony that they shaped was contested and fraught with the threat of violence.

As a colonial "periphery," the Sierra Norte of Oaxaca provides an ideal setting in which to examine the work of native intermediary figures. Traditionally, scholars have focused their studies on the metropolitan "centers" of colonial society, which were considered the hub of economic, political, and cultural processes. Yet as this book will show, it was in regions that scholars have tended to identify as "peripheral" that the dialectic between state formation and native autonomy was strongest, and, consequently, where colonial processes and negotiations were at their most dynamic. By adopting "peripheral vision,"[11] this book participates in an effort among scholars of the colonial Americas to redefine the designations of "center" and "periphery" and reimagine the relationship between the two.[12] In this regard, it joins an innovative and growing body of Oaxaca scholarship that situates this vibrant and ethnically diverse region at the heart of global, colonial, and national processes.[13]

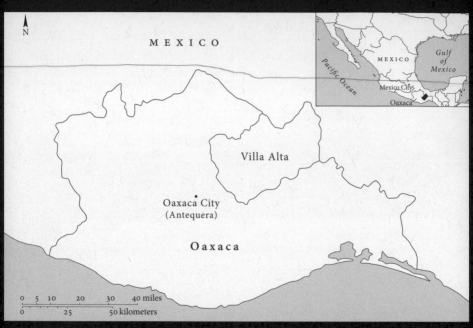

MAP 1 Map of Oaxaca, Mexico. Inset: District of Villa Alta, Oaxaca.

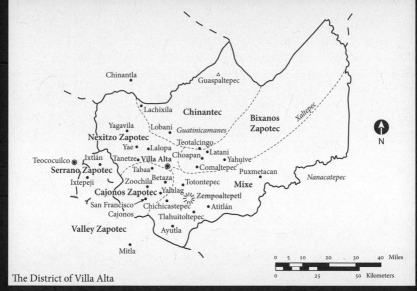

MAP 2 Map of the linguistic regions of the Sierra Norte.

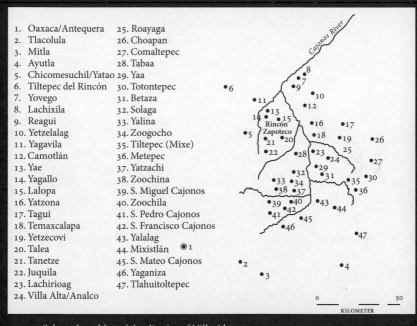

1. Oaxaca/Antequera
2. Tlacolula
3. Mitla
4. Ayutla
5. Chicomesuchil/Yatao
6. Tiltepec del Rincón
7. Yovego
8. Lachixila
9. Reagui
10. Yetzelalag
11. Yagavila
12. Camotlán
13. Yae
14. Yagallo
15. Lalopa
16. Yatzona
17. Tagui
18. Temaxcalapa
19. Yetzecovi
20. Talea
21. Tanetze
22. Juquila
23. Lachirioag
24. Villa Alta/Analco
25. Roayaga
26. Choapan
27. Comaltepec
28. Tabaa
29. Yaa
30. Totontepec
31. Betaza
32. Solaga
33. Yalina
34. Zoogocho
35. Tiltepec (Mixe)
36. Metepec
37. Yatzachi
38. Zoochina
39. S. Miguel Cajonos
40. Zoochila
41. S. Pedro Cajonos
42. S. Francisco Cajonos
43. Yalalag
44. Mixistlán
45. S. Mateo Cajonos
46. Yaganiza
47. Tlahuitoltepec

MAP 3 Selected pueblos of the district of Villa Alta.

Acknowledgments

This project owes a great debt to many people and institutions. A Fulbright-Hays Dissertation Grant for Research Abroad funded research in Oaxaca and Mexico City and a grant from the University of Pennsylvania facilitated research in Seville. A University of Pennsylvania History Department award, an Andrew W. Mellon write-up grant, and a Chimicles Fellowship in the Teaching of Writing made possible three years of hard thinking and writing that went into early versions of this manuscript. Grants from the College of Letters and Science and Vice Provost for Research at Montana State University allowed me to return to Oaxaca and Seville for further research and provided me with additional, precious time that I could devote to completing the manuscript. I want to express special thanks to Valerie Millholland, senior editor at Duke University Press, who has shepherded this project (and me) through the long journey from manuscript to book.

I benefited from the insight of many friends and colleagues in the departments of History, Anthropology, and Art History at the University of Pennsylvania, who read chapters at different stages of "gestation." In particular, I would like to thank Greg Urban, Laura Matthew, Anne Pushkal, Joan Bristol, Gabriela Ramos, Paulina Alberto, Luly Feliciano, Mike Hesson, Gene Ogle, Hilary Dick, Matt Tomlinson, Abigail McGowan, Shefali Chandra, Ian Petrie, Lorrin Thomas, Jesse Hoffnung-Garskoff, Deborah Augsburger, and Paja Faudree for pushing my thinking in fruitful directions.

Daniel Richter and Ann Farnsworth-Alvear read many early drafts of this manuscript and provided invaluable criticism and commentary. More recently, Susan Kellogg, John Chance, Peter Guardino, Michel Oudijk, Susan Schroeder, David Tavárez, Florine Asselbergs, Ethelia Ruiz Medrano, and Cynthia Radding have enhanced this project with insight, intellectual support, and warm collegiality. This book owes its greatest debt to Nancy Farriss, who over the years has shared with me her remarkable wealth of ideas and experience. She has been tireless in her commentary and suggestions and has helped to shape the project in many ways. Finally, my colleagues in the Department of History and Philosophy and in my women's writing group at Montana State University have welcomed me to Bozeman and have expressed enthusiasm for my work, for which I am grateful. Among them, I would especially like to thank Rob Campbell, Kirk Branch, Cindy Ott, Bridget Kevane, and Leah Schmalzbauer.

I am particularly indebted to friends in Oaxaca who opened many doors for me both personally and professionally. María de los Angeles Romero Frizzi demonstrated endless generosity in her willingness to share information and hash out ideas. Israel Garrido Esquivel and the staff at the Archivo del Poder Judicial de Oaxaca were always remarkably helpful and collegial, as were the staff at the Archivo del Poder General Ejecutivo and at the Archivo del Tribunal Superior. Francisco José Ruiz Cervantes, Daniela Traffano, and Alejandro de Avila Blomberg took time out of their busy schedules to answer questions and discuss a range of issues related to historical research and present-day Oaxaca and its more recent past. I am particularly grateful to Martina Schrader Kniffki and her husband John for introducing me to friends in San Juan Yaée and for sharing their knowledge and experience of the Sierra Norte. I learned a great deal from my discussions and travels with Flaviano Pérez Hernández and Genaro Hernández Hernández, and will always treasure their friendship and hospitality and that of their families. I would also like to extend my gratitude to the community of San Juan Yae for allowing me to participate in and enjoy fiestas, celebrations, *tepache*, and long conversations. The bustling, extended Girón family provided warm friendship and a wonderful home during our time in Oaxaca. I am also grateful to the friends and colleagues who shared work and recreational time with me and my family in Mexico and experienced with me the great adventure of archival research: in particular, Luly Feliciano, Mark Overmyer Velázquez, and Alonso Barros.

Elizabeth Fuller at the Rosenbach Museum and Library in Philadelphia graciously opened the New Spain Collection to me, and the staffs at both the Archivo General de la Nación in Mexico City and the Archivo General de las Indias in Seville were always helpful. I would like to thank Viola König and Michel Oudijk who introduced me to the Lienzo of Analco, Julieta Gil Elroduy, and Miguel Angel Gasca at the Biblioteca Nacional de Antropología e Historia who provided me with the images of the Lienzo of Analco that appear in this book, and Michel Oudijk for providing me with John Paddock's images of the Lienzo of Tiltepec.

Finally, and most importantly, the extended Yannakakis family, the Downeys, and Mary and Robert Gold, have provided me with essential moral support, as have a wonderful network of friends who are scattered across the country. I would especially like to thank my parents George and Zoena, my sisters Grace and Daphne, and my grandmother Clara Jordan. My husband Aiden Downey endured this long journey with me and supplied me with endless ideas and support. Over the last five years, my daughter Marianna has opened a new portal onto the world, and has blown my life and imagination wide open.

Introduction

By an art of being in-between, he draws unexpected results from his situation.

MICHEL DE CERTEAU, *THE PRACTICE OF EVERYDAY LIFE* (1984)

A native rebellion in colonial Mexico put two Zapotec Indians on the road to sainthood. On 14 September 1700, in the district of Villa Alta, Oaxaca, leaders of the Zapotec pueblo of San Francisco Cajonos led a mob of angry villagers to the door of the nearby Dominican monastery. The leaders of the mob demanded that the friars hand over Jacinto de los Angeles and Juan Bautista, two of their fellow villagers, who had taken refuge there. If the friars refused, the village leaders threatened to kill everyone inside. Angeles and Bautista served as *fiscales* (assistants) to the pueblo's Dominican priest, Fray Gaspar de los Reyes. The night before, Angeles and Bautista had reported to Reyes that a large gathering of natives, including the pueblo's municipal officers, had congregated at the home of Joseph Flores, a community leader. There, according to Angeles and Bautista, the gathered villagers committed a grave offense against the Catholic Church and royal authority: they performed and participated in native rituals, which the Church considered "idolatry."

In the eyes of the villagers, Angeles and Bautista had betrayed their community by reporting to the priest. In the eyes of the priest,

Angeles and Bautista had fulfilled their role as his eyes and ears. For the friars under siege in the monastery, however, the fiscales' service to the Church was counterbalanced by the hundreds of angry villagers outside the monastery. Terrified for their own lives, the friars turned out their trusted assistants. The crowd took the two fiscales away, and they were never seen again. Two years later, after a lengthy investigation and court trial, Spanish colonial judges convicted fifteen municipal officers and native leaders of the Cajonos region of the murder of the fiscales. On 11 January 1702, the Cajonos rebels were executed, and their bodies drawn and quartered. Their remains were displayed on the Camino Real (royal highway), as a warning to would-be rebels and idolaters. Three hundred years later, in 2002, Pope John Paul II rewarded Angeles and Bautista—the "martyrs of Cajonos"—for their sacrifice on behalf of the Church by beatifying them—often a first step toward sainthood—to the pride of some Zapotecs and the outrage of others. The intense debate about the meaning of the "martyrs'" life and death illustrates the degree to which the symbolic order constructed by Spanish colonialism in Oaxaca's highlands has endured over time; more pointedly, it reveals the centrality to that system of meaning of native people who dealt closely with Spanish priests, administrators, and colonizers.

This book asks how native leaders in the district of Villa Alta, like the "martyred" priest's assistants and "rebel" officials of San Francisco Cajonos, redefined native political leadership, shaped the dynamics of native rebellions, and co-constructed the symbolic order that allowed Spanish colonialism to endure for three hundred years. In the period that immediately followed the conquest of Mexico and Peru, the Catholic Church and the colonial state identified the native nobility as a caste of colonial intermediaries, who by virtue of their legitimacy among native peoples could help administer colonial society. What the Spaniards did not count on, however, were the limiting effects of the strong bonds of reciprocity between nobility and commoners. The sons of native nobles who learned to speak and write in Latin and Spanish and successfully petitioned the Crown to wear Spanish silks, carry a sword, and ride a horse had to answer not only to their Spanish overlords but also to the people who legitimated their authority in native society.

Through their roles in four colonial institutions—the *cabildo* (native municipal government), the *repartimiento* (the Spanish system of forced labor and production), the Catholic Church, and the legal system—native leaders mediated between the competing demands of Spaniards and indigenous people. In the process, they made colonial systems work and created a hybrid colonial culture. Native governors made the colonial economy function through the collection of tribute and oversight of the repartimiento. At times, however, they stood up to abusive Spanish officials and shielded their pueblos from the kind of violence and coercion that might provoke a native rebellion. Native schoolmasters taught their fellow villagers the Christian doctrine and Spanish language, but under cover of night some led their communities in native rituals. Their dual role facilitated the intertwining of Catholicism and indigenous religion. Native legal agents petitioned the Real Audiencia (royal court) in Mexico City to censor the Spanish magistrate for his interference in cabildo elections, all the while pursuing the interests of their own political factions. In doing so, they secured the political power of their lineages but also made their pueblos dependent on the Spanish legal system.

In these double-edged roles, native leaders served as cultural intermediaries and political brokers. More specifically, they held the colonial order in balance: most often, they defused tensions in colonial society, but on occasion, as during the Cajonos Rebellion, the pressures were such that they abandoned the middle ground. In these moments, the violence of colonialism came to the fore, and the material and symbolic force of that violence—the drawing and quartering of the Cajonos rebels, for instance— shaped the work of native intermediaries for decades to come. In this regard, native intermediaries provide answers to two questions that have occupied a generation of historians of Latin America: How can we explain three hundred years of Spanish colonial rule given the absence of a standing army and the prevalence of stark inequalities?[1] Why, in certain instances, did native peoples rebel?[2] These questions are particularly relevant for regions at the edges of the Spanish Empire, such as the district of Villa Alta. In Villa Alta, until 1700 only 10 percent of the district's one hundred native pueblos had parish priests, and a mere one hundred and fifty Spaniards were clustered in the district seat, cut off from administrative and economic centers by rugged mountainous terrain. This handful of Spaniards lived in a sea of thirty to forty thousand native people. By necessity, the Spaniards of Villa Alta relied on local native elites to facilitate the region's colonial order. In turn, these native intermediaries won the grudging consent of the district's native subjects and secured a political legitimacy for themselves. But as the Cajonos Rebellion reveals in the starkest of terms, the colonial order that they built with their Spanish counterparts stood on shaky and shifting ground.

NATIVE INTERMEDIARIES

Intermediary figures, such as agents, interpreters, missionaries, advocates, and traders, intrigued and repelled contemporary observers as well as those who came after them. As people of considerable linguistic talent, cross-cultural sensibility, and sensitivity to the more subtle aspects of human communication, intermediaries evoked a world of mobility and fluid boundaries. They also inspired suspicion. Not fully rooted in any locality or social group yet comfortable and competent in opposing camps, during the age of conquest and colonialism these remarkable people traveled under the presumption of betrayal and treachery. Cross-cultural competence made their cultural and political loyalties suspect, and when situations went sour, they met closed doors, recrimination, legal sanction, or worse.

Throughout the history of Latin America, intermediary figures have played a prominent role in sewing together and exploiting the differences among the political, economic, and cultural interests of peoples of indigenous, African, mixed race, and European origins. During the colonial period, European or mixed race intermediaries most often sought to secure a position among the elite. The exploitative nature of colonialism, based on a hierarchy of race, produced a society characterized by gross inequalities, traceable along cultural and ethnic lines. In the colonial period, parish priests, local magistrates, and itinerant merchants of European origins generally maintained and reproduced these structures. Despite the ability of some to learn native languages, adopt certain aspects of native lifeways, and even sympathize with native peoples, their mediation most often had the interests of colonial power in view.

Native intermediaries present a more ambivalent moral, political, and cultural landscape than their European counterparts. Scholars rightly have represented colonialism as violent and exploitative, as the underbelly of Western narratives of European progress and rationality.[3] Correspondingly, open or violent resistance to colonialism has been portrayed in heroic terms, as a testimony to the agency and resilience of colonized peoples. The social history scholarship of the last three decades, hand in hand with the almost century-long intellectual and political tradition of *indigenismo*, has valorized the culture, history, and experience of native peoples across Latin America, in particular in Mexico and Peru.[4] The immense contribution of this current of thought has provided a counternarrative to European triumphalism and has established a baseline for two generations of rich and innovative scholarship on native peoples. It has also obscured important aspects of colonial Latin American society. The heroic resistance implied by cultural survival, open defiance, and rebellion leaves little room for the ambivalence of cultural mediation. Whereas European intermediaries fit into our template for understanding colonialism, native intermediaries betray our expectations. At best, scholars have perceived them as enigmatic, but more often they have portrayed them as social climbers, tragic figures, power seekers, and lesser partners in the colonial enterprise.[5] In short, intellectual and popular discourses evince disillusionment with native intermediary figures.

No native intermediary figure has suffered more from disillusionment than Doña Marina, also known as La Malinche, the interpreter of Hernán Cortés, "conqueror" of Mexico. Doña Marina's image in history, particularly as portrayed by Mexican nationalists and intellectuals, is that of the traitor and the oversexed Indian woman lusting after a white man. In Mexico, to be a "Malinchista" is to allow oneself to be corrupted by foreign influences; it is to betray one's people. Octavio Paz, who emerged on the literary scene during the 1930s through the 1950s, when Mexican intellectuals were groping for answers to what they perceived to be Mexico's persistent conundrum—its failure to take its place among the world's "modern" nations—captured this attitude toward Doña Marina in "The Sons of La Malinche," a chapter in his well-known book *The Labyrinth of Solitude*.[6]

Paz situated Doña Marina in what he perceived to be a national culture and national psychology of inferiority and self-abnegation, born in part of violent conquest. He wrote that for Mexicans, Doña Marina is "La Chingada," the mother of the nation and "the mother forcibly opened, violated, or deceived."[7] He insisted that as a result of her simultaneous victimhood and betrayal, "the Mexican people have not forgiven La Malinche."[8] But whom did Doña Marina betray? She was a Nahua woman of noble origin, and as an adolescent, she was either sold (as a spoil of war) or gifted (in order to cement alliance with Maya-speaking people. Following exile from her kin and homeland, she was passed along two more times among the Maya. The last of these people, the Chontal Maya of Tabasco, finally gifted her to Cortés. So who were Doña Marina's people? Were they the Nahuatl-speaking nobility of her home region of Coatzacoalcos, or were they the Maya who passed her on to strangers from across the sea? Or were they Cortés and his entourage? Here, at colonial Mexico's moment of inception, as we consider Doña Marina's loyalties, the categories of "Spaniard" and "Indian" and their correspondence to the terms *conqueror* and *conquered* have little meaning.

Bernal Diaz del Castillo, a foot soldier who accompanied Cortés, highlighted the importance of Doña Marina's role in the conquest of the Aztec Empire by devoting an entire chapter of his chronicle to her life story and service to the Spaniards. At the end of the chapter, he states, "I have made a point of telling this story, because without Doña Marina, we could not have understood the language of New Spain and Mexico."[9] Since so much of the conquest of Mexico involved almost constant negotiation, first among Cortés and the emissaries of Moctezuma, then among Cortés and the enemies of the Aztec Empire, the most important of whom were the Tlaxcalans, and finally between Cortés and Moctezuma himself, the role of Doña Marina cannot be overemphasized. Without language, negotiation, and native allies, it is unlikely that Cortés's small entourage could have survived long on Mexican shores. Indeed, as recent scholarship has shown, the conquest of Mexico was as much an Indian affair as it was a Spanish one.[10] At the time, the Tlaxcalans and other allies of the Spaniards viewed the war against the Aztec empire as their own military campaign. And perhaps Doña Marina viewed the Spaniards as her people, as much as the Nahua and Maya people who had given her away.

The venom reserved for La Malinche in Mexican nationalist discourse has as much to do with Doña Marina's gender and the mythical status of the conquest in the Mexican national imagination as with her role as interpreter and cultural intermediary. Yet the associations remain: the native interpreter—*la lengua*—as a treacherous figure without clear loyalties. But there is a reverse side to the perception of Doña Marina as traitor, a counterpoint provided by ethnohistorical perspectives. For example, Frances Karttunen has rehabilitated La Malinche as a "survivor." She argues that as a Nahua woman uprooted from any meaningful network or community, La Malinche had to play by the rules of her overseers, whether the Chontal Maya or Cortés, in order to survive.[11] Her life possibilities diminished and her choices narrowed by her exile, Cortés presented her with an opportunity, and she filled the role required of her with aplomb. Karttunen's interpretation encourages us to consider that intermediaries were defined not only by their personal skills and attributes, but also by the dynamic and unpredictable situation on the ground, and their efforts and abilities to maximize the room for maneuver afforded by that situation. There have been other rehabilitations. Referring to Nahua renderings of the history of the Spanish invasion in the pictographic *Florentine Codex*, Matthew Restall argues that in the sixteenth century, "Malinche was portrayed neither as a victim, nor as immoral, but as powerful."[12] Camilla Townsend, in her analysis of the images of Malintzin (the Nahuatl name from which La Malinche was derived) in the native conquest pictorial, the Lienzo of Tlaxcala, argues the same.[13]

In her intermediary role, Doña Marina throws into question the categories of Spaniard and Indian, conqueror and conquered. She also represents the power of native intermediaries to ignite debate and produce divergent meanings. Yet the era in which La Malinche lived, the singular nature of the encounter that she mediated and, most important, her identity as an indigenous woman, set her apart from the native intermediaries who followed her. Over the course of the colonial period, as the Spanish state imposed a system of native government and a legal system that excluded indigenous women from roles like governor and interpreter general, and the Catholic Church came to rely exclusively on indigenous men as lay catechists and Church intermediaries, indigenous women became nearly invisible in the arena of formal institutional power.[14] As a result, indigenous men overwhelmingly exercised formal intermediary roles in both civil and ecclesiastical realms during the bulk of the colonial period.

The career of one of these men, Gaspar Antonio Chi, is worth examining because it provides a representative framework for understanding the balance of forces with which native intermediaries had to contend in colonial Mexico. Born sometime in the late 1520s into the noble Xiu lineage, Chi lived through the conquest of Yucatan, the Great Maya Revolt of 1546, and the violent and murderous Franciscan Inquisition of 1562 into Maya "idolatry" and alleged human sacrifice.[15] Like many of the native intermediaries of the sixteenth and early seventeenth centuries, Chi was educated in a Franciscan-run school for the sons of native nobility. The friars taught their native charges how to read and write Latin, Spanish, and their own native languages (in alphabetic writing). The objective was to create a cadre of schoolmasters who would teach their fellow natives the catechism and, just as important, would serve as Franciscan interpreters in the evangelical enterprise as well as agents and informants in the battle against "idolatry."

What is striking about the career of Gaspar Antonio Chi, who served as interpreter for Franciscan *Provincial* Fray Diego de Landa and then for Landa's great antagonist the bishop of Yucatan and Tabasco Francisco de Toral, and finally as governor of the Mani province, is the volatile political era in which he mediated among competing Spanish interests and competing Maya interests. When in 1562, rumors of human sacrifice and persistent idolatry reached Landa, a man who until this point had defended the Maya from the rapacity of Yucatan's *encomenderos* (Spanish colonists given rights to Indian labor by the Crown), he received the news as if his favorite children had betrayed him. He and the Franciscans of the peninsula went on what can only be characterized as a punitive rampage. During this violent period, Landa's interpreter, Chi, delivered countless sentences of torture, lashings, and hangings to both his own kinsmen of the Xiu lineage group and their mortal enemies, the Cocoms. One can only imagine what was going through the interpreter's head as he translated those words to "his people," the great Xiu lords. Had his education among the Franciscans erased his affinity for his Xiu roots? Was he totally committed to the Franciscan project?

Apparently not. Landa's violent campaign against idolatry alarmed the Church hierarchy so much so that Bishop Toral was sent to Yucatan to investigate Landa and rein him in. He asked none other than Chi to serve as his interpreter during the investigation. In this role, Chi translated and notarized countless documents indicting Landa, his former boss, and the Franciscans who had educated him for their role in the needless deaths of hundreds of Maya men and women. The irony could not have been lost on any of the men involved. Eventually Landa was sent packing back to Spain. Chi continued his varied career by making use of his Franciscan education as a tutor to the brother of an encomendero in Tizimin, a town in Yucatan. Later, he became governor of his home Mani province, and toward the end of his life he served as a respondent to the *Relaciones Geográficas* of 1579–

81, a royal survey of Indian lands, history, and culture. At the end of his life, he petitioned the Spanish king for a royal pension in view of his service to the Crown.[16]

We can only speculate as to the motives that drove Chi's stunning and unpredictable career. His actions and their context, however, are undeniable. Chi used his cross-cultural skills to leverage power, with serious consequences for local rule in Yucatan. Although it was not his choice to attend the Franciscan school, the skills he acquired there were indispensable to shaping a political situation in which the ground was constantly shifting. His acceptance of Toral's invitation to serve as his interpreter demonstrates a shrewd reading of the fluid power play of the colonial period in Yucatan. Having chosen the "winning" side, Chi participated in neutralizing what had been a dominant Franciscan power in the peninsula, and creating a more balanced relationship among the Franciscans, civil authority, and encomenderos of the region. Such a situation—in which the competing interests of the colonizers checked and balanced one another, and in which Chi as a broker and intermediary could play one off of the other—would prove more auspicious for him as a native governor. It also proved more favorable for the success of colonialism in Yucatan. Putting the brakes on the relentless Franciscan extirpation campaign—an unsustainable state of affairs given growing Maya resentment—avoided the very real possibility of a Maya rebellion. Chi shaped the balance of power of colonial institutions and shifted the delicate tension from overt Spanish violence and Maya rebellion to a Pax Hispanica.

CULTURAL MEDIATION AND VIOLENCE

The example of Gaspar Antonio Chi underscores the point that colonial power was not monolithic. Skillful native intermediaries could profitably exploit divisions among missionary orders, a secular Church hierarchy, Spanish colonists, local magistrates, the viceroy, and the Crown. They could also exploit divisions among native peoples: their rival lineage groups, communities, and caciques. In this regard, the term *survivor*, which Karttunen has also applied to Chi, appears insufficient.[17] Both Doña Marina and Chi did more than survive and interpret: they negotiated, brokered, and played decisive roles in changing the local societies in which they lived.

The complexity of forces with which native intermediaries had to contend constrained them; they were not free agents. Their social context in combination with their communicative skills situated them as brokers and negotiators, and as such, their positions entailed considerable power and risk. Daniel Richter has applied network theory to his analysis of "cultural brokers" in seventeenth-century New York in an effort to understand more precisely the social context that allowed intermediary figures to connect local systems to centers of power. Richter argues that cultural brokers could leverage power because of their "simultaneous membership in two or more interacting networks (kin groups, political factions, communities, or other formal or informal coalitions)."[18] Their position in multiple networks and coalitions meant that they were both varyingly situated and not situated at all: they occupied an "intermediate position, one step removed from final responsibility in decision making."[19]

In Richter's examination of the brokerage of New York–Iroquois relations in the late seventeenth century, negotiations by cultural brokers helped to consolidate the relationship among native groups with heterogeneous interests and two competing colonial powers (the Dutch and the English). In New Spain, from the mid-sixteenth century forward, the power relationships were much clearer. The Spaniards had claimed military victory (tentatively in some of the "peripheral" regions, but with confidence in the "centers") and had established the foundations of their colonial state. But the shape of local rule remained to be decided, and this is where native intermediaries played a considerable role in connecting the colonial state to localities. Their negotiations secured a role for them as local rulers and a role for the colonial state in local affairs.

Participating in social networks from an intermediate position required not only considerable communicative skills but also a "tactical" sensibility. Whereas a strategy is most often formulated from a space outside of and prior to direct engagement with an opponent or enemy, tactics are formulated from within, during contact. Michel de Certeau has applied "tactics," most often associated with warfare, to quotidian social relations, and in particular to acts of communication. He defines "tactics" as an "antidiscipline," an antidote to Foucault's vision of the totalizing and disciplinary power of the state. "Tactics" are the subtle, everyday actions undertaken by individuals to navigate, resist, and subvert authority. Although language and symbols provide the tactical arsenal for de Certeau's antidiscipline, he encourages us to move from a "linguistic" to a "polemological" frame in which acts of communication stand in for "battles" or "games" between social unequals.[20] This framework illuminates the work of native intermediaries, whose power rested in skillful and tactical communication with people who wielded considerable power. For example, in the cases of Doña Marina and Gaspar Antonio Chi, language, translation, and, for Chi, alphabetic literacy played vital roles in their negotiations with Spaniards and native lords. But as important as were their linguistic skills, the wider context of the communicative acts, such as comportment, performance, and cross-cultural competence proved equally critical to their success as intermediary figures. Here, the difference between language and discourse is critical. If we accept that discourse embodies a culturally specific system of signification (linguistic and nonlinguistic), then a facility with a range of Spanish and native discourses and their effective deployment constituted the primary tactics of cultural brokerage.

Richter has also examined the question of tactics, though independently of de Certeau's theoretical frame. He posits that the intermediate political and cultural space in which cultural brokers operated provided them with significant room for maneuver, which in turn occasionally led them to "promise more than they could deliver."[21] These "promises" proved a secret to successful brokerage. Richter's concept of "promise" fits well with the case of native intermediaries in colonial Latin America. Through their promises, native intermediaries opened a political space in which they could "promote the aims of one group while protecting the interests of another—and thus become nearly indispensable to all sides."[22] Through their promises and negotiations, native intermediaries bound native pueblos to the colonial state, and its right arm, the Catholic Church. As community leaders and cabildo officers, they were responsible for defending their pueblos from abuses *and* delivering tribute to the Crown, for maintaining reciprocal relations between their communities and the gods *and* making sure that their fellow villagers attended Catholic mass. Fulfilling these competing demands enhanced political legitimacy, social status, and material wealth. When the competing constituencies in question called native intermediaries to account, however, the political space closed around them, imperiled their intermediary role, and upset the fragile balance of power that they had negotiated.

Rolena Adorno has traced and analyzed the rhetorical strategies of native intermediary figures in her study of the written work of Guaman Poma de Ayala, Garcilaso de la Vega, and Fernando de Alva Ixtlilxochitl.[23] All of them lived in the seventeenth century, the first two in Peru, the last in Mexico, and all were products of the unions between Spanish conquerors and indigenous nobility. Despite their bicultural origins and their facility with Spanish language and customs, they remained rooted in an indigenous social context, largely because of Spanish social prejudice against *mestizos* and because of inheritance laws that privileged the children of the conquerors' Spanish wives over those of their indigenous wives or partners. In the face of this growing social and legal discrimination, these native chroniclers used the Spanish discourses of *relaciones de méritos y servicios* (accounts of merit and service) and *probanzas* (testimonies) of services rendered to the Crown to construct written defenses of the indigenous past and present. They established their legitimacy for their Spanish audience by using Spanish narrative genres, claiming fidelity to Christianity, and, in the case of Garcilaso de la Vega, reconstructing the Andean past as a prelude to the Catholic colonial present, much in the way that Renaissance humanists had recast classical antiquity as the seedbed for Christianity. By drawing on discourses intelligible to an official Spanish audience, ones that would be read sympathetically by Spaniards, they defended the rights and claims of their noble lineages, and in the case of the Andean chroniclers, countered discourses of idolatry which threatened to marginalize all indigenous people as "consorts of the devil."

Adorno aptly characterizes these men as "ethnographers" and "historians" of native culture and as "cultural mediators." The native chroniclers deployed writing and Spanish discourse to communicate a favorable cultural and historical identity for themselves, their lineage groups, and the societies of which they claimed to be a part in order to sway official opinion, attitudes, and ultimately, policy. In this regard, they provide a paradigmatic example of cultural brokerage. The analytical utility of their chronicles is limited, however, by the rarefied niche of these men and the relatively small number of such elaborately constructed texts. Further, Adorno's textually centered approach, which attempts to understand the chroniclers' colonial subjectivity, but probes little into the social relations and political struggles behind the text, leaves one with the impression of these men as individuals mediating in a space between two autonomous social and cultural groups. As a result, cultural legitimization appears to be a one-way process, as the native authors utilized their texts to appeal to the Crown.

In most contexts, native intermediaries had to appeal to at least two audiences who were often at odds: Spanish colonial officials and their own corporate groups. Native officials, priest's assistants, interpreters, and legal agents had to balance these competing accountabilities and construct a two-way legitimacy for themselves in order to maintain their positions as servants to the Crown and leaders of their communities. In regions like the Sierra Norte of Oaxaca, where colonial power was less centralized and more contested, they established their bifurcated legitimacy by forging a particular kind of relationship between their region and the state. This relationship is captured best by the concept of a fragile "colonial bargain": a degree of native political and cultural autonomy in exchange for a grudging consent.[24]

The cultural mediation performed by native intermediaries existed in tension with low-level and endemic violence, on the one hand, and the threat of more overt or organized forms of violence, on the other. As Murdo MacLeod has noted, in Spanish America, "revolts were rare, but violence was frequent," generalized, and underreported.[25] Some examples of this persistent undercurrent of violence include crime and punishment, domestic violence, whippings, floggings, and the many forms of psychic violence that accompanied colonialism. This undercurrent was related to the violent forms of peasant resistance that have captured the imagination of colonial historians: native rebellions.[26] Under certain conditions, floggings by priests or magistrates for failure to attend mass or meet repartimiento quotas could lead to localized uprisings or wider rebellion.

The fact and threat of violence, combined with the value that native peoples placed on local autonomy, positioned native intermediaries in a role complementary to that of state makers: they were also gatekeepers. Often, the objective of their political and legal activity was to keep the Church and state out of community life, and to mitigate against violence, objectives that required them to position themselves against parish priests or the Spanish magistrate. In regions where Spanish magistrates exerted their power through constant extortion and coercion, a political culture developed, characterized by "a steady but minor tension . . . which was never resolved but provoked a constant rumble of violence."[27] As this book will demonstrate, in certain moments, indigenous intermediaries could not hold violence at bay, and when it raged out of control, the political space that they had achieved through their promises and tactics closed, and they either positioned themselves as leaders in moments of violent resistance, or became primary targets of that violence.

INDIAN IDENTITY

The construction of a state system in Spanish America that could incorporate a loose confederation of culturally and ethnically heterogeneous peoples and achieve political consent owed a debt to medieval Iberia, where local semiautonomy and cultural and ethnic pluralism were legally recognized through municipal *fueros* (charters). This arrangement was transplanted to Spanish America with some modifications that allowed for a legal distinction between Spaniards and Indians, which the Spanish Crown institutionalized in the sixteenth century by creating two independent republics: the republic of Indians and the republic of Spaniards.

According to Spanish law, Indians held special status as wards of the Crown. In the early years that followed the conquest, death by disease and the excesses of encomenderos convinced the Spanish Crown that it should position itself between Spanish colonists and its indigenous subjects. The alternative might well have been widespread native rebellion and/or a continued native population decline, both of which would have posed serious problems for the Crown's evangelical and economic objectives. The Crown thus designated Indians as minors, perpetual children in need of protection from the abuses of Spaniards, *criollos* (American-born Spaniards), and people of mixed race (*mestizos* and *castas*). As wards of the Crown, they had privileges. For example, they were protected from slavery, were exempt from the Inquisition, and enjoyed limited political autonomy; non-Indians were not allowed to live in their pueblos. The Crown recognized communal rights to certain pueblo lands by issuing legal titles, and it established a special legal body, the General Indian Court, to address native grievances and conflicts.[28]

In colonial Spanish America, then, the term *indio* denoted a legal category, and did not map fully on to the concept of "race" in its nineteenth-century meaning, although it anticipated modern discourses of "race."[29] For example, the Iberian concept of "lineage," which referred to "bloodline," intersected with the legal definition of *indio* as a marker of social and cultural difference. Lineage marked differences among Spaniards, Jews, Moriscos, Indians, and Africans, and at the same time, it delineated social status (*calidad*), thereby distinguishing among nobility and commoners.

Although lineage marked difference in terms of group identities and qualities considered essential to those groups, it is important to note that lineage did not represent a biological category of difference. For this reason, Irene Silverblatt situates the Iberian discourse of difference, based in part on legal distinctions, and in part on lineage, as "race thinking."[30]

The category *indio* belonged to the colonial *sistema de castas* (caste system), which organized colonial society into a protoracial hierarchy according to their proportion of Spanish blood. The system emerged in response to the growing racial and socioeconomic complexity of the Spanish colonies during the second half of the sixteenth century. Three basic categories of difference—*indio*, *negro*, and *español*—provided the poles of the system, with anywhere from seven to forty categories of race mixture in-between. The exact origins of the caste system remain shadowy; most scholars pinpoint the mid-seventeenth century as the period during which it took institutional form. Immigration of Spaniards (many of them poor), increasing importation of African slaves, and growing "race-mixture" threatened the social exclusivity of Spanish and creole elites. The caste system provided a means by which to maintain social exclusivity in the face of blurring racial boundaries, and the growing dissymmetry between race and class due to the emergence of economically prosperous castas and the declining fortunes of some poor creoles. In theory, the caste system would encourage racial endogamy and insure that if race mixing occurred, the "cream" would rise to the top through a process of whitening. A premium on whiteness meant that poor Spaniards and creoles would be at the top of plebeian society, and that wealthy creoles and Spaniards would be at the top of the entire pyramid.[31] Most historians concede that this classificatory scheme did not work so neatly in social practice.

The relationship between the complex colonial social order on the ground and the colonial principles of social classification has been hotly debated by historians. Relying largely on quantitative analyses of marriage records, social historians in the 1970s and 1980s argued over the relative weight of caste (which they conflated with colonial racial cum legal categories) versus class in determining social hierarchy. Their approach to social identity was largely etic (focusing on ascribed status), and the debate centered on the degree of social mobility in a caste system prescribed by elites.[32]

More recent social historical and cultural approaches to the sistema de castas have transformed our understandings of race, class, and ethnicity by asking about the meaning and perception of racial categories, and the degree to which they were accepted or resisted by colonial subalterns.[33] This bottom-up approach led to a greater emphasis on ethnicity in colonial society; that is, how people produced and understood their own group identities through acknowledgment of shared history, territory, language, and religion, and how those identities provided a basis for social cohesion, conflict, and political claims.[34] Scholars came to recognize the fluid and "protean" nature of ethnic identities in colonial Latin America, and the ways they intersected with class, wealth, status, social occupation, and other markers of social identity.[35] In this light, the meaning of *indio* as a racial category depended in large part on its relationship to other social categories, like "Zapotec," "cacique" (native señorial lord), and "merchant."

In this book, I build on the cultural approach to race and ethnicity, which recognizes their interpenetration and the plurality of factors that determined social stratification in Spanish colonial society. As a rural colonial "periphery," the Sierra Norte of Oaxaca provides a different kind of historical setting than has been characteristic of most studies of race and ethnicity, which have focused on racially diverse and socially stratified urban and mining centers. In the sierra, the small size of *cacicazgos* (noble estates) and the relative lack of valuable resources meant that the gap between indigenous nobility and commoners was defined more by lineage and status than by wealth or class.[36] A plurality of ethnolinguistic groups made the Sierra Norte ethnically diverse, but the region was not racially diverse. Due to a very small Spanish, mestizo, and African presence, political and cultural struggle was primarily either an interindigenous or an indigenous-Spanish affair, and it often centered on a contestation of the racial and cultural categories of Indian and Spanish, and their related identities. As I will show throughout the book, the Zapotec, Mixe, and Chinantec people of the Sierra Norte of Oaxaca had their own systems of social organization and hierarchy, which they put to use in local governance, collective ritual, inter- and intrapueblo conflict and alliance, and disputes within the Spanish legal system. These varying forms of ethnic identity existed in tension with the racial category of *indio*.

In the Sierra Norte, in lieu of a fully functioning sistema de castas, Spaniards produced an informal classificatory scheme for "Indians," defined by the interpenetration of ethnicity and cultural traits. As such, the category *indio* was multilayered and locally specific, cross-cut by other Spanish categories of indigenous identity, such as *pueblo* (a self-governing, semiautonomous municipality, officially recognized by the Crown) and *nación* (nation). For example, the Indian pueblos that made up the republic of Indians were each entitled to elect their own cabildos. In matters of local governance, the Spanish state respected the autonomy of local custom (*costumbre*) if it did not contradict Catholicism. The preservation of local autonomy and custom in the native pueblo provided a bulwark against the cultural and ethnic homogenization implied by the overarching category of the "republic of Indians." *Nación* represented another collective category created by the Spanish state that mitigated against the homogenization implied by *indio* while reflecting Iberian notions of difference. As Lomnitz-Adler describes, "the Spanish concept of *nación* (nation) referred to a community of blood and it was distinct from the notion of *patria* (fatherland), which was merely the place where a person was born."[37] But the concept of nación could not be so easily disentangled from patria, as it folded language, region, and culture into the notion of lineage. So, for example, in the Sierra Norte, Spaniards referred to six different naciones: there was (in Spanish) the nación Zapoteco, which included the naciones Cajonos, Nexitzo, and Bijanos (three different strains of Sierra Zapotec language).There were also the naciones Mixe and Chinanteco. To each of these categories, Spanish Church and civil officials attributed certain kinds of cultural characteristics: for example, the "Indians" of the "nación Cajonos" were known to be "idolaters."

The cultural labeling of groups of "Indians" was a critical, and until recently, understudied classificatory scheme in the Spanish colonial state's overlapping hierarchies of difference, one that this book's analysis will further illuminate. There were officially recognized *indios conquistadores* (Indian conquerors) who had special privileges, and on the other end of the spectrum, there were *indios bárbaros* (wild or barbaric Indians) who had yet to be "conquered."[38] Spanish officials recognized the rights and privileges of *indios principales* (Indian notables), and judges accorded greater weight to their testimony than to that of native commoners. Spaniards also created unofficial categories of "Indianness." Indians whom Spaniards considered to be "loyal vassals" and "good Christians" reinforced colonial ideals of political expropriation of native peoples and their successful conversion. Conversely, Spaniards projected their deepest colonial fears on

Indians who were "rebels" and "idolaters." Finally, there was the category in-between: *indios ladinos* (hispanized Indians). For Spaniards and native peoples, indios ladinos represented the ambivalence and ambiguity of colonial society. With a foot in either world, these intermediary figures were assigned significant cultural baggage and remained under intense suspicion by Spanish officials and native people alike.

The Spanish colonial state's creation of the category *indio* thus co-existed uneasily with its recognition of ethnic and cultural pluralism, and it created serious tensions in Spanish colonial governance. In their inter-actions with the colonial state, Spanish America's native intermediaries profitably exploited the dissonances in "Indian" identity in pursuit and defense of variably defined collective interests and identities. The disso-nances in colonial Indian identity still lie at the heart of the relationship between Latin America's indigenous peoples and their respective states.[39] For this reason, colonial histories of indigenous peoples in Latin America are taking on increased significance as they enrich our understanding of the political, legal, cultural, and economic contexts in which indigenous peoples today "define themselves and their political projects."[40] One of the objectives of this book is to elucidate native intermediaries' political use of a multiplicity of "Indian" identities, and how their work shaped these iden-tities' fluid nature.

LOCAL RULE

Native intermediaries parlayed the Spanish colonial state's lack of a mo-nopoly on violence and the unevenness of its territorial hegemony into considerable political and cultural power for themselves. A glance at a map of the colony of New Spain would lead one to believe that the Spaniards controlled the territory from Baja California in the west across a rough line to Florida in the east, and south through all of present-day Mexico and Central America to the Isthmus of Panama. But maps can be deceiving. A more realistic representation of the geography of Spanish power would be blotchy. Mexico City, Puebla, Veracruz, and the mining centers to the north would stand out in greatest relief, and would be integrated through corridors or trunks of transportation and communication. Other regions would recede in varying gradations, depending on the exports that they could offer. This map, defined by the relationship of economic "cores" or "centers" to economic "peripheries," represents one way to conceptualize the geography of Spanish colonialism.[41]

The economic designations of "center" and "periphery" are undermined, however, by considerations of politics and culture. As Ida Altman has put it, "perception defined core and periphery as much as distance and resources."[42] For example, Spaniards in "peripheral" regions longed for a taste of the metropolitan culture available in the colonial centers, and felt their geographical and economic distance from the center in terms of a lack. Indigenous peoples, on the other hand, enjoyed the cultural and political autonomy that such distance afforded, and as a result of that distance had the space to negotiate with, resist, or ignore state institutions in the interest of maintaining local autonomy.

From a politico-economic perspective, the district of Villa Alta in the Sierra Norte of Oaxaca rested on the periphery of the Spanish colonial system, yet the *repartimiento* (system of forced production) of cochineal dye (*grana de cochinilla*) and cotton cloth (*mantas*) contributed significantly to the economic vitality of New Spain. As in other "peripheral" regions of New Spain and Guatemala with dense indigenous populations, the repartimiento was Villa Alta's primary economic engine, and generated a system of production and trade internal to the colony, as well as the production of valuable exports. In this manner, the system linked "peripheral" regional economies to the wider trans-Atlantic trade.

The Spaniards of Villa Alta established the repartimiento in the decades that followed the conquest. The system did not reach its peak production, however, until the eighteenth century. The system functioned in two main modes: as credit, and as a commercial transaction between Spanish agents of the repartimiento and indigenous producers. In Villa Alta and in Oaxaca in general, the repartimiento represented a system of forced production and consumption known as the *repartimiento de efectos* or *mercancías*, not to be confused with the labor draft also known as the repartimiento.[43] Jeremy Baskes has challenged the notion that the repartimiento in Oaxaca was coercive, arguing that it provided peasants with badly needed credit, and that as a result, peasant producers entered into the system voluntarily. Baskes's economic analysis reveals much about the previously unknown particulars of the repartimiento, but it does not take into account sufficiently the politics of the repartimiento, and the underlying coerciveness that defined Spanish-indigenous relations in Oaxaca. Further, Baskes acknowledges that in the collection of repartimiento debts, *alcaldes mayores* (Spanish magistrates) and their intermediaries often resorted to violence and coercion.[44]

The remarkable profitability of trade in cochineal and cotton cloth made Oaxaca one of the most lucrative regions in New Spain. Only the silver mining centers of Zacatecas and Guanajuato could provide greater profits to the Spanish magistrate lucky enough to get the post. The *alcaldía mayor* (office of alcalde mayor) of Villa Alta was therefore one of the most expensive in the colony, second only to the alcaldía mayor of Jicaya, Oaxaca, which also derived its value and high price from cochineal production.[45] In this regard, as a "periphery," the district of Villa Alta occupied a paradoxical position in Spanish America, captured by the term *internal periphery*.[46]

Despite the economic value assigned to the region and the riches that it offered to Spanish administrators, Spaniards considered the district of Villa Alta a cultural backwater. But for the indigenous people who lived there, it was a geographic, political, economic, and cosmic center. The indigenous society that made up the district of Villa Alta (including Zapotec, Mixe, and Chinantec ethnic groups) differed from the long-established, urbanized, and densely hierarchical pre-Hispanic societies that were found in central Mexico, the Mixteca, or in the Valley of Oaxaca. Indeed, Sierra Zapotec settlements appear to have been only recently established at the time of the Spanish invasion. Through close examination of Sierra Zapotec *lienzos* (genealogical records, maps, and histories transposed onto a tapestry-like form), Michel Oudijk has argued that Sierra Zapotec society emerged from political instability and warfare in the Valley of Oaxaca during the late postclassic period (1350–1521). This situation set off waves of migration to both the Isthmus of Tehuantepec and the Sierra Norte in the century prior to the arrival of the Spaniards. It appears that valley nobles migrated to the sierra with their followers in groups that native people referred to in later Spanish documentation as "parentelas," "cónyuges," or "primos" (all of which loosely translate as "lineage groups"),[47] and that Spaniards later referred to as "parcialidades." Upon arrival, they divided territory and established settlements, known in Zapotec as "yetze." There was a basic division in these settlements between nobles and commoners, but it appears that the finer social distinctions that characterized indigenous society in the valley of Oaxaca, the Mixteca, and Mexico's central valleys did not exist.[48]

Genealogical relationships dating from the original parentelas loosely bound the new populations, but these linkages never reached the complexity or depth of those of the Valley of Oaxaca. Intermarriage and other forms of alliance could not form deep roots due to the relatively short period between parentela settlement and the Spanish conquest (less than a century). As a result, small-scale, loosely interrelated *cacicazgos* (noble estates) and relative autonomy characterized political and territorial relations among Sierra Zapotec settlements.[49] The ethos of autonomy among sierra communities was bolstered by the fact that the sierra never fell under the direct control of the Aztec Empire.

We know less about the history of the Mixe and Chinantec peoples who inhabited the Sierra Norte. In his classic ethnology of the Mixe, Ralph Beals notes that prior to the Spanish invasion, some of the eastern Mixe had contact with Maya speakers, though little is known about how much cultural exchange occurred between the two groups. Beals characterizes Mixe and Chinantec societies as "simpler" than those of the Zapotecs of the Isthmus of Tehuantepec and the Valley of Oaxaca, and notes that their rugged geography limited contact with outsiders.[50] More recently, Frank Lipp has argued that the Mixe-Zoque–speaking peoples "played an integral role in the formation of the Olmec," the first major "civilization" of Mesoamerica, and more broadly, in the development of Mesoamerican culture.[51]

The ethnic diversity of the Sierra Norte was unusual in New Spain for an area of its size (12,700 square kilometers).[52] Ethnic divisions led to bitter warfare in the pre-Hispanic period, particularly among the Zapotecs and the Mixes, but also between Zapotecs and Chinantecs. Linguistic diversity complicated matters even further. Among the Sierra Zapotecs who resided in the district, three variants of Zapotec were spoken: Nexitzo, Cajonos, and Bijanos. The mountainous terrain isolated these Zapotec peoples from one another and most likely contributed to the development of this remarkable linguistic diversity.[53]

This geography played a role in separating the Sierra Norte from other regions of Mexico in both the pre-Hispanic period and afterward. Layers of mountains isolated the region from the Valley of Oaxaca. The difficult terrain combined with fierce local resistance made the Spanish conquest of the sierra a prolonged and bloody affair. Spanish conquistadors had to make at least three attempts to subdue and pacify the region. The first two forays, led by Rodrigo de Rangel in 1523–24, met with some initial success until native rebellion forced the Spaniards to retreat. A third campaign in

1526, led by Gaspar Pacheco and Diego de Figueroa, owed its partial success to the extreme force used by the Spaniards, most notably the deployment of mastiffs to hunt and devour Indian rebels, and the participation of a few hundred native allies from central Mexico. A war raging between the Zapotecs and Mixes of the region also contributed to the eventual military success of the Spaniards and their indigenous allies.[54] During the following year (1527), Pacheco and Figueroa established the Spanish seat of power at San Ildefonso de Villa Alta. The tiny settlement of Spaniards in Villa Alta (which never exceeded thirty families)[55] and its central Mexican native allies spent much of the sixteenth century attempting to achieve stability and establish the most basic foundations of colonial rule.

Once the region had been pacified militarily, the Spaniards carved the district's indigenous population into *encomiendas* (grants of labor and tribute rights given by the Crown) and initiated a regime of forced labor that resulted in a rebellion centered in the Nextizo Zapotec community of Tiltepec in 1531. The Spaniards and the Indian conquerors responded swiftly and cruelly, torturing and executing a number of community leaders. The Indian conquerors proved the centrality of their role in the prolonged conquest of the sierra as they helped the Spaniards to put down a general rebellion that shook the region in 1550, a second uprising that erupted in Choapan in 1552, and a fierce Mixe rebellion in 1570. The overwhelmingly destructive effects of epidemic disease on the indigenous population cannot be overemphasized as a factor in Spanish military success. In 1548, the region's population numbered 95,851. Twenty years later, this figure was reduced by a third. The indigenous population would eventually stabilize at between 30,000 and 40,000 (at its height in the eighteenth century).[56] The disarray of indigenous society and political leadership that accompanied the Great Dying eventually broke the back of native resistance in the Sierra Norte and facilitated the consolidation of Spanish power.[57]

Among the Spaniards of Villa Alta, the alcalde mayor held the most powerful post. Throughout the colonial period, the alcalde mayor served as the district's highest judge in civil and criminal affairs, and was responsible to the Crown, and at some levels to the Church, in matters concerning the administration and control of the region's indigenous population. His administrative responsibilities included the enforcement of rules of productive labor, land use, residency, and social order in Indian pueblos. In the judicial realm, he served as criminal judge, police commissioner, and royal investigator, and the arbiter of property relations and land transactions. Financial responsibilities accompanied administrative and judicial duties. The alcalde mayor was the guardian of the regional economy, supervising tribute collection, regional markets, and the local weights and measures used in market transactions.[58] But the small number of Spaniards available to fill the district's civil bureaucracy hampered the alcalde mayor's ability to fulfill the duties of his office, that is, to impose full social control in the region. For governing and for the administration of the repartimiento, the magistrate and the Spanish *vecinos* (residents) of Villa Alta relied largely on indigenous governors of the district's *pueblos de indios*.

The small size of the Spanish settlement and its anemic civil bureaucracy made the role of the Dominican missionaries who evangelized and administered the region from the military conquest until 1700 central to the colonial enterprise. But small numbers plagued the Dominican administration as well. Until 1700, less than 10 percent of the pueblos in the district of Villa Alta (around one hundred total) had a resident priest.[59] In this regard, the Dominican order, which served as a parallel state structure in the region, was also limited in its ability to establish social control. In order to be effective at all, the Dominicans had to form a partnership of sorts with the region's native nobility, a strategy that empowered native intermediaries, and complemented their mediating roles in the colonial economy and cabildo.

For Spaniards, then, the Sierra Norte was indeed a "periphery." But from the perspective of the Zapotec, Mixe, and Chinantec peoples who lived there, an alternative geography of ritual and political centers, markets (*tianguis*), and a spiritual topography of physical features of the land, such as mountaintops and caves, lent the region its own "central place hierarchy."[60] Maintenance of the semiautonomy of this indigenous world in the face of colonial pressures required native intermediaries to negotiate with the Spanish state and the Catholic Church. Through their negotiations, native intermediaries achieved more than the immediate goal of local autonomy; they actively shaped colonial political culture and the state itself. But negotiation produced a countervailing effect that worked against the objectives of political and cultural autonomy: by engaging with colonial institutions, native intermediaries brought the district of Villa Alta into the orbit of the state, creating a dialectic between local autonomy and colonial rule. This process was critical to the cohesion of empire. In this regard, this book examines the contradictions that inhered in the negotiations between "periphery" and "center," and considers how the intermediary figures responsible for those negotiations shaped forms of local rule.

SOURCES AND METHODS

The historical sources available for the Sierra Norte make it an attractive case study. The district archive of Villa Alta, housed in the Archivo del Poder Judicial in Oaxaca City, is one of the best documented in Mexico, distinctive both for its depth and breadth: it encompasses legal documentation, civil and criminal, for approximately one hundred pueblos de indios from the mid-seventeenth century through the national period. The Archivo del Poder Ejecutivo in Oaxaca City contains more cases from the region, as does the Rosenbach Museum and Library in Philadelphia. The Archivo General de la Nación in Mexico City provides documentation of appeals, the petitions of native nobility for special privileges, and other business that required mediation by the Real Audiencia. Finally, the Archivo General de las Indias (AGI) in Seville, Spain, boasts a rich collection of Oaxaca-related documents that recount conflicts and problems of governance overseen by the Council of the Indies. For this book, I used AGI documents that concerned two native rebellions, the administration of the Dominican order, the secular hierarchy's efforts to overhaul Dominican administration after 1700, Bourbon linguistic policy, and the privileges of the "Indian conquerors" of the sierra.

The rich ethnographic details that abound in the criminal and civil suits of Villa Alta have allowed me to connect the micropolitical to the macropolitical: to analyze the complexities of local politics and culture at close range and to examine the ways that native intermediaries articulated local concerns in a wider colonial context. Disputes can be traced over the span of decades, and alliances and conflicts can be mapped across linguistic regions. The careers of native intermediary figures and Spanish political and cultural brokers appear in three dimensions, as their names and signatures sprawl across a range of documentation. Through thick description and textual interpretation, I have attempted to bring these fascinating figures to life and to chronicle their roles in the quotidian tensions and conflicts that constituted colonial political culture.

My methodology is eclectic, borrowing from the disciplines of history and anthropology. I owe a debt to the rich tradition of colonial Latin American social history, ethnohistory, and historical anthropology. The call to study intermediary figures, issued specifically by William Taylor, grew out of this social historical and ethnohistorical tradition.[61] To understand the social networks that, in the words of Taylor, "connected localities to wider colonial systems," I piece together the fragmentary evidence of social networks, alliances, and rivalries that appears in the documents. I also pay close attention to how indigenous people identified themselves, and how others identified them (i.e., as belonging to a parcialidad, pueblo, or nación) in an effort to reconstruct a social history of Indian identity in the Sierra Norte.

Cultural history, with its focus on language and representation, has also influenced this book's methodology. For example, one of the central threads in the book is an interrogation of the term *indio ladino* (hispanized Indian). Studying Spanish correspondence and writing, indigenous testimony, and court-mandated witness identification, I analyze how the meaning of the term changed over time, and how it operated in a larger system of colonial representation. My focus on the political rhetoric of Spanish and indigenous officials and witnesses owes a debt to a growing subdiscipline in Latin American studies that focuses on political culture.[62] With an eye to the dynamics of colonial courtrooms, I use court cases to examine how people made arguments, communicated conflicts, presented themselves, and, through performance, constructed situational identities. Finally, I borrow from postcolonial theory. In a wider sense, the book explores how Spanish colonialism worked through language and how native peoples used Spanish discourses to subvert or use to their advantage Spanish notions of Indian identity.

In keeping with the book's focus on language, William Roseberry's reading of Antonio Gramsci's theory of hegemony provides one of the theoretical underpinnings of the book's methodology. Gramsci argued that hegemony—subordination and exploitation in the absence of overwhelming coercion—can be explained by the creation of a common set of understandings and values that united antagonistic classes on one level, and the people and the state on another.[63] Roseberry has argued that the "consent" implied by Gramsci's model does not mean the absence of struggle, nor is it static. Cultural and political struggles contribute to an ongoing reformulation of the terms of "consent," and hegemony constitutes a "common material and meaningful framework for living through, talking about, and acting upon social orders characterized by domination."[64] "Consent" thus coexists with resistance, and the signs and symbols meant to articulate the common understandings of hegemony can have alternative meanings across class and ethnic lines.[65] The common meaningful framework that constitutes hegemony also provides the tools for its transformation and even subversion.

Through legal and political struggles with the Church and state, native intermediaries shaped a hegemonic system in New Spain. Court records are ideal for analyzing this process because the courtroom, with its mutually understood procedures and language, constituted a common meaningful framework in which the tensions among, race, ethnicity, and cultural competence were hashed out. The court was a public space and, as such, a space for performance and micropolitics. Spanish, the language of the conquerors, was the hegemonic language, but native peoples learned to use it—often quite masterfully—in counterhegemonic ways.

GENDER AND INDIGENOUS WOMEN'S HISTORY

Indigenous women intermediaries are notably absent from this book. Part of the problem relates to observations made earlier: during the colonial period, Spanish notions of gender and power excluded indigenous women from intermediary roles in formal institutions, such as the Church, the cabildo, the repartimiento, and the legal system. Indigenous women did continue to exert power as *cacicas*, property holders, testators, plaintiffs, defendants, witnesses, and market vendors, but their power was often mediated by men: their husbands, legal representatives, or cabildo. Laura Lewis has shown that *casta* women, including indigenous women, played important intermediary roles in informal and forbidden aspects of colonial society, such as healing and witchcraft.[66] Matthew Restall and Marta Espejo-Ponce Hunt have argued that by learning Spanish ways and language, and teaching their own ways to "many a Spaniard," Maya women served as critical links between indigenous and Spanish society.[67] But as important as they were to the creation of a hybrid colonial culture, these realms of mediation stand outside of the scope of this book. Problems with documentation also interfere with efforts to get at the intermediary work of indigenous women. Lisa Mary Sousa has commented on the lack of women's testimony in Villa Alta legal documentation and posited that the absence may be attributable to the long and arduous journey from most indigenous pueblos to the district court in Villa Alta. The distance may have discouraged women from providing testimony in civil and criminal suits, since long absences would have precluded them from fulfilling their household and productive duties.[68] Yet it is important to keep in mind that lack of documentation does not necessarily mean the absence of historical agency, or the lack of women in powerful mediating roles.

Although indigenous women intermediaries do not grace the pages of this book, I use the concept of gender as a signifying system in different moments in my analysis. In chapter 1, as I examine the construction of languages of negotiation that native and Spanish intermediary figures used in their struggles with one another, I consider "honor" and "Indian" as gendered colonial discourses that constituted part of a common meaningful framework for political and cultural negotiation. In analyzing the Lienzo of Tiltepec (a Zapotec pictorial narrative) in chapter 4, I explore the gendered dimensions of changes in Sierra Zapotec iconography concerning ruling pairs and legitimate authority. Finally, in chapter 6, which focuses on the mediating role of the sierra's "Indian conquerors," I incorporate an analysis of how the Indian conquerors used the discourse of "conquest" to "feminize" the indigenous people of the sierra while identifying the "indios conquistadores" as masculine warriors, thereby bolstering the latter's claims to ethnic and cultural superiority over local "Indians."

CHRONOLOGICAL AND THEMATIC FRAMEWORK

The Dominican missionary project and the repartimiento established the broad outlines of colonial society in the Sierra Norte and situated native intermediaries at the heart of the colonial project during the first century after the conquest. Yet the profound trauma for the indigenous population brought on by conquest and early colonialism—disease, death, and the disruption of the program of *congregación* (forced nucleation of settlements)—impeded the development of a fully functioning colonial system. This, combined with the Sierra Norte's "peripheral" status, delayed the consolidation of colonial society in the sierra in comparison with the central regions of New Spain.[69] The dearth of Spaniards, the prolonged and late conquest, and the cultural autonomy afforded to native pueblos slowed the process of cultural change and the establishment of colonial institutions. In this regard, the Sierra Norte resembles other "peripheral" mountain regions in New Spain, such as the Sierra of Puebla and the Sierra of Guerrero, which experienced a different historical trajectory from "central" regions.[70]

Recovery of the native population (it had reached its nadir in the 1620s at 20,751) began slowly in the 1630s, and provided a baseline for the emergence of a more integrated colonial society.[71] The year 1660 marked a turning point in this process. In the spring of 1660, when the native population was still dangerously diminished, and the demands of the repartimiento had increased substantially, native pueblos in districts throughout Oaxaca—Tehuantepec, Nexapa, Villa Alta, and Ixtepeji—rose up against their native governors and the local magistrates. The uprisings, which varied from a full-fledged rebellion in Tehuantepec to more disjointed skirmishes in the neighboring districts, arose from a combination of demographic, religious, and political causes. María de los Angeles Romero Frizzi posits that the rebellion represented a crisis in native religiosity, in which native pueblos could not maintain the cult of the saints because of the population crisis and the demands of the repartimiento.[72] Héctor Díaz-Polanco and his coauthors contend that the rebellion expressed a profound confrontation between an extractive political economy and a long-standing tradition of native autonomy.[73] According to Judith Zeitlin, in the case of Tehuantepec, the spark that ignited this tinderbox was a startling and "unsupportable" increase in repartimiento demands for cotton cloth implemented by the alcalde mayor of Tehuantepec, Juan de Avellán, and the "failure of the political institutions of the colonial state to restore an acceptable level of economic burden on the populace."[74] Although these pressures were most acute in Tehuantepec, native peoples of other regions clearly felt them as well as they expressed their discontentment with their alcaldes mayores.

The historical arguments concerning the causes of the 1660 rebellion reinforce one another in their focus on the corrosive effects of the repartimiento on a central element of native collective identity: an indissoluble politico-religious autonomy. Native autonomy lay at the heart of the struggles between native intermediaries and Spaniards throughout the mid-late colonial period. The story that I tell in the pages that follow traces the period from the 1660 rebellion until the beginnings of the independence movement in 1810. In the district of Villa Alta, this century and a half was the most dynamic of the colonial era. The 1660 rebellion forced the colonial administration to rethink its ruling strategy. From 1660–1810, through violent rebellion, legal conflict, and political negotiation, native intermediaries and their Spanish counterparts forged a late-flowering colonial society characterized by a growing interpenetration of colonial institutions and what I will call a native "shadow system."

Part 1, "Conflict and Crisis, 1660–1700," follows the careers of native noblemen who asserted themselves as itinerant merchants, legal agents, interpreters, native governors, and religious leaders in the context of the Spaniards' efforts to consolidate their hold on the repartimiento and intensify the war against "idolatry." Chapter 1 explores how in response to native resentment of Spanish civil and Church officials, native intermediaries resisted Spanish interference in native political and ritual life. Through their political and legal work—declarations of fealty to the Crown, mobilization of interethnic alliances, and deployment of the discourse of native autonomy—they opened space for electoral independence, interpueblo integration, native trade, and native religiosity while enhancing their own power vis-à-vis the Spanish magistrate and parish priests.

Chapter 2 focuses on the Cajonos Rebellion of 1700 and its aftermath. The rebellion represented a violent native reaction to persistent Spanish interference in native affairs, and more pointedly to the violation of the principle of native autonomy. During the trial of the rebel leaders that followed the rebellion, Spanish officials and the cabildo officers of the Cajonos region struggled to impose their version of events. In the process, they produced divergent meanings of the rebellion, which shaped local politics in the half century that followed. The rebellion provided the Church and state with a pretext to impose a new colonial order and reminded both the Spaniards and the region's native inhabitants in the starkest of terms of the relationships of power that undergirded colonialism.

Part 2, "The Renegotiation of Local Rule: Strategies and Tactics, 1700–1770," examines the remaking of the local colonial order by native intermediaries, the bishop of Oaxaca, the local magistrates, and the Real Audiencia after the Cajonos Rebellion and in the wake of a native demographic boom. From 1702 to 1728, the bishop of Oaxaca, in partnership with the local magistrates, initiated policies of repression, extirpation, and administrative reform. These policies nearly doubled the parishes in the district and placed more parish priests on the ground. Chapter 3 traces how native intermediaries resisted parish reform through appeals to the Real Audiencia in which they deployed legal rhetorical strategies, such as bicultural (ladino) performance and "local custom" (*costumbre*). Chapter 4 focuses on how native intermediaries mediated the effects of a boom in the native population and an intensification of the repartimiento to create a growing interdependence between Spaniards and native people. As legal agents and cabildo officers, native intermediaries turned to the district court and creatively utilized the designations of *cacique* (nobleman) and *cacicazgo* (noble estate) to negotiate shifting relationships among native nobility and commoners and shape the outcome of interpueblo rivalries.

Part 3, "The Political Space Closes, 1770–1810," examines how native intermediaries shaped the local impact of the Bourbon Reforms, and how Bourbon legislation affected their intermediary roles. The reforms, which began in earnest in 1763, represented a move toward state centralization and direct rule of Spain's imperial holdings. Chapter 5 looks at how native intermediaries mitigated the combined effects of Bourbon economic and cultural reforms. The outlawing of the repartimiento and renewed state support for the mining industry converged with Bourbon hostility toward native languages and local custom to undercut the power of native cabildo officers. Chapter 6 examines how the "Indian conquerors" of Villa Alta—natives from central Mexico who helped the Spaniards to subdue the Zapotec, Mixe, and Chinantec peoples in the sixteenth century— resisted Bourbon efforts to eliminate their special privileges, including tribute exemption. In petitions to the court, the residents of Analco identified themselves as "Tlaxcalans" in an effort to link themselves with the most important native allies of Hernán Cortés. The courts ruled against them, and this moment marked a shift in their status from "Indian conquerors" to "local Indians."

Despite the efforts of some native intermediaries to resist political centralization and the homogenization of indigenous identity, the net effect of the Bourbon Reforms was to constrict the intermediary space that independent-minded cabildo officers, priest's assistants, legal agents, and the Indian conquerors had occupied. I suggest at the end of the book that by undercutting native intermediaries in their diversity of roles, the Bourbons weakened a lynchpin in the colonial system, and speeded the process of independence.

PART 1

Conflict and Crisis, 1660–1700

Chapter 1

"Loyal Vassal," "Seditious Subject," and Other Performances

On Palm Sunday, 21 March 21 1660, the native officials of Tehuantepec, the district seat of the Zapotec Isthmus of Tehuantepec, presented themselves at the administrative quarters of the *alcalde mayor* (Spanish magistrate), Juan de Avellán. There they issued a protest regarding the high production quotas and the low prices paid to native producers of cotton thread and cloth through the *repartimiento* system of forced production and consumption. The alcalde mayor, who was notoriously abusive, berated the officials and had them whipped publicly and imprisoned. The following morning, a crowd of over one thousand from Tehuantepec and its outlying settlements gathered in the town plaza and made its way to the municipal buildings. When the crowd encountered the alcalde mayor and two of his assistants, it turned violent and killed all three. The rebels then took control of the town. They organized a local government, garnered the support of surrounding pueblos, and for a year maintained a virtually independent native polity whose control extended into the outlying area. In the meantime, the rebellion spread, in the words of Spanish officials, like "wildfire" to the neighboring districts of Nexapa, Villa Alta, and Ixtepeji.[1]

Historians have debated the geographical scope of the rebellion and its political organization and objectives. Notably, Judith Zeitlin contends that the extent of the rebellion was grossly exaggerated by the lead investigator and judge (*oidor*) of the Real Audiencia (royal supreme court), Juan Francisco de Montemayor y Cuenca, for political reasons, and that Spanish conceptions of the rebellion as highly organized and premeditated reflected Spanish hysteria more than reality. Most historians concur that the rebels' objectives were localized and reformist rather than revolutionary and anticolonial. For the most part, native peoples directed their grievances toward the abusive practices of the alcaldes mayores and not against the colonial system writ large.[2]

In the districts of Villa Alta, Nexapa, and Ixtepeji, all of which were located in the Sierra Norte, the uprisings that coincided with the rebellion in the isthmus were not as violent as in Tehuantepec. Whereas the Zapotecs of the isthmus turned against their native governors who administered the repartimiento on behalf of the alcalde mayor, on the whole, sierra pueblos responded with community solidarity. Despite the abuses of some native governors, in general the commoners maintained their allegiance to their municipal governments, and directed their violence at the alcalde mayor and his agents. These differences may be attributable to the less stratified social relations in these districts, in which nobility and commoners were more tightly bound through the ethos of reciprocity than they were in the more complex social hierarchy of Tehuantepec.[3] But although the rebellion in Villa Alta did not reach the intensity of that in Tehuantepec, several smaller uprisings from 1659 to 1661, involving some four thousand natives, proved sufficient to put the alcalde mayor, parish priests, and the native officials of the region on notice.[4]

The choice of human targets for the rebellion's violence—native intermediaries and local Spanish officials—points to the perils of economic, political, and cross-cultural mediation in a largely indigenous, peripheral region where the demographic imbalance between Spaniards and Indians was stark, and where economic demands placed on native pueblos were highly coercive. Until 1660, the repartimiento had operated for well over a century without significant resistance, in large part because native and Spanish intermediary figures had struck a balance between the productive demands of the system and the maintenance of a degree of political autonomy in the region's pueblos. Once the demands of the system upset this delicate balance, the region erupted in protest, revealing a crisis in the political and economic mediation that had kept the system afloat.

The rebellion of 1660 generated a flood of letters, reports, and petitions written by and circulated among the bishop of Oaxaca, the viceroy, local Spanish officials, and native leaders. This documentation reveals a complex process of soul searching, finger pointing, and historical revisionism as Spanish officials struggled among themselves to come to terms with the root causes of the rebellion, propose solutions to the social unrest brewing in the four affected districts, and recast the events to their own political advantage. The effort to make meaning of the rebellion in its aftermath opened a forking path. Would the alcaldes mayores of the districts affected by the rebellion ease up on the repartimiento demands? Or would they continue to squeeze the native labor to which they were entitled and use the occasion to diminish native autonomy in the interests of tightening social control? Bishop Juan de Palafox of Puebla, who had written vociferously about the abuses of the alcaldes mayores of New Spain, used the occasion to renew his call for the abolition of the office of alcalde mayor and the repartimiento. No such measure was ever passed.[5]

Yet the official investigation that followed the rebellion made plain the risks inherent in failing to modify the coerciveness of the repartimiento. The lead investigator, Juan Francisco de Montemayor y Cuenca, detailed the abuses of the alcaldes mayores of the affected districts. Zeitlin argues that Montemayor's *relación* was intended not to remedy the abuses of the alcaldes mayores but to impugn those currently in office so that his own "cronies" would replace them. Montemayor's machinations bore fruit: the alcaldes mayores of Nexapa and Ixtepeji were replaced.[6] However, the alcalde mayor General Pedro Fernández de Villaroel y de la Cueva of Villa Alta was allowed to finish his term since the rebellion did not affect his district as acutely. It is also likely that his close relationship to the viceroy, the duque de Albuquerque (he was the viceroy's nephew) helped him to hold onto his office.[7]

The alcaldes mayores were not the only controversial figures to emerge from the investigation of the rebellion. In a 1661 report to the viceroy, the bishop of Oaxaca, Alonso de Cuevas Dávalos, who had a reputation as a defender of Oaxaca's Indians against the abuses of local officials and priests, cited other culprits for the violence—literate and bilingual native leaders who dressed in Spanish silks:

> And it is necessary to remedy the abuses that there are in many pueblos where some Indians, perhaps one or two in each pueblo, dressed like Spaniards and some with sword and with total authority, who having left their Indian clothing, and in the new clothing that they don, are in the habit of raising the spirits of the community, and come to be in the

pueblos the lettered men and superiors to whose will they have subordinated the other Indians. And in addition to being the leaches that suck the poor lifeblood of the Indians, they are the ones who absolutely lead and arrange whatever disagreement or uprising. To avoid this it appears very advisable not to give them the chance to change their natural attire and excite their pretensions so that they become the oracles of their pueblos, but rather that they live in equality with the rest.[8]

The bishop's description of these men was clearly influenced by Spanish prejudices toward the perceived pretension and duplicity of hispanized Indians, particularly those who were literate and used the legal system to stir up trouble. These men were known by Spaniards and natives as *indios ladinos*, a term that was at once descriptive, meaning bicultural, and pejorative, connoting duplicity. The term *ladino* carried significant symbolic weight and served as a political weapon for both Spaniards and native people who sought to cast aspersions on natives with a foot in either world.

The term *ladino* originated during the Roman period on the Iberian Peninsula and referred to those locals who learned to speak Latin with skill and refinement. The connotation of skillfulness broadened the applicability of the term *ladino* to include those "skilled or sagacious in any dealing."[9] During the Middle Ages, the term came to refer to Sephardic Jewish culture, and then expanded its range of meaning to include foreigners (such as *moriscos*, or "Moors") who mastered Castilian. Finally, following the conquest, the term was imported to Spanish America and applied to natives who learned the language of their conquerors. In the New World, *ladino* took on a range of associative meanings, varying regionally in its connotations.[10]

Throughout the seventeenth century, native elites of the district of Villa Alta petitioned the Real Audiencia for licenses to wear Spanish clothes, carry swords and daggers, and mount horses, things forbidden to Indians by the sumptuary laws of the time.[11] That native elites should seek to present themselves in a way that aligned them with colonial power makes sense given their desire to project social distinction from other Indians and to maintain their claims to authority in a context where older claims no longer had the same meaning. Both Spaniards and Indians considered ladinos to be "civilized Indians." Their noble status, rootedness in local political networks, and skillful use of Spanish legal discourses earned them respect from Spaniards and native people alike. However, native people also viewed ladinos' cross-cultural mobility with suspicion and resentment, associating it with trickery and taking advantage. From a Spanish perspective, ladino identity represented a threat to the colonial order. Not truly Spaniards, despite their language and dress, ladinos were seen to have suspect motives, and their cross-cultural and linguistic skills were considered dangerous.

Through the use of coded language—with which he accused indios ladinos of "raising the spirits" of the pueblo, "sucking the poor lifeblood of the Indians," and "arranging whatever disagreement"—the bishop made clear that one of the most dangerous roles that indios ladinos played was that of *apoderado*, someone to whom indigenous groups or individuals issued power of attorney. An apoderado, also known as an *agente* or *actor de oficio y cargo*, served as a liaison between those who hired him and the colonial court system. Apoderados penned petitions, managed legal documents, kept tabs on the Spanish lawyers (*procuradores*) who represented Indians officially in court (by law, Indians, who were considered minors, could not represent themselves in court), and ensured that the procurador remained on task and protected the interests of his clients. The absence of Spanish legal professionals in regions remote from urban centers forced indigenous individuals and groups in places like the Sierra Norte to turn to people in their own pueblos or in neighboring pueblos to fulfill this critical role. In the Sierra Norte, ladino legal agents tended to be caciques and were the most bicultural and linguistically skilled of any other intermediary figures in a given pueblo or parish. They also tended to have especially wide social networks, consisting of other native elites as well as Spaniards, and a fluency in Spanish law and the workings of the colonial bureaucracy. To the chagrin of Spanish authorities, native municipal governments financed the legal activities of apoderados through the community treasury (*caja de comunidad*), the economic "lifeblood" of the pueblo.

The long, transatlantic history of the term *ladino* and the historical nature of the role of indigenous apoderados, which dated back to the sixteenth century, make clear that the prejudices against ladino legal agents expressed in the bishop's report long predated the rebellion. The deployment of this rhetoric concerning apoderados at this particular moment, however, provided encouragement and justification for an aggressive stance toward these figures on the part of the alcaldes mayores. In this regard, in the wake of the rebellion, the symbolism of "ladino" identity worked in tandem with the historical agency of apoderados themselves to shape local politics.

The bishop's report helped to make meaning of the rebellion for local Spanish officials, the Audiencia, and Council of the Indies. By identifying ladino legal agents as a social and political problem with serious bearing on the maintenance of colonial order, the bishop's report justified the alcaldes mayores' persecution of these native intermediary figures, and in doing so, shaped the tense political climate in the district of Villa Alta in the decades between the rebellion of 1660 and the Cajonos Rebellion of 1700. During this period, the alcaldes mayores of the district identified two ladino legal agents in particular, with wide-ranging economic and political power— Felipe de Santiago and Joseph de Celis—as troublemakers. These men in turn pushed back with a vigorous campaign of political organizing and legal action.

The stakes in this mounting political, economic, and cultural confrontation among Santiago, Celis, the alcaldes mayores, parish priests, and other Zapotec rivals were quite high. From 1660 forward, the native population began to recover more fully, and the alcaldes mayores recognized the potential for greater profits from the repartimiento that more numerous native laborers could provide. An uprising in the sierra in 1684 reflected native resentment of these pressures and, more important, provided the alcaldes mayores with an excuse to intervene in pueblo elections, nominally to ensure regional security, but more pointedly to secure their own profits. To compound these political and economic pressures on sierra pueblos, after 1660, the bishops of Oaxaca, with the zealous cooperation of the alcaldes mayores of Villa Alta, reinvigorated their extirpation campaign and brought cases of idolatry against native ritual specialists.[12]

Santiago and Celis responded to these attacks on native autonomy with legal action aimed at opening political and cultural space for electoral independence, interpueblo integration, native trade, and native religiosity. Although they articulated these objectives in collective terms, the defense of local autonomy also enhanced their own wealth and power. But the pursuit of power proved to be quite dangerous: the magistrates and priests wielded the force of colonial law and Catholic orthodoxy, and used them to physically punish, imprison, and exile their native opponents. What follows is a close examination of the micropolitics of this high-stakes political struggle. The tactics used by both native intermediaries and Spanish officials shaped the emerging political culture and the colonial system of the district and set the stage for the conflagration of 1700: the Cajonos Rebellion.

THE MANY PERFORMANCES OF FELIPE DE SANTIAGO AND JOSEPH DE CELIS

Felipe de Santiago and Joseph de Celis first appear to us in a 1684 petition addressed to the king. In the many instances during the late seventeenth century in which the district court identified Santiago as giving testimony or submitting a petition, the notary described his comportment as "bastantamente ladino en la lengua castellana" ("very skilled in the Spanish language") and noted that he dressed in Spanish costume. His signature at the bottom of petitions and court documents evinced a practiced hand, indicating that he was most likely literate. During the many occasions in which Celis did business with the district court, the notary identified him as ladino, though no mention was made of his bearing or his dress, and less evidence exists as to his degree of literacy.

In their 1684 petition to the king, Santiago and Celis, both caciques from the pueblo of San Juan Yatzona, and another cacique, Juan de Alvarado from San Juan Yalahui, proclaimed their loyalty to the Crown and Church. Although they addressed their petition to the king, these men, all of whom were Nexitzo Zapotecs, performed their deference to Crown and Church in front of the alcalde mayor of Villa Alta, whose notary transcribed the words onto paper, asked the caciques to sign the document, and deposited a copy in the archives of the district court:

> In Villa Alta of San Ildefonso on the 26th day of the month of November of 1684, this petition was presented before said Spanish magistrate and auxiliary judge: Don Felipe de Santiago and Don Joseph de Celis, caciques of the community of San Juan Yatzona, and Don Juan de Alvarado, cacique of the community of Yalahui, of this jurisdiction appear before your Excellency in the best and most favorable form that that our rights afford us and we say that we present ourselves before your Excellency as persons who as Catholic Christians and loyal vassals of His Majesty may God our Lord preserve him many years as we have declared and declare, have lived under your sovereignty, and are prepared to shed blood for your Royal Crown.[13]

What is particularly striking about this declaration of fealty is that four years later, in 1688, Celis's defense attorney presented it as evidence of

Celis's loyalty to the Crown in a case of sedition against him. The same year, the magistrate brought Santiago up on charges of sedition as well.

Santiago's and Celis's long careers as native intermediaries, which spanned the years 1684 to 1702, express a complex social and political identity. The facet that appears to us through the historical documentation depended largely on two factors: their audience and the political moment. Facing the Crown, native intermediaries performed the role of "loyal vassal," but there were always native audiences in the balcony or in the wings to which native intermediaries directed performances that Spaniards failed to notice or understand. These audiences changed shape and composition depending on historical circumstances. They could be made up of regional alliances, interpueblo alliances, subpueblo units, kinship groups, clients, or fellow villagers.

Colonial courts provided a stage for the multilayered performances of native intermediaries. Legal cases were therefore complex social texts in which multiple performances and audiences were at play. The embedding of Celis's 1684 declaration of loyalty in a 1688 case of sedition provides a perfect example of this multilayered quality. In the dissonance between "loyalty" and "sedition" lay a hidden performance and a hidden history. A closer look at the events that transpired between the submission of the 1684 petition and the 1688 cases of sedition helps to uncover what was hidden by public acts of deference and defiance and to unravel the apparent paradox of Celis and Santiago as seditious loyal vassals.

Felipe de Santiago, Joseph de Celis, and Juan de Alvarado presented their petition to the alcalde mayor as a response to a 1684 native uprising in the town of Santiago Choapan, the second most important in the Sierra Norte after the district seat of Villa Alta. Since the pre-Hispanic era, the town had provided a hub of political and economic power because of its geographic position as a crossroads for highland and lowland trade routes and as a distribution center for the cotton-producing region of Chinantla. Choapan—not Villa Alta—hosted the sierra's most prominent market, drawing Indian traders from as far as the Isthmus of Tehuantepec, as well as Spanish merchants from the jurisdiction and beyond. It also served as a base for ecclesiastical and civil administration of the district's lowland region. Given the economic and strategic importance of Choapan, the alcaldes mayores of Villa Alta stationed special lieutenants there for much of the colonial period. These lieutenants had the reputation of being even more exploitative than the alcaldes mayores themselves.[14]

In November 1684, a crowd from surrounding native pueblos besieged Choapan's *casas reales* (administrative buildings) with the alcalde mayor of Villa Alta and a delegation of Spaniards inside. Although the motives for the uprising remain unclear, the rebels were most likely protesting excessive tribute and taxation. Colonial authorities in Antequera (Oaxaca City) sent two militias into the sierra to break the siege, which lasted only a few days.[15]

The Choapan uprising reverberated like an aftershock of the 1660 rebellion, and as such, represented more of a symbolic threat to local Spaniards than it would have if the 1660 rebellion had not preceded it. The 1660 rebellion had terrified the Spaniards of four of Oaxaca's districts, who lived as tiny minorities among a relatively large indigenous population, and planted a seed of fear in Spanish minds about the possibility of coordinated regional indigenous rebellion. The Choapan uprising appears to have rekindled these fears, which were sparked again during the Cajonos uprising of 1700. In this regard, the very material conditions of native rebellions shaped how Spaniards made meaning of and responded to the uprisings and rebellions that followed them.

During the crisis in Choapan, Spanish authorities turned to the region's native elites to assist them in restoring social order. Spanish officials and native elites realized that this required some symbolic work. Anxious to maintain their legitimacy in the eyes of Spanish officials, no matter the complexity of their political connections and allegiances, some native intermediaries abandoned the political middle ground—or at least they gave the appearance of doing so—and swore their loyalty to the king. Santiago and his cosignatories no doubt recognized the gravity of the political situation and, well aware of the long-standing fear among the sierra's Spanish residents of indigenous rebellion and the repression that such fear could provoke in the wake of an uprising, they performed their act of deference to the king, with the alcalde mayor and his lieutenants as their primary audience.

The petition demonstrates the signatories' ease with the reverential language of fealty to the Crown and Church. This language had long been used among the native elite of New Spain and Peru. During the sixteenth and seventeenth centuries, in countless *relaciones de mérito y servicio* and *probanzas* (proof of services rendered to the king), native elites throughout colonial Latin America enumerated and chronicled the contributions made by them or their ancestors to the conquest, evangelization, or administration of the Crown's American holdings. The most famous of these were Felipe Guaman Poma de Ayala's *Nueva crónica y buen gobierno*, El Inca Garcilaso de la Vega's *Comentarios reales de los Incas*, and Fernando Alva de Ixtlilxochitl's *Compendio histórico del reino de Texcoco*. Though rendered in a language that trumpeted the identity of these native noblemen as "loyal vassals" to the Crown, these texts were remarkably ambivalent in their cultural and political substance. Their authors used European written genres to critique the actions and comportment of the *conquistadores*, local *corregidores* (Spanish governors), and priests while at the same time maintaining allegiance to the Crown and the Spanish colonial enterprise, and pursuing the interests of their own lineages.[16] The ambivalence in these colonial narratives complicates the neat opposition between unqualified deference and open resistance. Through their powers of written expression, these men sought to negotiate with Spanish royal authority more than to resist it. Their goal was not to turn the world upside down but to arrive at a comfortable accommodation with their colonial rulers, or at the most provoke a reform of the established colonial order.

Like relaciones and probanzas, the 1684 petition to the king must be considered an ambivalent text and a tactic of political negotiation. As native leaders, Santiago, Celis, and Alvarado had to read, interpret, and publicly react to volatile political situations. Through their competent deployment of the language of fealty, the three caciques performed a role in accordance with the expectations of their Spanish audience. Their proclamation of fealty to the Crown and Church cleared them of Spanish suspicion of disloyalty. But loyalty to the Crown did not fully define their position, nor were the magistrate and the king their only audiences.

As native leaders, Celis, Santiago, and Alvarado were answerable not only to the Crown but also to local groups. Clearly, there was sufficient discontent in the area surrounding Choapan to provoke a native uprising. As local notables of regional reach, these men were keenly aware of pressures from below. Depending on the level of native discontent and the degree of state intervention in local affairs, they faced the possibilities of violence from below and sanctions from above if they failed to carry out the apparently contradictory roles of defender of community against colonial abuses and loyal vassal to the Spanish king and servant of the Catholic Church. In the years that followed the Choapan uprising, Santiago's and Celis's competing audiences tested the limits of their powers as intermediary figures and power brokers. From 1685 until 1690, Santiago and Celis waged a political campaign against the alcaldes mayores of the district, which brought on charges of sedition against both of them.

THE STRUGGLE OVER ELECTORAL AUTONOMY

The 1684 uprising gave the alcalde mayor of Villa Alta license to intervene in native affairs in the interest of local security. In fact, the uprising ushered in a short and intense period of colonial interference in pueblo politics through attempts to manipulate elections of native *cabildos* (native municipal governments). In 1685, one year after the Choapan uprising, *principales* (native notables) from the pueblos of Latani and Yaveo complained to the Audiencia that the alcalde mayor had refused to recognize the election of new governors in their pueblos. The Real Audiencia supported the alcalde mayor's intervention and ordered that the outgoing governors remain in power since they were to the liking of the alcalde mayor. The Audiencia justified its decision by citing the recent rebellion and expressing concern over the threat of renewed unrest.[17]

The Audiencia's stance was most likely a reaction not only to the 1684 Choapan uprising but also to the 1660 rebellion. By supporting the alcalde mayor in his efforts to control native resistance and sedition, the Real Audiencia abrogated the right that native pueblos throughout New Spain had enjoyed since 1622—and would continue to enjoy until the Bourbon Reforms—to elect their own cabildos without the interference of outsiders like the alcalde mayor and parish priests. We should assume that from 1685 to 1690, the alcalde mayor of Villa Alta intervened at least intermittently in pueblo elections given the 1685 decree discussed above and given that in 1690, the Audiencia, in response to a petition from ninety pueblos of the jurisdiction of Villa Alta that demanded an end to the intervention of Spanish officials in municipal elections, ordered the alcalde mayor, his lieutenant (*teniente*), and parish priests to allow the pueblos of the jurisdiction to elect their officials without interference.[18]

In the Sierra Norte, as in other regions of New Spain, the notion that the cabildo was "elected" proved largely a euphemism.[19] The nobility of a pueblo, consisting of *caciques* (señorial lords) and *principales* (nobility of lesser status), determined who among them would hold office during any given year, and rotated in and out of the most powerful posts. The office of governor was most prized because of the access it afforded to community resources. Governors, with the assistance of magistrates (*alcaldes*) and councilmen (*regidores*), oversaw a community treasury (*caja de comuni-dad*), the collection of taxes and tribute, and, most important, mediated the repartimiento. In general, only caciques held the post of governor and were exempt from holding other offices, whereas principales more fre-quently filled the posts of alcalde and regidor. Commoners could hold the lowest offices. During their years out of office, the remaining caciques and principales constituted either a "shadow government," serving as advisors to the elected municipal authority, and/or situated themselves as an op-positional faction.[20]

The composition of the cabildo was of strategic importance not only to the caciques and principales of native pueblos, but also to the alcalde mayor, his lieutenant, parish priests, and some powerful Spanish local residents (*vecinos*) in Villa Alta, in large part because of their reliance on the cabildo to collect tribute, ensure social order, and, most important, mediate the repartimiento. During the lieutenant's rounds to the district's pueblos, he provided eight pounds of cotton and a cash advance of eight reales to the native governors, alcaldes, and regidores, who in turn dis-tributed the raw materials and cash to each head of household. The lieu-tenant returned in a stipulated amount of time (usually a few months) to collect finished cotton cloth and cochineal dye from the cabildo. A second form of the repartimiento involved distribution of goods, such as livestock (cattle and mules, for example) by Spanish merchants (often vecinos of Villa Alta) to native heads of household, with payment expected within six months to a year.[21] The lieutenant and the alcalde mayor wanted native officers in power who could ensure the delivery of repartimiento quotas and cash debts. Beyond the mediation of the repartimiento, native gover-nors and alcaldes were often expected to siphon money and goods from their pueblos to the storehouses and pockets of Spanish officials, either through the repartimiento or illicit forms of extortion. John Chance has argued that many native officials also kept a pound or so of cotton, one real, or a mule for themselves, and that other elites tolerated the officials' actions in the expectation that they would have the same economic oppor-tunities once they became officials.[22]

The objectives of a pueblo's caciques and principales (or factions thereof) vis-à-vis the composition of the native cabildo at times clashed with those of the alcalde mayor and *teniente*. Conflicts of interest and competition for power appear to have been exacerbated by the political climate of the district after 1685, during which time the alcalde mayor interfered in pueblo elections with impunity. This power imbalance likely prompted a group of unnamed principales of the district to bring a petition to the Audiencia in August 1688, complaining of the "troubles, offenses, and humiliations" perpetrated by the alcalde mayor Juan Manuel Bernardo de Quiroz. The judges ordered Quiroz to appear in front of them to answer the charges.[23] In addition, the municipal officials of Yatzona, Yahuio, and other pueblos brought a legal case to the Audiencia against Quiroz, which the Audiencia heard in 1689. According to the petition brought by the plaintiffs, the alcalde mayor had taken goods such as hens and chicks, and had demanded services such as the cutting and carrying of firewood from the pueblos closest to the town of Villa Alta—Yatzona, Roayaga, Tagui, Temascalapa, Yalahui, Yaa, Yatee, and Lachitaa—without proper compensation.[24] As events unfolded, it became clear that Felipe de Santiago, Joseph de Celis, Andrés Martín of Yatzachi, and Gabriel Martín of Choapan were the unnamed principales who organized the legal cases against the alcalde mayor. Santiago acted as apoderado and the other men collected funds from the signatory pueblos to pay for the litigation.[25]

The four caciques' ability to mobilize and unite ninety of the district's one hundred pueblos against the alcalde mayor over the cause of electoral autonomy is stunning in light of Villa Alta's ethnic complexities and current understandings of native politics and identity during the colonial period. The district of Villa Alta was home to three ethnic groups (Zapotec, Mixe, and Chinantec) and five linguistic groups (the Zapotecs of Villa Alta spoke three linguistic variants: Nexitzo, Cajonos, and Bijanos) with a long history of interethnic tension and enmity. The scholarship on native politics in New Spain paints a picture of inward-looking native communities whose identifications were highly localized and rooted in the pueblo. This form of identity has been compared to "ethnonationalism," the emphasis being on its tendency to fragment and produce conflict rather than unite over common causes.[26] William Taylor and others have argued that this localized or atomized native identity precluded coordinated rebellions of regional scope.[27] The campaign against the alcalde mayor of Villa Alta paints a different picture. Although rooted in the pueblo, as evident in myriad interpueblo disputes, native identifications in Villa Alta could also prove quite fluid and situational in the late seventeenth century and, given the proper circumstances, could produce regional strategic alliances that cut across linguistic and ethnic boundaries.

The Audiencia proved itself a sympathetic ally to the cause of native autonomy when in December 1689 it issued a royal decree (*real provisión*) that forbade Quiroz to coerce labor or extort goods from the pueblos and ordered him to provide the plaintiffs with proper compensation for their goods and services. A day earlier, the Audiencia responded to the petition of the ninety sierra pueblos with a decree for the reinitiation of free elections in the jurisdiction, without the interference of the alcalde mayor, his lieutenant, or the parish priest. In the same decree, the Audiencia warned Quiroz not to seek vengeance on the authors and organizers of the petition, in particular Joseph de Celis and Gabriel Martín.[28] In March 1690, the Audiencia issued three more royal decrees [*reales provisiones*]. The first forbade the alcalde mayor and his tenientes to harass residents of the pueblos of Choapan, Chinantla, and the rest of the jurisdiction, and insisted that the Indians of the jurisdiction be paid proper prices for their products. The second prohibited the collection of tribute before the designated time. The third insisted that the alcalde mayor and his tenientes leave the native governors, alcaldes, and the pueblos of the jurisdiction in peace, that they should be allowed to live in their houses (presumably without threat of exile), and that those who were entitled should not be prevented from wearing Spanish dress, riding a mount with saddle and bridle, or using mules.[29]

Celis's and Santiago's political organizing and legal efforts on behalf of local autonomy and against the heavy-handed demands and interventions of the alcalde mayor required two important calculations. First, they had to accept that the alcalde mayor would interpret their actions as an all-out political campaign against him, and that, as a result, they might suffer serious sanctions. The Audiencia certainly recognized this likelihood in its 1690 decree, when it forbade the alcalde mayor to persecute Celis and Martín. Second, they were well aware that the Real Audiencia situated itself as protector of its Indian subjects against the abuses of local magistrates. Santiago and Celis presumed with good reason, therefore, that the high court might support their demands.

THE ALCALDE MAYOR STRIKES BACK: THE POLITICS OF REPUTATION

Felipe de Santiago and Joseph de Celis were right on both counts: they won the support of the Audiencia, but at a high cost. The alcalde mayor was incensed by the political campaign waged against him and attempted to silence Celis and Santiago through intimidation and coercion. Once again, the courts proved to be the theater in which this political drama was enacted. Eighteen months before the Real Audiencia found in favor of the first petition against the alcalde mayor, both Santiago and Celis were brought to criminal court on separate charges. During the alcalde mayor's pueblo inspections, some principales in the jurisdiction denounced Celis's efforts to organize the petition against the alcalde mayor. In response, the alcalde mayor leveled charges of sedition against Celis.[30]

Curiously, and perhaps not coincidentally, eight days later, a Spanish resident of Villa Alta claimed that Felipe de Santiago had stolen mules from her. During the trial, witnesses from a number of different pueblos claimed that Santiago and Celis had been seeking power of attorney to bring a petition against the alcalde mayor. At this point, the court expanded the criminal charges against Santiago to include sedition.[31]

On the one hand, the alcalde mayor's deployment of criminal charges against Santiago and Celis points to the ways the courts could be mobilized for political purposes. On the other hand, the charges also reveal how the intermediary position of men like Santiago and Celis, which in this case encompassed trade and legal mediation, made them vulnerable to legal sanction. According to his own admission, Santiago traded in cochineal dye in the neighboring district of Ixtepeji.[32]

Santiago's commerce in cochineal, the highly valued commodity produced by the repartimiento, situated him as an economic competitor vis-à-vis the alcalde mayor, teniente, parish priests, and other Spanish vecinos who had a stake in the region's political economy. In the 1688 case against Santiago for mule theft, witnesses testified that he compounded his wealth by selling mules, which he also utilized for his commercial activities.[33] As we saw earlier in this chapter, mules represented another commodity circulated via the repartimiento. Spanish merchants traveled to native pueblos throughout Oaxaca providing mules, oxen, and other beasts of burden on credit. Since draft animals were valuable and expensive, few natives had sufficient means to make good on the credit six months later, which often indebted them further while expanding the profits of the merchants. By trading in mules, Santiago not only positioned himself as an economic competitor to the Spaniards who sold draft animals, he also equipped himself to engage in the long-distance trade of cochineal dye, and thereby threatened the alcalde mayor's monopoly. Finally, by selling mules to local people on credit, Santiago exploited native villagers. The role of economic exploiter places the role of defender of pueblo autonomy in a different light. By defending the district pueblos' electoral independence from the alcalde mayor, Santiago may well have been clearing the way for his own profits.

The economic dimension of Santiago's power helps to explain the hostility of Spanish officials toward him. John Chance notes that in the late seventeenth century, a group of itinerant Indian merchants, most of cacique or principal status, and some of whom dressed as Spaniards, appeared on the scene in the district of Villa Alta. They traded in chile, salt, shrimp, cotton, soap, dishes, and *guaraches* (leather sandals), and appear to have had contacts or lieutenants in pueblos throughout the sierra. Their economic ascendance occurred at the same time that the Spanish magistrates were working to eliminate their economic competition in the district.[34] The charges of mule theft against Santiago take on a different meaning in this context of Spanish-native competition. In the sierra, commerce was impossible without mules, horses, or donkeys because of the difficult terrain and the distance to commercial centers. Only natives with the economic wherewithal to purchase and maintain these animals could sustain a career in long-distance trade or in the trade of the mules themselves. By challenging the legality of Santiago's possession of and trade in mules, the alcalde mayor could cripple an economic competitor. Economic competition may explain why from 1650 to 1701, in addition to Felipe de Santiago, at least twelve native men, many of whom were of elite status, were brought up on charges of mule theft in the district court of Villa Alta.[35] The plaintiffs were most often other native elites or Spanish vecinos.

Apparently Santiago was not the only one with a reputation for theft. In an effort to build the case of sedition against Celis, the prosecuting attorney invoked Celis's criminal record (bear in mind that this was the same case of sedition in which the defense attorney had attempted to play up Celis's identity as a "loyal vassal" by presenting as evidence the 1684 petition to the king by Celis, Santiago, and Alvarado). Allegedly, during the tenure of alcalde mayor Cristóbal del Castillo Mondragón, Celis had broken into the community church under cover of night and stolen the silver *pedestal de la custodia* (base of the monstrance).[36]

To steal the base of the monstrance—a valuable silver object used in

Catholic mass—was an act replete with economic, political, and religious meaning. As a commodity, the base of the monstrance straddled two categories: it was both a high-value luxury good and an implement of the sacred. The monstrance as a whole was the object that displayed the holy Host—the wafer that would become, through the sacrament of the Eucharist, the body of Christ. During the mid-seventeenth century—the height of the Baroque period—a new style of monstrance came increasingly into use. The Baroque monstrance consisted of a base from which arose a narrow column, which in turn gave rise to what appears a sunburst, a halo of silver or gold rays emanating from the glass circle at the center, the space intended for the Host.[37] The base of the monstrance allowed the Host to be displayed on the central altar during mass. The Host could then be removed from its base when necessary and processed by the priest during public celebrations such as the festival of Corpus Christi. The monstrance allowed a large congregation to gaze on the host, which produced a simultaneously public and visual experience of the Eucharist. In this regard, the Baroque monstrance symbolized the apotheosis of two developments in seventeenth-century Catholicism: the preeminence of the Eucharist as the most important sacrament and the centralization of sacred authority in the hands of the parish priest.[38]

The allegations of theft of the monstrance must be considered in the context of an intense struggle during the second half of the seventeenth century between native people and the Catholic Church over what the Church considered to be a preponderance of idolatry in native pueblos. The widespread persistence of native religious practices in Villa Alta, often under the leadership of cabildo officers, has been well documented, and was very present in the minds of Spanish authorities throughout the seventeenth and eighteenth centuries.[39] Whereas extirpation campaigns in New Spain had lost much of their steam by the end of the seventeenth century, in the region of Villa Alta, the campaign against idolatry escalated from the 1660s through the 1730s.[40] Of note was the existence of networks of "ritual specialists" who interpreted and utilized sacred texts and calendars for individual and community needs.[41] A subregional pattern of ritual specialization appears to have existed, in which the *doctrina* (Church district) of Villa Alta (of which Celis's and Santiago's home pueblo of San Juan Yatzona was a part) served as a hotspot for divination and home to a cadre of native priests.[42] In contrast with the central regions of Mexico or the Valley of

Oaxaca, there was no division in the district of Villa Alta between the priestly and political classes; the two appear to have been intertwined.[43] Given their literacy, political leadership in interpueblo networks, and enmity with the parish priest, it is possible that Celis and Santiago were part of that elite cadre of ritual specialists.

If Celis was indeed a native ritual specialist, then the parish priest of Villa Alta represented a competitor, much as the alcalde mayor represented a political and economic rival. To steal the base of the monstrance deprived the parish priest of an implement of his power. More pointedly, it crippled the Host, which could not be displayed on the altar without the monstrance's base. The separate components of monstrances were not interchangeable, so the base of another monstrance would not do.

In the context of an intense extirpation campaign, to accuse a native leader of stealing the base of the monstrance was to accuse him of egregious disobedience of Spanish authority. As such, it makes sense that the allegations against Celis of stealing the base of the monstrance reappeared in the text of his 1688 sedition case. The symbolic linkage between sedition and the theft of the base of the monstrance becomes crystal clear in an exchange between Celis and the prosecutor during the sedition case. In the opening passages of Celis's testimony, the prosecuting attorney asked him a series of questions concerning the charges of sedition against him. Celis did not deny that he had traveled through the district and had visited with community leaders, but he claimed that these visits were of a personal rather than a political nature. Immediately following this exchange, the prosecuting attorney asked Celis if he remembered the case brought against him some years before regarding the theft of the base of the monstrance. Celis replied, without admitting guilt, that yes, he remembered the case, and that he had paid. The attorney went on to ask him how he had paid. According to Celis's own account, he had paid quite dearly: he had been condemned to be whipped publicly and to be sold into service. He did not remember how many lashings he had been given, but he did remember that he served one year of hard labor in the mines, three months of service in the church, eight months of personal service for Hernando de Chaves, a mestizo from the pueblo of Lahoya, and eight months of personal service for Chaves's son Miguel, whom his own wife also served for four months.[44]

At least a quarter of Celis's testimony in the case of sedition against him was taken up with questioning and testimony concerning the theft of the base of the monstrance and Celis's harsh punishment. As such, the story was an important aspect of the prosecutor's rhetorical strategy, the thrust of which was to criminalize Celis's political challenge to the alcalde mayor during 1688, when Celis and Santiago brought the case to the Audiencia demanding that the alcalde mayor refrain from interfering in pueblo elections. In this regard, the magistrate's tactics represent what Scott has called the "politics of reputation," "in which a good name is conferred in exchange for adherence to a certain code of conduct."[45]

But in a colonial situation, more than one code of conduct was at play. How did the villagers of Yatzona and other pueblos in the district interpret the allegations of theft against Celis and the criminal trial and punishment that ensued? Although we do not have access to native reactions and interpretations, as a hidden audience, they took in and made meaning of the drama around them. Native interpretations of Celis's story may well have had reverberations in the tense decades that followed.

The association of both Celis and Santiago with sedition and thievery make clear that rivalry between native and Spanish power brokers involved symbolic warfare and a high-stakes game of perception. At the conclusion of their 1688 criminal trials, the alcalde mayor found both Santiago and Celis guilty of sedition (he also found Santiago guilty of mule theft), for which they received severe sentences. Santiago was publicly sentenced to one hundred lashes—some convicted criminals did not survive one hundred lashings—in public view in the town of Villa Alta, and afterward, to labor in the construction of the church of Our Lady of Solitude in the city of Antequera. Keenly aware of the symbolic power of such punishment, the alcalde mayor made clear in his pronouncement of the sentence that Santiago's public beating was meant to serve as an example to political agitators.[46] Celis was sentenced to two years of exile during which time he could not enter or conduct commercial activities in the jurisdiction.[47] We do not know for sure if these sentences were carried out. Celis appealed to the Real Audiencia. Two years later, in 1690, the judges of the Audiencia chastised the alcalde mayor for pronouncing a sentence in a criminal case without first consulting the high court.[48] This was the same year that the Audiencia forbade the alcalde mayor to demand labor and services without compensation, prohibited his interference in pueblo elections, and proscribed the persecution of Celis and Martín for their petition against him.[49] For Celis, then, the Audiencia's admonition came two years too late. In the case of Santiago, we do not know whether he ultimately suffered the lashings or performed the hard labor.

As the cases of theft and sedition against Santiago and Celis demonstrate, leveraging power was a dangerous game. For native intermediaries, the threat of sanctions from below complemented the threat of sanctions from above. In 1698, Santiago found himself at the center of a standoff between the pueblo of Lachirioag and the alcalde mayor Capitán Juan Antonio Mier del Tojo. At issue were the three legal documents (the royal decrees) that were won in 1690 by the pueblos of the jurisdiction through Santiago's legal mediation. In 1698, the cabildos of Choapan and Yatzachi presented a royal order (*real despacho*) demanding that all three 1690 royal decrees be turned over to the possession of the two pueblos. According to the petition submitted by the cabildos, the case that Santiago, Celis, and Martín had organized against the alcalde mayor Juan Manuel Bernardo de Quiroz had been brought to the Audiencia in the name of the pueblos of the entire jurisdiction, but it had been spearheaded in particular by the cabildos of Choapan and Yatzachi, who had hired Santiago as their apoderado. In their petition, the principales of Choapan and Yatzachi made clear that they felt that the royal decrees were rightfully theirs.[50]

Alcalde Mayor Mier del Tojo agreed to the terms of the royal decree and sent his interpreter to inform Santiago, then governor of San Juan Yatzona, of the terms of the royal order, and to request that Santiago make the royal decrees available to the cabildos of Choapan and Yatzachi. According to the interpreter's report, Santiago informed him that he was not in possession of the royal decrees; rather, the pueblo of Lachirioag had them.[51]

According to the interpreter's testimony and the testimony of three principales of Yatzona, Santiago traveled with the interpreter and the principales to the pueblo of Lachirioag and asked that the royal decrees be turned over to their legal owners. As Santiago discussed the issue with the cabildo of Lachirioag in the village plaza, a crowd gathered, led by the alcaldes of the previous year and the governor of the nearby pueblo of Tabaa. The witnesses claimed that the mood was tense, and that, sensing trouble, the alcaldes of Lachiroag attempted to placate the crowd, which murmured and then shouted its opposition to handing over the royal decrees. A scuffle ensued, resulting in jailing Santiago and the alcaldes of Lachirioag.[52]

When news of the illegal imprisonment reached the alcalde mayor, he decided to travel to Lachirioag himself with some of his lieutenants and intervene. He reported that he was shocked and incensed to find that the crowd refused to release the prisoners. When he asked the leaders of the crowd why, they replied that the 1688–90 litigation against Alcalde Mayor Juan Manuel Bernardo de Quiroz had cost the pueblo ten thousand pesos, and that given this economic sacrifice and the fact that the petition against the alcalde mayor had been made in the name of the pueblos of the entire jurisdiction and had been won by all, it seemed an injustice that the three documents should remain in the hands of only two pueblos. The crowd stood firm and refused to release Santiago until the moment that Celis, Gabriel Martín, and Andrés Martin, who had been responsible for collecting the funds for the litigation, appeared in the pueblo.[53]

According to his own report, the alcalde mayor, through the intervention of his interpreter, prevailed on the leadership of the mutiny to release the alcaldes, and eventually to release Santiago. As the three former prisoners provided their testimony to the alcalde mayor, they emphasized what they claimed were the very real possibilities of a violent uprising over the issue of the royal decrees. They testified that through the prison window, they could hear the crowd's leaders making plans to contact the pueblos of the Rincón, Cajonos, and Mixe regions to come to their aid should a violent standoff ensue. The alcalde mayor ruled that since no one would claim responsibility for the events in Lachirioag, the entire pueblo was guilty of disobedience.[54]

In this particular moment, the alcalde mayor took a pragmatic stance. He ordered that the originals of the three royal decrees be placed in the district archive so that any pueblo could have official copies made. He then declared that the pueblos of Lachirioag, Yatzachi, and Choapan could have any portion of the documents that they desired reproduced.[55] A receipt made out to the pueblos of Yatzachi, Lachrioag, and Betaza dated 30 May 1700, indicates that at least these three pueblos took him up on the proposition. But it also appears that the cabildos of Yatzachi and Choapan were not satisfied with this arrangement, and that they appealed to the Audiencia. On 14 October 1701, in compliance with the Audiencia's orders, the alcalde mayor turned over the originals to the officials of Yatzachi and Choapan.[56]

The standoff in the pueblo of Lachirioag demonstrates the fragility of interpueblo alliances, and points to what Van Young has characterized as a persistent tension between solidarity and conflict in native social and political life.[57] Although Santiago, Celis, and the other organizers of the 1688–90 campaign against Alcalde Mayor Quiroz were able to create a united front among the pueblos of the jurisdiction, they clearly built this unity on a shifting foundation. The anger of the crowd in Lachirioag toward Felipe de Santiago demonstrates that there was little unanimity regarding the provision of funds to support the litigation, and money may have been extracted from villagers who knew or cared little about district-level politics and the intricacies of litigation in Mexico City. To put the alleged ten-thousand-peso cost of the 1688–90 litigation in perspective, María de los Angeles Romero Frizzi has estimated that during the seventeenth century, the average salary for an unskilled Oaxacan peasant on a hacienda was one real (8 reales = 1 peso) per day, and that the average cost of a machete was 6 reales.[58] The three royal decrees were therefore won at a very high cost indeed.

The stubborn refusal of the crowd to give over the documents hints that there may have been several motivations and expectations associated with the 1688 litigation against the alcalde mayor. Whereas the high officers who agreed to participate may have supported the explicit political goals of the case, lesser officials and commoners had a complementary goal in mind: obtaining and keeping the documents themselves. Whether penned in the municipal halls of remote sierra pueblos or in the ornate chambers of the Real Audiencia, legal documents had high material and symbolic value to native individuals and groups. Royal decrees, land titles, and wills often represented the only legal claim of an individual, group, or pueblo to special privileges, rights, land, or an inheritance. In particular, royal decrees and land titles also embodied the authority of the king, and as such represented the material and symbolic reach of imperial culture into remote locales.

Although they embodied colonial authority, legal documents could also challenge it. As in the case of the royal decrees won by Santiago, Celis, and Martín, legal documents often represented victory in long and hard-fought legal battles against a Spanish magistrate or parish priest, and thereby preserved the memory of resistance to colonial injustices. In other cases, over time, knowledge of the specific content of legal documents faded.

Since many of those who possessed wills, land titles, or even royal decrees could not read them, they relied on oral tradition and historical memory for knowledge of their substance. In this process, the documents took on new meanings, and those new meanings in turn shaped local forms of identity and shared concepts of the past. Joanne Rappaport describes twentieth-century Andean-produced histories as "palimpsests in which the distant past, the recent past, and the present are layered, in which the political maneuvers of ancient chiefs and the labors of artisans of just thirty years ago complement each other, and in which written and oral modes of communication are interwoven with practical action." These interpretations of local history by local peoples "spring from the interface of the indigenous community and the state," and "the bridge that connects community and state is paved with papers and with interpretations of them."[59] As Rappaport's study demonstrates, the centrality of legal documents to collective identity, history, and political struggle appears to have been a feature of native cultures throughout Mexico and the Andes from the colonial period up to the present.

As in other regions, in the district of Villa Alta, legal documents represented a precious patrimony for sierra pueblos and kin groups, to be closely guarded from the ravages of termites, dampness, and political enemies in warm and dry ovens or church safe boxes. In a 1696 land dispute in the pueblo of Tagui, a litigant explained the charred appearance of a will as follows: "women keep their papers in the oven to keep them free from termites and so your lordship will in time see women bringing smoked papers from various places." The blackened will had led the man's opponents in the case to charge that the claimant had forged the will and "smoked" it in order to make it look old.[60] The contestation over the validity of the document and the reference to its safekeeping speak to the range of conflicts that written documents could engender at the level of the pueblo.

Legal documents constituted part of the common symbolic framework produced by native intermediaries and Spanish officials in the process of political struggle. Given their quasi-sacred status, it makes sense that the crowd gathered in the plaza of Lachirioag threatened and risked violence to maintain possession of the hard-won royal decrees. Through their actions, the crowd in Lachirioag pushed back against the power of their legal agent, Felipe de Santiago, and the alcalde mayor. Their defiance hints at the divergent meanings of legal documents, at once instruments of colonial authority, embodiments of local identity, and inspiration for subversion.

A SHADOW SYSTEM: INDIGENOUS POLITICS

The political mediation of Santiago and Celis during the last decades of the seventeenth century raises important questions. First, how did they go from being self-proclaimed loyal vassals to the Crown in 1684 to perpetrators of sedition in the years that followed? Second, why did they risk so much for the cause of local autonomy, particularly since their risks did not secure the allegiance of the people they represented, as evidenced by the imprisonment of Santiago by the villagers of Lachirioag?

In response to the first question, following the Choapan uprising, Santiago and Celis proclaimed their fealty to the Crown and the Church, and not to the Spanish magistrate. This represented a strategic alignment with the highest powers in the realm, both of which had ambivalent relationships with the colony's alcaldes mayores. The Church often viewed the alcaldes mayores as obstacles to its objectives in the countryside. The repartimiento of the Spanish magistrates directed pueblo funds and resources away from parish churches, Church revenues, and community-level Church activities. The abuses of the alcaldes mayores—demands for production at overcapacity, whippings of community leaders who did not comply, underpayment, and overcharging for goods—threatened the delicate social order over which the Church presided in the countryside through the incitement of resentment toward local representations of colonial authority and sometimes open rebellion. For these reasons, the Church hierarchy intermittently recommended to the Crown abolition of the *alcaldías mayores* (office of alcalde mayor) and the repartmiento. It should be remembered, however, that there were exceptions to the general animosity of the Church toward the magistrates. In the war against idolatry in the district of Villa Alta, the Church and the magistrates were allies.

The Crown recognized the threat to the Pax Hispanica that abusive alcaldes mayores represented, but it also recognized that without the rural magistrates, there would be no civil authority in the countryside. As I mentioned earlier, the Crown's solution to this dilemma was to position itself as a defender of its Indian subjects against the offenses of alcaldes mayores. The system of judicial appeal that allowed the Crown's indigenous subjects access to the Real Audiencia was intended to check the power of the alcaldes mayores and to channel cause for rebellion into nonviolent forms of expression.

Santiago and Celis were well attuned to these cleavages in colonial power. In their view, there was no contradiction between fealty to the Crown and Church and opposition to an alcalde mayor or parish priest who misrepresented the authority of the Crown or Church. For Santiago and Celis, the Audiencia, if approached properly, represented a strategic ally. Their sedition—their legal campaign against the interference of the alcalde mayor in pueblo affairs—was therefore an act of political brokerage, a playing off of competing colonial powers in order to influence local rule.

The response to the second question—Why risk severe sanction for the cause of local autonomy, and in particular electoral autonomy?—lies in Santiago's and Celis's rootedness in local indigenous political structures and their efforts to open a political space to pursue locally oriented political goals. This hidden history can be pieced together through incidental references in the legal cases in question and must be considered in two dimensions: regionwide alliances and conflicts, and pueblo-based politics.

Native intermediaries mediated native interests and brokered regional alliances and local political conflicts whose roots were often hidden from Spanish view. For example, in 1696, the governors of Yatzona, Temascalapa, Yalahui, Tabaa, and Yalalag brought charges of sedition against Miguel de Santiago, governor of Santiago Yagallo. They complained that during the market day in San Juan Yae, he had slandered their legal agent, Felipe de Santiago. Witnesses in the case made cryptic references to political factions (*parcialidades*) of regional reach headed by Felipe de Santiago and Celis. According to the testimony, Miguel de Santiago was trying to convince and even intimidate the witnesses to join the parcialidad of Celis because it was rumored that by order of the alcalde mayor, Felipe de Santiago was soon to be imprisoned in the jail of San Juan de Ulua in Veracruz for unspecified crimes.[61]

Reference to Felipe de Santiago's parcialidad surfaced again twice in the legal documentation of the period. In a land dispute in Temascalapa, according to their own admissions, the witnesses—almost all of whom were from Yatzona—were divided in their allegiances along parcialidad lines, hinting at lineage or patronage connections between the two pueblos.[62] The witnesses identified the leaders of the parcialidades as Felipe de Santiago and Pablo de Vargas, another cacique of San Juan Yatzona. In the fifteen years that followed the Choapan Uprising, Vargas had enjoyed the support of Yatzona's parish priest and the alcaldes mayores Alonso Muñoz de Castilblanque (1684–86), Juan Manuel Bernardo de Quiroz (1687–91), and Miguel Ramón de Nogales (1692–96), which ensured his more or less continuous tenure as governor of Yatzona from 1684 to 1696, as well as governor of the nearby pueblo of Reagui. Vargas's cozy relationship with the alcaldes mayores and parish priests, which compromised Yatzona's pueblo autonomy, positioned him as a longtime rival of Santiago, until Vargas hired Santiago as apoderado in 1695.

Further evidence of Felipe de Santiago's regional networks appears in a 1696 decree, in which the Real Audiencia forbade Santiago to serve as apoderado or interpreter anywhere in the district because of alleged abuse of authority. Apparently, the cabildos of Choapan, Yalahui, and other pueblos had brought a case against Santiago and Nicolas de la Cruz, another principal from San Juan Yatzona who served at the time as the interpreter general for the jurisdiction. According to the petition, Santiago and Cruz had taken advantage of their positions as apoderado and interpreter to encourage legal disputes for their own economic benefit, and to extort money and cotton cloth (in the sierra, a commodity second in value only to cochineal dye) from the petitioning pueblos.[63]

These incidental documentary references suggest that Felipe de Santiago's role as a legal intermediary was intertwined with native forms of social organization based on interpueblo lineage and patronage connections, which Spanish interpreters glossed as "parcialidades." Although the Spanish model of the pueblo came to provide the formal and legal structure of social and political relationships in the sierra during the colonial period, aspects of older and local forms of social organization persisted, albeit in modified form.[64] Pueblo-based parcialidades appear to have intersected with and crosscut interpueblo parcialidades. In the case of San Juan Yatzona, pueblo-based parcialidades expressed competition through legal battles over election results from 1676 until 1702. The years 1692–1702 marked a particularly tense period during which Yatzona's political factions brought six cases of electoral fraud, sedition, embezzlement, or bad government against one another.[65] Reference to the parcialidades of Celis, Santiago, and Vargas pepper the hundreds of pages of testimony taken in these cases.

The petitions and testimony found in the cases that chronicle Yatzona's electoral disputes provide rich evidence of colonial political culture in the making. The rhetoric that Vargas, Santiago, Celis, and their competing parcialidades used against one another drew on a growing pattern of maligning native leaders for compromising pueblo autonomy through political conspiracy, economic exploitation, and close connections with local Spaniards. In a 1695 case brought by Vargas and Santiago (acting as apoderado) against Celis's parcialidad, they accused Celis of directing via "ill-intentioned advice" the actions of the municipal government and of holding meetings at his home rather than in the municipal buildings so as to conduct illicit business and concoct lawsuits in privacy. They claimed that Celis utilized legal cases as a means to "extort money and rob us of the few reales that we have, to the point of sucking our life blood." They also accused Celis of initiating legal cases in the name of the entire pueblo when in fact there was no consensus behind the suit. Even more serious, Celis had also allegedly given power of attorney in the name of the pueblo, without its consent, to Pedro Boza de los Monteros, the teniente of Villa Alta.[66]

In their petition against Celis, Vargas and his associates played on the native villagers' resentment of Boza for the role he played in the repartimiento. Vargas and his associates claimed that in order to pay Boza for his legal services to the pueblo, Celis had demanded fish and hens from the pueblo's households, dissimulating that they were payment for the alcalde mayor. According to the petition, Celis and the deposed government also verbally and physically abused those who did not comply with their wishes. Finally, the petitioners complained that through the bad example that he set as a "ladino," Celis had corrupted a young principal who worked in his house by taking him to "Mexico City for lawsuits and for these reasons [Celis] has been teaching him many things about the disobedience of civil officials and priests alike."[67]

Vargas and Santiago then made the very serious rhetorical move of linking Celis with the potential for native rebellion. Apparently, during the electoral dispute, Celis had been imprisoned in the district jail of Villa Alta on unspecified charges. In response, members of the municipal government allegedly abandoned the pueblo of Yatzona, thereby abdicating their civic responsibilities, and moved to Boza's house in Villa Alta. There, they allegedly plotted Celis's release, or if necessary, his escape from jail. According to Vargas and Santiago, the cabildo also contacted Celis's allies in other pueblos, such as Choapan and Yatzachi, asking them to come to Villa

Alta to help spring him from jail. In the words of the accusers, such a situation could result in a regional rebellion.[68] Given the weighty memory of the 1684 Choapan uprising and the 1660 rebellion, these were not allegations to be wielded lightly.

Vargas and company also accused Celis of crimes of corruption. They claimed that he extorted money—for his own benefit and that of Boza and other Spanish vecinos—through the repartimiento. They also charged that on Celis's orders, Yatzona's governor went to Mexico City to get a royal decree that would allow them to sell cabildo offices to whomever would pay, and they accused Celis of nepotism in appointing an incompetent choir master (*maestro de capilla*). Finally, to the great moral outrage of the accusers, Celis and his allies in the cabildo refused to allow the burial of Joseph Mendes, a political enemy of Celis, in the community church. Instead, they allegedly ordered that his body be thrown over a cliff to be eaten by vultures,[69] an act that clearly flew in the face of notions of Christian decency.

The accusations against Celis made a caricature of him, an idealized social type who represented one pole of native leadership in a colonial context. As such, Celis came to stand in for what James Scott has called a "social banner," a human symbol of "good" or "bad" personal and political conduct. The accusations against Celis, which were articulated in legal testimony in the form of stories and anecdotes, must be recognized "as cornerstones of an ideological edifice under construction. They embody, as ideology, a critique of things as they are as well as a vision of things as they should be."[70] The portrayal of Celis as an exploitative legal agent who sold out the community through political conspiracy with Pedro Boza, and who had abandoned all pretensions to good leadership, such as the commitment to community harmony, Christian decency, and peace in the district, constituted a message within a message: This man is a bad Indian, and we (his accusers) are everything that he is not. Of course this message did not necessarily correspond to reality; ten years prior, while the governor of Yatzona, Pablo de Vargas, Celis's chief accuser, had been on the receiving end of similar accusations.[71]

The construction of Celis as a "bad Indian" relied largely on the gendered discourse of "honor." "Honor," a code of conduct of Mediterranean origins, as applied to Iberian colonial society, prescribed certain behaviors for racially defined groups, women and men, and different classes. In this way, "honor" maintained a sense of race-, status-, and gender-based hierarchy (in which Spanish men were on top), while allowing for hierarchy in different social groups, defined by those who followed the code of honor and those who flaunted it. As Sarah Chambers has put it, "more than reflecting internal virtue, honor was a social attribute that increased in value as it was recognized publicly by others."[72] By adhering to codes of honor, Spain's colonial subjects competed for social and cultural capital while legitimizing Spanish rule.

Gender as a symbolic system permeated the discourse of honor and worked together with the discourses of status, race, and Christianity in contradictory ways. For example, the identities of women, children, and "Indians"—the groups that Iberian law classified explicitly as "dependent minors"—were often closely linked through the discourse of honor. The distinction between "good" and "bad" Indians thus intersected with the distinction between "Spaniards" (gendered masculine) and "Indians" (gendered feminine). To be a "good Indian" meant to take on Spanish (masculine) attributes such as "loyal vassalage" and "Christian decency." To be a "bad Indian"—"seditious," "rebellious," or "idolatrous"—invoked the unruly child defying the patriarch, or the religious "neophyte" in need of discipline and further education. Yet "Indian" identity conflicted with legal and social definitions of "masculinity," meaning that "good Indians" always fell short of the social ideal ("Spanishness"). In this regard, the discourse of honor embodied what Carolyn Dean has called "the colonizer's quandary": "the paradoxical need to enculturate the colonized and encourage mimesis while, at the same time, upholding and maintaining the difference that legitimizes colonization."[73]

As in all of the litigation inspired by pueblo factionalism, the audiences for the stories about the ill deeds of one faction or another were the alcalde mayor and the Real Audiencia. As such, the accusers crafted their stories in such a way as to cast the accused's actions in language that would alarm or offend Spanish sensibilities. In effect, Spaniards provided native litigants with the rhetorical arsenal that they deployed against one another for the benefit of a Spanish audience. For example, the portrayal of Celis as an immoral and troublesome legal agent fit well in the parameters of Bishop Cuevas y Dávalos's unflattering portrait of ladino apoderados following the 1660 rebellion. The accusers sought to convince the magistrate that in the interest of the smooth functioning of the pueblo and the district, and an end to bothersome litigation, he needed to sanction Celis and empower his accusers. Through their stories about Celis, Vargas and his allies aimed not only to convince the alcalde mayor, but also to control him and bend him to their purposes: "to control by convincing."[74] This strategy was successful. The Audiencia found in favor of Vargas and his allies, and Vargas continued as governor of Yatzona despite retaliatory cases brought by Celis's parcialidad.[75]

In light of the electoral disputes in San Juan Yatzona, it appears that Santiago's and Celis's 1688–90 campaign against the alcalde mayor, Vargas's alliances with a series of alcaldes mayores during the 1680s and 1690s, and Celis's alliance with teniente Pedro Boza during the 1690s were means to clear the way for the electoral ascendance of these native intermediaries' respective lineage groups or parcialidades. This conclusion requires us to resist viewing electoral factionalism wholly from the perspective of Spanish officials or interpreting alliances and rivalries in terms of Spanish political goals alone or in terms of political goals oriented outward, toward the realm of Spanish officialdom. We must also resist the assumption that the alliance of Boza and Celis and of Vargas and Quiroz represented the co-optation of native leaders by their more powerful Spanish counterparts. The historical evidence speaks eloquently to the political assertiveness and skill of Santiago, Celis, and Vargas. As much as Spanish officials were casting native leaders in their colonial dramas, native leaders were casting Spaniards in dramas of their own making. In doing so, Santiago, Celis, and Vargas performed a deft act of political and cultural brokerage: they worked to accommodate a colonial order in a native political landscape.

CONCLUSION

During the years 1660–1700, native intermediaries and Spaniards struggled over political power, economic resources, and sacred practices. At the heart of it, this struggle was uneven, since the alcalde mayor and parish priests represented the long reach of colonial institutions in the region. From the perspective of native intermediaries, the struggle was not pointless, however, since the demographics of the district precluded a Spanish monopoly on power and afforded native intermediaries room for maneuver. From this political space, native governors and legal agents deployed a range of tactics in order to pursue locally defined goals. The alcaldes mayores and parish priests struck back with their own weapons, as did local people. In the process of this struggle, native intermediaries, Spanish officials, and native villagers constructed and shaped a meaningful framework through which to negotiate and continue to struggle over the shape of local rule. The circulation and deployment of discourses—ladino identity, fealty, criminality, and political conspiracy—all contributed to a broad symbolic juxtaposition between native autonomy and colonial control.

Autonomy had divergent meanings and material implications. Freedom from political interference of the alcalde mayor did not free native pueblos from exploitation; rather, it opened a space for the economic and political ascendance of native brokers at the expense of local people. In winning their case on behalf of native electoral autonomy in 1688, Felipe de Santiago and Joseph de Celis opened space to pursue their economic and political interests and those of their parcialidades, space that had been significantly constrained by the rebellion of 1660 and the Choapan uprising of 1684. Santiago used this space to intensify his economic rivalry with the alcalde mayor, and Santiago, Celis, and Vargas rekindled electoral rivalries during the 1690s through shifting alliances with one another and Spanish officials. The local effects were more factionalism, more litigation, and more resources spent on resolving local conflicts.

Yet to cast native intermediaries as colonial exploiters behind a native veneer oversimplifies the local political order in Villa Alta as much as does casting them as defenders of native autonomy clothed in Spanish silks. As native intermediaries opened political space to pursue their own interests, they faced considerable risks, as evident in the 1688 criminal cases, convictions, and punishments of Celis and Santiago at the hands of the alcalde mayor. In general, Spaniards did not have to worry to the same degree about imprisonment, exile, and corporal punishment, an inequality that always made the political calculations of native intermediaries more complex.

Native intermediaries also faced consequences from below, making them accountable to local people in ways that Spaniards were not. Local people could push back against their native legal agents and impose their own form of sanction on native leaders with whom they were disaffected, as happened in the village square of Lachirioag in 1698. In this regard, commoners could exercise some constraint on the exploitation they suffered at the hands of their own elites. By responding to competing pressures and answering to their many constituencies, native intermediaries

defused the political tinderbox created by the coerciveness of the repartimiento, Catholic evangelization, and tensions in native society. More often
than not, their Spanish counterparts exacerbated and inflamed them. Ultimately, the political opening and balance of power achieved by Santiago
and Celis during the 1690s was short-lived. In 1700, the tinderbox ex-
ploded, shattering the accommodations achieved in the prior decades and
initiating a new cycle of struggle over the terms of local rule. This story will
be taken up in the next chapter.

Chapter 2

"Idolaters and Rebels," "Good and Faithful Indians"
THE CAJONOS REBELLION AND AFTER

On 15 September 1700, a seismic shift in the balance of political forces shook the district of Villa Alta, Oaxaca. In response to an intensified campaign against "idolatry" by Spanish priests and their native assistants, the Zapotec residents of the parish seat of San Francisco Cajonos and many others from surrounding pueblos rose up in a violent rebellion that shocked and unsettled the small population of Spanish and mestizo *vecinos* (local residents) in the administrative seat of Villa Alta. More than one hundred and fifty years after the conquest of the Sierra Norte, it appeared that Spanish colonial control and the Spiritual Conquest were not a fait accompli. The events of 1700 ruptured the Pax Hispanica of the region by unleashing Spanish repression, administrative reform, and native resistance. The official investigation of the incident, the trial of the rebels, the grisly punishments, and the material rewards bestowed on the families of the priest's assistants, whose denunciation of an act of "idolatry" had provoked the rebellion, reconfigured the region's symbolic order. The rebellion had other political effects as well: it reflected and intensified jurisdictional disputes between ecclesiastical and civil authorities as well as the secular Catholic hierarchy and the Dominican order. It also initiated a renegotiation of the terms of local rule among Zapotec intermediaries, the Church, and the state during the eighteenth century.

"IDOLATERS," "REBELS," "MURDERERS": THE SPANISH STORY

The Rebellion

The story of the Cajonos Rebellion comes to us from the letters of Fray Alonso de Vargas, the Dominican *superior*, and Fray Gaspar de los Reyes, the Dominican priest of San Francisco Cajonos, addressed to the *provincial* of Santo Domingo in Oaxaca, as well as from the declarations of seven Spanish witnesses and one African slave who happened to be in the pueblo during the uprising.[1] Documents related to the subsequent investigation conducted by the Real Audiencia and the trial of the suspected murderers and rebels conducted in the district court provide additional narratives of the uprising and its aftermath.[2] These official records offer a more faithful picture of how the Spanish saw the Indians in Villa Alta than they do of the events themselves, or of the motivations of the *fiscales* (priests' assistants), the pueblo officials, or the crowd. From the Spanish perspective, however, we can discern a connection between Spanish fears of "idolatry" and rebellion, which shaped how Spaniards reconfigured the local colonial order in the district of Villa Alta in the wake of the rebellion.

Of particular import in this story are the roles of the fiscales who sparked the uprising by denouncing an act of idolatry in the pueblo of San Francisco Cajonos, and the *cabildo* (native municipal government) officers of San Francisco Cajonos who led the uprising. In chapter 1, we analyzed in detail the strategic middle ground occupied by cabildo officers and legal intermediaries. The intermediary role of the fiscal shares some features with that of the cabildo officer and legal intermediary, but it diverges in significant ways.

Throughout New Spain, the *fiscal de iglesia* represented the most important native office related to the Catholic Church. Fiscales were expected to "promote the cult" of Catholicism in native pueblos. Since the parish priest could not be everywhere at once, these men were afforded considerable latitude in their work. They served as the priests' eyes and ears, and as his "tireless constables" who monitored the moral and religious behavior of native parishioners.[3]

As with the role of native governor, the role of fiscal could prove controversial at the level of the pueblo. Fiscales administered corporal punishment on behalf of the priest: they whipped fellow villagers for failure to attend mass, public drunkenness, and other offenses. They also collected clerical fees and parish taxes, actions that incurred resentment from parishioners already overburdened by tribute and *repartimiento* demands. In the spiritual realm, fiscales assisted the priests with the sacrament and instructed fellow villagers in the Catholic faith. These roles could lead to "spiritual confusion," as some fiscales used their visible and central role in Catholic rituals to position themselves as spiritual rivals to the parish priest. Other fiscales used their authority to oppose community leaders who participated in and led native rituals.[4]

In the district of Villa Alta, during the sixteenth century, Dominican clergy established a school for the sons of Indian nobles and Spanish residents of Villa Alta.[5] As in comparable schools for the sons of indigenous nobility in other regions of New Spain, the friars likely taught their students spoken Spanish, the Christian doctrine, and how to read and write Latin script. In this manner, they groomed them to be fiscales. The Dominicans, like other missionary orders, believed that the social status, political authority, and biculturalism of trained native nobility would uniquely equip them to communicate Christian principles to their fellow natives.

Dominican Fray Pedro de Guerrero, a central figure in the consolidation of Dominican power in the Sierra Norte and vicar of Villa Alta from 1561 to 1576, was the first to appoint fiscales de iglesia in the native pueblos of Villa Alta. As in other regions of New Spain, the fiscales served as the friars' chief assistants and were responsible for the liturgy and catechism. Initially, the Dominicans paid them a small salary. In their role, the fiscales exercised considerable authority, even over the *principales* of their pueblos. They ensured that everyone married in the Christian manner, that unmarried men and women did not live together, and that no religious sacrifices or public drunkenness occurred. They assembled villagers to teach them Catholic doctrine, and punished those who did not conform to Christian norms.[6]

Only a handful of Dominican clerics administered the pueblos of Villa Alta during the late sixteenth and seventeenth centuries. As such, many of the district's natives saw a priest seven or eight times a year at the most.[7] Thus, the power and autonomy of fiscales in the district was considerable, a fact that may have led many to abuse their position or use it for their own purposes. As Taylor puts it, for fiscales, "there was a temptation to bring down local rivals and enemies by charging them on the flimsiest of evidence with violations of the faith."[8]

The fiscales of San Francisco Cajonos thus occupied a strategic intermediary role, and they exercised their power in a manner that provoked a violent clash between Dominican priests, Spaniards, and their native allies, on the one hand, and the villagers of the Cajonos region, on the other. The narrative of the Cajonos Rebellion as told by Spanish witnesses begins on 14 September 1700, when Jacinto de los Angeles and Juan Bautista, the fiscales of the pueblo of San Francisco Cajonos, reported to the parish priest Fray Gaspar de los Reyes that Joseph Flores, the mayordomo of the cofradía of Saint Joseph, was hosting a feast on the patio of his house, and leading his guests in "idolatrous" rites in celebration of the end of his term as mayordomo.[9]

Reyes reported the news to the Dominican superior, Fray Alonso de Vargas, who then called on seven Spaniards and an African slave for assistance. Together, they took off toward the house of Joseph de Flores, bearing swords and guns.[10] The raiding party testified that they arrived at the house undetected, and in the instant before they confronted the celebrators, they claimed that they saw a multitude of people of all ages—men, women, and children—repeating prayers that Sebastian Martín, the choirmaster, read from a parchment inscribed with large, "blood-colored letters." Dressed in *huipiles* that "looked like the white habits worn by priests," and with headscarves, the governor and two *alcaldes* of the pueblo—Joseph de Celis (no apparent relation to Joseph de Celis of San Juan Yatzona), Christóbal de Robles, and Juan Hernández—stood out from the rest of the crowd.[11]

The Spaniards reported that after taking in the scene, they burst into the house. Startled, the crowd dispersed quickly. The Spaniards and the fiscales investigated the remains of the feast and confiscated what they perceived to be evidence of idolatry.[12] The next morning, anticipating trouble, Fray Alonso de Vargas and Fray Gaspar de los Reyes sought reinforcement from a handful of Spanish residents and trusted native officials in neighboring pueblos. Shortly thereafter, a Zapotec crowd, yelling, beating drums, and sounding a horn—all of which were traditional signals to war—besieged the monastery.[13]

The crowd, armed with rocks and machetes, overwhelmed and entered the building despite the shots fired by Spaniards. First, they took back the food and implements confiscated from Flores's house the night before. Then threats ensued: either the Spaniards would turn over the fiscales, or the crowd would burn down the monastery and kill everyone inside. The

Spaniards later identified the governor and alcaldes of San Francisco—Celis, Robles, and Hernández, as well as a principal named José de Mendoza—as the leaders of the crowd. Among the crowd, they identified the other principales of San Francisco Cajonos and many native residents of San Pedro, San Miguel, Santo Domingo, San Pablo, and San Mateo. Terrified for their lives, the Spaniards complied with the wishes of their antagonists. The two fiscales asked the friars to give them their final absolution and Communion. Afterward, the crowd whipped Jacinto de los Angeles and Juan Bautista at the post (*picota*) in the village plaza. They then took the men into their custody and traveled with them to San Pedro. The two fiscales were never seen by Spanish eyes again.[14]

We should pause to consider why the villagers of San Francisco Cajonos responded violently to the fiscales' denunciation and the aggressive disruption of the feast by the friars and Spaniards, given the considerable risks that such violence entailed. Part of the explanation lies in the accumulation of grievances among native elites and villagers in the district of Villa Alta in response to an extirpation campaign led by Dominican friars in concert with Spanish magistrates and secular officials throughout the diocese of Oaxaca.

The extirpation campaign began just after the Rebellion of 1660 and continued until the 1730s. During these years, ecclesiastical and civil authorities intensified the war against idolatry in response to what they perceived to be the recalcitrance of the native populations of the region to the ongoing process of Catholic evangelization.[15] David Tavárez has noted that the most "visible monument" to their efforts to wipe out community ritual practices was the Prison of Perpetual Idolatry, in use from 1686 to 1690, reconstructed by Bishop Angel Maldonado after the Cajonos Rebellion, and used until the mid-eighteenth century.[16] Escalation of the war against idolatry in Oaxaca and in other parts of the Spanish America during the mid-late colonial period overturns the conventional wisdom that the extirpation of idolatry had lost momentum by the seventeenth century.[17]

How resistant were the native populations of Oaxaca to the friars' efforts to impose Catholic orthodoxy and wipe out native ritual in comparison with inhabitants of other regions of the Spanish Empire? As has been shown for the Andes and New Spain, to the chagrin of the missionary orders and the Church hierarchy, and to the detriment of the reputation of the "Spiritual Conquest,"[18] not only did native ritual coexist with Catholicism in a syncretic fashion, but in many regards, it appears that native cosmology continued to provide the primary framework into which aspects of Catholicism were incorporated.[19] Where the Spiritual Conquest was partially successful was in driving native ritual out of the public sphere and into a clandestine domain.[20] In the case of the Sierra Norte of Oaxaca, Alcina Franch and Tavárez have demonstrated that at least until 1700, native ritual practices occurred in clandestine settings, but these rituals remained public in the sense that they often involved the entire community or subgroups within the community. Cabildo officers often led these semiclandestine public rites,[21] and native ritual specialists used ritual texts and calendars to interpret and forecast events in individual lives and the life of the community.[22] Dominican friars and the Church hierarchy in Oaxaca were well aware that these activities took place, though they were perhaps unaware of their ubiquity.

Semiclandestine native ritual challenged the hegemony of Christianity and clearly defied colonial rule. As Tavárez has argued, by the eighteenth century, Zapotec elites and the elites of other indigenous groups could not be accused of nepantlism (*nepantla* being the Nahuatl word for an in "in-between" state, such as that between Christianity and their own religion), nor could they use it as a defense. It was absolutely clear to them that when they engaged in native ritual acts in the privacy of a home or on a mountaintop, they were doing something forbidden.[23] In the case of San Francisco Cajonos, there is no doubt that the villagers considered the fiscales' denunciation of the gathering as a breach of the community boundaries and solidarity necessary to preserve a space for semipublic native ritual, or more broadly for native autonomy. For these reasons, the villagers of San Francisco Cajonos risked the severest of sanctions in their siege of the monastery. In order to defend an autonomous native space, the villagers had to punish the fiscales for their actions.

The Aftermath

Once the Spaniards turned the fiscales over to the Zapotec crowd, the siege of the monastery and the violence abated. José Martínez de la Sierra, the *alguacil mayor* (bailiff) of Villa Alta, arrived in San Francisco Cajonos on 16 September, accompanied by auxiliaries. In a report to the *alcalde mayor* of Villa Alta, Capitán Juan Antonio Mier del Tojo, Sierra described the pueblo as practically empty of inhabitants, save Christóbal de Robles, the alcalde. Robles warned the bailiff that tensions were running high in the Cajonos region, and that if he tried to arrest anyone, the residents of all six pueblos would flee into the mountains. That afternoon, a crowd of about eighty Indians arrived armed with sticks and stones, and demolished the houses of Juan Bautista and Jacinto de los Angeles. Lacking sufficient backup, and not wanting to further provoke the crowd, the bailiff did nothing.[24]

According to Spanish witnesses, that evening Robles initiated negotiations with the Spaniards and padres ensconced in the monastery. He asked what the pueblo of San Francisco could do to right the wrongs committed during the previous days. When asked about the fiscales, he responded that the crowd had set them free on the condition that they leave the region, and go either to Chiapas or Guatemala. The officials of San Mateo followed Robles's lead in attempting reconciliation with the Spaniards and the friars.[25]

Fray Gaspar de los Reyes and José Martínez de la Sierra continued to relay their version of events via letters to the Dominican Provincial and the alcalde mayor. From where they stood, restoring calm to the region's pueblos was the most important objective. In the interest of keeping the peace, Sierra and the friars responded positively to Robles's efforts at conciliation by pardoning the crowd for its actions. But they demanded that the crowd return the fiscales. The crowd claimed to have no knowledge of the latter's whereabouts, an answer that Spanish authorities let stand for the time being. The next morning, the friars opened the church and told the Indians to put aside their differences and their bad feelings toward the fiscales. Then the assistant priest (*padre vicario*) absolved them of their actions after they performed an act of faith and contrition. They returned to their homes, but established a set of conditions of their own. If the Spaniards arrested anyone, they would be forced to defend them, and villagers would flee their homes.[26] Spanish fears of continued unrest were bolstered by Sierra's report of rumors that all eighteen of the Cajonos pueblos were in alliance over the incident, and that the remainder of the pueblos in the district, with the exception of the Mixe, would come to the aid of the Cajonos pueblos if a confrontation ensued.[27]

The alcalde mayor and the Dominican provincial and cabildo endorsed a conciliatory approach through which they hoped to buy time for a militia to arrive from Antequera and occupy the Cajonos region. Although he

asked for armed reinforcement, the alcalde mayor perceived the risks inherent in a coercive response. He pleaded with the resident lawyer of the
Real Audiencia in Antequera, Don Francisco Manuel González, to proceed
with caution given what he perceived to be the high passions running in
the pueblos of the district. The alcalde mayor's ideal approach to the situation combined the carrot and the stick. He hoped to lure back to their
homes the villagers of the six Cajonos pueblos who had fled to the mountains out of fear of Spanish reprisal.[28] The notion of renegade Indians in the
forbidding mountains of the sierra was clearly unacceptable to colonial
officials obsessed with restoring social control.

Spanish officials paired their strategy of conciliation with a concerted
investigation to determine the fate of the fiscales and the identity of the
leaders of the rebellion. In a letter to Sierra, who oversaw the initial investigation, Tojo encouraged him to proceed with subtlety and caution, and to
preserve the veneer of reconciliation and forgiveness.[29] In the meantime,
the alcalde mayor moved quickly to bring the case of idolatry, rebellion,
and murder to the attention of the viceroy.[30] González, the lawyer for the
Real Audiencia, instructed Tojo to lose no time in taking depositions concerning who led the uprising, the complicity of other pueblos in the uprising and the murder of the fiscales, and the whereabouts of the fiscales in
order to secure their return, dead or alive.[31] On orders of the Audiencia,
the alcalde mayor enlisted the help of Spanish officials in the neighboring
districts of Ixtepeji and Teotitlán in the search for the fiscales.[32]

From September through November, six Spaniards and six Indians provided testimony to the alcalde mayor of Villa Alta. Two Indians from Villa
Alta who resided in Antequera provided their own testimony to the corregidor of Oaxaca. In Villa Alta, the witnesses reported rumors that they
had overheard regarding the uprising and the whereabouts of the fiscales.
In Antequera, the two witnesses, identified as *indios ladinos*, provided
testimony on the identities of so-called *maestros de idolatría* in the district
of Villa Alta. The consensus that emerged from the testimony given in
Villa Alta was that a crowd from San Francisco Cajonos and its surrounding pueblos had murdered the fiscales in a gruesome way. According to the
rumors, the mob of Indians seized the fiscales, cruelly whipped them,
imprisoned them, and then took them to a mountain where they cut off
their arms and cut out their hearts, which they threw to dogs. Since the
dogs were unwilling to eat the hearts, they disposed of them in a river and

lit the corpses on fire.[33] This sensational account became the official story in the Spanish judicial system.

In December 1700, the *fiscal del crímen* (akin to an attorney general) of the Real Audiencia, José de Espinoza, presented the case to the viceroy. He foregrounded the murder of the fiscales as a primary concern, and recounted the alleged act in the sensational terms recounted by Spanish and native witnesses, which he attributed to the vague provenance of the "voz común" (popular version).[34] Meanwhile, Joseph Patiño de las Casas, the lawyer who represented the Cajonos defendants in the Real Audiencia, began his arguments on behalf of his clients, and asked the viceroy for justice. He had his work cut out for him. The net effect of Spanish and native testimony in the case thus far and the rhetoric with which the alcalde mayor, Church officials, Audiencia, and viceroy framed the events of 14 September 1700 was to cast the defendants as "idolaters," "rebels," and "murderers." De las Casas laid out an argument designed to inject an element of dissonance about the meaning of the uprising and to challenge the official story.

The argument presented by de las Casas in March 1701 narrated a version of events organized around a single theme: *rivalry* among the elite of San Francisco Cajonos provided the explanation for the violence, not *idolatry*. He argued that Jacinto de los Angeles and Juan Bautista falsely denounced the gathering at the house of Joseph Flores as "idolatry" because the two fiscales were the "enemies" of his clients. There was no idolatry at the gathering; rather, it was a celebratory dinner of traditional Indian foods, and the blood from the deer was intended for a traditional dish known as *morzillas*. Further, the mob from San Francisco Cajonos had not killed the two fiscales. Rather, the latter were in hiding, allowing Spanish officials to believe that they had been murdered. The fiscales' motives were twofold: first, to avenge themselves on the community, and second, to avoid paying a debt.[35]

De las Casas's argument was certainly plausible. Tavárez has noted the role of intense factionalism in idolatry cases in Yalalag, Betaza, Yalahui, Lachitaa, and Lachirioag during the late seventeenth and early eighteenth centuries.[36] Indeed, we should consider that if semiclandestine native ritual practices were commonplace and public knowledge among all residents of native pueblos, why would the fiscales of Cajonos choose this particular moment to denounce their fellow villagers? It certainly is possible that other factors, such as community rivalries or unpaid debts, were involved.

The truth of de las Casas's argument is beyond our reach. But its plausibility, particularly in Spanish eyes, constituted its strength. Spanish officials assumed that sierra pueblos were prone to a generalized rivalry and factionalism. They believed this because of the inordinate number of legal cases brought to the district court by local pueblos concerning election disputes, sedition, abuse of authority, and conflict over land. Spanish understanding of "factionalism" and "rivalry" was, however, overly simple. As I discussed in chapter 1, native legal intermediaries and cabildo officers learned to use tropes and discourses intelligible to Spaniards to express what was in fact a more complex social reality in their pueblos. Conflict over a debt, if it existed, may have represented the tip of the iceberg in a complex web of alliance and conflict in the pueblo of San Francisco Cajonos.

One week later, the alcalde mayor of Villa Alta reported to the viceroy on the state of affairs in the Cajonos region. He stated that the pueblo of San Francisco Cajonos and its allied pueblos maintained a veneer of calm, but beneath this the people were vigilant, inquiring as to the resolution of the conflict and protecting the principle suspects. Although he had tried to arrest the men through various means, he had been unable to do so. Without their imprisonment, he argued, there was no way to conduct a thorough investigation of the murders of the fiscales. In order to secure their imprisonment, he needed a reinforcement of two hundred armed men from the district of Oaxaca.[37]

The alcalde mayor then made a political argument. He claimed that apprehending, trying, and punishing the men was worthwhile despite the risks to peace in the district. Most of the Indians of the diocese were idolaters, he argued, and this was particularly true for the district of Villa Alta. He highlighted this last point with reference to pending criminal cases of idolatry against Cajonos natives. When these idolaters and allies of the Cajonos pueblos saw armed militias moving through the district, they would take pause and realize that disobedience of the Crown and Church would not be tolerated. Further, apprehending and punishing the leaders of the rebellion for their crimes would send a message to the district's Indians that idolatry, rebellion, and murder carried the severest consequences.[38] It would also send a message to the "good Indians [*buenos indios*]" that Spanish authorities would protect the denunciation of idolatry. Finally, he argued that the descendants of Bautista and Angeles should be rewarded, so that "their deaths and torments would appear to faithful Indians not as horrific, but rather as incentive to emulate them."[39] It appears that the Audiencia followed this recommendation. From 1774 to 1775, a descendant of Jacinto de los Angeles presented a claim for exemption from tribute by virtue of a prior exemption granted by the alcalde mayor and *juezes contadores* to all of the descendants of the martyred fiscales.[40]

The alcalde mayor made clear in his report that in its formulation of a response to the Cajonos uprising, the Spanish colonial administration had been presented with a powerful political opportunity. A generalized, violent response to the rebellion was no longer practically necessary, or politically advisable. By March 1701, the Cajonos pueblos had become peaceful and did not constitute a direct threat to the administration of the alcalde mayor or the Dominican order. But the alcalde mayor believed that the disobedience of the cabildo officers and elites of the Cajonos region required a selective violence for symbolic purposes. Through the punishment of the Cajonos officials and the reward of the descendants of the fiscales, the Spanish administration could make clear the distinction between "good and faithful Indians" and "rebels and idolaters." They could also, the alcalde mayor appears to have believed, through symbolic violence, discipline and transform "rebels and idolaters" into "good and faithful Indians." The corregidor of Oaxaca took a similar political line in his report to the viceroy. He advocated a war of terror of sorts, in which the rebellion's leaders should be severely punished such that the natives of the jurisdiction would view their errors and crimes with "horror."[41]

In the meantime, the criminal investigation of the Cajonos defendants continued. In May 1701, de las Casas presented sixteen defense witnesses, most of who were principales and current or former office holders of pueblos in the Cajonos region.[42] In aggregate, their testimony mirrored the claims made by de las Casas in his 10 March statement. They characterized the gathering at the house of José Flores on the evening of 14 September as nothing more than a celebratory feast, and cast the disruption of the feast by Jacinto de los Angeles and Juan Bautista as motivated by political enmity.[43]

Most of the witnesses also claimed that the crowd that eventually took custody of the two fiscales was justifiably angered by the abrupt and violent disturbance of the feast, and by the fact that the two fiscales owed money (most likely to the community treasury). They went on to say that the mob whipped the fiscales and then took them to the prison in San Pedro Cajonos. Eventually, the fiscales were released in response to the pleas of their relatives, and now their whereabouts were unknown. Witnesses for the defense cast Christóbal Robles, alcalde of San Francisco Cajonos, as a voice of reason throughout the events. In an effort to prevent vigilante justice, he had ordered, to no avail, that the men not be whipped, and that they be taken to the bailiff of Villa Alta to answer for their debts.[44]

The arguments made by defense lawyer de las Casas and the witnesses countered the official version of the events as "idolatry," "rebellion," and "murder" by positing another scenario: community rivalry, conflict over debt, and the irrationality of the crowd versus the reasoned actions of the leadership. As with the trope of community rivalry and factionalism, the trope of the impassioned native crowd, unresponsive to the rational exhortations of native elites, was in keeping with deep-seated Spanish prejudices about Indians and peasants. Class and racial prejudices mixed to create Spanish fears of out-of-control Indian mobs. These fears were particularly unsettling because they revealed a deep Spanish dependence on native elites to "control" native commoners. Spanish nightmares came to fruition when native elites chose to incite rather than control.

The play of the witnesses and lawyer on Spanish tropes and fears foils any attempt on the part of the historian to use the testimony as a means to get inside the native perspective of the rebellion, or the native version of what happened. But we can use the testimony to interpret the ways native people attempted to challenge the symbolic order that the alcalde mayor and Spanish administration tried to impose in the wake of the Cajonos incident. The political stakes cannot be overemphasized. If the alcalde mayor could indeed impose a symbolic order through which to empower "good and faithful Indians" and disempower "idolaters and rebels," then the struggle on the part of native intermediaries like Felipe de Santiago to accommodate Spanish power in a native framework would be lost. In fact, Santiago encountered the symbolic power of "idolater and rebel" in a final standoff with the alcalde mayor in the wake of the Cajonos incident. Just months into the investigation, the aftermath of the Cajonos Rebellion collided with Santiago's political career.

FELIPE DE SANTIAGO: RECAST AS "IDOLATER" AND "REBEL"

In June 1701, nine months after the Cajonos Rebellion, Santiago sat in the Episcopal jail of Antequera, the region's capital. He had been conducting legal business there when by request of the alcalde mayor of Villa Alta, he was imprisoned on very serious charges. As we know from chapter 1, this was not Santiago's first experience of prison; in fact, he knew the walls of Villa Alta's district jail quite intimately. Nor was it his first encounter with the law: Santiago was one of the sierra's premier legal intermediaries, having penned many petitions on behalf of indigenous litigants. On this occasion, however, he turned his pen toward the purpose of freeing himself from prison and an idolatry accusation. As the first step in his own defense against the charges of idolatry and sedition brought against him by the alcalde mayor, he issued power of attorney to Miguel Martín, identified by the scribe as an "indio ladino" originally from Antequera and residing in the town of Villa Alta.[45]

When we left San Juan Yatzona in chapter 1, the elites of the pueblo were bitterly divided over the legality and outcome of the municipal elections of 1696, a conflict that they had taken to the Audiencia. The Audiencia upheld the continuation of Pablo de Vargas as governor of Yatzona, but its decision met with serious opposition. In 1699, Phelipe López and Nicolas de la Cruz, former officials of Yatzona, brought a case against Vargas and his two alcaldes, accusing them of having imposed a head tax for church construction, but then having used it for other purposes. In an unexpected twist, the case evolved to include criminal charges against Vargas's *apoderado*, Felipe de Santiago. Vargas and his alcaldes claimed that they had given Santiago the funds for the church and that he had defrauded them and misappropriated the money.[46] The case against Vargas, Santiago, and associates continued until at least July 1702, at which point the Audiencia had not arrived at a decision.[47]

The case against Santiago may have been linked to a land dispute that he and his cousin Gaspar de Vargas brought against two members of their own pueblo, Nicolas Martín and Nicolas Mendes. In the dispute, which began in 1697 and picked up again in 1699, Santiago claimed that Martín and Mendes had usurped land that was part of his *cacicazgo* (noble estate).[48] It is not clear whether the land dispute represented an effort by Santiago and Gaspar de Vargas to protect their cacicazgo, or an effort on their part to expand their cacicazgo at the expense of less powerful villagers. Santiago brought the case to the district court and then to the Audiencia, but eventually lost. Santiago may have used the money that Governor Pablo de Vargas had entrusted to him for the reconstruction of the church to fund his litigation against Martín and Mendes. It is also possible that the litigation engendered bad feelings against Santiago in the pueblo and prompted the charges against him.

Just prior to the Cajonos Rebellion, the alcalde mayor Antonio Mier del Tojo conducted inspections of the pueblos of the district of Villa Alta. In response, an unspecified number of unnamed indigenous plaintiffs brought a petition to the Real Audiencia complaining of the alcalde mayor's repressive conduct (*vejaciones*) during the inspections. It seems that the alcalde mayor presumed that Felipe de Santiago was one of the chief organizers of the petition or the apoderado for the group and ordered his imprisonment for having "incited" and "agitated" pueblos throughout the district.[49] Santiago appealed to the Real Audiencia to override the Spanish magistrate. As had happened before, Santiago's strategy of appeal to the Real Audiencia as enforcer of laws protecting the Indians worked to his advantage. The royal court ordered his release.[50]

But the Audiencia rendered this decision during troubled times, and consequently its action met with resistance. In defiance of the Audiencia's order, which was pronounced six days after the Cajonos uprising began, the alcalde mayor refused to free Santiago. The Spanish magistrate justified his continued imprisonment on claims that Santiago, who was reputed to "agitate" and "bring together" the pueblos of the Cajonos region, had participated in idolatry and in the Cajonos uprising.[51] The magistrate presented no evidence or testimony to support these claims, and we do not know who accused or denounced him. Santiago denied the accusation and claimed that the alcalde mayor issued the charges for political reasons. But here, the alcalde mayor's strategy worked, at least temporarily. Accusations of and association with the uprising and idolatry in the Cajonos region kept Santiago in jail until 1702, as he pursued numerous appeals.[52]

A question that hovers over Santiago's imprisonment is who denounced him as an "idolater." The intense political factionalism in San Juan Yatzona during the 1690s and the land dispute between Santiago and Vargas, on the one hand, and Martín and Mendes, on the other, suggests that Santiago was not short on political enemies. In a situation in which "good and faithful Indians" had been encouraged to report the identities of "rebels and idolaters," the temptation to denounce a political rival must have been quite high. Of interest was the denunciation of Vargas, Santiago's cousin and coplaintiff in the land dispute, as a "maestro de idolatría" in the extirpation campaign that followed the Cajonos uprising.[53]

As evident in the fate of Felipe de Santiago, the Cajonos uprising provided a pretext for the alcalde mayor to subdue native rivals like Santiago. But Santiago recovered his footing and eventually emerged from prison to serve as legal agent in a land dispute in Temascalapa in 1702.[54] From there, however, Santiago's documentary trail goes cold. Illness or advanced age might have caught up with him. Or the chilling effect of the Audiencia's and the bishop's response to the uprising (to which we will now turn) may have closed his room for maneuver completely, requiring a full retreat from his role as legal intermediary.

DANGER AND DISCIPLINE: NATIVE INTERMEDIARIES AND THE SHADOW SYSTEM

Alcalde mayor Antonio Mier del Tojo imprisoned Felipe de Santiago because he considered him dangerous and a direct threat to his interests. Santiago positioned himself as Tojo's antagonist through his defense of an ideal of native autonomy, which he enacted in his role as legal agent, and organizer of legal efforts to keep the alcalde mayor out of the affairs of native pueblos. But Santiago represented another kind of threat to the alcalde mayor. As a native leader, he embodied an alternative form of authority. So too did the "rebels" of San Francisco Cajonos. This alternative form of authority, more than direct challenges to the alcalde mayor's power, undermined the Spanish vision of colonial rule. For these reasons, the alcalde mayor advocated that Santiago and the defendants in the Cajonos case should be disciplined in order to undercut their power. As leaders of a rebellion, the Cajonos defendants faced a much harsher form of discipline than did Santiago.

Three months after Felipe de Santiago issued his power of attorney to Miguel Martín, the defendants in the Cajonos case faced a grim destiny. It is clear that some time between May 1701, when the defense witnesses provided their testimony, and December 1701, Spanish authorities apprehended the defendants. It is also clear that the Audiencia did not take seriously the testimony provided on their behalf in May 1701. We know this because on 12 December 1701, the defendants confirmed their "confessions" in the case under torture.[55]

The use of torture to extract confessions in cases of idolatry, superstition, or sorcery was quite rare. Tavárez notes that with the exception of the extensive use of torture on Maya defendants in the inquisition conducted by Bishop Diego de Landa in 1562 in Yucatan, the use of torture in central

Mexico and Oaxaca appears in only seven trials, all of which occurred prior to 1561.[56] Torture does stand out, then, in this case and needs to be explained.

In the case of the defendants of San Francisco Cajonos, torture had both practical and symbolic value. The central obsession of Spanish authorities throughout the investigation—the fate and whereabouts of the fiscales—had not yet been resolved. More important, from a Spanish juridical perspective, one of the central charges against the Cajonos defendants—murder—had yet to be established by any kind of physical evidence. The defendants and their fellow villagers had maintained a remarkable wall of silence on the issue, and this no doubt frustrated the alcalde mayor. It revealed to him the degree of solidarity and resistance that the native people of the district were capable of mustering given the proper circumstances. It also threatened to undermine his legal case. Torture of the defendants might provide him with the information that he sought. At the very least, it might lead the defendants to corroborate through legal confession the official line on the gruesome murder of the fiscales attained via hearsay in the months after the rebellion. If the alcalde mayor could obtain a confession, then the gap in the story—a gap that revealed a hole in Spanish power and that threatened the murder conviction—would be filled.

On a symbolic level, the alcalde mayor likely sought to punish the officials of the Cajonos region for failing to uphold colonial authority, as their role required. They had failed in two respects. First, they had transgressed the teachings of the Church by overseeing a clandestine public ritual. Second, they had either led or failed to squelch a violent uprising that had resulted in the murder of native servants of the Church.

Thus it is likely that legal concerns and political calculation led the alcalde mayor to torture the Cajonos defendants. Other motives, such as religious zeal, which one might assume played a central role, were probably secondary. Inga Clendinnen has argued that shock, feelings of betrayal, and religious zeal largely motivated Fray Diego de Landa and his fellow Franciscans to torture cruelly hundreds of Maya men and women for their participation in "idolatry" during the extirpation campaign of 1562.[57] But this horrific episode occurred early in the evangelical enterprise, when the religious orders had naively and grossly overestimated their powers of conversion. In 1700, this naiveté had largely given way to pessimism and cynicism among civil and ecclesiastical officials alike. The alcalde mayor of Villa Alta could not have been surprised that the cabildo officers of San Francisco Cajonos participated in and led acts of "idolatry." The campaign against idolatry waged during the final decade of the seventeenth century made clear that disobedience to colonial authority was the norm among the native pueblos of the district, and the alcalde mayor himself admitted that it was widely known that the villagers of the Cajonos region were "idolaters." What became important in the aftermath of the crisis, therefore, was less the act of "idolatry" than *how* Spanish authorities would respond to what accompanied it: rebellion and murder.

In this respect, the aftermath of the Cajonos incident became a critical exercise in symbolic warfare. Taken together, idolatry, the multipueblo rebellion, and the presumed murder of the fiscales threatened the perception, if not the fact, of Spanish control in the region. Indeed, the Cajonos Rebellion was more a perceived threat to Spanish rule than an actual one. The actions of the Cajonos rebels demonstrate that they were interested in one thing: exacting retribution against the fiscales. They did not kill the friars or other Spaniards in the monastery, though they had sufficient opportunity, nor did they broaden the scope of the uprising to target Spanish authorities outside of San Francisco, most notably the alcalde mayor or any other Spanish officials, civil or ecclesiastical. As for the spread of rebellion to other pueblos, in the days following the uprising, most residents of the Cajonos region chose to flee rather than fight.

What was particularly dangerous about the Cajonos Rebellion in the eyes of colonial authorities was that it challenged a Spanish political ideal in which native officials—governors, alcaldes, mayordomos, and choirmasters—served Spanish authority unequivocally. The combination of an illicit semipublic gathering in which the officials of San Francisco presided over unsanctioned rites, and the vigilantism in which those same officials oversaw the punishment of the fiscales, provoked the ire of Spanish authorities precisely because it revealed the existence of a shadow system over which they had no control. In this shadow system, "idolatry," "rebellion," and "murder" were not transgressions but rather legitimate means by which to enact alternative forms of authority. For a significant Zapotec constituency, "idolatry" represented community ritual, "rebellion," a means of self-defense, and "murder," the enactment of justice.

Spanish civil and ecclesiastical authorities were painfully aware of the central role played by native elites and intermediary figures in the maintenance of this colonial shadow system. Leadership in ritual life fulfilled community expectations of native elites and grounded their political legitimacy. Farriss has detailed the role of the choirmasters (*maestros cantores*) of Yucatan, who "were the first bridge between the old and new religious forms, leading a dual existence as deputy curates in the Christian structure and also participating in the proscribed rituals—at least one of them as the principal *ahkin* (chief priest)."[58] Tavárez has drawn a parallel for the case of Oaxaca in his analysis of *sacristanes, cantores de iglesia*, and other principales who authored, interpreted, and circulated clandestine ritual texts. He notes that these figures decided to lead a dual life as members of certain importance in the public sphere of Christian practice and as possessors of these texts, linking the "public sphere of orthodox Christianity with the marginal social spheres, a space that transcended the domestic sphere without becoming totally public."[59]

This dual life placed native religious intermediaries on a tightrope. Those who succeeded in exercising their dual roles did so through considerable discretion, by enacting the illicit aspects of their roles in secret or in a semiclandestine public sphere. Others, through bad luck, or through a bold assertion of the sacred into the public sphere, suffered at the hands of the colonial justice system.

Spanish fears of the dual role of native religious intermediaries and their association of this duality with idolatry and conspiracy had deep roots in Oaxaca. The Dominican friar Francisco de Burgoa expressed these long-standing cultural fears in his chronicle of Catholic evangelization in the diocese of Oaxaca. Burgoa writes that during a 1652 visit to the pueblo of San Francisco Cajonos that he conducted while provincial, he encountered a cacique from the Cajonos region. Burgoa's description reveals that in the eyes of many Spaniards, no matter how "hispanized" (and by extension, "civilized") some natives might become, they could not shed their Indian identity, in particular, their attachment to their own religion:

> Among other principales came a very old one, lord of his community, and in the clothing the most splendid of all, dressed in silk in the Spanish style. They respected him with much care, and coming to me to give welcome and the report of the administration of the parish of his community, I recognized that he was very ladino. And for some circumstances that experience had taught me, I suspected the true Christianity

of his faith, so much that I asked the curate, without letting on to the friars my suspicion, what kind of a person was that venerable old man. He spoke to me so positively about his conduct, that I attributed my suspicion to my fragility and repented. I excused myself; but I could not put it aside, and while taking my leave I asked the curate to be very vigilant to insure the good opinion of this cacique, treating him with love, because if he was as he had told me, he was deserving of it, and if not, he would have it with well-disposed tenderness without horror and fear of emendation. A few months had not passed before the truth was discovered that he was the greatest dogmatist and priest of idols in this land, and his community the famous synagogue of the nation.[60]

Burgoa's 1652 description of this hispanized cacique cum "idolater" reveals a deep-seated anxiety among Spaniards in Oaxaca and in other parts of New Spain: those Indians who appeared to be "good and faithful" on the surface could be in reality "idolaters and rebels." Burgoa's narrative also augured and complemented the 1661 characterization of the bishop of Oaxaca, Alonso de Cuevas y Dávalos, in his report to the viceroy concerning the causes of the 1660 rebellion of Tehuantepec discussed in chapter 1. In his report, Cuevas had complained that native apoderados threatened the colonial order by "raising the spirits of the community" and "leading and arranging whatever disagreement or uprising." Taken together, the writings of these two churchmen cautioned Spanish audiences against the twin dangers posed by hispanized Indians: idolatry and rebellion.

How accurately, however, did this view reflect social reality? Does "duplicity" capture the role played by the "rebels" and "idolaters" of San Francisco Cajonos? Does "loyalty" capture the role played by the fiscales? Were these figures Manichean opposites: non-Christian versus Christian, seditious subjects versus loyal vassals? To what degree were the Spaniards inscribing their own fears, prejudices, and agendas onto the events of 1700 and onto the Zapotecs involved in those events?

From a Spanish perspective, the native intermediary figures who were the protagonists of the Cajonos rebellion—the fiscales, Jacinto de los Angeles and Juan Bautista, and the leaders of San Francisco Cajonos, Christóbal Robles, Juan de Mendoza, Joseph Flores, and others—were classified in terms that made sense to their colonial rulers: "good and faithful Indians" or "idolaters" and "rebels." As the Spaniards saw them, these men were mirror images of one another. The fiscales were the good Indians, trusted collaborators, loyal. For the Spaniards, the alcalde, cantor, and mayordomo represented the Janus face of the fiscales and expressed Spanish fears of even their most trusted Indian civil and ecclesiastical servants. But were these men really so different in reality? Might they have been using the Spaniards for their own purposes?

The fiscales clearly had their enemies in the community, and their denunciation of the gathering at the house of José Flores united much of San Francisco Cajonos and the surrounding pueblos against them. Their actions in that particular moment cast them as traitors, but this identity may have been situated rather than permanent. After all, the fiscales had their allies in the pueblo as well: their immediate kin who pleaded for their lives during the initial hours of the rebellion, perhaps others from their barrio or extended family group, and perhaps other elites who may have been close allies of the parish priest. Community conflict or rivalry may have situated the fiscales and their enemies in more rigid categories in relation to their Spanish overlords, but these alliances and allegiances may have been temporary and utilitarian. The story of Santiago, Celis, and Vargas, as told in chapter 1, reveals the fluidity and contingency of native enmity and alliance.

Crisis and conflict intensified this fluidity, and positioned native brokers at the center of fast-changing events. Not only were they instigators of conflict, as in the case of the fiscales and the officials of San Francisco, but they also came to represent a way that both Spaniards and Indians understood colonial conflict. In short, they were lightning rods after the fact, and often written in as sources of conflict in both native and Spanish accounts of violence and political rancor.

In the Spanish view, the Cajonos defendants were both protagonists of the rebellion and powerful symbols of cultural conflict. As such, they had to bear the full brunt of the law in order to restore the public face of the region's colonial order. And their suffering had to mirror the alleged suffering of the "good and faithful Indians" they had supposedly murdered. Torture on the rack went some way toward turning the symbolic order upright again, as Spanish authorities asserted themselves over their Zapotec rivals.

Not surprisingly, under torture, the defendants' confessions of 12 December 1701 contradicted the argument of their defense lawyer and the testimony of the witnesses presented on their behalf, and prejudiced their defense. According to these tortured testimonies, the cabildo officers, principales, and commoners of San Francisco Cajonos, as well as those of

San Mateo, San Pablo, Santo Domingo, San Miguel, and San Pedro met in the house of a man named Sebastian Martín to figure out how to kill and dispose of the fiscales. They went to San Pedro, where the two men were imprisoned, took them out of their cell to a mountaintop, killed them, a few people drank their blood "so that they would be empowered" (*para que pudiesen andar bien*), and then mutilated their bodies.[61]

The ratifications under torture confirmed the gruesome rumors about the murder of the fiscales that circulated around the district in October and November 1700 and the Audiencia's initial report of the events in December 1700, based on those rumors. Given the use of torture, and the wide circulation of these rumors, it is quite possible that the tortured prisoners were telling the Spaniards what they wanted to hear. In her analysis of the bloody 1562 extirpation campaign in Yucatan, Clendinnen argues that the confessions of dozens of Maya under torture "reveal more about the shaping power of Landa's imagination than the actual behavior of Indians."[62] Carlo Ginzburg has also demonstrated how Catholic inquisitors, through psychological coercion, the implicit threat of physical coercion, and leading questions elicited "confessions" from the *benandante* of rural Italy that conformed to received narratives about "sabbat" (devil worship).[63] If we assume that coercion significantly shaped the details of the confessions, then we should consider the possibility that the narrative of the ritualized murder of the fiscales, involving the drinking of their blood in order to enhance the power of their murderers, may have been as much a reflection of Spanish preconceptions about "idolatry" and native ritual, and their preoccupation with native disobedience and violence, as the facts themselves.

The testimony of 12 December 1701 given by twenty-five prisoners under torture left the defense lawyer with little ammunition. He resorted to well-worn Spanish conceptions of Indians by arguing that their "incapacity, misery, and ignorance" explained their actions and should excuse them. In a last ditch effort, he adopted a familiar defense strategy for native elites caught up in Indian uprisings: blame the commoners (*macehualaje*). He argued that experience had shown time and again that the commoners of Indian pueblos banded together, and against the orders of their alcaldes and officials, do whatever "appetizes them [*les antoja*]." As principales, his clients had attempted to dissuade the crowd from killing the fiscales, but to no avail.[64]

The Audiencia was not convinced by this argument. Indeed, the official correspondence and documentation of the previous year and a half make clear that a guilty verdict was a foregone conclusion. The judges pronounced their sentence in January 1702. The Audiencia condemned fifteen of the thirty-four defendants to death without appeal. Fourteen of the men were natives of San Francisco Cajonos: Christóbal de Robles (the alcalde of San Francisco Cajonos), Nicolas de Aquino, Francisco Lopes, Joseph Luis, Nicolas Bartolo, Bartolomé de los Angeles Gastila, Francisco Hernández alias Francisco Lucas, Joseph de Mendoza (the mestizo cantor), Martín de los Angeles alias de la Cruz, Ciprian de Aquino, Geronimo Francisco, Ambrosio Hernández, Nicolas Hernández, and Pedro Pablo. Nicolas Antonio, the fifteenth, was a native of Santo Domingo Xagasia.[65]

The Audiencia appears to have taken pains to craft a death sentence that would have the maximum symbolic effect with the least political risk. The judges avoided a public execution, which might have incited a crowd of native spectators to attempt a rescue of the condemned men or to react with outraged violence against the alcalde mayor. Instead of a public hanging, the condemned were to be garroted (strangled) within the confines of the jail. Then, their heads were to be cut off and placed on stakes around the perimeter of the central plaza of the pueblo of San Francisco Cajonos while the town crier publicly proclaimed their crimes. The right hands of Nicolas de Aquino and Francisco Lopez, the men who allegedly killed the two fiscales, were to be placed on stakes as well. Then, the bodies of all of the condemned were to be drawn and quartered, and their body parts placed in trees and on stakes along the Camino Real while the town crier proclaimed that if anyone removed the bodies, they would suffer the same fate.[66]

The Audiencia's sentence of the fifteen principal defendants reflects a hybridization of classical and modern approaches to criminal punishment. Michel Foucault has argued that in classical jurisprudence, such as that exercised in medieval and early modern Europe, public torture and executions were spectacles through which the sovereignty of the king was established. As such, public torture and executions served more than a juridical function: they were "political tactics" and "political rituals," "ceremonies by which power was manifested."[67] Foucault notes the centrality of the body of the condemned in a politics of "terror." The tortured body was intended "to make everyone aware, through the body of the criminal, of the unrestrained presence of the sovereign. The public execution did not reestablish justice; it reactivated power."[68]

However, public torture and execution always entailed political risk: "the great spectacle of punishment ran the risk of being rejected by the very people to whom it was addressed."[69] Foucault argues that the spectacle often aroused sympathy for the condemned among the crowd, and that solidarity rather than sovereignty could result. The risk of solidarity appears particularly potent in a colonial situation where resistance to colonial authority was a constant threat to legitimacy and by extension, sovereignty. In colonial contexts, therefore, the state may have been more painfully aware that public execution could constitute "a hearth in which violence bursts again into flame." Foucault argues that this risk explains why punishment became the most hidden part of the modern penal process. By avoiding public punishment, the modern justice system avoids "public responsibility for the violence that is bound up with its practice."[70] Colonial functionaries may have realized this earlier than their metropolitan cousins. In this regard, as some scholars have argued, colonialism may well have been the midwife of modernity.[71]

In the case of the Cajonos defendants, the Real Audiencia combined a hidden punishment with all of the symbolic flair of a public execution. By killing the condemned men behind closed doors, Spanish authorities defused what might have been an explosive situation had they decided to execute the men publicly. Yet the desecration of the men's corpses through decapitation, drawing and quartering, and the public display of their body parts preserved some of the effects of execution as public ritual: "the body of the condemned man [became] the place where the vengeance of the sovereign was applied, the anchoring point for a manifestation of power, an opportunity of affirming the dissymmetry of forces."[72]

The Audiencia extended its economy of terror through its sentencing of seventeen other Cajonos defendants, one of whom was Joseph Flores, in whose house the gathering was held on the night of 14 September. These men were to suffer the same fate as the principle fifteen, but the Audiencia allowed them the right of appeal. The seventeen were natives of pueblos throughout the Cajonos region, including San Francisco, San Miguel, San Matheo, and San Pedro Yaeche.[73]

The remaining two defendants, Ambrosio Contreras of San Francisco Cajonos and Gabriel Flores de los Angeles of Santa Lucia, were sentenced to two hundred lashes, ten years of exile from the district, on pain of death, and depravation of municipal office for life. The two men were to be publicly humiliated: they were to be whipped and then paraded around the town of Villa Alta with pointed hats, covered in honey, chile, salt, and feathers. Then they were to be tied to scaffolding and exposed to the sun for an hour.[74]

Finally, the Audiencia saw fit to punish in a largely symbolic fashion the villagers of San Francisco Cajonos. The villagers of San Francisco were to demolish the house of Sebastian Martín, where the conspiracy to murder the fiscales was allegedly hatched. Then they were to painstakingly and at their own expense reconstruct the houses of the fiscales, which they had destroyed during the uprising. Finally, in the center of the plot where the house of Sebastian Martín stood, the villagers were to construct a shrine with two large crosses in honor of the two fiscales.[75]

On 14 January, the Spanish officials of Villa Alta carried out the sentence against the fifteen condemned men.[76] In an effort to avoid a similar outcome, by 11 July, the defense lawyer had begun appeals for the seventeen remaining condemned.[77] Tavárez notes that in a cruel irony, the bishop of Oaxaca, Angel Maldonado, "obtained a commutation [for the remaining seventeen] from the Audiencia, tried eleven of them for idolatry, and selected one of the former 'teachers of idolatry' to proclaim his clemency across the region."[78]

In the years that followed the execution of the Cajonos defendants, the decisions and actions of the Audiencia and the alcalde mayor created "a battleground around the crime, its punishment, and its memory."[79] The rebellion and its aftermath also provided local native people with what De Certeau might call a tactical arsenal for "polemology," or linguistic battles in a context characterized by asymmetries of power.[80] For example, in a 1703 dispute in the cabildo of San Juan Tabaa, the alcaldes imprisoned their governor, Pascual García, for being a "troublemaker," "gossip," and "liar." According to the opening petition of the alcaldes, regidores, and other principales, García had maligned community members and threatened to bring them before the bishop of Oaxaca for idolatry and other crimes. As a result, many had fled into the mountains out of fear of punishment by the alcalde mayor and religious authorities.[81]

Pascual García defended himself with a petition to the alcalde mayor in which he claimed that the alcaldes conducted a late night roundup of García and his supporters, and imprisoned them in the village jail. According to his account, the next day, the wife of one of the imprisoned men challenged the alcaldes with these fighting words: "[you are] not Christians, if [you] were so powerful, [you] should kill [my] husband and all of us who are imprisoned, like the community of San Francisco Cajonos had done with the two men who denounced them." According to García, this verbal assault, which likened the position of García's allies to that of the fiscales of San Francisco Cajonos, earned the unfortunate woman a day in solitary confinement and a public whipping, followed by another day in jail. Whether García invented the verbal barrage for the benefit of the court, or whether the woman who was allegedly responsible for the words actually spoke them, it is clear in this case that the Cajonos Rebellion had made its mark in the tactical and rhetorical arsenal of native villagers. In the context of the extirpation campaign, it is not surprising that the dispute in Tabaa evolved into a criminal case of idolatry and sedition against the alcaldes and their allies. The Audiencia found in favor of García and sentenced the alcaldes and regidores to two hundred lashes and terms of personal service of four to six years and/or work in a nearby *obraje*. Eleven others were either sentenced to six years' exile from the pueblo or fifty lashes. All were prohibited from ever holding office in the future.[82]

THE BISHOP'S TURN: PARISH REFORM AND EXTIRPATION

Much as the Cajonos Rebellion provided a political opportunity for the alcalde mayor and Audiencia to discipline the district's native population, it provided a political opportunity for the secular Church hierarchy in Antequera to discipline both an "idolatrous" native population and a wayward Dominican order. In 1702, the new bishop of Oaxaca, Fray Angel Maldonado (1702–28) arrived from Spain with the immediate goal of changing what he perceived to be the misadministration of the Sierra Norte. His strategy was to launch a bold policy of administrative reform and a more wide-ranging and systematic extirpation campaign of the pueblos of the district of Villa Alta.[83]

Maldonado's most significant achievement was the overhaul of the loose, understaffed, and geographically diffuse administration of the Dominican order in the district of Villa Alta. A long-standing power struggle between the Dominican order in Oaxaca and the bishops who in theory presided over the evangelization of the region helps to explain the ambition with which Maldonado designed his program of parish reform. Maldonado's designs were part of a larger struggle throughout New Spain between the mendicant orders, the secular Church hierarchy, and the Spanish Crown. In the remote regions of New Spain, where formal state structures tended to be absent, the missionary orders had considerable economic and political power, and ran remote areas as small fiefdoms. Their interests often clashed with those of the Crown and the Church hierarchy, and as a result, these two arms of the Spanish empire periodically attempted to curtail their power. The accession of the Bourbon hierarchy to the throne in 1700 marked a watershed in this process as the Bourbons centralized power in the hands of the secular Church hierarchy, which answered to the king. This process occurred at the expense of the missionary orders over the course of the eighteenth century.

Since the conquest, with the exception of the Rincón region in which secular priests (priests who did not belong to a religious order) ran the parishes of Tanetze and Yae, the Dominicans had staked their claim to the Sierra Norte. During the early colonial period, despite occasional flare-ups between the jurisdiction of the Dominicans and civil authority, the Crown and the bishops of Oaxaca were content to allow the Dominicans to serve as colonial overlords in the sierra. However, beginning in the early seventeenth century, the bishops of Oaxaca made sporadic attempts to rein in Dominican power. With the support of the Crown, Bishop Juan Bartolomé de Bohórquez e Hinojosa (1617–33) and Bishop Bartolomé de la Cerda Benavente y Benavides (1639–52) attempted to subject the Dominican parishes to the direct authority of the bishops, but the Dominicans mounted a vigorous and largely successful resistance.[84]

The Cajonos Rebellion provided an opening for the renewal of this power struggle and an opportunity for the Church hierarchy to wrest power from the Dominicans. Bishop Maldonado framed the incident as proof of the insufficiency of the Dominican presence in the sierra. As a remedy, he replaced Dominican curates with secular clergy, and increased the number of parish priests in the district, from twelve prior to 1702 to twenty-one by 1705. As he increased the number of parish priests, he increased the number of parish seats (*cabeceras*). Between 1705 and 1707, the six Dominican *doctrinas* (parishes) of the sierra (Villa Alta, San Francisco Cajonos, Choapan, Totontepec, Juquila Mixes, and Quetzaltepec) and three secular doctrinas (Tanetze, Yaée, and Yagavila) were expanded to eighteen secular parishes between 1705 and 1707. By the mid-eighteenth century, there were twenty parishes.[85]

Maldonado's parish reform constituted a serious threat to the native political order of the district of Villa Alta. One of the most important changes he introduced was the enforcement of the *cabecera-sujeto* parish

structure. Throughout New Spain, the Spanish model of spatial organization relied on the centralized and hierarchical cabecera-sujeto structure as
a means of organizing tribute collection and evangelization. Cabeceras
tended to be the power and population centers of a particular region or
jurisdiction, and as such, governed their smaller neighbors and collected
tribute for the Crown from the settlements that surrounded them. In
addition to their political and administrative roles, cabeceras also served as
the parish seats of the Catholic Church. Given their position, they had the
right to demand financial contributions and labor from their sujetos for
the maintenance of the parish church and the celebration of religious
festivals, obligations often resented by the subject pueblos.

John Chance has noted that the cabecera-sujeto structure of the district
of Villa Alta was largely undeveloped in comparison with other regions of
New Spain.[86] As a result, the native pueblos of the sierra were not ac-
customed to the rigid hierarchy that defined cabecera-sujeto relations. A
reinvigorated cabecera-sujeto structure implied a reordering of relationships of power among sierra pueblos and, as we will see in chapter 3, the
enforcement of the cabecera-sujeto model engendered long-term conflict
between the parish seats and their neighbors.

A near doubling of the number of parish priests in the district was
another radical political change. Parish priests presented a constellation of
overlapping burdens for native pueblos. Native villagers were required to
provide food, labor, and personal services to the parish priests who lived
among them. Parish priests demanded fees, either in kind (goods) or in
cash for services such as baptism or marriage. These fees were highly
burdensome for native villagers, and became a point of contention in
lawsuits and local uprisings from the mid-eighteenth century. Many parish
priests took advantage of their position of power in native pueblos to set up
their own personal repartimiento apart from that of the alcalde mayor.
Parish priests often meddled in cabildo elections. In the absence of Spanish
civil authorities in far-flung parishes, parish priests were required to ratify
the results of cabildo elections. If the pueblo elected a governor who was at
odds with the parish priest, the priest could declare the election null and
void. Finally, parish priests were hostile to native ritual. Their presence in
the community compromised efforts to maintain a semiclandestine public
space for native rites.

Replacement of Dominican priests by secular clergy issued in yet another political change. Chance has noted that conditions under the secular clergy were much more oppressive than under the Dominicans. Most secular clergy did not bother to learn native languages and many resented their placement in what they perceived to be the barbaric parishes of the Sierra Norte. They tended to charge exorbitant fees for their services and physically abused parishioners. For example, during the late eighteenth century, parish priests empowered fiscales and Church *topiles* (constables) to administer penalties of six to sixteen lashes on male parishioners who failed to attend Mass, rosary recitations, or doctrina classes; who got drunk; who beat their wives; or who disrespected their parents or the curate. These kinds of abuses led to uprisings against parish priests on at least four occasions during the second half of the eighteenth century.[87]

Bishop Maldonado attempted to institute a program of pueblo nucleation (*congregación*) as a complement to administrative centralization. With the support of the alcalde mayor of Villa Alta, Diego de Rivera y Cotes, Maldonado recommended to the viceroy that the district's pueblos be congregated into settlements of at least four hundred heads of household each; that each pueblo have a Spanish teacher; and that the alcalde mayor should have the right to place lieutenants in pueblos where he deemed it necessary. The viceroy approved the proposal in 1706 to a flurry of protest from Villa Alta cabildo officers.[88] The protestations of sierra cabildos may have had some effect, since it appears that of these proposals, only the one concerning the stationing of schoolmasters appears to have been implemented.[89]

In sum, Maldonado's parish reform effected a political centralization of the district's native pueblos under the control of the secular hierarchy of the Catholic Church. In this regard, the decade that followed the Cajonos rebellion resembled a second conquest of the Sierra Norte, and anticipated the secularization program of the Bourbon administration during the second half of the eighteenth century. Maldonado believed that a tighter administrative ship—more priests, more parish seats, more densely populated settlements (in a word, centralization)—would establish greater social control, leading in turn to the eradication of idolatry. The establishment and enforcement of a more rigid hierarchy among indigenous pueblos, in which cabeceras would serve as command centers, and their superior position with regard to their subject pueblos, would be clearly demarcated and maintained, further bolstering efforts at social and political control. This program of centralization chafed against the long-standing political autonomy of the pueblos of Villa Alta and displaced the decentralized administrative structure that had been the rule in the region prior to the tumultuous events of 1700.

Maldonado opened another front in his reconquest of the sierra: he sought to purge the pueblos of the district of Villa Alta—notoriously some of the most "idolatrous" in Oaxaca—of non-Christian practices. As an immediate response to the Cajonos uprising, he conducted a parish inspection in the jurisdiction of Villa Alta, and enlisted the help of Joseph de Aragón y Alcántara, curate of Ejutla (an administrative center in the valley) and a renowned extirpator. During this first visit, Maldonado implemented an "innovative and unorthodox" strategy of extirpation. He offered a general absolution and legal amnesty for any pueblo that turned over its maestros of idolatry and ritual implements. On returning to the sierra in 1704, the bishop reaped the benefits of this strategy. From 1704 to 1705, Aragón y Alcántara recorded verbal and written confessions concerning "idolatrous" practices from all of the district's pueblos, with the exception of the Chinantec region, and confiscated ninety-nine ritual calendars, "idols," and other sacred objects. The calendars were sent to Spain and the sacred objects burned in the plaza of Villa Alta to the horror and dismay of the region's population.[90]

One cannot underestimate the chilling effect of the "confessions" and the destruction of the sacred objects. Confessions and denunciations gave expression to and deepened divisions in native pueblos as different parcialidades and factions used accusations of "idolatry" as political weapons. The burning of sacred objects must have caused tremendous spiritual trauma, and must have affected the legitimacy and authority of native ritual leaders. Indeed, Chance has argued that the extirpation campaign drove native ritual underground and secured a monopoly in the public sphere for Catholic ritual and the cult of the saints.[91] In some instances, the extirpation campaign led to violence and abuse of authority on the part of native authorities. For example, in 1704, María Gutiérrez brought a criminal case against Juan de la Cruz and Augustín Hernández of Yalalag. She claimed that the governor of the pueblo ordered the two men to set fire to her house while she and her daughters slept inside because her husband was a "known idolater."[92]

In addition to conflicts over the identities of "idolaters," from 1703 to

1753, native residents of the pueblos of Lalopa, Yalahui, Lachitaa, Yalalag (two cases), and Zoogocho brought cases of idolatry against fellow villagers.[93] In the two cases from Yalalag, the accused were cabildo officers. These denunciations make clear that Maldonado's extirpation campaign provided a fruitful context in which to express asymmetries of power, cultural differences, political rivalries, and/or personal conflicts.

CONCLUSION

Historically, violence has had the potential to reorder society and to shake up political and cultural systems. The Cajonos Rebellion achieved this with regard to the colonial order in the district of Villa Alta, but less through the violence of the rebellion itself than through the symbolic warfare and political reforms that characterized the rebellion's aftermath. The political and cultural system that emerged from the Cajonos Rebellion did not resemble the semiautonomy that the rebels sought to preserve, but rather a colonial order that the Spanish church and state had sought to impose for a century and a half.

The Cajonos Rebellion provided the climax to the political tensions that had been mounting in the district of Villa Alta since the rebellion of 1660. The violence represented the culmination of a forty-year breakdown in the norms that had governed Spanish-native relations: a semiautonomous space for clandestine native ritual, semiautonomous native elections, and the moral economy that had governed the repartimiento. This breakdown offered the Church and state an unprecedented opportunity to reconstruct a political order that served their interests. Part of that reconstruction involved the imposition of a symbolic order that pitted "good and faithful Indians" against "rebels" and "idolaters." The torture and punishment of the leaders of the rebellion, the material rewards provided to the descendants of the fiscales of San Francisco Cajonos, and the purges and confessions that accompanied the extirpation campaign reinforced this colonial ideal.

This highly polarized situation, in which native leaders were either one with the colonial order or its mortal enemies, provided little room for native intermediaries like Felipe de Santiago. His imprisonment from 1699 to 1702 reveals the extent to which the political space for cultural mediation and political brokerage had shrunk by the end of the seventeenth century. The Cajonos Rebellion closed it completely.

But as much as the rebellion allowed the alcalde mayor, the bishop of Oaxaca, and the Audiencia to design and implement a reconquest of the Sierra, it also opened political opportunities for some native intermediary figures. The descendants of the fiscales of San Francisco Cajonos are one example. The schoolmasters installed in pueblos throughout the district in the aftermath of the rebellion are another. The governors and cabildo officers of the newly formed cabeceras are a third. As the cabecera-sujeto system established greater hierarchy among the native pueblos of the district of Villa Alta, the leadership of the new parish centers benefited from the resources, services, labor, and prestige that accompanied cabecera status. In response, the cabildos and community leadership of the sujetos mounted significant legal resistance, a story to which we will now turn.

PART 2

The Renegotiation of Local Rule: Strategies and Tactics, 1700–1770

Chapter 3

Reform, Resistance, and Rhetoric

The Cajonos Rebellion was a watershed in the process of state formation in the district of Villa Alta. It provided a pretext for a secular takeover of what had been a Dominican district, and for tighter ecclesiastical and civil control of native social, political, and cultural life. The rebellion also legitimized the war on idolatry and invigorated the campaign against native ritual specialists, and the political atmosphere that it engendered allowed the *alcalde mayor* to take a more interventionist and aggressive stance toward his native antagonists. Finally, Bishop Angel Maldonado's reorganization of parishes challenged the long-standing relationships of space and power in the district. In response to these changes, after 1700, *cabildo* (native municipal government) officers and legal agents turned their attention to renegotiating the terms of local rule.

The next two chapters focus on the strategies and tactics that native intermediaries used to renegotiate local rule. This chapter examines communicative strategies, in particular the legal rhetoric and oral performances deployed by native legal agents and witnesses in an intermittent civil suit in the parish of San Juan Yae–San Juan Tanetze over parish relationships, provoked in part by Maldonado's reforms. Much more was at stake in the lawsuit than *cabecera-sujeto* relationships (i.e., those of the parish seat to its subject pueblos). The legal case provided a forum in which native intermediaries could struggle to preserve native autonomy from Church and civil intervention, and simultaneously negotiate their identity as colonial subjects. These two objectives were related. As I discussed in chapter 2, the alcalde mayor used the Cajonos Rebellion as a political opportunity to reorder symbolic relationships in the region, and to juxtapose "idolaters and rebels" with "good and faithful Indians." On the basis of this symbolic framework, Spanish civil and ecclesiastical officials undercut native leaders whom they considered threats to the colonial order and the centralization of political power. In the decades that followed, native legal agents, pueblo officials, and native witnesses resisted Spanish policies by presenting themselves as good Christians committed to the "ancient customs" of the region. Through their legal rhetoric, they argued against the centralization of parishes and the ideological framework that threatened their political and cultural semiautonomy.

PARISH REFORM: A POLITICAL OPPORTUNITY

The Cajonos Rebellion and the repression and reforms that followed it represented a political disaster for native ritual specialists and their allies among the native elite of Villa Alta. At the same time, this intense five-year period represented a political opportunity for the bishop and alcalde mayor to centralize political power in a region where Church and civil power had been relatively diffuse. The rebellion and its aftermath also provided a political opportunity for the native allies of parish priests and the native elites of pueblos designated as new cabeceras.

Cabecera status entailed significant power and privilege. In cabeceras, parish priests took up residence and, from this seat of power, taught the Christian doctrine and celebrated the major religious festivals of the Christian calendar. Although priests were often meddlesome and burdensome, they were also powerful spiritual and political figures. Their residence in cabeceras lent these pueblos significant prestige, as did the celebration of religious fiestas. Advantages of a cultural nature also adhered to the privilege of having the parish priest reside in one's pueblo. In addition to the curate, cabeceras were staffed by a schoolmaster (*maestro de escuela*) who taught the Christian doctrine and Spanish language to native youth. Education in the Spanish language provided an invaluable skill and vehicle to power for cabildo officers of the *principal* status group, whose role it was to mediate between the pueblo and Spanish institutions. The cabecera also enjoyed commercial and economic benefits since it usually hosted the regional market. Cabeceras were also entitled to demand material resources and labor from their subject pueblos to help with church maintenance and preparations for major religious celebrations.

Considering the advantages of cabecera status, native leaders throughout New Spain decided that cabecera-sujeto relationships were worth fighting over (at least in the courts). Especially during the eighteenth century, cabildos and legal agents of subject pueblos engaged their communities in a wave of secessionist litigation against their cabeceras. Their goal was to establish independent pueblos, without financial, labor, or religious obligations to a larger entity. Scholars have identified this process as "atomization," "fragmentation," "particularism," and "secession."[1]

The demographic recovery of New Spain's indigenous population during the second half of the seventeenth century and the penetration of the Church into deeper levels of indigenous society during the middle and late colonial periods contributed to the process of secession. As the population increased, the smaller settlements that had been sujetos acquired the critical mass of residents necessary for their community to become independent, and even be established as a cabecera in its own right. The increase in church construction in sujetos provided further incentive for independence. Subject pueblos resented the labor and resources required of them for the maintenance of the parish seat, since increasing numbers of them had their own church to maintain and adorn.

As their churches became central to communal identity and political activity, subject pueblos made their cases for independence, casting the obligations required of them by their cabeceras in terms of greed and political abuse.[2] The Real Audiencia tended to abet secessionist efforts. Reduction of native jurisdiction to the cabecera-sujeto relationship was a central goal of colonial administration. The Crown's acknowledgement of new cabeceras therefore converged with indigenous aspirations for local autonomy and played on a long-standing tension in Mesoamerican society between centralization and fragmentation.

The cabecera-sujeto struggles of eighteenth-century Villa Alta share some commonalities with trends in other regions. The demographic and economic recovery of the pueblos in the Sierra Norte during the second half of the seventeenth century and a population boom at the turn of the eighteenth century provided the material conditions necessary for competing claims to cabecera status: the critical mass of population required to support a resident priest and to engage in lengthy litigation. From 1622 to

1703, the population increased from 20,751 to 36,396, and by 1742 reached its century high at 49,135.[3] This demographic boom coincided with a relative stability in the number of native settlements in the district, which meant that native elites had to find new mechanisms or resort to old ones in order to accommodate the new population in existing social and political structures. Carmagnani has examined the process of demographic recovery and consolidation of native society throughout Oaxaca from the perspective of a reconstitution of native ethnic identity based on a reinvigorated relationship among native pueblos, territory, and sacred space from roughly 1630 to 1720. He contends that native pueblos adopted strategies of "fragmentation and recomposition" to accommodate changing relationships among population, land, and resources. The reconfiguration of cabecera-sujeto relationships was an important strategy in this process.[4] The establishment of a system of local markets (*tianguis*), another process that characterized eighteenth-century Villa Alta, figured into struggles over cabecera-sujeto relationships, since it was often the cabecera that hosted the markets.

Despite the common factor of demographic recovery and boom, the history of cabecera-sujeto relationships in the district of Villa Alta differs considerably from central regions of New Spain, and even from other regions of Oaxaca. Political decentralization characterized pueblo relationships and colonial administration in the district until the eighteenth century, and the cabecera-sujeto structure was quite underdeveloped in comparison with other regions. During the sixteenth and seventeenth centuries, a sparse clerical presence and the relative poverty of the region's pueblos discouraged the formation of more than a handful of parishes, the backbone of the centralized and hierarchical cabecera-sujeto structure. As a result, a pattern of "small, relatively independent villages," organized in somewhat horizontal, decentralized relationships of power, persisted and even intensified until Maldonado's reforms reshaped the political landscape.[5]

Maldonado's effort to (re)impose a hierarchical structure on the decentralized parishes of the district of Villa Alta bears greater comparison with the histories of parish formation in mountain regions of New Spain like the Sierra of Puebla, as well as with rural areas of Europe.[6] In these regions, the political implications of elevating a single ritual and administrative center in a cluster of villages had made the process of parish reform (or formation) quite contentious. The centralization of ritual and political power from a plurality of ritual sites to a single site, and the flow of material and labor resources from the outside to the center, provoked considerable resistance from local people.

In the district of Villa Alta, Maldonado's reforms converged with *longue durée* power struggles among native pueblos in the parish of San Juan Yae– San Juan Tanetze in the region of the Sierra Norte known as the Rincón Zapoteco (Zapotec corner).[7] Cabildo officers, legal agents, and other native elites took advantage of or resisted Maldonado's policies in light of local histories of struggle and cooperation. From the start of the Catholic evangelical enterprise, the establishment of parishes in the Rincón Zapoteco created political tensions among the region's pueblos. When the first Spanish missionaries arrived in the Zapotec Rincón in the 1530s, they established two parishes, both secular, in the pueblos of Tanetze and Yagavila. In doing so, the Church administration followed what it assumed was the pre-Hispanic pattern of regional power relations, Tanetze and Yagavila having been the most populous communities in the region at the time of the conquest. At a certain point, Church authorities split the parish of Tanetze in two, and installed a secular priest in the pueblo of Lalopa. In a few years, however, they moved the parish seat to San Juan Yae, another pre-Hispanic population center, and designated it as the second cabecera on the eastern side of the Cajonos River.[8] By dividing the parish of Tanetze, the Church hoped to facilitate evangelization by allowing two resident priests to share the large expanse of territory that made up the eastern Rincón. For the local residents, however, this meant double the burden; they had to provide the livelihood for two curates and pay for their services, a substantial expense and drain of local resources.

The extent of the burden of maintaining two priests on the surrounding pueblos became clear in 1617 when the cabildos of the pueblos of Yae, Lalopa, Lahoya (Xaca) petitioned the Real Audiencia to rejoin the parishes of Yae and Tanetze under the cabecera of Tanetze. Their request was demographically and economically driven. During the previous decade, a *congregación* had taken place, resulting in the deaths of many inhabitants of the Rincón, particularly in the region around Yae. As a result, Yae's residents could no longer pay the tribute required to maintain a parish priest. The aggregation of the parishes that ensued rearranged the region's relationships of power. By demoting Yae to a subject pueblo of Tanetze, the Church reinforced loose horizontal political relationships between Yae and its neighbors; as of 1617, they were all subject to the authority of Tanetze.[9]

Eighty years later, the situation could not have looked more different. The population of the region had recovered, and the material conditions in the region's pueblos had improved. Bolstered by these developments, Yae's cabildo in 1695 petitioned the bishop of Oaxaca, Isidro de Sariñana y Cuenca, and the Real Audiencia for recognition as cabecera. The colonial Church and state concurred, thereby resurrecting Yae as a hub of colonial ecclesiastical and political administration.[10] But this recognition of Yae as cabecera was de jure and not de facto: none of the surrounding pueblos recognized it as such.

The cabildos of the surrounding pueblos justified their refusal to recognize Yae as cabecera through claims to a local tradition of pueblo autonomy and egalitarianism. In lieu of a hierarchical cabecera-sujeto model, a variety of local arrangements provided a degree of political, commercial, and religious integration among Rincón pueblos and shared power among its elites. A multipueblo religious brotherhood—the cofradía of the Virgin of Yabee—provides one manifestation of this horizontal form of inter-pueblo integration.

Cofradías—Catholic brotherhoods that oversaw the care of a particular saint—were an important setting for the work of native intermediaries and a framework for indigenous social organization. Cofradías often drew their leadership from a bicultural native elite, and in this regard, at the level of leadership, shared much of the same personnel with the native cabildo. That these two bodies constituted complementary forms of power makes sense given that both Mesoamerican and European cultures shared a concept of political authority intimately intertwined with that of the sacred. Like the native cabildo, cofradías oversaw pueblo funds, often with the supervision of the parish priest. These accounts were designated for the care of the saints, such as wax for candles, and clothing and accessories for the saints themselves. As guardians of significant funds, cofradías served as credit and lending institutions in many regions of Spanish America.[11] They also integrated the kin networks, neighborhoods, and outlying settlements of native pueblos into the institutional fabric of the Catholic Church. But as with schoolmasters, priest's assistants (*fiscales*), and other Church intermediaries, cofradías were often double-edged institutions. On the face of it, their purpose was in keeping with Catholic parish life. Beneath the surface, their purpose was often multifold, including the care of a native deity, ancestor cult, or the perpetuation of native rituals.

The Virgin of Yabee (the Virgin of the "mountain of butterflies") was a local deity whose veneration became integrated with that of the Catholic Virgin Mary over the course of the colonial period. Rincón pueblos designated a hilltop above Yae as the site for her veneration and built a shrine dedicated to her. The region's elites formed the cofradía to serve as custodian of the shrine and to maintain and adorn the Virgin's image. Each of the pueblos represented by the cofradía bought and contributed expensive decorations and ornaments for the cult of Yabee.[12]

The leadership of the cofradía, represented by the governors of six Rincón pueblos, also oversaw the local market (*tianguis*) held in Yae. In fact, the question of Yae's cabecera status was intimately tied to a conflict over the location of the market in the Northeastern Rincón, and the material wealth that belonged to the cofradía of the Virgin of Yabee. In 1696, the local market was held in Yae and overseen by the leadership of the cofradía of the Virgin of Yabee. After the dissolution of the cofradía in 1703, the market continued to be held in Yae, to the chagrin of the pueblos of the Eastern Rincón. In 1735, the pueblos that had formed part of the cofradía of Yabee went to court over the division of the jewels (*alhajas*) and ornaments (*ornamentos*) used to adorn the Virgin.[13] During the same period, a series of lawsuits brought by the regions' pueblos argued that the market in Yae was inconvenient in terms of its location, and that the officials of Yae did not oversee the market properly, allowing fraud and abuse. In 1744, the cabildo officers of San Juan Tanetze, with the support of the pueblos of Lalopa, Yagallo, Lachichina, Yaviche, Lahoya, Yatoni, Talea, Juquila, Yotao, Cacalotepec, and Roavela, sued to have the market moved to Tanetze because of that town's long-standing cabecera status.[14]

These interpueblo conflicts make clear that parish reform was embedded in larger changes that engulfed the district. As we examine the legal strategies of Zapotec witnesses, cabildo officers, and legal agents in the litigation over Yae's cabecera status, we must keep in mind that their legal arguments addressed a range of issues characterized not only by a struggle between Spanish officials and Zapotec pueblos, but also among these pueblos themselves. In this context, the case against San Juan Yae represents not only resistance to parish reform, but also local efforts to challenge Yae's pretensions to political and economic power.

The phenomenon of multiple cabeceras in the Rincón region of the

Sierra provides another manifestation of the district of Villa Alta's decentralized political system. Part of what defined the region's political relationships was the unusually peripatetic nature of its parish priest and the claim that the priest had no fixed residence. It appears that the priest without fixed residence was not unique to the parish of San Juan Yae–San Juan Tanetze. On the western side of the Cajonos River, the parish of Yagavila (also part of the Rincón Zapoteco) shared a similar tradition. In 1691, Yagavila's officials complained to the Real Audiencia that the major religious celebrations surrounding Easter should be held in Yagavila, the cabecera, since carrying the paraphernalia for these celebrations to subject pueblos posed a hardship.[15]

The Rincón custom of the mobile parish priest had its parallels across New Spain. In remote, rural regions, priests often traveled extensively in order to serve the far-flung pueblos of their parishes, but most had a permanent residence in the cabecera. What set the Rincón custom apart was that according to both Spanish officials and Rincón Zapotecs, the parish priest of the *partido* of San Juan Tanetze–San Juan Yae did not reside permanently in the cabecera. Rather, he moved from pueblo to pueblo, every few days or so, such that in the thirty years that he had served the parish, he had never spent more than a month in one pueblo. Since he was always on the move, the priest celebrated major religious festivals in the pueblo that he happened to be in on the appointed day of the festival, rather than celebrating them in the cabecera. In his testimony to the Real Audiencia during a 1734 investigation of parish relationships in San Juan Tanetze–San Juan Yae, the alcalde mayor made clear that he found the peculiarities of the Rincón custom to be an administrative nightmare. He characterized the region as a "monster with four heads [*un monstruo con cuatro cabeceras*]" in which at least four pueblos felt that they had the "privileges of a cabecera [*fueros de cabecera*]."[16]

The priest's constant movement must have had significant symbolic value for the region's residents, demarcating multiple loci of sacred power, and reinforcing the horizontal nature of political relationships in the region. On closer scrutiny, the "monster with four heads" appears to have been what Marcello Carmagnani has called an "ethnic district"—native territory governed according to native concepts of space and power—whose composition and political organization eluded the understanding of Spanish officials.[17]

After the Cajonos rebellion in 1700, San Juan Yae's efforts to reestablish and reinforce its status as cabecera coincided with Maldonado's efforts to regularize the diffuse cabecera-sujeto structure of the district, and reconfigure the district along the lines of a strict cabecera-sujeto blueprint. In this sense, the reforms that followed the Cajonos Rebellion represented a political opportunity for native elites in San Juan Yae. In a petition presented to Maldonado dated 7 December 1702, the officials of San Juan Yae requested that the parish priest observe all major religious feast days in San Juan Yae, the cabecera. A second petition presented to Maldonado by the officials of San Juan Yae in April of 1703 requested that Maldonado uphold Sariñana's provision of 1695, which recognized San Juan Yae as cabecera. Apparently eager to tame the "monster with four heads," Maldonado insisted on the recognition of three cabeceras (Tanetze, Yagavila, and Yae) in the Rincón region, and that Yae's de jure status as cabecera should be de facto.[18] In response, the pueblo of Santiago Lalopa and later the pueblo of Santiago Yagallo, both of which under Maldonado's plan were designated as subject pueblos of San Juan Yae, led a legal rebellion against the bishop's order.

PERFORMANCE AS RESISTANCE:
COURTROOM POLITICS AND STATE FORMATION

The convergence of the long-term history of parish formation, the Cajonos Rebellion, and Maldonado's parish reforms shaped the renegotiation of power relationships in the parish of San Juan Tanetze–San Juan Yae during the eighteenth century. The Cajonos Rebellion focused the centralizing and reformist gaze of the state and Church hierarchy on the district of Villa Alta and pushed Zapotec intermediaries in pueblos designated as "sujetos" to reassert the political autonomy of their communities. As for so much of the colonial history of New Spain, the legal system provided the arena for the enactment of political struggle and negotiation between state and pueblo, and Spanish law and legal discourse provided the rhetorical tools.

In the parish of San Juan Yae–San Juan Tanetze, resistance to Maldonado's reforms and San Juan Yae's pretensions to cabecera status through recourse to the legal system began in 1705, when Santiago Lalopa, one of the "four heads," refused to recognize Yae as parish seat and appealed to the Audiencia for recognition of its own status as cabecera. The Audiencia found in favor of Lalopa, though we do not know why since we do not have access to the language of the decision in this case. Tensions between Lalopa and Yae persisted until 1709 when the cabildo and legal agent of Lalopa submitted a petition to the alcalde mayor requesting that Yae stop demanding that the villagers of Lalopa comply with their obligations as a subject pueblo. In their petition, the cabildo and legal agent of Lalopa claimed that the pueblo did not recognize Yae as cabecera because Lalopa itself was a cabecera of old (*cabecera antigua*) and Yae was a recently established cabecera (*cabecera moderna*). The Audiencia accepted this argument and exempted Lalopa from any obligations that it owed to Yae as a subject pueblo.[19]

From the time of Maldonado's reforms until 1734, resistance to Yae's status as cabecera continued. As with Santiago Lalopa, at least three of Yae's other subject pueblos refused to attend the major religious celebrations in the disputed cabecera. This stalemate came to a head in 1734 when, in response to complaints by the officials of San Juan Yae that three of its subject pueblos—Yagallo, Yaviche, and Lachichina—did not attend the major religious celebrations in Yae, but rather celebrated them in their own pueblos, the alcalde mayor ordered an investigation and discovered that the three pueblos in question openly refused to recognize Yae as cabecera.[20]

In response to the alcalde mayor's 1734 inquest, the cabildo of Santiago Yagallo presented four witnesses, all principales of the Rincón region, to testify as to the "local custom [*costumbre*]" that governed parish relationships in San Juan Yae–San Juan Tanetze. Their testimonies, given on 18 September 1734, presented a picture of regional relationships that argued against Yae's cabecera status. These few moments of testimony allowed the witnesses to communicate much more to the court than the case required. Through this oral performance, they contested San Juan Yae's status as cabecera, demonstrated their rhetorical skills, and negotiated their personal identity as native intermediaries and colonial subjects.

The negotiation of personal identity constituted a political act and an act of resistance. Spaniards had hoped that through their harsh punishment of the Cajonos "rebels" and the rewards they offered to the families of the fiscales, they could establish a symbolic order that drew a sharp distinction between "idolaters and rebels" and "good and faithful Indians." This distinction established a rhetorical gauntlet of sorts for the witnesses who testified in the 1734 investigation of parish relationships and the ensuing civil suit. How could they present an argument that contradicted the bishops' policies and simultaneously maintain the semblance of "good and faithful Indians"? Through skillful self-presentation and rhetoric—"oral performance"—these men worked to achieve this end. In the process, they linked micropolitics (the politics of the courtroom) to macropolitics (the politics of the district and the colonial state).

Oral performance denotes "a mode of communication, a way of speaking, the essence of which resides in the assumption of responsibility to an audience for a display of communicative skill, highlighting the way in which communication is carried out, above and beyond its referential content."[21] The emphasis on communicative skill, the relationship between the speaker and audience, and implicit meanings beyond the explicit content of the oral text make oral performance a particularly powerful tool for analysis of legal testimony as a mode of cross-cultural communication. When native intermediaries provided testimony in Spanish courts, they walked a fine line between pursuing their individually and communally defined interests and demonstrating their cultural authority and political legitimacy in the eyes of their Spanish audience. This balancing act, in which accommodation, resistance, and negotiation were in constant play, required the deployment of a range of communicative skills, verbal and nonverbal. We have access to elements of both the text and context of indigenous testimony thanks to the court scribe who wrote down not only the witness's words, but also certain details about the witness and the act of giving testimony itself.

The oral performances of Zapotec witnesses connected the social interactions and power dynamics at play in the district courtroom of Villa Alta on 18 September 1734 with the highly charged cultural and political conflicts brewing in the district during the first half of the eighteenth century. Like any form of communication, "performance carries the potential to rearrange the structure of social relations within the performance event and perhaps beyond it."[22] In the courtroom context, the potential to affect change was heightened, as were the social and political stakes involved in giving testimony. By virtue of their performances, witnesses had the power to affect judicial decisions. Furthermore, if evaluated positively, the skill of the witnesses translated into valuable social currency: cultural authority and political legitimacy in the eyes of the Spanish court. These attributes were particularly prized given the witnesses' subaltern identities as Indians and colonial subjects, and given the recent history of the Cajonos Rebellion.

During oral performances, the relationship between performer and audience produces a dynamic relationship between the text of the oral performance (narrated events) and the social context of the narrative (narrative event). When Zapotec witnesses provided court testimony, they "keyed" or "framed" their performances toward both the narrated events (the history of parish relationships) and the narrative event (the act of giving testimony in the courtroom).[23] On that day in the district court, Spaniards constituted the bulk of the courtroom audience. The alcalde mayor represented the ultimate judicial authority in the room, but the short period of his appointment—five years—positioned him as an outsider and placed significant limits on his knowledge of local affairs. As a result, he had to rely on the testimony of local witnesses, and the local knowledge of indigenous elites and long-term Spanish residents in order to make his judgments. The Spanish *vecinos* (local residents) who served as the alcalde mayor's eyes and ears occupied the important roles of scribes, interpreters, and *testigos de asistencia* (in lieu of an official notary) in the district court.

For some of the Zapotec legal agents, cabildo officers, and witnesses, the Spaniards they encountered in the district court were very familiar. These Spanish vecinos came from families that were long established in the region (*encomenderos*, merchants, *ministros de justicia*). As local notables, they participated in the justice system as lawyers and legal counselors. Their local knowledge and interests represented both danger and opportunity for elite indigenous witnesses who often engaged in economic, political, and social relationships with these men, albeit not on equal footing.[24] The porous social boundary between native power brokers and Spanish vecinos formed an important element of the courtroom context: the Spaniards and elite native witnesses, plaintiffs, and defendants were not anonymous to one another. Rather, the workings of justice were highly personalized.

Francisco de Aldas was the first witness to testify on 18 September 1734 on behalf of Santiago Yagallo and the other subject pueblos of San Juan Yae in the alcalde mayor's investigation of parish relationships. Before Aldas and other witnesses gave their testimony, the court asked them to identify themselves. A brief court identification complemented the witnesses' self-identification. Although an apparent formality, this very basic protocol of witness identification allowed a witness to perform his or her social status and cross-cultural competence. Most of the witnesses in the case were elders in their pueblos (in their fifties, sixties, or seventies), of *principal* status, and former or current holders of high cabildo office, such as fiscal, gobernador, alcalde, or *maestro de doctrina* (schoolmaster).

Perhaps most important, according to the court notary, three out of the four witnesses who testified on 18 September 1734, including Aldas, were identified as "indios ladinos." In the case of Aldas, the court identified him as a sixty-two-year-old principal, "indio ladino," dressed in Spanish costume, and residing in the long-recognized cabecera of San Juan Tanetze. His Spanish dress and speaking skill in Spanish impressed the court interpreter who noted his bearing, describing him as "very competent in the Spanish language and dressed as a Spaniard [*bastantamente ladino en la lengua castellana y vestir traje de español*]." As a result of his language skills, he addressed the court directly without using an interpreter. Two other witnesses who testified on this particular day performed their identity in a similar way. Furthermore, all of the witnesses, whether indios ladinos or not, signed their names to their testimony.[25] In a region in which spoken Spanish and literacy were rare skills, this act projected significant cross-cultural competence, Spanish notions of civility, and power.

Ladino performance helped Aldas and other witnesses to battle the "language ideology" of the courtroom. Language ideology—the "perception of language and discourse that is constructed in the interest of a specific social or cultural group"[26]—was another critical element of the courtroom context. In New Spain, given the predominance of Spanish as the language of power, the use of spoken Spanish by indigenous witnesses and litigants was expressly political. Spanish represented "civility" in opposition to indigenous "barbarism," and served as a primary marker of Indian or non-Indian identity and an idealized boundary between colonizer and colonized. Spanish was the language of the Crown, the legal system, and the Church. To provide testimony in Spanish—as did Aldas and most of the witnesses throughout the civil suit that followed the 1734 investigation—denoted and projected power in the courtroom. Testifying in Spanish also addressed Spanish doubts about the credibility of indigenous witnesses. One of the pervasive prejudices of Spanish jurists and legal functionaries was the notion that natives were prone to perjury. Demonstration of hispanization could circumvent this prejudice to some degree. For these reasons, the ladino identity of witnesses undoubtedly was part of the performative strategy of the plaintiff pueblos' legal teams.

Ladino performance provided a critical legitimizing function for Aldas and other witnesses: it established the cultural authority necessary to persuade the Spanish judges. Ladino performance "keyed" Aldas's narrative toward the implicit cultural context surrounding the text: the Spanish notion that in light of the Cajonos uprising, the rebellious and idolatrous native peoples of the district of Villa Alta needed to be disciplined and brought into line with Catholic orthodoxy. Aldas, a Zapotec *principal*, from the long-recognized cabecera of San Juan Tanetze, who testified authoritatively in Spanish about the history and customs of the region, may well have lent a note of dissonance to these Spanish attitudes.

As he addressed the court, Aldas faced a difficult rhetorical task. According to the petitions of the attorney for the plaintiff pueblos and according to the witnesses themselves, the pueblos had agreed to send laborers, wood, branches, and other materials to San Juan Yae in preparation for the celebration of Corpus Christi in the year 1731 despite the fact that the plaintiff pueblos claimed not to recognize San Juan Yae as cabecera. The cabecera-sujeto relationship was defined in part by the material obligations and labor requirements owed by the subject pueblos to the cabecera during major feast days. Aldas had to explain why these pueblos provided labor and materials to San Juan Yae if they did not consider it a cabecera:

> The parish of San Juan Tanetze is made up of twelve pueblos but because of very ancient custom, the parish priest does not reside in any of them. Since the time of Francisco Pacheco de Silva, the witness has seen that in practice, the parish priest passes three days in one pueblo and three in another and in this way he spends time in all of them, and does not have residence in any of them because he celebrates Holy Week and the fiesta of Corpus wherever he happens to be. And there, the rest of the pueblos gather, except the ones which coincidentally happen to be celebrating the same fiesta with the two other priests in this parish who celebrate Christmas, Holy Week, and Corpus Christi in pueblos that request them. In this, there is no stability. Further, they celebrate the titular fiesta annually in each pueblo, such as San Juan Tanetze, or Yae, or Santiago Yagallo, and in this way in each of the pueblos, they cele-

brate the day of their patron saint. And this witness, having seen so, knows that in 1731, they gathered in the pueblo of Yae for the fiesta of Corpus, and the municipal officials of the pueblos of Yagallo, Lachichina, and Yaviche brought the common folk from their pueblos so that they could help those of Yae build the arch made of branches for the procession. But they did this because the parish priest, who celebrated the fiesta of Corpus there, asked them to do so, and not because of obligation to them or custom. Although they have attended this fiesta and others sometimes when they were celebrated in the pueblo of Yae, it has been voluntarily. The pueblos that make up this parish do not recognize a cabecera, nor do they subject themselves to the authority of any pueblo because in the case of recognizing a cabecera, it appears to the witness that they should recognize his pueblo of Tanetze which has been cabecera since they conquered this land and to which not only this parish of which we are speaking has been subjected but also that of Yagavila.[27]

The narrative structure of Aldas's testimony reveals his central rhetorical objective: to explain the apparent contradiction between the actions of the subject pueblos and their refusal to recognize San Juan Yae as cabecera. His primary strategy for meeting this objective was to establish his own cultural authority in the eyes of the Spanish court, a task that was difficult to achieve since he was in effect providing a justification for open resistance to Church policy.

Aldas's testimony established that the parish priest had no fixed residence, and it justified this through reference to ancient customary practice. It also established that the priest celebrated the major religious fiestas "wherever he happen[ed] to be," and that he celebrated the titular fiesta of each community in its pueblo. Aldas legitimized these practices by attributing them to very ancient custom and indirectly to the former *cura beneficiado* of the parish of San Juan Yae–San Juan Tanetze, Francisco Pacheco de Silva. Pacheco de Silva was notable in the religious history of the region for his publication in 1687 of *Doctrina christiana en lengua zapoteca nexitza*.[28] He was also a reknowned extirpator of idolatry, and during the investigation and extirpation campaign that followed the Cajonos Rebellion, cabildo officials of the Rincón pueblos of Yae, Lalopa, and Yaviche credited him with putting an end to community-based native ritual in their pueblos.[29]

By implying that the practice of the excessively wandering priest began after the tenure of Pacheco de Silva, Aldas suggested a kind of historical causality between the (in)famous Pacheco de Silva and local custom. These elements combined to produce an overall rhetorical thrust: contingency and instability with regard to parish structure and hierarchy had been the legitimate custom of the region. Thus it was by coincidence that in 1731, the parish priest happened to celebrate Corpus in San Juan Yae (and not because Yae was cabecera). The attendance and the contributions of the allied pueblos to the celebration of Corpus in Yae were voluntary, and were provided at the request of the parish priest.

Finally, Aldas's testimony referenced a long-standing local power struggle of which this case formed a small part. By referring to Church history, Aldas capitalized on the opportunity to reinforce and promote the political preeminence of his own pueblo—San Juan Tanetze—which was the original cabecera in the Rincón region: "because in the case of recognizing a cabecera, it appears to the witness that they should recognize his pueblo of Tanetze which has been cabecera since they conquered this land." Immediately following, he claimed: "to which not only this parish of which we are speaking [Yae] has been subjected but also that of Yagavila." Through this rhetorical move, Aldas deployed the weight of history to position his pueblo as the powerful cabecera in opposition to the pretensions of Yae or any other pueblo. The historical question of cabecera status for San Juan Yae and San Juan Tanetze reflects the multiple and overlapping political contexts referenced by Aldas's testimony and deconstructs the veneer of witness disinterest. Although he was not from the pueblos directly involved in this phase of the litigation, he had a powerful interest in its outcome, rooted in a long history of pueblo power struggles.

Aldas's use of historical discourse provided a narrative framework of regional history intelligible and acceptable to Spanish authorities: conquest, the establishment of parishes in the region, and reference to important local Church figures, like Pacheco de Silva. Yet he also claimed Church history as part of a local history of pueblo relationships, in which he situated his own pueblo, San Juan Tanetze, in a position of local preeminence. By making Church history local, he lent a degree of ambivalence to the position of the Church: Was it a local institution or a foreign one? This ambivalence cast a shadow of doubt on the dominion of colonial power over the local: On what basis did the alcalde mayor, the Real Audiencia, or the secular hierarchy of the Catholic Church claim the authority to reform local Church practices, to change "very ancient custom" and contradict the "will" of the region's pueblos?

Aldas's narrative of ambivalence—the appropriation of Church history under the rubric of local custom—provided an opening, or rupture, for his characterization of the local customs that structured parish relationships: "no stability," "voluntarily," "not because of obligation," "nor do they subject themselves to the authority of any pueblo," "the parish priest does not reside in any of them." Taken together, this language appears dissonant in a colonial context in which stability, hierarchy, obligation, and submission were expected of native colonial subjects.

Undoubtedly, Aldas realized that most Spanish authorities would view this situation as chaotic, disorderly, and undisciplined, akin to the alcalde mayor's characterization of the parish as a "monster with four heads." But Aldas had positioned these parish practices as "custom [*costumbre*]," a realm that according to the laws of the Indies was supposed to be autonomous in relationship to Spanish law. The relationship between native custom and Spanish law had a long history in Spain's American empire. It was codified in three articles in the New Laws of 1542 and again in the *Recopliacion de las leyes de las Indias* in 1680:

> That the laws and good customs [*buenas costumbres*] that the Indians had in the past, and those that they have made since they were Christians, and any new laws that they make if these laws do not conflict with Christianity, nor with the laws of this book be respected.[30]

> That in lawsuits among Indians, there should be swift and summary determination of the case, maintaining their customs [*usos y costumbres*] as long as they are not clearly unjust.[31]

> That with particular attention, the Spanish governors and judges make note of the order and manner of living of the Indians, their government and form of maintenance, and inform the Viceroys or Courts, and respect their good customs [*usos y costumbres*] that are not contradictory to our sacred faith.[32]

Aldas's testimony put the question to the court in this way: Should Spanish notions of order prevail, or should the costumbre of the district's natives prevail, as provided for in the *Recopilación de las leyes*? The recent history of the Cajonos Rebellion might have tipped the scales in favor of the imposition of a strict cabecera-sujeto model, but Aldas's narrative strategy presented a local alternative cloaked in the legitimacy of Spanish law.

COSTUMBRE AS RHETORICAL STRATEGY

Through Aldas's skillful use of costumbre in his 1734 testimony, he provided a legal foundation for the legitimation of local parish relationships in the Zapotec Rincón of the district of Villa Alta, and for a rejection of San Juan Yae's claims to cabecera status. He also inserted the regional politics of the district of Villa Alta in a larger eighteenth-century debate about the status of costumbre. Costumbre as a Spanish legal concept embodied the principle of local autonomy in the face of an increasingly state-centered legal system in Spanish America. As such, it constituted both a metaphor for local autonomy and a rhetorical tool for its defense. Costumbre as it was applied in the Americas by Spanish jurists and indigenous litigants had its roots in the medieval period of the Iberian Peninsula, a pluralistic society of Catholic, Muslim, and Jewish municipalities, held together in a loose and uneasy coexistence through the recognition of local cultural and political autonomy. As Woodrow Borah has pointed out, on the eve of the conquest of America, the Iberian Peninsula was a patchwork of laws, customs, and competing jurisdictions.[33] As the Reconquista brought more towns and settlements under Christian rule, each community adopted its own *fuero* (body of customary law), which codified laws and procedures related to local governance, including punishment of crime and sexual misconduct, and the criteria and process for selection of officers of municipal cabildos.[34] Whether Christian, Muslim, or Jewish, the fueros drew heavily from the tradition of Roman law, such that despite local particularities, they were remarkably consistent.[35] The coexistence of royal law and local custom in combination with jurisdictional plurality (secular and religious) lent a significant elasticity and complexity to the Iberian legal framework.

Despite the general flexibility and decentralization of this legal system, from the thirteenth century forward, costumbre existed in increasing tension with royal authority. During this period, the Crown attempted to shift the balance away from the fueros in favor of royal authority by issuing the Fuero Real and the Siete Partidas, and by asserting its role as the court of appeal. The Crown increased its judicial power further in 1348 with the

Ordenamiento de Alcalá, which established an order of precedence for sources of law, the most important of which was the superiority of royal law to fueros. In practice, however, local custom continued to inform most judicial decisions. Where the Crown exercised its greatest legal influence in local matters, then, was through its role as a court of appeal, a role that it would continue to play in the Americas through the institution of the Real Audiencia.[36]

The preeminence of royal law converged with an officially prescribed respect for native custom, creating a legal system during the first quarter century of Spanish colonial rule characterized by "strong legal pluralism": a clearly established hierarchy among sources of law.[37] In the abstract, the Spanish Crown reproduced the relationship between the fueros of medieval Castile and royal authority: in the realm of self-government, native custom under the supervision of the administration of the Indies could be preserved as long as it did not challenge Christianization.

However, much changed between the 1542 promulgation of the New Laws and the publication of the *Recopilación de las leyes* in 1680. The formal and legal respect for native custom expressed in the *Recopilación* was mitigated by all of the transformations wrought by evangelization and colonialism itself. Native relationships of power, suprapueblo alliances and rivalries, commerce, and social relations at all levels were changed by the attack on native politico-religious hierarchies at the time of the conquest. In short, colonialism severely curtailed the autonomy of native custom in relationship to Spanish law. By the seventeenth century, recourse to native custom by Spanish jurists had been confined primarily to procedures for local elections and disputes over cabecera-sujeto relationships.[38]

The continued valorization of costumbre in theory despite its erosion in practice (at least at the higher levels of the Spanish judiciary) can be attributed to the influence of the seventeenth-century Spanish jurist Juan de Solórzano Peréira. Solórzano's *Política indiana* (1647), republished three times during the eighteenth century, was considered by jurists and legal practitioners of the time to be one of the most important sources on the laws of the Indies other than the *Recopilación*. Solórzano can be considered the last great Spanish jurist to champion costumbre. Trained in the Humanist and Renaissance tradition, and espousing a conservative approach to the law, Solórzano sought continuity with what he perceived to be the great tradition of the Siete Partidas in his effort to strike a balance between the primacy of royal authority and respect for local custom. The wide circulation of *Política indiana*—it could even be found in the judicial libraries of the remote borderlands of Northern New Spain[39]—ensured that Solórzano's theories provided inspiration and rhetorical tools to legal agents and lawyers throughout eighteenth-century Spanish America who asserted the authority of native custom in the face of increasingly centralized royal political and legal power.[40] The text also provided a resource for alcaldes mayores who in general were far less educated in the law than the judges of the Audiencia and less up-to-date on the most recent juridical trends. As a result, they used whatever textual resources were available to them and employed a combination of local custom and pragmatism rather than current legal theory or doctrine (*doctrina*) when making legal decisions.[41]

The diminution of native custom throughout the colonial period produced a shift in the legal framework of the Audiencia of Mexico from one of "strong legal pluralism" to a "state-centered legal order," in which "the state has at least made if not sustained a claim to dominance over other legal authorities."[42] But this increasingly state-centered legal order maintained some of the flexibility and loopholes that had characterized the strong legal pluralism of medieval Iberia and the early colony, largely through a decentralized legal structure. The decisions of individual local magistrates rather than judicial precedent and previous case decisions determined the enactment of justice in the *alcaldías mayores* of New Spain. Each decision was in effect autonomous from what had gone before and judges ruled based on specific enactment or codified clause. If there were none available, the Crown, Audiencia, or viceroy could issue a *cédula*, *auto acordado*, or ordinance of good government, respectively.[43]

The practice of specific enactment in combination with the power of both local and royal jurists to interpret Indian custom made "jurisdictional jockeying"—playing local and ecclesiastical courts off of the Real Audiencia, and playing civil and ecclesiastical courts off of one another—an effective strategy for indigenous litigants.[44] "Costumbre" could be interpreted differently by judges in different jurisdictions or stages on the ladder of appeals. The decentralized nature of the legal system made for a cycle of endless litigation. It also made costumbre potentially unstable, subject to the interpretation of a range of legal opinion.[45] Both the plaintiffs and the defendants in the case of Santiago Yagallo and allies versus San Juan Yae utilized jurisdictional jockeying and deployed legal arguments based on costumbre. Their procedural and rhetorical strategies help to explain the long duration of the case, as judges across legal jurisdictions interpreted and reinterpreted the custom governing cabecera-sujeto relationships in the district.

The deployment of costumbre as a legal rhetorical strategy by the plaintiff pueblos and San Juan Yae, and its interpretation and application by Spanish judges during this three decade–long cabecera-sujeto case, produced a struggle over the meaning of the term. In petitions, *probanzas*, and testimony, the legal agents, lawyers, and witnesses of the plaintiff pueblos rendered costumbre in what Paola Miceli has called its "romantic" and "primordial" connotations. In its romantic connotation, costumbre emerged spontaneously from the will and practices of the people. The primordial connotation located costumbre in a distant past. Together, the romantic and primordial connotations presented a picture of long-established consensual and popular practices that emanated from everyday life since time immemorial. Miceli urges us not to take the romantic connotation of costumbre at face value. She argues that contrary to scholarly and popular assumptions, costumbre did not originate in the popular will and practices of the people of medieval Castile but rather had its origins in Castilian legal institutions, and was used as a juridical tool for controlling diverse peoples.[46]

The plaintiff pueblos (Santiago Yagallo and associates) deployed a number of rhetorical oppositions to render costumbre in its romantic-primordial connotations. According to their case, local custom defined power relations among pueblos in the region as flexible, contingent, and reciprocal—as a set of horizontal relations. Not surprisingly, the legal case of San Juan Yae also rested on a romantic-primordial definition of costumbre. But rather than present "la costumbre muy antigua" in terms of horizontal relationships among the pueblos of the district, the legal team of San Juan Yae presented a vertical model that squared with the model of pueblo relations intended by the Spaniards: one parish and administrative seat to which the surrounding pueblos contributed labor and material resources.

From 1695, when resistance to San Juan Yae's cabecera status began, until the Audiencia's decision in 1769, Spanish jurists found in favor of both interpretations of costumbre. But over time, the balance tilted in favor of Yae, and in favor of a universal reading of costumbre, applicable to all regions of New Spain regardless of local conditions or temporal considerations. As my analysis will elucidate, struggle over the meaning of costumbre had significant repercussions for power relationships in the district of Villa Alta and the relationship between costumbre and royal legal authority.

THE CIVIL SUIT: A DEBATE OVER
PARISH RELATIONSHIPS AND STATE POWER

In the year that followed the alcalde mayor's 1734 investigation, the cabildos of Santiago Yagallo and other neighboring pueblos brought a civil suit against San Juan Yae over the question of Yae's cabecera status. As the case makes clear, in the intervening years between the investigation and the civil suit, Yae had continued to insist that its neighbors comply with the obligations required of them as subject pueblos. Romantic-primordial costumbre provided the cornerstone of the case presented by the plaintiffs. The themes of contingency, reciprocity, and flexibility that had characterized local practice in the 1734 testimony of Francisco de Aldas came to dominate the probanzas, petitions, and testimonies produced by the lawyer, legal agent, cabildo officials, and witnesses for Yagallo and its fellow plaintiffs.

Spanish law prescribed the identity of the historical actors involved in pueblo-state conflicts: according to the law, indigenous people could not represent themselves in court. Questions of cross-cultural competence also limited the direct participation of indigenous people in the legal system. Many community elites, particularly in peripheral regions of New Spain, did not have the technical skills—bilingualism, literacy, and familiarity with legal protocols—to pursue legal cases effectively. Intermediary figures, both Spanish and indigenous, remedied these obstacles to indigenous litigation and often profited significantly from their roles. Cabildo officers and community elites hired *apoderados* or *agentes* (individuals given power of attorney by the cabildo) to facilitate a case through the first stage of litigation. This most often involved the drafting and presentation of a petition to the alcalde mayor in the district court. Commoners participated through their contributions to the *caja de comunidad* (community treasury), which often provided resources for lengthy litigation.[47] *Derramas* (head taxes) and other forms of illicit taxation also provided funds for costly and lengthy legal cases (we must remember that the legal insurance of the General Indian Court was available only for individual Indian commoners, not for legal cases involving an entire pueblo or a member of the Indian nobility).[48] Commoner discontent over *derramas* could fuel pueblo factionalism through manipulation by one elite faction or another. Elites often deployed such discontent as a weapon against a governor or alcalde who pursued a legal case too aggressively.

In the district of Villa Alta, apoderados and legal agents were often caciques or principales from the pueblo engaged in the litigation or, if the pueblo was small, from the cabecera of the district. Spanish and mestizo vecinos from Villa Alta also served frequently as apoderados and agentes, although less so over the course of the eighteenth century, most likely as a result of a general increase in the number of indigenous elites who possessed the necessary skills to perform the intermediary role. If the litigation progressed beyond the district court, cabildo officials hired a lawyer (*procurador*), usually a Spaniard from Villa Alta or Antequera, since Indians could not by law represent themselves in court. If the case went to appeal in the Real Audiencia, they generally hired a lawyer in Mexico City to represent them in the royal court.

The activity of native legal intermediaries demonstrates that indigenous litigation was not necessarily a pretext for Spaniards to manipulate native grievances for their own profit, as some historians have suggested, although Spanish judges often assumed this was the case in large part because of their prejudices toward Indians as highly suggestible and incapable of independent thought or action. In the case of Villa Alta, indigenous apoderados and governors often traveled to the district seat of Villa Alta or to Antequera to consult with Spanish lawyers. If the case went to appeal, indigenous legal agents migrated to Mexico City and resided there for months or even years in order to keep tabs on the case that they had been hired to follow. This does not mean that litigation was not an exploitative affair; indigenous legal agents could take advantage of their role for their own profit as easily as Spaniards. Rather, the presence of intermediaries who by definition of their role were accountable to the people who hired them and were required to mediate between their clients and Spanish lawyers and officials indicates that native litigation was a collective, interethnic affair, mitigated by bonds of debt and obligation. The technicalities of litigation—legal strategy, rhetorical strategy, presentation of witnesses, composition of petitions—were as often the product of collective strategizing by community elites, legal agents, and lawyers as they were the full creation of a powerful Spaniard. Experience made native legal intermediaries and cabildo officers remarkably savvy about the law. As Enrique Florescano has eloquently put it, for indigenous peoples, the court was "a school where they learned to use the laws, the procedural and juridical memory of the conquistador."[49]

The consistent and skillful deployment over almost four decades of costumbre as a legal rhetorical strategy in the cabecera-sujeto dispute of San Juan Yae and its neighbors was attributable to a collective process in which an interethnic legal team participated. Documents signed by the cabildos of Yagallo, Yae, and other pueblos involved in the litigation authorized local indigenous notables from Yae and Tanetze with power of attorney, and eventually authorized lawyers in Mexico City to take over the case. For example, on 29 July 1744, the cabildo of San Juan Yae gave power of attorney to Juan de Mendoza, a cacique of Yae, "so that he find and retrieve from the archives of the courts of the Church, monasteries, and pueblos the titles, royal decrees [*reales provisiones*], papers, books, and other documents that demonstrate that San Juan Yae has been and is the cabecera of this parish."[50] A day later, the cabildo of Yae issued a second power of attorney to Joseph Sanchez Pizarro, a legal agent in Mexico City, for the express purpose of representing Yae in the Real Audiencia in the case against Yagallo and associates over the matter of cabecera status.[51] On the same day, the cabildos of the plaintiff pueblos gave power of attorney to Antonio de Aldas (no relation to Francisco de Aldas), a cacique from San Juan Tanetze.[52] The interethnic legal teams appointed by the cabildos of the plaintiffs and defendants, in concert with community elites and witnesses, produced the rhetoric of the case with reference to a rich repertoire of Spanish legal discourse.

In June 1741, the Spanish lawyer for Santiago Yagallo and associates, with the likely cooperation of the legal agent and high-ranking officials of Yagallo and the other plaintiff pueblos, presented to the court a list of questions intended to structure the testimony of the witnesses who testified on their behalf. Two questions, asked in succession, addressed the customary relations between pueblos of the region. The first question asked whether the festivals of Corpus Christi, Christmas, Holy Week, and others are celebrated in the pueblo in which the "padre cura happens to be since he has no fixed residence in any of the pueblos of the parish (with the exception of the titular saint's day which is celebrated in the pueblo of the patron saint)." The second question asked whether the help (*asistencias*) provided during these Church events is or has been given "freely due to the good relations obtaining among the pueblos of my clients and San Juan Yae and due to the style [*estilo*], practice [*práctica*], and custom [*costumbre*] that when there is an event in one of these pueblos, the villagers of Yae attend, and when there is one in Yae, the villagers of the other pueblos attend."[53]

The language of the questions is reminiscent of that of the 1734 testimony of Francisco de Aldas. Contingency (celebrations are held in the pueblo where the "padre cura happens to be") as opposed to fixity ("he has no fixed residence") is one of the major thematic oppositions and rhetorical tools of the questions. Free will as motive for attendance of the fiestas in Yae (the help has been given "freely") and reciprocity ("good relations") represent a second set of rhetorical tools. In these questions, costumbre is not a "fixed thing [*cosa fija*]," imposed from above, but the "estilo, práctica" of the people, emanating from below.

The lawyer and legal team of the plaintiff pueblos deployed a discourse of costumbre that embedded its purportedly local characteristics—contingency, flexibility, and free will—in a standardized legal discourse about costumbre. Solórzano's legal theory informed the rhetoric of their questions and the responses of the witnesses. In *Política indiana*, the Spanish jurist and champion of costumbre elaborated a specific vocabulary that accompanied the use of costumbre in colonial-era legal cases in Castile and Spanish America. Drawing on Solórzano's vocabulary, lawyers and legal agents routinely utilized the words *práctica*, *estilo*, and *uso* interchangeably with costumbre, reinforcing its roots in local practice. Legal agents and lawyers also used *modo* (style), *manera* (manner), and *orden* (order) interchangeably with costumbre, but with less frequency. In addition to this catalogue of synonyms around which the meaning of costumbre was constructed, Solórzano identified a number of verbs—*introducir* (introduce), *guardar* (maintain), and *observar* (observe)—used to express a range of relationships between costumbre and royal authority. A legal conservative and proponent of tradition, Solórzano favored *guardar* over *introducir* in matters concerning *costumbre*.[54] If he had rendered the decision in this case, he would likely have found in favor of Santiago Yagallo and the other plaintiff pueblos.

Given the wide circulation of *Política indiana*, the lawyer for Santiago

Yagallo may well have read Solórzano, or relied on the *Recopilación*'s codification of costumbre, replete with some of the vocabulary elaborated by Solórzano. In his study of costumbre, Victor Tau Anzoátegui claims that the *Recopilación* was often the only legal text to be found in most cabildos in the viceroyalty of the Rio de la Plata from the last decade of the seventeenth century until the Crown issued the Real Ordenanza de Intendentes in 1784.[55] The *Recopilación* enjoyed a wide circulation in the viceroyalty of New Spain as well. Nearly every territorial jurisdiction had "at its disposal" a copy of the *Recopliacíon*.[56] In the 1734 petition presented on behalf of Santiago Yagallo, the legal team contested the right of outsiders to impose custom from above by claiming that "much unanimity" was needed to "introduce" (*introducirse*) costumbre. Here, the legal team deployed *introducir* negatively as a rhetorical device for legitimizing the popular roots of costumbre. Furthermore, by utilizing the vocabulary most frequently associated with the legal concept of costumbre, the legal teams of both sides of the dispute strengthened their legal claims through a demonstration of legal competence and familiarity with the language of the law.

The thematic oppositions embedded in the questions served to structure the testimony of the witnesses, who in their responses expressed the particularities of local custom in the parameters of Solórzano's standardized rhetoric of costumbre.[57] If we consider the relationship between the questions presented in probanzas and the testimony of witnesses in musical terminology, the questions provided simple themes on which witnesses could improvise. The sum of witness testimony, then, served to rehearse the same themes, while preserving the individuality of each witness's improvisation. Repetition of major themes balanced by a diversity of details provided the building blocks of a strong legal case. Ideally, by the end of the series of testimony, the Spanish judge would be able to recite the particularities of local custom from the perspective of the plaintiff pueblos, and would consider the violation thereof as an injustice.

The witnesses presented by San Juan Yae replicated the romantic-primordial interpretation of costumbre deployed by the legal team of the plaintiff pueblos, but changed the relevant content. They attempted to persuade the court of the antiquity of Yae's cabecera status by refuting the picture of reciprocity and contingency painted by the witnesses for the plaintiff pueblos and replacing it with a picture of a romantic-primordial custom of hierarchy and obligation.[58] To complicate matters, Juan Bartolomé, a *principal* from Yatoni and witness for Yae, stated that the reason that the pueblos of Lachichina, Yagallo, and Yaviche did not attend the major religious fiestas was because of a dispute between Antonio de Saavedra, the parish priest, and Juan de Mendoza, the governor of Yae. Out of disgust with Mendoza, Saavedra asked the subject pueblos not to provide the customary labor and materials for the fiestas.[59] Another witness for Yae, Francisco Javier de Medina, a Spaniard and resident of the city of Oaxaca, who had been living in the parish of San Juan Yae for eight years, testified that during the celebration of Corpus Christi in 1733, the alcalde of Yae asked the parish priest to send an order to Yagallo, Lachichina, and Yaviche that required them to comply with their obligations to Yae. Saavedra refused, arguing that he did not want the pueblos to provide help since Yae "was not the cabecera, nor had it ever been."[60]

If the testimonies of Bartolomé and Medina were true, by turning a blind eye to or even encouraging Yagallo, Lachichina, and Yaviche to resist complying with their obligations as subject pueblos, the parish priest may have been a primary player in the conflict. The invocation of the priest as puppeteer who encouraged the pueblos of Yagallo, Yaviche, and Lachichina to ignore their obligations as sujetos undercut earlier claims of Yaviche's cabildo that it had independent motives for bringing the case against Yae. This scenario would indeed be in keeping with Spanish prejudices about Indian disputes, some of which have been adopted by modern historians: wherever there was an Indian dispute, a Spaniard was most likely pulling the strings. But ethnohistorical research has shown that more often, long-standing political rivalries and disputes, sometimes centuries long, simmered beneath the surface structure of colonial administrative and political organization, often without the full knowledge or understanding of Spanish judges and officials. In this particular case, given the long-standing tensions over Yae's cabecera status, dating back at least to 1617, it seems more likely that if the priest was indeed involved, his meddling provided a spark for the long fuse of power struggles in the district, and opened a space for Yae's neighbors again to resist its claims to cabecera status.

THE AUDIENCIA'S DECISION

In December 1743, the Audiencia rendered its decision, ruling in favor of San Juan Yae's claims to cabecera status. The Audiencia justified its ruling with an interpretation of costumbre that eschewed contingency and reciprocity in favor of a hierarchical set of relations defined by "obligaciones" and "asistencias" owed to cabeceras on the part of their subject pueblos.[61] But despite its decision in favor of Yae, the Audiencia made clear that it still awaited a title (*título*) that the legal team of Yae had promised to produce that would prove their town's cabecera status and detail the obligaciones and asistencias owed them by their subject pueblos. The very notion that costumbre could be ascertained from a legal document reveals the gulf between the concepts of costumbre deployed by the legal teams of Yagallo and the Audiencia, respectively. From the perspective of the plaintiff pueblos, romantic-primordial custom was legitimized by social practice over time, not by legal fiat.

The Audiencia's definition of costumbre as obligaciones and asistencias reveals the limits of romantic-primordial costumbre as rhetorical strategy on the part of native litigants. In the eyes of the Audiencia, in cases of cabecera-sujeto relations, costumbre could only be interpreted in one way: the hierarchical cabecera-sujeto model imposed by the Spaniards themselves. This use of costumbre makes clear that as a legal concept it served the needs of empire more than it reflected the practices of indigenous groups or protected their autonomy. By the eighteenth century, in the hands of the Audiencia, costumbre had been rendered neutral as its meaning had come to eschew the inconveniences and subtleties of local practice, and to reflect the imperial imperatives of standardization, centralization, and universality.

The lawyer for Yagallo and its allies recognized this tension between his own use of costumbre and that of the Audiencia. In a 1744 petition to the Audiencia appealing the 1743 decision, he protested the homogenization and universality of the concept as applied by the Audiencia: "What is this custom and what are the asistencias and obligaciones that have constituted custom? Because according to its nature and as delineated in Royal law, judges must not and cannot impose custom. Rather, habitual acts and deeds repeated over the long term constitute custom, which is why Indians do not observe the same custom. Rather, the customs that they observe are as numerous and diverse as are the pueblos themselves."[62] The struggle over the meaning of costumbre captured so pointedly by the lawyer for the plaintiff pueblos may be traced again to Solórzano and a tension in his elaboration of the concept. Solórzano defined costumbre as both a juridical norm and as a habit acquired by doing something continuously over time. As royal legal authority became increasingly centralized, it appears that the Audiencia interpreted costumbre as juridical norm rather than as long-standing local practice. In an effort to combat the Audiencia's interpretation, the petition penned by the lawyer of the plaintiff pueblos echoes Solórzano's articulation in *Política indiana* of costumbre as practice and costumbre as regionally variable: "No less different are the customs of each region than the winds that bathe them and the municipalities that divide them."[63] Solórzano's favorable reading of romantic-primordial costumbre marked the end of an era. A rationalist trend in legal theory launched an assault on romantic-primordial costumbre that coincided with the case of Santiago Yagallo and associates versus San Juan Yae.

The trend toward the centralization of legal power (*la potestad legislativa*) in the hands of the king and away from local custom that had begun in medieval Castile accelerated substantially during the eighteenth century. Bourbon devotion to enlightened absolutism and the rationalization of imperial rule may in part explain the divergent legal interpretations of costumbre apparent in the case of Santiago Yagallo and allies versus San Juan Yae. A *real cédula* dated 13 December 1721 and issued to the Audiencia of México emphasized the primacy of royal law and the importance of its literal interpretation and application.[64] Twenty-one years later, in 1742, the Council of the Indies warned the viceroy of New Spain "to observe without exception the laws of the Kingdom, no matter the custom [*práctica, uso o costumbre*] introduced or intended by the Viceroys and Ministers."[65]

In tandem with the centralization of legal power in the hands of the king, royal jurists in the second half of the eighteenth century increasingly abandoned or disregarded local custom as a legitimate source for legal decisions in favor of an instrumentalist application of costumbre that served the enlightened absolutist policies of the Bourbon kings. From 1747 to 1774, four royal jurists—Tomás Manuel Fernández, Manuel Silvestre Martínez, Juan Francisco de Castro, and Juan Antonio Mujál y de Gibert—launched an attack on costumbre that embodied the rationalist spirit of the period.[66] In particular, Castro's treatise, *Discursos críticos sobre las leyes y sus intérpretes*, reflects the legal trend:

> We do not need to go far in order to demonstrate the dim uncertainty in matters of custom. Far from finding solace in custom, litigants frequently experience major frustration. It is more useful for the republic

to adorn itself with the laws that are the fruit of the sleepless nights of our wise legislators than to vacillate due to a system of law that is so uncertain and rife with variations, as is the case with custom. . . . it would therefore serve the public peace to banish all custom since it is derogatory to the law.[67]

In the last two decades of the century, as the Bourbon Reforms rationalized the administration of the Indies through the system of intendencias, Spanish jurists such as José Pérez y López and El Conde de la Cañada continued their attacks on costumbre in favor of la potestad legislativa. By the turn of the century, the consensus of Spanish jurists centered on the absolute power of royal authority in legal matters and left little room for recourse to local custom.[68]

The shift toward rationalist legal theory in the metropole may have had some effect on the Audiencia's decision in the case of Santiago Yagallo and associates versus San Juan Yae. The chronology of the shift appears to coincide to some degree with the chronology of the case, although it is difficult to be sure, since the timing of the appeals remains somewhat shadowy. The plaintiff pueblos appealed the Audiencia's 1743 decision in 1744.[69] The documentation of the case, however, ends in 1745, when the Audiencia rejected the appeal of the plaintiff pueblos.[70]

Legal cases from 1750 and 1769 suggest, however, that the dispute continued after the Audiencia's 1744 decision. In 1750, Christóbal Flores, governor of Yae, and a number of Yae's officials and principales brought a case of abuse of authority against their legal agent Francisco de Mendoza (the same man who had served as governor in the 1730s and had quarreled with the priest, Antonio de Saavedra). Armed with the pueblo's power of attorney from 1733 until 1750, Mendoza had played a central role in the case against Santiago Yagallo and associates. Flores and his allies complained that Mendoza had asked them to authorize legal business—and therefore further expenses—without explaining the exact content of said business. It is possible that Mendoza had continued to conduct legal business related to the cabecera-sujeto dispute in response to the plaintiff pueblos' continued appeals.[71]

A legal document from 1769 further suggests that the appeals may have continued until that date. The last of the 104 pages of the document records the request by the procurador for Yae and the return by the Audiencia of the provisions and decrees that Yae's legal team had submitted in support of their claims to cabecera status. The first 103 pages contained copies of petitions, testimony, and appeals on the part of the litigants from 1731 to 1744, as well as a copy of the royal decree from 1743. This amalgam of the case may have represented what the judges reviewed for final appeal sometime between 1744 and 1769.[72]

If not directly influenced by the 1764 and 1765 treatises of Martínez and Castro, the decision of the Audiencia may have reflected ideas that were in the air or brewing during this period. Even if there was no direct connection between legal theory in Spain and the Audiencia's decision in the case (which would be difficult to believe), it is interesting to note that the political conditions obtaining on the ground in the district of Villa Alta from 1700 forward spoke directly to the political debates in Spain concerning the validity of local custom and native autonomy versus royal legal authority and the centralization of political power. This is not surprising when one considers that the centralizing and authoritarian policies of Bishop Maldonado (Oaxaca's first Bourbon bishop) and their deleterious effects on native autonomy brought the spirit if not the letter of the Bourbon Reforms to the district of Villa Alta earlier than to other parts of New Spain. Bourbon efforts during the 1740s and 1750s to secularize and centralize parish administration throughout its American holdings mirrored Maldonado's attacks on Dominican hegemony in Villa Alta.[73] The case of Santiago Yagallo and allies versus San Juan Yae represented a response on the part of the litigants on both sides of the case to these new conditions and an impulse to negotiate a favorable outcome for themselves.

CONCLUSION

By examining the dialectic between local custom and Spanish royal law, this chapter contributes to an important comparative dialogue in the study of legal regimes as global structures that change over time. Lauren Benton's ambitious comparative work on colonial legal regimes posits that colonialism as a global phenomenon concerned itself largely with the construction of legal institutions that emerged as a negotiation between local legal orders (what colonizers recognized and labeled as "custom") and state legal orders. Benton argues that across a spectrum of European colonial projects, from 1400 to 1900, plural legal systems helped to bring colonial states into being and maintain their viability over time.[74] Colonial states and legal institutions did not exist as static monoliths, but rather emerged over time in dialectic with native litigation and politico-legal culture. Native intermediaries provide a point of entry for examining the formation, maintenance, success, and limitations of colonial legal regimes.

As native legal intermediaries negotiated with the colonial state and Catholic Church over matters of local concern, they linked native political structures in the Sierra Norte to wider ones. Through legal mediation, they both responded to and actively sought the intervention of colonial courts in indigenous affairs. By turning to the colonial legal system to resolve local disputes, legal intermediaries incorporated the power of the Crown and Church into regional and pueblo politics, thereby making colonial rule a two-way dynamic rather than a one-way process with power flowing only from the center outward. They thus participated in the formation of a common cultural and political terrain—a "legal culture"—in which they, local Spanish officials, parish priests, and the Crown and Church hashed out forms of local rule.[75]

In the case under study in this chapter, the Audiencia's decision in favor of San Juan Yae diminished native autonomy in the Rincón region of Villa Alta, a process that had begun in the aftermath of the Cajonos Rebellion. The principles of fixity, obligation, and hierarchy championed by Maldonado, the legal team of San Juan Yae, and the Real Audiencia overshadowed the principles of contingency, consensus, and reciprocity put forth by Santiago Yagallo and associates in defense of local autonomy. The legal decision in favor of colonial domination in this particular case must be understood as multilayered. The legal team of San Juan Yae asserted the pueblo's right to dominate its subject pueblos, much as the Audiencia asserted its right to impose an instrumentalist interpretation of custom, and to shape local relationships of power through legal fiat. If the Audiencia's decision was actually enforced in local practice, a more pointed form of domination came to define the relationships among the Zapotec pueblos of the Rincón in the second half of the eighteenth century as much as it did Spanish-indigenous and state-pueblo relations. But the Audiencia's decision in this long-term, cabecera-sujeto struggle should not lead us to believe that costumbre no longer mattered to Spanish judges in New Spain. Although increasingly discounted by the Audiencia over the eighteenth century, local magistrates continued to rely on costumbre in cases that they decided on their own, without referral to the Audiencia. In the case of Villa Alta, as we shall see in chapter 5, costumbre still held sway in the magistrates' decisions in electoral disputes.

Chapter 4

The Pact

CACIQUE AND CABILDO

In 1730, Miguel Fernández de Chaves, a cacique of Tiltepec, dressed in Spanish clothing and speaking fluent Castilian, appeared in front of the *alcalde mayor* of Villa Alta, Antonio Blanco de Sandoval. Deathly ill, he claimed that a guilty conscience had led him to the district court. He confessed that he had deceived the *cabildo* (native municipal government) of his pueblo with false promises that had been given the force of law through a Spanish legal document known as an *escripta de convenio y obligacion* (a contractual agreement or pact). Now, as a "good Christian," he sought to make amends for his actions. He proceeded to authorize a last will and testament that entitled the pueblo of Tiltepec to his *cacicazgo* (noble estate).[1]

The pact between Chaves and the cabildo of Tiltepec was a tactic for the renegotiation of local rule in Zapotec pueblos in the face of the sweeping material changes that characterized early eighteenth-century Villa Alta. The terms of the pact reinstituted Chaves, who had been absent from the district for many years prior to the Cajonos Rebellion, as cacique of San Miguel Tiltepec, his pueblo of origin, in exchange for his legal services in a land dispute with the neighboring pueblo of San Francisco Yovego. The problem that brought Chaves to the alcalde mayor in the last months of his life was that in enacting the pact, he found himself in a political bind common to intermediary figures: he promised more than he could deliver, and the people on whose behalf he had negotiated called him to account. Through further negotiation, however, Chaves and the cabildo officers salvaged the terms of the pact and forged a mutually beneficial agreement. This thirty-year process of negotiation and renegotiation had significant effects on the form of local rule at the pueblo and interpueblo level. It reordered not only the territorial relationship between Tiltepec and Yovego but also the traditional system of authority that governed relations among the hereditary nobility, municipal officials, and commoners of Tiltepec. Chaves's story reveals the power of the cacique as a symbol for the renegotiation of territorial rights and political and economic power in eighteenth-century Villa Alta.

DEMOGRAPHIC CHANGE, LOCAL MARKETS, AND LAND CONFLICT

The Cajonos Rebellion was a political watershed in the district of Villa Alta that ushered in a wave of state- and Church-sponsored reform, native resistance, and interpueblo conflict. Native intermediaries took center stage in this tumultuous political process. As critical as the Cajonos Rebellion was as an engine of change, so too were a constellation of material changes, which also had significant bearing on the political landscape of the district of Villa Alta in the eighteenth century, and added new dimensions to the role of the district's native intermediaries. The population boom in the late seventeenth and early eighteenth centuries (discussed in chap. 3) put pressure on land and heightened demand for subsistence goods, resulting in an increase in land conflict and the creation of a system of local markets.

These changes dovetailed with the political changes wrought by the Cajonos Rebellion and subsequent reforms. Together, they pressured the native leadership of the district's pueblos to respond to the new political and demographic realities through interrelated strategies: claims to the status of *cabecera* or parish seat (as in the cases of San Juan Yae, Santiago Lalopa, and Santiago Yagallo), territorial expansion, and petitions for the rights to host a local market. Through litigation, large pueblos ate away at and sometimes swallowed whole the territory of their smaller neighbors. Conversely, previously marginal settlements such as *barrios* or *ranchos*, with recently added population, brought legal cases to the Audiencia in an effort to break away and form their own pueblos. Through a similar dynamic of fragmentation, *sujetos* ceded from their cabeceras, demanded to be recognized as cabeceras, and sought licenses to hold a market day.

Strategies of fragmentation and consolidation opened a world of opportunity to native legal intermediaries, since their objectives required the stamp of legitimacy that only the legal system could provide.

In the final years of the seventeenth century, the cabildo of San Miguel Tiltepec responded to the doubling of the pueblo's population[2] in two ways: a petition to the Audiencia for the rights to hold a local market, and through a land dispute with the neighboring pueblo of Yovego. The assertiveness on the part of Tiltepec's cabildo may have been fueled as much by historical memory as by material changes. According to Michel Oudijk and John Chance, in the pre-Hispanic period, Tiltepec was one of the power centers of the Zapotec Sierra, notable for its large population and military prowess. Its military reputation only grew in the course of the Spanish conquest of the sierra. Relying on Bernal Díaz's account of the conquest of New Spain, Chance notes that at Tiltepec, the first Spanish *entrada* made up of one hundred Spaniards led by a Spanish conquistador named Captain Briones was routed. During the following two entradas, the population of Tiltepec continued to lead a fierce Zapotec resistance to the Spanish conquerors and their native allies from central Mexico. This martial spirit was immortalized in the Lienzo of Analco, a pictographic history of the conquest of the sierra, commissioned by the sierra's Indian conquerors sometime during the sixteenth century in their effort to record, promote, and defend their special role and privileges as Spanish military allies. According to Oudijk's description, one of the striking features of the lienzo is the depiction of a battle at Tiltepec in which the native artist rendered the pueblo as a black hill covered with Zapotec soldiers on the offensive against the Spanish conquerors and their native allies. The resistance of the Zapotecs of Tiltepec did not end with the Spanish conquest. In 1531, the caciques of Tiltepec led an uprising against the foreign invaders, which was serious enough that the alcalde mayor had to call in reinforcements from Antequera. Once they had succeeded in repressing the revolt, the Spaniards executed the offending caciques and rebels.[3]

The resistance of the pueblo of Tiltepec to early Spanish rule provoked the first alcalde mayor of Villa Alta, Luis de Berrio, to characterize the pueblo's inhabitants as "the worst Indians of the land."[4] It is likely that in the years following the 1531 uprising, this reputation elicited sufficient Spanish repression to erode Tiltepec's preeminent position in the sierra. Unlike the town of Choapan, which had also been a military power during the pre-Hispanic era, and which was transformed during the colonial period into an administrative and commercial center, Tiltepec's role as a power center diminished significantly in the century and a half that followed the conquest. Claims to commercial, territorial, and political power on the part of Tiltepec's intermediaries in the late seventeenth and early eighteenth century may therefore have been driven by both demographic change and a memory of past glory.

In 1696, the same year that San Juan Yae petitioned Bishop Isidro de Sariñana y Cuenca to reinstate it as cabecera, the cabildo of San Miguel Tiltepec petitioned the Audiencia to grant a market day in their pueblo. The cabildo justified its request by its growing population and a lack of basic foodstuffs.[5] Chance's population figures for Tiltepec corroborate the claims of the petition. In 1622, the population stood at 352; in 1703, it was 736. Population figures for the district as a whole grew from 20,751 to 36,396 during the same years.[6] The petition argued that a market day would help to ease the pressures created by this population boom by making goods such as fish, salt, lard, pork, tomatoes, jitomates, plantains, custard apples (*chirimoyas*), and corn available to the residents of Tiltepec and its surrounding pueblos, who were also suffering from a lack of staples. The cabildo of Tiltepec secured the testimony of local power brokers, like the governor of the cabecera of Yagavila, Joseph de Santiago, who signed his testimony with an impressive flourish, a regidor from Yovego, and alcaldes from Lahoya and Yagallo. Each of these men agreed that a market day in Tiltepec would benefit the region as a whole.[7] The same year, the Audiencia conceded to the demands of the petition, granting a market day in Tiltepec.[8]

Petitions for market days in the Rincón region streamed into the district court of Villa Alta and then on to the Real Audiencia throughout the eighteenth century: Yaviche in 1709, Yagavila in 1734, and Tanetze in 1741.[9] The Rincón region of the sierra demarcated a commercial zone because of its relative proximity to Ixtlán and Antequera, and as a result, a cadre of native elites filled roles as commercial intermediaries. Chance notes that this group of native merchants appeared on the scene in the 1690s, about the same time as the Indian market system.[10] It is not surprising, therefore, that Rincón cabildo officers sought to expand commerce in their region by establishing market days in major pueblos. However, the commercialization of the district during the eighteenth century appears to have had a double-edged effect on the economic position of native merchants. Chance has noted that the increasingly monopolistic practices of the alcaldes mayores in the cochineal trade squeezed out native and Spanish competitors during the eighteenth century.[11] If native merchants were to benefit from the development of a market system in the district, they would do so as small-time intermediaries in the cochineal trade or in trade outside of the cochineal market.

In August 1698, the cabildo of Tiltepec followed its bid for a market day with an effort to appropriate land that it claimed had been taken from Tiltepec unjustly by the neighboring pueblo of San Francisco Yovego. According to an August 1698 petition in which they laid claim to a parcel known as Leahbichitoag in Zapotec, and Caltepeque in Nahuatl, the pueblo of Tiltepec had acquired the parcel and other lands during the pre-Hispanic Zapotec war of expansion against the Chinantecs and Mixes. The parcel had been in Chinantec territory, and according to the cabildo of Tiltepec, their ancestors had won the parcel through "force of arms."[12]

The Tiltepec cabildo's claim to Leahbichitoag, a parcel that according to their petition had a long, meaningful, and contentious history, points to the mutually reinforcing material and cultural value of land for native peoples throughout Latin America. Land served obvious economic purposes, the most basic of which were subsistence and the provision of goods and income for tribute payment, religious fiestas, and the maintenance and adornment of community churches.

Beyond its economic value, land mediated concepts of time, ancestry, collective identity, and the sacred. In the voluminous documentation of land disputes in the district of Villa Alta, one is struck by the intimacy of indigenous knowledge of and relationship to the land. Each parcel had a name, recognized by at least a pueblo's *principales* and by neighboring principales. Elites and perhaps some commoners knew the land as if it were an old friend or member of the family and could narrate its contours, rises, and dips, texture, boundaries, stone features, and how it was situated with respect to other parcels. In situating land use and ownership in space, indigenous witnesses and litigants also made territorial claims by reference to time and lineage, invoking possession "since time immemorial" by virtue of the labor of their ancestors, who could be real or mythical, and often divine. In this way, litigants made land, time, and lineage—all elements of the sacred—central to their conception of property "rights."

Lineage constituted an especially important aspect of property "rights" and a rhetorical strategy for claiming those rights. Primordial titles—complex narratives of history, genealogy, and territory which native leaders produced during the colonial period in response to Spanish demands that they codify communal landholdings—represented this rhetorical strategy in action. Many of the sierra's primordial titles of the end of the seventeenth and beginning of the eighteenth century were either produced by local caciques or by cabildos that referred to caciques and pre-Hispanic *coquis*. In some late primordial titles, native cabildos whose members could not claim direct descent from cacique lines laid claim to land through rights "since time immemorial [*desde tiempos imemoriales*]."[13] "Time immemorial" skirted around the issue of bloodline by invoking the principle of lineage through reference to antiquity. In this way, the history of the lineage became the history of the pueblo, and by extension, the pueblo became the inheritor of the cacique's lands.

The high value assigned to land made territorial disputes the primary expression of inter- and intrapueblo conflict in the district of Villa Alta during the colonial period, and especially during the eighteenth century, although it is important to note that some subregions of the district and some pueblos experienced more land conflict than others. Oaxaca's major indigenous regions—the Valley of Oaxaca, the Mixteca, and the Sierra Norte—have been noted for the persistence of indigenous landholding. As a result, unlike other parts of Mexico where land disputes often involved the defense of Indian territory against encroachment by Spaniards, criollos, or mestizos, in Oaxaca, for the most part, indigenous individuals, groups, and pueblos fought for land among themselves. This was especially true in the Sierra Norte, where the Spanish and mestizo population was so proportionately small.[14] The thesis that indigenous engagement in land conflict served a defensive purpose, uniting Indian pueblos against rapacious outsiders, thus cannot be applied to the Sierra Norte, even during the eighteenth century.[15]

Land disputes were complicated legal processes that required mastery of particular forms of knowledge originating in both Spanish and indigenous conceptions of land tenure. With the exception of a handful of legal professionals and long-term Spanish residents of Villa Alta, the biculturalism of native intermediaries uniquely positioned them to mediate litigation over land. Their knowledge of the intricacies of local genealogy and the indigenous names of the land parcels, including how a particular parcel of territory was situated in relation to other parcels, made them indispensable participants in land disputes. Mastery of Spanish property law such as inheritance rights and legal mechanisms for the transfer of land, including wills, bills of sale, land transfer, and donation made them effective legal agents and complemented their local knowledge. Most important, their biculturalism allowed them to present this array of confusing information with coherence and intelligibility sufficient for their cases to convince the local magistrate and the Real Audiencia.

As mediators of land disputes, native legal agents controlled a critical point of articulation between native peoples and the colonial state. Territorial rights, as defined by Spanish law, served two important purposes in reinforcing state influence in Indian pueblos. First, this body of law made the state indispensable to Indians. Without state sanction of territorial possession, indigenous people had no secure claim to their land. Second, land disputes provided the state with an important means of affecting power relationships in and among Indian pueblos. By deciding in favor of one litigant over another, the Audiencia could empower a well-represented "upstart" individual or pueblo, or diminish the economic power of a traditional noble family or cabecera.

The competing narratives of the history of the parcel Leahbichitoag in the 1698 land dispute between Tiltepec and Yovego make clear that land disputes provided a key forum for the negotiation of the interests of the colonial state and its native subjects over the long term. According to the 1698 petition submitted by the cabildo of Tiltepec, in the decades that followed the conquest, Cristóbal de Chaves, a resident of Antequera who served as alcalde mayor of Villa Alta during the years 1549 and 1551, incorporated Leahbichitoag into his sierra holdings. Chaves caused problems for the community by introducing livestock onto the parcel. The animals overran land that belonged to the pueblo of Tiltepec, creating physical damage and ill will. Further, Chaves, who had a reputation for abuse and misadministration, appointed a native as his assistant (*fiscal*), whose task it was to entice Indians from Tiltepec and surrounding pueblos through promises of tribute exemption to leave their land in order to live and work on his estate. The cabildo of Tiltepec complained to the Audiencia about Chaves's abuses. In 1555, the Audiencia issued a royal decree (*real provisión*) that ordered an investigation. Another royal decree, issued in 1590, granted possession of the parcel to the pueblo of Tiltepec.[16]

In the 1698 petition, the cabildo of Tiltepec claimed that from 1590 until 1650, the pueblo had been in possession of the parcel. During this period, a number of Yovego residents rented the land. In 1650, an epidemic hit Tiltepec hard, leaving no more than thirty-five households. The petition asserts that at this point, residents of the pueblo of Yovego took advantage of the weakened position of Tiltepec, crossed the Rio Grande (the local name for the Cajonos River), the river that divided the two pueblos, and began to cultivate the parcel, among others, without paying proper rent. Eventually, the villagers of Yovego claimed the parcel as their own.[17]

In legal testimony, the Yovego officials mounted an aggressive counterargument: they accused the cabildo of Tiltepec of fraud. They claimed that the disputed parcel had always belonged to them and their ancestors, and that the pueblo of Tiltepec had in 1555 presented a deliberately confusing picture to the Real Audiencia in order to win the royal decree that was granted them in 1590. They pointed to two anomalies in the royal decree of 1590. First, in the text of the decree, which drew its language from the original petition, the land under dispute had been identified as being within the confines of the pueblos of Tiltepec and Caltepeque. The cabildo of Yovego argued that they never had any knowledge that the parcel Leahbichitoag also bore the Nahuatl name Caltepeque. They also claimed that as far as they knew, no pueblo named Caltepeque had ever existed. Second, according to the text of the royal decree, the petition had arrived at the Audiencia through the auspices of the corregidor of Mixapa. The cabildo of Yovego objected that no such corregidor existed in the sierra.[18] In short, the cabildo of Yovego asserted that the legal team of Tiltepec had presented a fraudulent petition to the Audiencia, and that the Audiencia had issued the royal decree based on false premises.

The Yovego cabildo's accusation of fraud illustrates a shift in legal culture and indigenous legal strategies in New Spain during the second half of the seventeenth century. Susan Kellogg has argued that in the case of central Mexico, rather than focus exclusively on proving ownership by inheritance or sale, native litigants placed new emphasis on corruption of legal procedure in their efforts to discredit their opponents' cases. *Rebeldía* (failure to meet deadlines) and fraud, including the presentation of forged documents, figured prominently among these legal arguments.[19]

Even if the accusations of fraud constituted part of their legal strategy, the objections to the substance of the royal decree raised by the Yovego legal team carried weight in themselves. No record of a pueblo of Caltepeque in the mid-sixteenth century exists, nor is there a record of a corregidor of Mixapa. It is therefore quite possible that the Spanish lawyer or the native legal agent hired by the cabildo of Tiltepec had invented or fudged these details in the 1555 petition to the Audiencia, with or without the full knowledge of the cabildo.

Finally, the cabildo of Yovego resorted to another legal rhetorical strategy popular among native litigants: the invocation of a history of inter-pueblo discord as a motivation for retaliation or revenge. The members of the Yovego cabildo argued that the pueblo of Tiltepec bore them ill will and wanted to cause them frustration and expense because they had refused to come to an agreement with them to open a road from Yovego to the border of the two pueblos. The new road would join the road that Tiltepec had built from their pueblo to that point.[20]

In October 1699, the Audiencia issued a royal decree in which the judges ordered the alcalde mayor of Villa Alta, Juan Antonio Mier del Tojo, to conduct a full investigation into the land dispute. In particular, the Audiencia wanted to know who had been in possession of the land before the alleged takeover by the pueblo of San Francisco Yovego following the 1650 epidemic.[21] On 15 February 1700, the legal team of Tiltepec presented prominent Zapotec witnesses from pueblos whose lands bordered the parcel under dispute. Miguel de Santiago, cacique of Yagallo; Phelipe de Mendosa, cacique and governor of Lachixila; Francisco Mendosa, principal and alcalde of Lachixila; Pedro de la Cruz, principal of Lachixila; Nicolas de Santiago, principal of Teotlasco; Gabriel Pablo, Juan Martin, and Juan Chaves, all principales from Yagila; Pedro Sanches, a principal from Yagavila; and Sebastian Lopes, a principal from Talea, all answered affirmatively the same set of questions posed to them by the lawyer for Tiltepec. Each confirmed that he knew of the land dispute, that the land in question, Leahbichitoag, had belonged to the pueblo of Tiltepec since time immemorial, and that residents of Yovego had crossed the Rio Grande, which divided the pueblos of Tiltepec and Yovego and marked the border of the parcel, in order to cultivate the land. Each also confirmed the existence on the parcel of the remains of the houses of Tiltepec residents and of the former encomendero. Finally, each confirmed that until four years previously, residents of Yovego had cultivated the land and paid rent on the parcel to the pueblo of Tiltepec.[22]

Notably, the Yovego legal team did not present any Zapotec witnesses to argue in favor of their possession of the parcel. Instead, it presented two letters from Dominican friars. The first, dated 8 December 1699, was written by Fray Joseph de Cardona, resident priest for the doctrina of Villa Alta and a twenty-year veteran of the Dominican order in the sierra. He stated that for the twenty years that he had worked in the district, he had assumed that the parcel known as Leahbichitoag belonged to the pueblo of Yovego, in part because he had heard it said among the residents of Yovego and neighboring pueblos and in part because of the way he understood the borders of the pueblos of Yovego, Tiltepec, and Yagavila. According to his understanding, all of the land between the cross on a hilltop known as Latiyeya, which marked the boundary between Yagavila and Yovego, including the parcel Leahbichitoag and the pueblo of Yovego, belonged to the pueblo of Yovego. To his knowledge, the distance from the cross to the territory of Tiltepec was three leagues, and did not include Leahbichitoag. He also noted that on many occasions, when he had to cross the Rio Grande to go to the pueblo of San Gaspar Xagalazi on business, he had seen residents cultivating Leahbichitoag, and that they had done so peacefully and without conflict until the present day. He closed his letter noting that he had written it at the behest of the governor and alcaldes of Yovego.[23]

In a letter dated 15 February 1700, Fray Miguel de Roxas interjected his version of the dispute into the legal proceedings. According to his narrative, the testimony of the governor and principales of Lachixila was compromised because of a conflict between the pueblos of Lachixila and Yovego over the celebration of Holy Week. The leadership of Yovego had by request secured the celebration for its pueblo the previous year (1699), to the chagrin of the leadership of Lachixila, which wanted the priest to celebrate Holy Week in their own pueblo. Out of ill will, the governor, alcalde, and a principal had testified against Yovego in the land dispute.[24]

In his closing argument, Lieutenant Francisco Lopes de Orosco y Asevedo, a lawyer for the pueblo of Yovego and a Spanish resident of Villa Alta, reiterated the main points of the friars' letters and attempted to discredit the testimony of the witnesses presented by Tiltepec, calling some of them "notorious drunks," claiming that others had been bought, and that others were prejudiced in favor of Tiltepec because of kinship or marriage.[25] However, the close ties that bound many of the Spaniards of Villa Alta—

Dominicans and *vecinos* (local residents) alike—should lead us to question the allegiances of the Dominicans who wrote the letters on behalf of Yovego, and likely at the behest of their lawyer. In a small-scale society like that of Villa Alta, it would be difficult to find neutral witnesses among the native elite and the even smaller group of Spaniards.

Based on his investigation, on 3 March 1700, the alcalde mayor ruled that the lands should be restituted to the pueblo of San Miguel Tiltepec. The cabildo of Yovego objected to the decision and appealed to the Real Audiencia.[26] But then the unexpected happened. First, a prodigal son of San Miguel Tiltepec, Miguel Fernández de Chaves, a cacique and "indio ladino" who had been residing in the Valley of Oaxaca and in San Pedro Nexitzo in the district of Ixtlán, returned home to lay claim to his extensive landholdings, including the parcel known as Leahbichitoag. Within weeks, the Cajonos Rebellion and the extirpation campaign that immediately followed it swept the district. As a result, the course of the land dispute, the relationship between Yovego and Tiltepec, and the lines of authority in the Tiltepec leadership shifted quite radically.

MIGUEL FERNÁNDEZ DE CHAVES: CACIQUE AS INTERMEDIARY

Miguel Fernández de Chaves was a cacique among caciques in the Sierra Norte. What set him apart from other caciques in the district of Villa Alta and in the pueblo of Tiltepec was the wealth and size of his *cacicazgo* (noble estate), which encompassed territory in the pueblos of Tiltepec, Santa Maria Lachichina, and San Pedro Nexitzo.[27] Throughout New Spain, cacicazgos not only delimited territory, they also embodied crucial aspects of political power, privilege, and prestige, the rights to which were determined by noble lineage. In general terms, a cacicazgo embodied the "sum and combination of all traditional rights, duties, privileges, services, lands and properties pertaining to the title of native ruler, natural lord or cacique whose right to the title was established by verification of direct descent from antecedent supreme lords of designated areas."[28] For example, caciques were often exempt from communal labor and taxes and had the right to have commoners perform personal services for them such as cutting firewood and running mail. In effect, the cacicazgo not only determined landholding, it also shaped a social system characterized by specified social roles, statuses, and clearly defined power relations.

The composition and ownership of cacicazgos in the Sierra Norte differed considerably from the better-studied regions of New Spain. In the sierra, multiple caciques collectively held the rights to a hereditary noble estate, recognized as a cacicazgo by Spanish law.[29] From the pre-Hispanic era through at least the middle of the eighteenth century, elite corporate kin groups, designated by the Spaniards as *parentelas*, *cónyuges*, or *primos* jointly administered and ruled over sierra cacicazgos.[30] In each kin group, several if not all members carried the title of cacique.[31] This system of land tenure and social organization contrasts with the regions of Central Mexico, the Mixteca Alta, and the Valley of Mexico, where native pueblos most often recognized only one cacique as their noble lord who had individual rights to his (or in the case of the Mixteca Alta, her) cacicazgo. An exception to this rule was the Sierra of Puebla, where land ownership by elite corporate kin groups also existed.[32]

The cacicazgos of the Sierra Norte also differed from those of other regions of New Spain in their small size. Due to the relative poverty of cacicazgos in the sierra, it appears that pre-Hispanic political power came from leadership in warfare rather than landholding.[33] During the colonial period, with the decline of warfare as a means of defining elite status, entitlement of cacicazgos by the Real Audiencia became the most common means to legitimize noble status, although few sierra cacicazgos ever received official recognition. The social structure and system of land tenure may explain the region's lack of legally titled cacicazgos. Since colonial law sanctioned landholding on the part of Indian pueblos and private individuals—but not on the part of corporate kin groups like parentelas, conyuges, and primos—the Audiencia did not have a legal mechanism by which to recognize corporately owned cacicazgos. In land cases in which elite corporate ownership was claimed, Spanish administrators tended to privatize ownership, thereby fragmenting corporately owned parcels of land.[34] The net effect of the legal decisions in land disputes favored the accretion of land into the hands of pueblos or individuals within pueblos, often at the expense of cacicazgos or larger, corporately owned parcels.[35]

Miguel Fernández de Chaves's ancestors were therefore successful where others were not when the Audiencia recognized their cacicazgo. The multicommunity scope of his cacicazgo, unique to the region, contributed to his lineage's special standing. Since it is one of the few cacicazgos in the region that existed from the pre-Hispanic period through the eighteenth century, the changes in its territorial composition over time can be traced.

An obvious question is how Chaves came to possess cacicazgo territory in the three pueblos of Lachichina, Tiltepec, and San Pedro Nexitzo.

Chaves interjected himself into the land dispute between Tiltepec and Yovego sometime during September 1700. Although we are uncertain as to the exact date of his entry into the case, the lawyer for Yovego referred to a request by Chaves and the cabildo of Tiltepec for approval of certain legal documents and procedures in the district court during September 1700, so we can assume that he appeared on the scene around that time.[36] Chaves's lawyer argued in a petition to the Real Audiencia that Leahbichitoag was neither the property of Yovego or of Tiltepec, but of his client, whom he identified as a cacique of Lachichina who had rights to the land by virtue of having inherited the cacicazgo of Tiltepec. According to respected elders from both Tiltepec and Yovego who had testified for the court, Juan de Mendoza had long been the cacique and governor of Tiltepec. According to his last will and testament, which had been translated for the Audiencia, he had no sons and had therefore left his land to his nephew, Francisco de Chaves, a cacique of Lachichina. On Francisco's death, the land would go to his sons, Juan, Nicolás, and Miguel, in succession. Miguel Fernández de Chaves was the last of this line and, as such, the sole proprietor of both the cacicazgos of Lachichina and Tiltepec.[37]

The Lienzo of Tiltepec, one of five known lienzos of the Sierra Norte region, provides a different perspective on Chaves's genealogical and territorial claims and the claims that witnesses made on his behalf. Lienzos were painted renderings of community history, territory, and ruling genealogy on cloth. Colonial-era native artists adapted elements of European iconography into a native template in order to make lienzos legible for a Spanish audience. Indeed, Spanish judges constituted the target audience for these culturally hybrid documents, which were often submitted as evidence in land disputes during the sixteenth century. By the early seventeenth century, European-style documents such as the land title and the last will and testament came to replace the lienzo as a preferred form of legal evidence. But it is important to note that like lienzos, these documents bore the markers of cultural hybridity.

The Lienzo of Tiltepec is simultaneously a map and a genealogical record whose overall structure bears considerable resemblance to the Lienzo of Tabaa, also from the sierra. As is the case with most lienzos from Oaxaca, both emphasized "dynastic foundations and genealogies of ruling

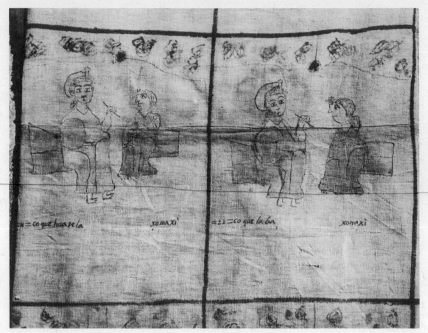

FIGURE 1 Precolonial-era *coqui* and *xonaxi*, Lienzo of Tiltepec. This photo and the photos in figures 6 and 7 were taken by the anthropologist John Paddock in 1955. COURTESY OF MICHEL OUDIJK.

families, going back four or five centuries before the Spanish conquest," a feature that sets them apart from the lienzos of central Mexico, which tend to focus on more recent history, much of it related to the Spanish conquest.[38] Oudijk argues that the lienzos of Tiltepec and Tabaa are actually pictographic translations of primordial titles.[39] Primordial titles and lienzos were legitimizing strategies used by caciques and cabildos to shore up the political power of their lineages or *parcialidades* in opposition to competing lineages, parcialidades, or neighboring pueblos.

The Lienzo of Tiltepec narrates the genealogy of the community's noble lineage through thirty-six compartments, each of which depicts a seated noble couple dressed in white. The lienzo establishes a clear transition from the precolonial to the colonial period. In the final seven compartments, the ruling *coqui* (male lord or cacique) wears a hat and colonial-style clothing, and no longer carries the staff carried by the precolonial coquis in the earlier compartments. Further, the colonial *xonaxis* (female lords or *cacicas*) no longer wear ornate headdress, and they are portrayed frontally rather than in profile (see figs. 1 and 2).[40] These stylistic changes

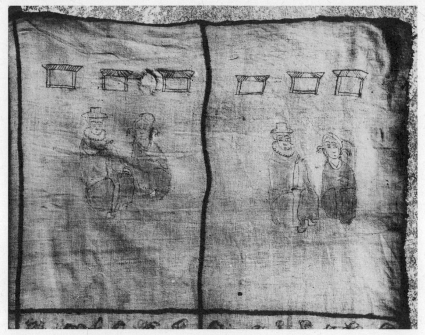

FIGURE 2 Colonial-era *coqui* and *xonaxi*, Lienzo of Tiltepec. PHOTO BY JOHN PADDOCK. COURTESY OF MICHEL OUDIJK.

may have been intended to signal transformations in the power and legitimacy of Sierra Zapotec nobility, and in particular of noble women, brought on by conquest and colonialism.

In this regard, the Lienzo of Tiltepec represents a gendered discourse that chronicles changes in indigenous political power after the conquest by showing the diminution of indigenous noblewomen's status. Scholars of colonial Latin America widely recognize that colonialism transformed gender as a set of social relations and as a system of representation.[41] During the pre-Columbian period, in the Inca Empire and in Mesoamerica, relations between men and women of the nobility were characterized by complementarity and parallelism. Complementarity denotes a number of meanings simultaneously, including "the sense of two halves 'constituting the whole,'" the notion of men and women "mutually completing each other to achieve a certain status in society," and finally, the idea that men and women "produce effects in concert that are different from those produced separately."[42] Parallelism refers to the "parallel lines of authority and institutionalized positions of leadership held by women and men."[43] In keeping with these gendered ideologies, women wielded formal political and ritual power, often through their own institutions parallel to those of men. Female deities were revered and celebrated. Like their male counterparts, they were often represented with both female and male attributes, and even with both sets of genitalia, or the genitalia of the opposite sex, thereby blurring Western notions of a binary male/female opposition.[44]

Although distinct from contemporaneous European systems of gender hierarchy, Mesoamerican and Andean gender complementarity and parallelism should not evoke an illusion of gender equality; indeed, patriarchy coexisted with them. In various pre-Columbian contexts, the most powerful rulers and gods were men, and men held the most important posts in the political-religious hierarchy.[45] In the highly militarized society of the Aztec Empire, men performed the all-important role of the warrior, and the Mexica came to use a "gendered discourse to describe victory as masculine and defeat as feminine."[46]

Spanish colonialism transformed gender complementarity and parallelism, and strengthened patriarchy in Mesoamerican and Andean societies. The colonial legal and political system precluded indigenous women from exercising formal political power as governors or cabildo members. Catholicism as a symbolic system celebrated male power while denigrating that of women, and excluded women from Church hierarchy. In exclusive schools for the male indigenous nobility, the friars taught their students skills that would empower them in colonial society, such as Spanish language and writing. This education further increased the disparity between the power and authority of indigenous men and women in the colonial context, and ensured a gender exclusive role for indigenous men as intermediaries between their communities and Spanish institutions. Although indigenous women did exercise some power through the legal system as plaintiffs, defendants, and witnesses in civil and criminal disputes, their influence in this context declined over the course of the colonial period.[47] Finally, Spanish demands for labor and tribute also appear to have had a negative impact on indigenous family life and the authority of women.[48]

The Mixtec region of Oaxaca provides an exception to the decline of the power of indigenous women, at least at the level of the nobility. Ronald Spores and Kevin Terraciano have documented the remarkable political power and landholding of Mixtec cacicas until the eighteenth century.[49] Spores notes that the wealth and power of some Mixtec cacicas

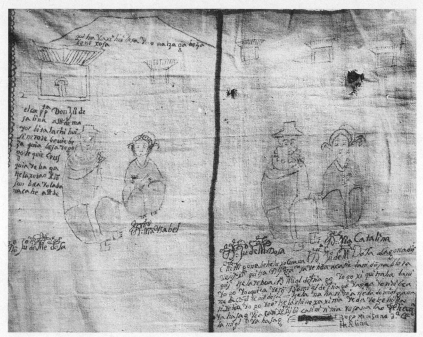

FIGURE 3 Colonial-era ruling pair with Zapotec gloss, Lienzo of Tiltepec. PHOTO BY JOHN PADDOCK. COURTESY OF MICHEL OUDIJK.

equaled that of some high-status Spaniards, encomenderos, and Dominican priors.[50] By contrast, in the Sierra Norte, cacicas do not appear to have wielded much power during the colonial period. They appear much less frequently than their male counterparts as plaintiffs, defendants, or witnesses in land disputes or other civil cases. For this reason, the title *cacique* proved considerably more useful as a symbol for the negotiation of power in the sierra than the title *cacica*. The Lienzo of Tiltepec hints at this imbalance, representing Zapotec noblewomen in diminished costume and posture.

Beyond its pictorial commentary on relationships of gender and power through time, the Lienzo of Tiltepec documented other significant aspects of Zapotec colonial and precolonial society. It contains historical scenes, geographical referents, and Zapotec glosses. Oudijk believes that some of these glosses were added during the 1699 land dispute between Tiltepec and Yovego and that the lienzo was likely used by the legal team of Tiltepec as evidence in the dispute (see fig. 3). For example, a Zapotec gloss in compartment 29 refers to the parcel of land named Leahbichitoag that belonged to the encomendero Christóbal de Chaves. This gloss squares with the narrative history of Leahbichitoag provided in the petition presented by the cabildo of Tiltepec in the early stages of the 1699 land dispute with Yovego.[51]

Miguel Fernández de Chaves and the legal team of Tiltepec may also have used the genealogical information portrayed by the lienzo to support their case. Oudijk contends that Juan de Mendoza of Tiltepec commissioned the Lienzo of Tiltepec in 1591.[52] Not surprisingly, the lienzo clearly depicts Mendoza's line. Indeed, Mendoza may have submitted the lienzo as evidence in response to the Audiencia's order of 1591 that the alcalde mayor of Villa Alta investigate his claim to cacique status.[53]

The witnesses who testified on Chaves's behalf claimed that Mendoza was the uncle of Chaves's father, Francisco de Chaves, cacique of Lachichina. As utilized by the witnesses, the Spanish term *tío* (uncle) may have represented a generic claim to ancestry that had no temporal or generational specificity considering that Mendoza lived at the end of the sixteenth century.[54] By linking Chaves to Mendoza, the witness may also have been linking Chaves to the version of history and territorial rights portrayed in the lienzo.

Chaves's claims to the cacicazgo of Tiltepec were ultimately successful. In August 1704, the Audiencia granted him title to Leahbichitoag. On 2 December 1705, in response to a request by Chaves's lawyer that Pedro Boza, the alcalde mayor's lieutenant, and Juan Martín de la Sierra, who was the district's bailiff, refrain from inciting the cabildo of Yovego to continue with the lawsuit, the Audiencia ordered that no one should interfere in or motivate the Indians' engagement in further litigation.[55] The Spaniards named by Chaves's lawyer were likely profiting from the lawsuit as legal advisors, or they may have had some vested interest in the outcome of the case.

Having won an initial victory, Chaves pushed his case further. In 1709, he extended his cacicazgo claims to other parcels of land, which he claimed he inherited from his father and grandfather.[56] Chaves's efforts to consolidate the cacicazgo likely constituted part of the *composiciones de tierras* of 1709. Through its program of composición, the Crown sought to generate revenue by requiring any individual or corporate group without proper title to its land to pay a fee commensurate with the value of the land to the royal treasury for a legal land title.[57] The *pueblos de indios* did not participate in the early composiciones (1591, 1635, 1643) because the Crown considered them too poor to pay the required fee. However, native people did participate in significant numbers in the composiciones of 1709–17, such that the acquisition of official land titles by the pueblos de indios was nearly complete by 1730.[58]

The cabildo of Tiltepec abetted Chaves's expansionism. Three witnesses from Tiltepec, one of them the current alcalde, provided testimony to the effect that since Chaves was the nephew of Juan de Mendoza, the pueblo of Tiltepec recognized him as their cacique and that as such he was entitled to the lands in question. In May 1709, the Audiencia granted him title to these lands and officially recognized him as cacique of Tiltepec. Throughout the course of Chaves's legal victories, the officials of Yovego had protested, both through legal petitions and, according to a September 1709 legal complaint by Chaves, through their refusal to pay him rent on the parcels that they were cultivating. Their protests won no concessions from the Audiencia, and Chaves expanded his cacicazgo effectively unopposed.[59]

Miguel Fernández de Chaves's story is a striking one. Many scholars of New Spain's indigenous peoples have argued that during the eighteenth century the political power of the native hereditary nobility and its land-holdings declined in large part because of a "revolt" against the caciques led by the cabildos of the pueblos de indios. During the early sixteenth century, the Crown transformed the source of wealth of New Spain's hereditary nobility. In the pre-Hispanic era, the nobility generated its wealth from tribute. After the conquest, the Spanish legal system converted this tributary wealth to landholding through the entitlement of cacicazgos. In the Valley of Oaxaca and the Mixteca Alta, during the sixteenth and seventeenth centuries, native commoners provided for themselves and their families by renting cacicazgo lands. The rents generated considerable income for the caciques, who became a seniorial landholding class along European lines.[60]

With the recovery of the native population during the second half of the seventeenth century, new pressure on the land created conflict over this landlord-tenant system and between caciques and commoners. The cabildos of the pueblos targeted the holdings of the caciques in an effort to gain a degree of economic independence from the seniorial lords, generating a boom in land disputes and lawsuits. Through this legal assault, the pueblos succeeded in diminishing if not wiping out the old hereditary nobility. As a result, the second-tier nobility that staffed the cabildos came to replace the caciques as the political leadership of the pueblos de indios. Cacicazgo lands devolved to the pueblos, and traditional lines of hierarchy in native communities were replaced by Spanish ones, in particular the cargo system.[61]

The story of Miguel Fernández de Chaves adds a dissonant note to this narrative of class conflict and hispanization. Given the presumption of the demise of the cacique status group during the eighteenth century at the hands of antagonistic cabildos, it is remarkable that Chaves could resurrect his cacicazgo with the help of Tiltepec's cabildo and return to Tiltepec as its cacique. This counternarrative of cooperation and negotiation between cacique and cabildo points to variability among different regions and within a specific region in the historical trajectory of the status of New Spain's hereditary nobility.

Recent scholarship also emphasizes significant variation in the political power and wealth of caciques over the colonial period. Nancy Farriss, Robert Haskett, and Arij Ouweneel have argued that in Yucatan, Cuernavaca, and Anahuác pueblos de indios maintained significant social hierarchy during the eighteenth century and that caciques still dominated native government, though the latter changed form.[62] Ouweneel characterizes the fungibility of cacique power in terms of a transition from *tlahtocayotl* (the form of rule of the hereditary nobility) to *gobernadoryotl*. In short, during the eighteenth century, the caciques of Anahuác channeled their power into the office of governor and maintained their wealth and status, despite the disappearance of their cacicazgo lands, through the apportionment of pueblo lands (*fundo legal*) to their kinship group.[63] Kevin Terraciano asserts that in the case of the Mixteca, within a general context of decline in status, many caciques adapted successfully to colonial circumstances, maintained and profited from extensive landholdings, and continued to enjoy the benefits of traditional labor systems.[64] Judith Zeitlin contends that on the Isthmus of Tehuantepec, caciques met with mixed fortunes over the colonial period. In the pueblo of Tehuantepec itself, the cacicazgo disappeared, and with it hereditary nobility, whereas in other isthmus pueblos, caciques held the highest cabildo offices, maintained significant wealth, and played a central role in community religious life by funding fiestas associated with the cult of the saints.[65] For the Valley of Oaxaca, William Taylor has documented the "enduring wealth and prestige of caciques," and for the Sierra of Puebla, John Chance has argued that disputes over cacique status during the late eighteenth century indicate the continued power and importance of caciques.[66]

The story of Miguel Fernández de Chaves supports the contention that across New Spain, and in particular in regions where Spanish settlement was sparse, many caciques proved remarkably adept at molding themselves to new political and economic conditions, and reconstituting their sources of power. Chaves engineered his return to the sierra from a distance, while residing in Antequera. Clearly, he had decided at some point that his fortunes would be better served if he left his pueblo of origin. It is noted throughout the documents that Chaves was a hispanized Zapotec: he penned his own petition to the Audiencia in 1709, spoke Spanish, and wore Spanish clothing. His ease in Spanish society may be indicative of his participation in a network of interethnic relationships. For instance, he may have had commercial interests in the Valley or in Ixtlán that took him away from the sierra. As the youngest male of his generation, he may have assumed that it would be more profitable for him to engage in commerce than to gamble on the early death of his two older brothers and wait for the possibility of inheriting a cacicazgo. Once the cacicazgo did in fact materialize for him, he may have surmised that the land could yield more wealth through rents and other forms of income than whatever he had turned his energies to outside the sierra. Further, the cabildo of Tiltepec encouraged him to rejoin the life of the community for reasons that I will discuss below.

Chaves's biculturalism and the mobility and flexibility of his life career indicate that the category *cacique* had changed and expanded over the colonial period to include both Spanish and traditional markers of power. In this regard, Chaves is emblematic of the ways some caciques transformed themselves, in the face of the exigencies of colonialism, into archetypal cultural intermediaries. Their ability to read and adjust to changing political and economic circumstances explains their long-standing role as power brokers. The timing of Chaves's interjection into the land dispute—within weeks of the Cajonos Rebellion—raises questions about how he interpreted the political situation unfolding in the district of Villa Alta on the eve of the eighteenth century. If he arrived just prior to the rebellion, had he heard from his relations and contacts in the sierra that political tensions between the alcaldes mayores, Church officials, and native elites had reached a point of crisis? Did he anticipate that this crisis might shake things up in the district? Once the rebellion was over and the extirpation campaign had begun, did concern over the survival of the traditional native power elite provide him with extra incentive to acquire legal title to the cacicazgo of Tiltepec? Although speculative, these questions are meant to evoke the uncertain and changing political landscape with which Chaves had to contend as he returned to the district of Villa Alta.

Finally, in light of the assumption that caciques and cabildos were generally antagonistic during the eighteenth century, we need to consider how the municipal officials and principales of Tiltepec might have viewed the return of their cacique. On the surface, his return posed a challenge to their power: he had effectively acted as an interloper in their land dispute with Yovego and had claimed the land as his own. Further, as a cacique he was entitled to certain privileges and authority to which they were subordinate. One might assume that they would resist his claims to cacique status and to the cacicazgo of Tiltepec rather than support them. Why, then, did the alcalde of Tiltepec support the power grab of a potential rival in his 1709 testimony on behalf of Chaves?

THE NEGOTIATION OF CACIQUE STATUS

In the years that followed Chaves's legal successes, a fuller story of his return to the sierra emerged. He came back to Tiltepec not on the basis of a traditional concept of noble authority, but rather via a political and economic deal. His return represented a process of negotiation between cacique and cabildo rather than cultural continuity. This process of negotiation proved fragile. It eventually unraveled, pitting the cacique and cabildo against one another. As quickly as the deal unraveled, however, the cacique and cabildo arrived at another agreement, and renegotiated their relationship.

From 1714 to 1729, Chaves engaged in legal action once again, but this time against the pueblo of Tiltepec. Over the course of these fifteen years, he petitioned the alcalde mayor and the Audiencia repeatedly to enforce an official "pact" or "agreement [*escripta de convenio y obligacion*]" that he had made with the municipal authorities of Tiltepec. Although we are never given a date for the pact, the alcalde mayor referred to the document in an inventory of legal evidence provided by Chaves. The terms of the pact were as follows. First, the cabildo of Tiltepec agreed to pay Chaves 2,708 pesos in order to pursue the land dispute against Yovego, but under the rubric of the reclamation of his cacicazgo. Once he had won the suit, they would provide him with the accounts of the money earned from renting the land; furnish his sustenance from the land; sow for him crops of corn, chile, and cotton; and either turn over to him the harvest or fifty pesos per crop. Finally, they would rebuild his house so that he could live in the pueblo. According to Chaves's petitions of 1714, 1718, 1727, and 1729, the officials of Tiltepec had failed to live up in full to any part of this bargain.[67]

In September 1729, the officials of Tiltepec presented their own version of the pact. They claimed that Chaves had tricked them into allowing him to intervene in the land dispute and claim Leahbichitoag for his own. The officials and the witnesses that they presented argued that the cabildo of Tiltepec had paid Chaves an exorbitant four thousand pesos to be their legal agent, and that he had promised them that once he won the dispute against Yovego, the land would be theirs again as it always had been. They took this promise to heart and dedicated the money earned from rent of the land to pay for a *retablo* of the Virgin of the Rosary. They argued further that no officials of Tiltepec had ever agreed to a legal document that outlined a pact or agreement with Chaves, and that the document was fraudulent because it did not bear the signature of Martín de la Cruz y Arriola, who had served the pueblo as scribe for forty years. Finally, they had gone to the alcalde mayor of Villa Alta to request a copy of the document from the district archive, and the document could not be found, at which point Chaves left Tiltepec and never returned.[68]

Shortly following this exchange, Chaves radically altered his strategy. Suffering from what he claimed to be an attack of conscience, he abruptly dropped his case against the pueblo and donated all of his lands to it. In 1730, less than a year after the acrimonious debate over the pact, a series of illnesses overcame him, and sensing that the end was near, he composed his last will and testament in front of the alcalde mayor of Villa Alta. In the text of the will, he specified what had been weighing on his conscience. He claimed that he had on false pretenses taken the 2,708 pesos from the pueblo of Tiltepec to pursue the land dispute with Yovego in the Real Audiencia. The lands, he claimed, had always been theirs, and he had appropriated them unjustly through his assertion of his title of cacique. As a "Catholic and a Christian, fearful of the tremendous judgment of God," he had repented and donated his cacicazgo to the pueblo of Tiltepec a year earlier, with the caveat that the pueblo would sustain him with some corn and other necessities for the few years of his life that remained.[69]

The problem with this land transfer was that it could not take place officially without the titles and documents pertaining to the land. These were in Mexico City, where they had been submitted to the Real Audiencia in the course of the legal disputes of the previous few years. Chaves had sent for them and in the interim had been invited to travel to the pueblo of Yovego. While in Yovego his health worsened, and he was forced to stay there under the care of the "enemy."[70]

During his stay in Yovego, the situation became more complicated. According to Chaves's testimony to the alcalde mayor, a number of residents of Yovego, with the collusion of the priest Marcial Carrera, forced him to authorize a last will and testament that named the pueblo and its church as the legitimate inheritors of Leahbichitoag and another parcel named Yhoxitag. Despite Chaves's protests, Carrera insisted and pressured him to the extent that he became confused and agreed to bequeath the land to Yovego. To pressure the dying cacique further, the *padre beneficiado* Antonio Xiron, under the pretext that the bishop had demanded that Chaves travel to Antequera in order to make the bequest official, tricked Chaves into authorizing the last will and testament in the ecclesiastical court of Antequera. Chaves insisted that fear also played a role in his compliance with the wishes of the padres and the residents of Yovego. Chaves worried that if he did not do as they asked, the residents of Yovego would stop caring for him and leave him to die of hunger or neglect.[71]

Apparently eager to undo what he had done under duress, Chaves presented himself in front of the alcalde mayor to reiterate his desire to donate the lands to Tiltepec, again with the stipulation that they use the lands in part to provide him with sustenance for the remainder of his life. The officials of Tiltepec agreed to these conditions, also agreeing to pay a small debt that they owed to Chaves and to pay another small debt that Chaves owed to the pueblo of Yovego. According to the terms of this will, then, on the death of the childless Miguel Fernández de Chaves, the cacicazgo of Tiltepec would die, too, becoming part of the communal holdings of Tiltepec.[72] Chaves and the cabildo thus salvaged their negotiated settlement with yet another negotiation.

CONCLUSION: CACIQUE, CABILDO, AND THE STATE

The conflicts and negotiations among Miguel Fernández de Chaves, the cabildos of Tiltepec and Yovego, and the priests of the district marked important changes in Zapotec concepts of legitimate authority. Jorge Guevara Hernández has posited that the conflict reflected the coexistence of two opposing power structures: one of pre-Hispanic origin, sustained by genealogical relationships, and the other of Iberian origin, with the municipality as the agent of political power. In the end, it was the Iberian form that won out. For Guevara Hernández, the fact that the pueblo of Tiltepec did not provide Miguel Fernández de Chaves with services commensurate with the status of cacique and stipulated in the legal agreement, at least until 1730, provides evidence of Chaves's powerlessness in the face of an ascendant Iberian-style cabildo and Iberian notions of property rights.[73]

This interpretation charts a process of acculturation in native concepts of legitimate authority and property rights that does not adequately capture the historical trajectory. The case of Chaves indicates that the hereditary nobility may have disappeared in its old form, but that those caciques with the requisite cultural skills persisted as a new kind of elite by adapting to a political order in which their sources of power were culturally hybrid, rather than "indigenous" or "Iberian."

A closer reading of the legal dispute among Tiltepec, Yovego, and Miguel Fernández de Chaves reveals that far from suffering from a lack of power, Chaves exerted significant power. Through his legal skills and, by his own admission, duplicity, he appropriated the land disputed by Tiltepec and Yovego, exacted significant payment for his legal "services" (which for the short run benefited him entirely), persuaded the Audiencia to recognize him as cacique of Tiltepec, and, at least on paper, through a pact with the cabildo of Tiltepec, laid claim to the traditional privileges and services to which caciques were entitled. This was a remarkable feat of legal ingenuity and negotiation, both with the Spanish legal system and the Zapotec cabildo. It also represented a skillful combination of old markers of power—the cacicazgo and the title of cacique—with a new marker: legal knowledge and competence. It would be difficult to argue, then, that Chaves lacked power because the increasing authority of the cabildo had eroded his basis of political authority as a member of the sierra nobility. Rather, Chaves illustrates the flexibility of some members of the sierra nobility in his ability to integrate different markers of power, and to adapt to sierra pueblos' new expectations of political leadership.

Chaves's power rested on his ability to advocate for and protect his pueblo's interests in colonial institutions. From 1700 to 1730, Chaves undermined his own authority through a common tactic of cultural and political brokerage: the dynamic of promise. Through promises, native intermediaries opened a political space in which they could "promote the aims of one group while protecting the interests of another—and thus become nearly indispensable to all sides."[74] According to the testimony of the cabildo of Tiltepec and consistent with Chaves's confession at the end of his life, Chaves had promised that once he had won the disputed parcel, the land would belong to Tiltepec. Ultimately, this proved true, but not for at least twenty-six years after the Audiencia issued its 1704 royal decree that gave Chaves title of the land, and not without a renegotiation of the "pact" between Chaves and the cabildo in the last months of Chaves's life.

Chaves's story also suggests that although the cacique status group may have declined as a whole over the colonial period, the symbolic power of the category *cacique* remained potent in the eyes of Spanish administrators through the middle and even late eighteenth century. As demonstrated by a flurry of late colonial-era litigation in which elites in the Sierra Norte of Oaxaca and the Sierra of Puebla claimed cacique status and the exemptions and privileges that accompanied it, native litigants knew well that the term *cacique* still resonated with their highly status-conscious colonial overlords.[75] It appears that the cabildo of Tiltepec banked on the continued salience of *cacique* in the colonial symbolic order. In the case of Miguel Fernández de Chaves, the cabildo of Tiltepec knew that a hispanized cacique, an effective outsider familiar with the courts of Antequera and Mexico City, could serve them not only through his extensive knowledge and skills, but also through his self-presentation as cacique and indio ladino. The Spanish legal system may have been recognizing cacicazgos with less frequency, but Chaves's claims to cacique status proved convincing enough for the Audiencia to recognize his title and grant him his lands. Chaves's clothing and his impressive mastery of Spanish language and writing may well have bolstered his legal claims. As the case of Chaves demonstrates, *cacique* represented an effective rhetorical strategy by native litigants in their negotiations with the colonial state over questions of land tenure, office holding, and privileges.

At a broader level, the land dispute examined in this chapter points to a trend in the relationship between native society in the sierra and the state during the eighteenth century. As the Cajonos Rebellion and demographic changes transformed old systems of authority, land disputes allowed native intermediaries to shape a new system of authority from which they could benefit. In doing so, they defined their interests against those of native society as a whole. Although interindigenous land conflict could mean short-term gains for a particular pueblo, or for particular individuals, those gains always came at the expense of the victor's neighbors. Furthermore, gains were often accompanied by substantial costs: exorbitant legal fees, a tendency for land disputes to magnify and exacerbate divisions among and within native pueblos, and a loss of local autonomy as the state became the ultimate arbiter of these disputes, imposing its own framework of "rights" and law as the means to resolve conflict. In this regard, an expanded role for native legal intermediaries during the eighteenth century did not coincide with an increase in native autonomy. Rather, the trend toward legal entitlement of lands intimated by the composiciones de tierras, and compounded by inter- and intrapueblo conflicts, allowed the state to creep further into native affairs. The strengthening of the state's hand in the district of Villa Alta complemented the process of centralization that began after the Cajonos Rebellion and accelerated with the Bourbon Reforms.

PART 3

The Political Space Closes, 1770–1810

Chapter 5

Bourbon Officials

On 27 February 1790, Pablo de Ortega, the *alcalde mayor* of Villa Alta, appointed Juan Felipe de Santiago, an aging *principal* and a native of San Juan Tabaa, as governor of his pueblo. The magistrate's decision came in response to a legal conflict over the election results of 1789 in Tabaa, in which the pueblo's two *parcialidades* could not agree on the suitability of municipal officials for that year.[1] The appointment of a native governor by an alcalde mayor was a rare occurrence, justified only in extreme cases such as a native uprising. If circumstances dictated that alcaldes mayores resort to this option, they generally postponed the elections until the crisis passed.[2] Was the pueblo of Tabaa in a state of crisis? Did electoral results have some bearing on the security of the district?

The Bourbon Reforms provided a political climate that encouraged and justified the alcalde mayor's encroachment in 1789 into the realm of native political autonomy in San Juan Tabaa. The Bourbon administration implemented cultural, political, and economic reforms designed to subordinate and hispanize native officeholders, squeeze more revenue from native pueblos, and subject native peoples to new labor regimes. Reform, combined with shifts in the political economy of the district of Villa Alta, required native intermediaries to respond to a changed political landscape with strategies that ranged from compliance, to cooperation, to resistance. Juan Felipe de Santiago's position arose from his compliance with the alcalde mayor's wishes, his hispanized self-presentation, and his avowed "distance" from parcialidad rivalry in San Juan Tabaa. Indeed, as the case unfolded, it became clear that Juan Felipe de Santiago was far less rooted in Zapotec political culture, traditional noble prerogatives, and parcialidad organization than Felipe de Santiago had been when he served as governor of San Juan Yatzona one hundred years before. Unlike Felipe de Santiago or Miguel Fernández de Chaves, Juan Felipe de Santiago's position was not rooted in a bifurcated or culturally hybrid legitimacy. Rather, his appointment by the alcalde mayor made him accountable to Spanish expectations at the expense of native ones. As a consequence, his legitimacy, which derived from Spanish mandate, rested on shaky ground, and provoked resistance and political unrest in the pueblo of Tabaa. Santiago's unstable position suggests a shift in the role of native intermediaries during the era of the Bourbon Reforms. He represented a new kind of native officer: a Bourbon official. Bourbon reformers did not look to their native officers to exercise power primarily through cultural mediation or brokerage. More than their Hapsburg predecessors, the Bourbons intended them to be ciphers of Spanish policies and interests.

THE BOURBON REFORMS

The Bourbon Reforms represented a wide-ranging effort on the part of the Bourbon kings to tighten their control over their American holdings and make the colonies as profitable as possible after the economic decline and commercial and strategic losses to other European powers that followed the Seven Years' War (1756–63). The most important reforms were initiated during the reign of Charles III (1759–88), whose program of colonial governance has been described as "Enlightened Absolutism." In keeping with the spirit of economic rationality championed by Adam Smith, and with a spirit of governance that favored royal control over republicanism, the Spanish Crown centralized power in its own hands and instituted a rule of law that held individual property rights at a premium.

The Bourbon reformers' economic program aimed to revive colonial industries, especially mining, to regularize and increase taxation and royal revenues, and to reinstate a monopoly of trade between the American colonies and Spain. The program of political reform that complemented economic reform was both decentralizing and centralizing. The Bourbon reformers sought absolute power through a rationalization of the mechanisms of government (a larger, "expert," loyal bureaucracy) and an attack on political competitors. The Catholic Church represented the most powerful of these. The Bourbons put an end to the Hapsburg tradition that provided for the near equal power of *las dos magestades* (the Crown and the Catholic Church) by making the Church subordinate to the Crown. Bourbon tactics included reigning in the power of the missionary orders and attacking the *fueros* (legal privileges) and property of the Church. The expulsion of the Jesuit order from the Spanish Empire in 1767 was the most visible (and controversial) effect of the state's hostility to Church power.

The Bourbons subdued other political competitors, such as the alcaldes mayores. Recognizing that the economic and political interests of the local magistrates were often at odds with those of the Crown, they abolished the *repartimiento* and replaced the alcaldes mayores with *subdelegados*, a new kind of local bureaucrat. The Bourbons also established the intendancy system, which provided an additional layer of bureaucracy between the subdelegados and the viceroy. The *intendentes* closely oversaw the administration of the subdelegados and answered directly to the Crown. Legal formalism accompanied political centralization. As I discussed in chapter 3, the Bourbons attempted to replace diverse customary practices with a standardized rule of law.

The Bourbons styled themselves as social and cultural reformers as well. In particular, they targeted Indian pueblos and New Spain's lower orders as economic and sociocultural objects for reform. In order to monopolize revenues in native pueblos and undercut the political and cultural autonomy of native elites, the Bourbons confiscated *cajas de comunidad* (community treasuries) and *cofradía* accounts. They also instituted fee schedules, which impinged on a range of pueblo affairs. Pueblos had to pay new fees to the subdelegados for approving elections, fees to parish priests for a range of services, and salaries to the schoolmasters who were installed in every pueblo. They prohibited the elaborate fiestas that formed part of the cult of the saints on the grounds that they were a serious drain on pueblo resources, and they instituted a Spanish language–only policy for official pueblo business.[3] In urban settings, the Bourbons attempted to "discipline" unruly plebeians in order to make productive workers out of them. The Reform program attacked crime and heterodoxy, policed public rituals and behavior, reordered urban space, and regulated marriage, gender, aesthetics, and cultural production.[4]

Historians have debated the effectiveness of this ambitious Bourbon

Reform project. Most agree that the Bourbons succeeded in implementing significant economic and administrative change. The Bourbon attack on merchant monopolies, led by José de Gálvez, freed capital for investment in the mining industry, stimulating a mining boom in New Spain. In effect, the Bourbon Reforms constituted a "Revolution in Government" and a "second conquest" of the economic and political power of criollos, many of whom lost their government posts to peninsular Spaniards.[5] The Crown's expropriation of the ecclesiastical jurisdiction during the Bourbon Reforms alienated secular clergy and turned them against the Crown at the close of the colonial period.[6]

The Bourbon Reforms also had significant effects on native society, although these proved to be uneven across the empire. For instance, the reforms had a widely divergent impact on native society in Yucatan and Cuernavaca. Farriss argues that the Bourbon era was particularly hard on the Maya of Yucatan, and she suggests that this may have been the case for peripheral native regions that had enjoyed significant autonomy earlier in the colonial period. The intendancy system and the confiscation of community treasuries and cofradía accounts reduced the political and economic sources of the Maya elite's legitimacy.[7] For the case of Cuernavaca, Robert Haskett argues that the Bourbon Reforms had a negligible effect on the fortunes of the region's native ruling elite. He claims that the significance of the Bourbon Reforms has been overemphasized and that although they attacked the autonomy of native pueblos in principle and, according to the letter of the law, in practice, there were never enough Spanish officials on the ground to enforce new regulations on native elections and politics.[8] For the case of the Andes, Scarlett O'Phelan Godoy has chronicled the effects of the Bourbon taxation regime across a range of social sectors, linking the rebellion of Tupac Amaru II to unpopular fiscal policies.[9]

Ambivalence and contradiction characterize yet another register of the effects of the Bourbon Reforms on native society. Sergio Serulnikov's study of the Potosí region reveals that the Bourbon Reforms fostered popular mobilization in Andean communities: although Bourbon legislation produced a fiscal squeeze, it also opened new avenues for collective protest, largely through the legal system.[10] In his analysis of the effects of the Bourbon Reforms on the district of Villa Alta, Peter Guardino argues that abolition of the repartimiento ended two and half centuries of a particular kind of economic servitude for the native population, but Bourbon efforts to curb native religious celebrations and control community resources had adverse effects on native autonomy.[11] These ambivalent effects demonstrate that rather than representing a coherent ideological project, the Bourbon Reforms constituted an "inherently ambiguous and ambivalent endeavor": "less an ideological blueprint than a series of contested practical applications."[12]

In this chapter, I examine how the Bourbon Reforms shaped the tactics deployed by native intermediaries and Spanish officials in politico-cultural struggle in the district of Villa Alta. In particular, I look at how one Bourbon cultural reform in particular—a Spanish language–only policy[13]—dovetailed unexpectedly with Bourbon efforts to revitalize mining. The net effect was to enrich the magistrate's (and later, the subdelegado's) political arsenal, and to diminish that of pueblo officials. The Bourbons would have viewed the disempowerment of native intermediaries in the mining districts of Villa Alta through the convergence of royal economic and cultural programs in a favorable light. The Bourbons harbored significant antagonism toward native intermediary figures (and intermediary figures of all sorts), whom they perceived as corrupt and inimical to the efficient functioning of empire.[14]

MINING AND LABOR DRAFTS

Bourbon cultural and legal policies worked together with economic policies and shifts in the political economy of Villa Alta to ramp up the pressure on native pueblos and their *cabildos* (municipal governments) in the 1780s. Electoral conflicts in San Juan Tabaa over the results of cabildo elections in 1784 and 1789 provide insight into how these historical processes reinforced one another at the expense of native autonomy and the power of native cabildos. In January 1784, the officials and principales of San Juan Tabaa petitioned Pablo de Ortega, who had just begun his term as alcalde mayor, to declare the results of the most recent elections in their pueblo null and void. The newly elected officials had refused to pursue a legal suit against Juan Francisco de Echarrí, owner of the mine of Santa Gertrudis, discovered in 1777 near the Rincón pueblo of Talea.[15] Though a relatively small operation in comparison with the great mines of northern and central Mexico, Santa Gertrudis became the most profitable mine in the history of the region.

Echarrí's operation emerged in the context of Bourbon efforts to revitalize mining. New Spain experienced a remarkable silver boom in the late
eighteenth century that can be attributed in part to royal policy but especially to general economic trends that had begun in the 1670s, such as
technological advances, a decline in the cost of labor, and a rise in the value
of precious metals. A series of Bourbon initiatives buttressed these trends.
In an effort to cut production costs, the Crown slashed silver royalties
and the price of mercury. The Bourbons also sponsored technical education, instituted state-organized credit banks, and created privileged mining guilds (despite Bourbon hostility toward guilds in general). As added
incentive, the Crown awarded noble titles to successful miners.[16]

Echarrí benefited from these state initiatives, which likely encouraged
him to pursue his claim at Santa Gertrudis. One perk in particular—the
right to labor in nearby native pueblos, which he maintained from 1783
until his death in 1807, thanks to his contacts in the Bourbon administration[17]—had significant effects on electoral politics in Tabaa in the 1780s.
As owner of the mine, Echarrí had the right to demand a labor repartimiento of eighteen pueblos of the Rincón for service in the mine, and of
three pueblos in the Cajonos region—Tabaa, Yojovi, and Solaga—for service on the hacienda that supported the mine. Of the other Cajonos pueblos, Yalalag, San Francisco Cajonos, and its five sujetos did not provide
laborers to Santa Gertrudis, most likely because they were subject to a
labor repartimiento for mines in their own region. The Rincón pueblos had
to provide weekly work crews equal to 4 percent or 2 percent of their populations, depending on the production levels set by the foreman. Each week,
Tabaa, Yojovi, and Solaga rotated the responsibility for sending workers to
the hacienda of Santa Gertrudis. Workers in the mine and on the hacienda
would be paid for their labor, and although their labor was supposed to be
"voluntary," they really had no choice in the matter since the alcalde mayor
oversaw the system.[18]

Echarrí's operation embodied "the internal contradictions" of the Bourbon Reforms. Despite Bourbon hostility to guilds and corporatism in general, Echarrí's mine was subject to oversight by a special mining deputation
(which Guardino characterizes as "toothless" and largely ineffective) in
Antequera, of which Echarrí was an officer.[19] The provision for native labor
also proved contradictory to the spirit of the Bourbon Reforms, whose
emphasis on economic modernization, individual liberty, and freedom of

economic choice stood in stark contrast to involuntary servitude. However, when the villagers of the Rincón and Cajonos pueblos subject to the labor draft pursued their economic freedoms in court, the Bourbon administration subordinated political principle in favor of the maximization of profit. In many ways, these decisions were not out of step with the way labor had been allocated in the district during prior centuries: although the law had protected Indians from "involuntary" or "personal service" for years, involuntary service by native pueblos in the form of repartimiento obligations had been the custom of the land since the mid-sixteenth century.[20]

The Cajonos pueblos of Tabaa, Solaga, and Yojovi had a relationship with mining that predated the Santa Gertrudis operation. The discovery of mines in Tabaa and Solaga in 1729 led to labor drafts from the pueblos in the region, and eventually to complaints by cabildo officers concerning the low wages, harsh working conditions, physical injury, sickness, and death that characterized labor in the mines. The officials of Yojovi complained to the alcalde mayor that the labor drafts forced villagers to neglect their fields of corn and cochineal, prohibited the pueblo from constructing the town church, and led to the disbanding of ten cofradías for lack of funds. From 1750 to 1793, nine more mines were discovered and claimed in the Cajonos region, though it appears that only a few actually operated.[21]

Native villagers resisted exploitation at the hands of the mining industry through litigation in some cases and violence in others. In 1782 the pueblos of Juquila, Tabaa, Yojovi, Solaga, and Yae threatened to kill their Nahua foreman over poor wages and dangerous working conditions. In 1783 native villagers in Tabaa, Yojovi, and Solaga rioted in protest over the labor repartimientos, even as they were engaged in litigation against Echarrí over ill treatment.[22] The Rincón pueblos brought their own suit against Echarrí in 1788.[23] In the aggregate, these actions did little to modify the labor drafts or their ill effects.

On 24 July 1783 the Real Audiencia issued a royal decree (*real provisión*) that required an investigation into the complaints against Echarrí brought by the cabildos of Tabaa, Solaga, and Yojovi. In the meantime, the three pueblos were to continue to send their laborers as required by law, and Echarrí was to pay them properly and refrain from any abuses.[24] The intervening period between this royal decree and another royal decree in favor of the three Cajonos pueblos proved particularly tense for local politics since the cabildo officers found themselves torn between their communities' expectation that they would defend them from Echarrí's abuses, primarily through recourse to the courts, and the expectation of the alcalde mayor and Echarrí that they would enforce the labor requirements of Santa Gertrudis.[25] As intermediary figures, these cabildo officers had little room for maneuver.

Since the officials elected for the year 1784 had refused to pursue the suit against Echarrí, and even worse, in the eyes of their opponents, had vowed to enforce Echarrí's labor draft and to publicly whip anyone who resisted it, the principales of the opposing parcialidad had declared the election illegitimate and had held a new one. As they articulated in their petition, they perceived it to be the officials' duty to pursue the litigation in order to "defend all of our rights, our common liberty, and to repudiate the slavery and involuntary servitude to which we are subjected in the mines." Josef Sánchez, the alcalde who had been originally elected and who had vowed to punish recalcitrant laborers, challenged their actions in court, and the alcalde mayor found in favor of Sánchez and the originally elected officials since there was nothing in his view that disqualified these men from holding office.[26]

It is highly likely that Echarrí, well connected and economically powerful (he addressed the alcalde mayor in his formal correspondence as his "good friend"), exercised some influence on Pablo de Ortega's decision in the 1784 election dispute. In a 22 May 1783 document concerning the case against Echarrí, Francisco Marty, the outgoing alcalde mayor, came to his defense, lamenting the injurious pride and the excesses of the Indians who had brought the suit.[27] In October 1784, in a move that favored Echarrí considerably, the new alcalde mayor, Ortega, declared it illegal for the officials of Tabaa, Yojovi, and Solaga and of the Rincón pueblos to institute head taxes (*derramas*) to pay for lawsuits against Echarrí. He met with little resistance from the compliant officials of Tabaa, whom the alcalde mayor had reinstated in office earlier that year, and who had vowed to enforce the labor draft and drop the legal complaint against the mine owner.[28]

Of note in the case of the Cajonos pueblos against Echarrí was the role of Padre Avendaño, the parish priest of Tabaa. Guardino notes that Avendaño supported the villagers in their resistance to Echarrí's labor draft, "complaining that Echarrí had posted men on the roads to Oaxaca, and had kidnapped his parishioners on the pretext that they were fleeing their mine service," and that conditions in the mine had caused fatalities. He also complained that the Indians fled into the mountains in despair, missed Sunday masses, and neglected their fields and their work.[29]

Avendaño's concern for his parishioners may have been motivated by self-interest, since fewer parishioners meant fewer fees, but like many parish priests, he may have been motivated both by self-interest and a genuine concern for his parishioner's well-being. These complex motivations may explain why Avendaño positioned himself differently in relationship to different aspects of the Bourbon Reforms. Whereas Avendaño opposed the labor draft supported by the Bourbons, as we shall see in the next section, he supported Bourbon legislation regarding the standardization of clerical fees. The opposing factions in San Juan Tabaa also positioned themselves against one another in response to those same laws. The apparently contradictory responses of local brokers like parish priests and cabildo officers to the Bourbon Reforms were not contradictory at all if viewed from a local perspective. Bourbon legislation could be used selectively for the purposes of local conflict, and in the process could exacerbate or generate new disputes.

COSTUMBRE VERSUS BOURBON LANGUAGE POLICY

On 15 December 1789, the date on which the pueblos of the district of Villa Alta were to report their election results to the alcalde mayor, the principales and officials of San Juan Tabaa presented themselves to the alcalde mayor as a house divided. The electoral rancor of 1784 had apparently resurfaced. The two parcialidades of the pueblo could not agree on the results of the election in their pueblo. Clemente López, assistant priest (*cura vicario*) of Tabaa, accompanied the leaders of Tabaa to the district court as a representative of Avendaño, the parish priest. The padre's presence was routine in that Bourbon law dictated that election results were only valid if approved by local priests. The priest's ratification of pueblo elections would in fact prove a sticking point, as part of the lawsuit over the election results concerned his role in pueblo politics.[30]

Before proposing a solution to the electoral crisis, Ortega, the alcalde mayor, tried to educate himself as to the *práctica* and *costumbre* of elections in Tabaa by asking each side to explain the electoral process.[31] In general, the Audiencia, the Council of the Indies, and other legal bodies staffed by peninsular Spaniards steeped in the juridical theories of their time had by the 1770s seriously begun to discount the legitimacy and status of costumbre as a legal framework for resolving indigenous claims or conflicts. The Audiencia's decision in the case of Santiago Yagallo and allies versus San Juan Yae (discussed in chap. 3) reflects these shifts in legal theory during the Bourbon era.

At the local level in Villa Alta, however, costumbre still factored significantly into the alcalde mayor's decisions in native conflicts, in particular over pueblo elections. John Chance has argued that conflicts over municipal offices heated up considerably during the eighteenth century in Villa Alta, in large part because of an increase in repartimiento demands and cochinilla production. As intermediaries in the repartimiento, native officers often skimmed money or cochineal off the top, and as a result, the post of governor and alcalde in particular held increasing appeal as repartimiento production boomed during the years 1740–90. In many pueblos, electoral custom held that caciques could bypass the lower offices in the cargo system and enter at the level of alcalde. Not surprisingly, many of the electoral disputes were intertwined with claims to cacique status made by an increasing number of aspiring governors and alcaldes.[32]

As the alcaldes mayores considered the growing number of cases concerning pueblo elections and noble status during the second half of the eighteenth century, they adopted two tacks. First, as outsiders unfamiliar with the intricacies of and variations in native electoral practices (which often differed from pueblo to pueblo), they tended to yield to local custom in matters of electoral conflict in an effort to avoid embittering the locals on whom they relied for their huge profits. Second, when aspiring officers presented claims to cacique status, often with scant legal evidence, the alcaldes mayores tended to grant them such status. Again, commercial self-interest motivated their acquiescence, since without the cooperation of native governors and alcaldes, the repartimiento would grind to a halt. In this regard, increase in the repartimiento encouraged a more symbiotic and interdependent relationship between the alcalde mayor and the native elite during the second half of the eighteenth century.[33]

The case of Villa Alta suggests that the Audiencia and local magistrates differentially applied Bourbon legal theory concerning costumbre in the late eighteenth century. In the economic realm, the Bourbon Reforms varied in their effects at the local level; regions that depended on mining or the hacienda system were affected acutely, whereas economically peripheral regions felt much less impact. The effects of the Bourbon legal and cultural programs have been less studied, but it does appear that local legal decisions often depended largely on local colonial circumstance. Contrary to the prevailing legal culture in the metropole and the Audiencias that favored legal centralization, alcaldes mayores in remote regions where local custom prevailed and persisted well into the eighteenth century found it politically and economically expedient in certain situations to respect costumbre.[34]

In the case of the 1789–90 electoral dispute in San Juan Tabaa, the warring parcialidades presented to the alcalde mayor two different versions of local electoral custom. The first parcialidad explained that the officials who currently held office proposed candidates who they thought were best suited for the offices of governor, alcalde, and *regidor*. The second parcialidad claimed that the officials who currently held office consulted with the eligible male voters of principal rank (*el común*) first, and then proposed candidates. Faced with these different versions, the alcalde mayor responded that since he had no way of verifying which version represented the truth, he would propose a new process: each parcialidad would elect an alcalde and regidor, as well as a suitable candidate for governor. The office of governor would then be decided by lottery. The second parcialidad agreed to this proposal, but not the first. Unable to reach an accord, the alcalde mayor referred the case to Manuel Fernández de Pantaleón, legal advisor of the Real Audiencia.[35]

When the alcalde mayor referred the case outside of his local jurisdiction, the playing field shifted considerably. Jurists and legal advisors of the Audiencia were much less sympathetic to the vagaries of local custom, and Fernández de Pantaleón's decision reflected as much. He suggested that in order to resolve the conflict, the alcalde mayor should not approve or decide on the election results until he investigated the "qualities and qualifications" of the candidates for governor, alcalde, and regidor. In particular, he advised the alcalde mayor to ascertain whether the candidates "knew the Spanish language" and whether "they dedicated themselves to agriculture or industry." This was to be done in front of impartial witnesses. If those of the first parcialidad had a problem with the results of this process, then they would have to file suit in the district court within twenty days of the decision.[36]

Fernández de Pantaleón's recommendation to evaluate the qualifications of the candidate as defined by Spanish criteria reveals the gap between the Audiencia's inclination to impose solutions grounded in Spanish law and culture and the magistrate's preference for costumbre. In particular, his insistence on the evaluation of the officials' linguistic criteria drew its inspiration from a *real cédula* of 1770, which required all elected native officials to speak Spanish. In fact, the legislation sought a much more thoroughgoing reform of political culture at the level of the native pueblo. Not only were elected officials to be ladino, but the Spanish language was to completely replace native languages in all native dealings, official, commercial, and quotidian.[37] Through this measure, the Bourbon administration sought to erase native languages from the face of their empire. As such, native cabildo officers were to represent and embody Spanish law and culture in a culturally homogenous empire, rather than mediate between Spanish and native worlds.

Spanish policy on the relationship between native and Spanish languages had a long history. In sixteenth- and seventeenth-century legislation, the Hapsburgs laid the foundation for native acculturation on two related fronts: spiritual and linguistic. A 1550 law mandated the training of an elite corps of native schoolmasters, who, after a rigorous examination of their linguistic abilities, would teach natives the Spanish language and the Christian doctrine in Spanish. After years of trial and error in the process of evangelization, ecclesiastical and civil authorities were convinced that the Christian doctrine had to be taught in Spanish. If rendered in the native language, too much was lost in the translation, and as a result dangerous misunderstandings of the Catholic faith proliferated. A 1634 law directed the archbishops and bishops to pursue Spanish-language education and catechization wholeheartedly, and to instruct their parish priests to teach the Indians Spanish using "gentle methods." The Crown hoped that Spanish-language instruction would effect an improvement in native government and lifeways.[38]

The primary objective of the Hapsburg legislation was successful evangelization. A bilingual native government would emerge organically, as a by-product of Christianization. This gradualist view was in keeping with the Hapsburg spirit of indirect rule, legal pluralism, and respect for native semiautonomy. By the late eighteenth century, the spirit and the letter of imperial language policy had changed significantly. The Bourbon administration identified reform of native government and culture as a primary concern. From the perspective of the Bourbon state and Church, 250 years of evangelization by the missionary orders had failed to dampen the spiritual recalcitrance of the Indians, and a precise understanding of the mysteries of the Catholic faith remained elusive to a largely monolingual native population. Worse, monolingual native officials could not be trusted to serve the Crown efficiently or unequivocally. Civil and ecclesiastical authorities were therefore poised to renew the effort to spread the Spanish language. In this regard, as was often the case with the Bourbon Reforms, the Bourbons merely reanimated Hapsburg programs that had either failed or not been enforced. This time, however, linguistic plurality was not the objective: in the era of the Bourbons, Spanish-language instruction was intended to wipe native languages off of the linguistic map.

In a letter to the Council of the Indies dated 27 June 1769, Viceroy Marqués de Croix voiced the complaints of the archbishops and bishops of New Spain that despite the laws and ordinances mandating the teaching of the Christian doctrine in Spanish, native languages continued to prevail in native pueblos, making it difficult for priests to do their work, and making it necessary for the bishops to assign assistant priests (*curas vicarios*) conversant in native languages to many native parishes. He enumerated some potential benefits of a renewed Spanish-language campaign: the natives would be able to confess in Spanish and understand the Christian doctrine in Spanish, such that in a few years, interpreters would no longer be needed for those purposes; bishops would be understood in all of the pueblos of their dioceses; Indians would not take advantage of one another in their dealings, commerce, and legal disputes; priests would be on more equal footing (presumably, this referred to the practice of assigning a priest of lesser qualifications because he spoke the native language); the friars would reap the rewards of their work; and the empire would be governed with greater facility. He proposed a method to achieve these effects: all of the natives elected to office annually had to speak Spanish, and Spanish magistrates as part of their duties of office would be required to enforce this law. To ensure its observance, all elections would have to be confirmed by the viceroy. Bishops, priests, jurists of the Audiencia, and local magistrates would be instructed to denounce any election that failed to live up to the letter of the law.[39]

Francisco Fabian y Fuero, the bishop of Puebla, sent his own letter to the Council of the Indies on 19 September 1769 regarding the matter of Spanish-language instruction. He reiterated the point made by the viceroy that in order to govern effectively, the empire should "speak one tongue." He went further than the viceroy, however, in his denigration of native languages and by extension in his conviction that Spanish needed to replace native languages even in markedly native realms. He asserted that the Indians had no legal right to maintain their languages since they had been conquered and incorporated into the Spanish Empire. He made the familiar and long-standing argument that Indian languages were barbaric, evidenced by a lack of alphabetic writing, and that among all of the native languages, including Mexicano (Nahuatl), not one was capable of expressing "Knowledge" (*Sabio*) or of being part of the "Republic of Letters." Although the spiritual conquest of the early years of the colony had justified the teaching of the Christian doctrine in native languages, that justification had now passed. If the Indians did not learn Spanish, they would be not only less knowledgeable of "Civil Law" but also of the Christian doctrine, and more likely to fall back on their old ways. He lamented that even though some Indians knew Spanish, they preferred to speak their own languages, a problem that he felt should be addressed by requiring Indians to speak Spanish in their everyday dealings, a practice that would make them more law-abiding.

Finally, the bishop made a striking point about what he characterized as native misconceptions of how Spaniards perceived natives who spoke Spanish. He remarked that contrary to native perception, parish priests and other Spaniards did not consider it discourteous for natives to speak Spanish to them. Rather, failure to do so indicated a lack of respect. Spaniards, as the "social superiors" of natives, took pleasure in seeing the natives imitate them. Instead of assuming that the native who spoke Spanish was putting on airs, the Spaniard would interpret this gesture as a sign of obedience. As an added incentive, natives should speak Spanish so that they would have access to and be better prepared to fulfill the honorable and often profitable posts of governor, alcalde, and principal.[40]

The bishop's assertion that Spaniards viewed Indians who spoke Spanish in a favorable light was somewhat disingenuous. Spaniards harbored long-standing prejudices and ambivalent attitudes toward *indios ladinos*, whom they considered duplicitous. They believed that despite the outward signs of acculturation, ladinos persisted in their "barbarity" and "idolatry," and sought to undermine Spanish authority. Why, then, did the bishop argue otherwise? In the bishop's vision of a new imperial order in which

Spanish would be spoken by all imperial subjects, there would be no middle ground for ladinos to stand on. It was this middle ground occupied by native brokers—the ground between a monolingual native world and a monolingual Spanish world—that caused anxiety for Spaniards. Ladinos were dangerous not only for speaking Spanish but because of their cultural mobility. The bishop appears to have assumed that without linguistic boundaries, the native world would melt into the Spanish one, and as such native brokers would no longer be privy to their threatening source of power: biculturalism.

If the bishop of Puebla marshaled Spanish cultural prejudices toward native languages as a justification for a Spanish-only language campaign, then the archbishop of Mexico, Francisco Antonio Lorenzana, mobilized what I will call an "imperial argument" in his letter to the Council of the Indies dated 6 October 1769. He deployed his rhetorical flourish in an effort to communicate the urgency of the problem:

> Two and a half centuries since the conquest of this empire, we lament that we feel as if we were the illustrious conquistador Hernán Cortés. We need Interpreters of the tongues and languages of the Indians in even greater numbers than in the beginning, since with Gerónimo de Aguilar and Doña Marina, the conquistador understood the languages of many of the provinces from Yucatan to Central Mexico, and from here to Guatemala. But now, in one sole Diocese, the languages have multiplied such that in order to hear the confession of a prisoner in jail, we can rest assured that neither a Church official nor an interpreter could be found to perform the task.[41]

He noted that the problem was most acute in the diocese of Oaxaca and Puebla, where many languages other than Nahuatl were spoken.

In the body of his letter, the archbishop elaborated the imperial rationale for imposing the Spanish language on the native populations of Spain's American holdings. His reliance on examples from the Greek and Roman empires reflected Enlightenment interest in classical history. He argued that in the history of the great empires of the world, such as those of Greece and Rome, a linguistic conquest always accompanied a military conquest. If the Romans could make Latin the lingua franca through the enormous and diverse swath of territory of the Roman Empire, such that it still remained the language of the educated and erudite, then imperial

Spain should achieve the same. With references to Biblical and "profane" history, he pointed to the perils of not imposing a single language. Where imperial subjects maintained their own languages and customs, sedition and rebellion took root. By contrast, speaking the same language created fraternity and facilitated commerce, government, and helped the conquered to forget their enmities toward each other, and their resentment toward those who ruled them. In short, the archbishop argued that one language was necessary for a stable and peaceful empire.[42]

The logistical realities of the work of the Church also entered into the archbishop's argument. He pointed to the difficulties of being a parish priest when parishioners did not speak Spanish. He assailed the role of the assistant priests (*clérigos vicarios*), to whom he referred derogatively as "ministers of Language." He claimed that they made frequent mistakes of translation and contributed to the persistence of idolatry. Was it not more sensible to have "the sheep understand the voice and the whistle of the pastor" than the other way around? Furthermore, if a bishop could not speak all of the languages of his diocese, how could he effectively perform parish inspections? In the beginning of the evangelical enterprise, the missionaries had to learn Indian languages to convert the Indians. This was no longer the case now that Indians had ample access to Spanish-language education through the *maestros de escuela*.[43]

The archbishop also touched on what he identified as a central political problem with the empire's linguistic plurality: the disproportionate power of interpreters, scribes, and *apoderados*:

> In the political realm, his Excellency the Viceroy and the jurists of the Real Audiencia cannot hear or understand the complaints of the Indians, who pretend to be mute. An interpreter compounds the problem by twisting the matter at hand, dissimulating, or divulging a secret. They [here, the archbishop is presumably referring to Indian interpreters, scribes, and apoderados] dishonor with one blow and with horrendous calumny parish priests, alcaldes mayores, and all manner of officials. They draft petitions for people of questionable repute in the rustic fashion of the Indians. In the courtyards of houses, the Indians and their scribe, with his paper on his knee, concoct petitions that inflame passions in the courts. All of these injurious problems emerge from the Indians' ignorance of spoken Spanish, and they become even more ignorant everyday because of the distrust they feel toward their superiors.[44]

The archbishop's anxiety about native legal intermediaries was not new; rather, it echoed the concerns of the bishop of Oaxaca, Alonso de Cuevas Dávalos, who in 1661 had blamed the rebellion of Tehuantepec on the bicultural apoderados who had "inflamed the passions" of the Indians by fomenting legal disputes.

On 7 March 1770, the Council of the Indies approved the measures proposed by the archbishop: the most qualified priests would be assigned to native parishes, even if they did not speak the Indian language; native officials had to speak Spanish in order to hold office; Spanish-language schools would be established in native pueblos; and the role of *vicario* (or "minister of language") would be abolished. Civil and ecclesiastical authorities presented a united front on the matter, stating that "the Council of the Indies, the Crown's representatives, the Viceroy, and the Archbishop of Mexico agree on the grave necessity of abolishing the great diversity of languages spoken by the Indians of America and of making the vassals of the King of Spain of that vast dominion monolingual in Spanish."[45]

The real cédula concerning Spanish-language policy reached the alcalde mayor of Villa Alta on 11 December 1770. The document instructed the magistrate to cooperate with the bishop to enforce the laws concerning the teaching of Spanish to the Indians and of the Christian doctrine in Spanish, and the requirement that native officials be Spanish speakers and use the Spanish language in all of their dealings.[46] One year later, all of the municipal authorities of the district of Villa Alta pledged that they would comply with the law.[47] A 1781 *cordillera* reinforced the Spanish language–only requirement, mandating that cabildo officers be Spanish speakers, men of "good customs and habits," and that the election results had to be approved and signed by the parish priest.[48]

The 1789–90 election dispute in Tabaa demonstrates that compliance with the letter of the law was elusive. According to native testimony in the dispute, none of the officials originally elected in December 1789 spoke Spanish. And this was the case in a *cabecera*, a parish seat and administrative center, where acculturation was most likely to take place. In fact, compliance with the Bourbon linguistic policy concerning the election of Spanish-speaking officials was for most pueblos in the district totally unrealistic. With the exception of the Rincón pueblos where due to intense commercial contact with Spaniards a plurality of the principales were ladino, in the district at large, most principales and candidates for village office were monolingual.[49]

This did not mean, however, that Spanish-language legislation had no effect on district politics. As Fernández de Pantaleón's recommendation to the alcalde mayor in the electoral dispute of San Juan Tabaa makes clear, as in the case of costumbre, Spanish-language legislation could be selectively applied to resolve politically contentious situations. The case of San Juan Tabaa reveals that the "Spanish-only" requirement for village officials provided a useful political tool for Spanish magistrates. If applied successfully, it could legitimize the handpicking of village officers by the alcalde mayor in troublesome villages.

The political elite of San Juan Tabaa may have sensed the threat to their political autonomy that lurked in the solution proposed by Fernández de Pantaleón. In fact, his recommendation met with oblique resistance from the officials who had most recently been elected and who represented the first parcialidad. In an effort to deflect a heavy-handed intervention on the part of the alcalde mayor in village politics, they presented an alternative explanation for the electoral discord in a petition dated 19 December 1789. They claimed that the whole community had gotten together to discuss the candidates. As they divulged the criteria that they had applied to the candidates in their deliberations, it became quite clear that they contrasted with the criteria proposed by the legal advisor. "Good conduct [*buena conducta*]" and "honorable comportment in the past [*honra de bien en los años pasados*]" were the customary markers of suitable candidates. Nowhere was there mention of Spanish-language abilities.[50]

If Spanish-language legislation did not register among the principales of Tabaa in their efforts to decide on a suitable candidate for governor, Bourbon legislation concerning clerical fees did figure into the villagers' electoral rancor. Whereas Spanish-language legislation provided a tool with which the Audiencia's lawyer and the alcalde mayor could intervene in Tabaa's elections, clerical fees provided a rationale for natives to contest the alcalde mayor's proposal for a new electoral process. In their 19 December 1789 petition, the first parcialidad denied that the electoral discord arose from parcialidad rivalry, insisting that the parish priest of Tabaa, Padre Avendaño, had fomented it. According to the account of the first parcialidad, Avendaño encouraged the second parcialidad to contest the elections out of revenge. Apparently, the first parcialidad had brought a case against the priest in the ecclesiastical court in Antequera for forcing villagers to perform involuntary services and other abuses rather than collect the standard clerical fees mandated by law.[51]

The contentious issue of clerical fees created political turmoil not only in the pueblo of San Juan Tabaa, but also throughout Spanish America. Local custom had it that native parishioners would compensate priests through the performance of agreed-on services, the provision of food and other goods, and payment during feast days. The Bourbon administration attempted to regulate the potential for abuses (of which there were many) of this flexible and locally defined system by issuing a standard fee schedule for payment of parish priests. In the case of Villa Alta, the 1781 cordillera concerning village elections mandated that the village officials had to collect the fees twice a year, at Easter and Christmas, and if they did not succeed, officials from the district seat would be sent to collect them on their behalf.[52]

Throughout Spanish America, many parish priests protested the imposition of the fee schedule because it represented an incursion into their relationship with their parishioners, not to mention, the potential restriction of their income in kind. Parishioners, on the other hand, both resisted the fee schedule and complied with it, depending on local circumstances, such as the relationship of the native cabildo to the parish priest, or the comparative burden of the customary arrangements versus the new fee schedule. Whatever the local particulars, the issue of clerical fees constituted one of the more controversial of the Bourbon Reforms in native pueblos in New Spain and the Andes, and generated considerable litigation.[53]

The possibility that Padre Avendaño had interfered in pueblo elections should not surprise us, then, since the outcome of the elections had serious implications for the litigation against him. Furthermore, it should alert us to the continuum of political change in the district of Villa Alta, particularly with regard to the effect of parish priests on pueblo politics, which began with Bishop Maldonado's reforms and continued through the Bourbon Reforms. Prior to Maldonado's reforms, there were only six Dominican-administered parishes in the district, and two secular parishes in the Rincón. The bishop claimed that the Dominicans had only twelve resident friars. In 1705, after Maldonado's reforms, there were twenty-one parishes, which eventually had resident priests.[54] Tabaa was one of these new cabeceras. Maldonado's program, which translated into a greater presence of priests in native pueblos, and Bourbon insistence on the ratification of pueblo elections by parish priests worked together to impinge on native political and cultural autonomy.

In response to the December petition of the first parcialidad, members of the second parcialidad presented an argument that centered on their opponents' disregard for "local custom" and reliance on litigation as a means of imposing their will. In a petition to the alcalde mayor dated 20 December, they complained bitterly that the first parcialidad had ignored the custom of discussing new candidates among the entire *común* before proposing them for election. As a result, over the past two years, the first parcialidad had come to monopolize village offices, excluding members of the second parcialidad from political power. They identified the lawsuit against the parish priest as the root of the discord over electoral practices. They aligned themselves with the padre, arguing that the charges brought against him by the first parcialidad were false and that the reason that the first parcialidad had excluded them from the elections was that they had refused to participate in the illegal *derrama* (head tax) collected for the purpose of pursuing the suit against the priest.[55] In addition to these charges, the petition went into lengthy enumeration of other abuses, among them the misappropriation of funds collected for the celebration of San Juan, the village's patron saint, and unjustified whippings and abuse of villagers of the second parcialidad.[56]

The electoral dispute in San Juan Tabaa demonstrates the extent to which certain aspects of the Bourbon Reforms—such as clerical fees and the increased power of the parish priest in pueblo elections—elicited native resistance and provoked discord in the pueblo. As political turmoil increased, native leaders turned to the legal system to express and resolve disputes. But litigation itself often exacerbated community conflict. In the case of San Juan Tabaa, parcialidad enmity produced litigation, and the refusal of one party to participate in legal conflict—in this case in a derrama intended to fund the suit against the parish priest—deepened divisions and created another legal dispute over election results. This dispute, in turn, motivated the alcalde mayor to go outside his own jurisdiction and turn to the Audiencia for a solution. The result was the imposition of the Bourbon Spanish-only criteria for the selection of native officers at the expense of costumbre and native autonomy in San Juan Tabaa.

NEW FORMS OF POLITICAL COERCION

As the struggles over election results in San Juan Tabaa demonstrate, in the eyes of native villagers, one of the most important qualifications for an elected official was a willingness and ability to pursue litigation in the interest of the pueblo or a faction thereof. This included rallying the community to the unpopular task of providing a head tax to fund the litigation. In two instances within five years, the elected officials' unwillingness to live up to these expectations was sufficient cause to remove them from office, at least in the eyes of the parcialidad that favored the legal dispute. In both circumstances, the alcalde mayor disagreed with this justification. In 1784, he reinstated those officials who spurned litigation and favored the economic interests of a local mine owner. In the dispute over the 1789 elections, he would also arrive at a solution—although through different means—that favored an official compliant with Spanish interests.

On 20 January 1790, alcalde mayor of Villa Alta Pablo de Ortega selected Juan Felipe de Santiago, an "impartial" principal and seventy-year-old native of Tabaa to help him determine the qualifications of the candidates of the first parcialidad who had been elected the previous month. Of Santiago, Ortega remarked that he spoke "Spanish, knew how to read and write," and was in Ortega's estimation "the person with the greatest abilities and of the best circumstances in this pueblo, with the singular attribute of not having taken sides in either parcialidad." As they considered the elected officials, Santiago informed the magistrate that Pedro Morales, who was elected governor, was older than Santiago, and that he and José Hernandes, who was elected alcalde, were behind on their tribute payments. Morales had "some abilities," but Hernandes was poor, and neither knew Spanish, although both were honorable men, of good habits and customs, and dedicated themselves to agriculture. Marcial Morales, the other elected alcalde, did not speak Spanish either, but he was a man of good habits and customs. However, he had not been living in Tabaa for some time, but rather had been living in various pueblos in the district until his wife died in Roayaga the year before, at which point he had returned to Tabaa. Domingo Gerónimo and Salvador Pérez, the two regidores who had been elected, did not know Spanish either; they were farmers and men of good habits and customs.[57]

Juan Felipe de Santiago's assessment of each of the elected officials did not reflect well on their qualifications for office in light of the Bourbon policy: none of them spoke Spanish. It is not surprising then that on 4 February, the Audiencia's legal advisor, Villaseñor of Antequera, recommended that the alcalde mayor appoint Juan Felipe de Santiago himself as governor since he spoke Spanish and in the alcalde mayor's estimation was the most apt and best qualified of all of the principales of Tabaa; more to the point, he was above the fray, without parcialidad affiliation. In light of the discord in the pueblo, the legal advisor added that Santiago's mission throughout the year should be to end the rancor and the internecine conflicts in the pueblo, to promote peace, and to punish troublemakers. Elections would be held shortly for the other offices, and each parcialidad could elect an alcalde and regidor to represent its interests.[58]

Resistance to the alcalde mayor's imposition of a governor emerged immediately. The same day that Juan Felipe de Santiago received his staff of office, Juan López, Antonio Morales, and Manuel Fabian, the governor and alcaldes who had been elected in December, arrived in the district court, accompanied by Juan Felipe de Santiago, and stated that although the alcalde mayor had ordered that Santiago should be governor, they refused to comply. The alcalde mayor responded by imprisoning Juan López. Then, in order to make his authority as kingmaker perfectly clear, he demanded that all of the principales and commoners of Tabaa appear in the district court. At 7:00 that evening, the alcalde mayor addressed most of the adult males of the pueblo of Tabaa, who were crowded into the doorway of the *casas reales*. He ordered them into the courtroom where he read the order of the intendente that Santiago should be governor. Once again, he gave the staff of office to Santiago and admonished the onlookers to end their discord and respect their new governor. The elections for the other offices were held on 4 March.[59]

Echarrí's mining interests affected the election results of 1789, as they had five years before in the electoral dispute of 1784. Earlier that year, the Audiencia had issued a royal decree in favor of the pueblos of Tabaa, Solaga, and Yojovi, and in favor of San Juan Yae and its neighboring pueblos in separate cases against Echarrí. The Audiencia admonished Echarrí to order his administrators and foreman to abstain from forcing any Indians from the three pueblos in question to work involuntarily in the mines; in addition to paying them the customary day wages, Echarrí was to compensate them for the distance traveled to and from the mines; refrain from assigning them to dangerous posts; regulate the weight they were forced to carry (in keeping with their "weak constitution"); refrain from whipping them under any circumstances and from imprisoning them; and pay them the appropriate rent for the mules and horses that they provided for the mine and hacienda labor.[60]

It is unclear to what extent Echarrí respected this decision, but the pueblos of Tabaa, Yojovi, and Solaga brought no further litigation against him after the 1789 royal decree. This may have been because Echarrí did in fact improve working conditions in compliance with the Audiencia's mandate. Or it may have been that in his role as the new governor of Tabaa, Juan Felipe de Santiago had obeyed the mandate of the alcalde mayor, which was to smooth over pueblo divisions and punish troublemakers. These orders may very well have been a euphemism for ending the litigation against Echarrí and punishing those who refused to comply with the labor draft and the mandate against derramas.

The appointment by the alcalde mayor of Juan Felipe de Santiago as governor of Tabaa points to a new kind of "political coercion" in the district of Villa Alta during the Bourbon Reforms, which resembled the kind of coercion at work in the mining regions of the Andes.[61] Rodolfo Pastor coined this term in order to describe the politico-economic vise in which the alcaldes mayores—by virtue of their triple role as agents of the repartimiento, local judges, and political administrators—held indigenous leaders.[62] The obligation of the governor and alcaldes to distribute the *reales* and raw materials and collect and deliver the finished products to the alcalde mayor's lieutenant worked against elite political resistance to the economic regime. In the last decades of the eighteenth century, cabildo officers found themselves positioned as economic middlemen once again, but in a new kind of enterprise and labor regime. In order to curry the political favor of the alcalde mayor, they had to provide bodies for the mines, an obligation to which fellow villagers put up considerable resistance. Cabildo officers' room for maneuver was marginal, and their only recourse was to bring a suit to the Real Audiencia, an option that the alcalde mayor attempted to close off.

Another difference in the economic mediation performed by native officials in the case of the mining labor draft versus the repartimiento concerned the potential profits to be made by natives participating in each system. In the case of the repartimiento of cochineal and cotton cloth, native officials profited by keeping goods or cash for themselves. There was little resistance by pueblo elites who were out of office, since it was understood that once they came to hold office, they too would profit from their role as intermediaries. Not so in the case of the labor draft. Since principales were not exempt, and since there was no economic transaction in which to serve as middlemen, there was little economic or political incentive to comply willingly.

The new form of political coercion imposed by the mining labor drafts of the late eighteenth century coincided with a shift in the political economy of the district of Villa Alta. By 1782, cochinilla production in Villa Alta had begun a sharp decline from which it would never recover. Brian Hamnett attributes the general decline in the cochineal industry in Oaxaca as a whole to (1) Church attempts to raise the tithe (for Spaniards) on cochineal from 4 percent to 10 percent, (2) threat of a reform of the *alcabala* which would have made transactions more costly, (3) the widespread famine and inflation that plagued New Spain in 1785–87, (4) the establishment of the intendancy system of 1786, and (5) the prohibition of the *repartimiento de efectos*.[63] Chance notes that all of these general trends applied to Villa Alta. In 1790, when the prohibition of the repartimiento had taken root in the district, cochinilla production and trade had declined by half. By 1810, the district, formerly one of the top cochineal producers, had dropped off of the roster of Oaxaca's major cochineal regions. Production and trade in cotton cloth, the district's second most important industry, also declined considerably during the last decades of the eighteenth century and the first years of the nineteenth century. From 1787 to 1828, production and trade in mantas was between one-third to one-fifth of former levels.[64]

Decline in the repartimiento did not mean that the system disappeared. In particular, the repartimiento of cotton cloth occurred by other means. From 1790 forward, the *subdelegados* of Villa Alta, eager to reproduce the profits of the alcaldes mayores before them, demanded tribute payment in mantas (*mantas de tributo*), a long-standing tradition in the sierra.[65] They then sold the mantas on the market for considerable profit. Payment of tribute in mantas presented both a burden and an opportunity to the cabildo officers who mediated the transaction. As with the repartimiento, they could skim mantas and reales off the top.[66] The labor demands of manta production proved quite onerous, however, especially for native women who were forced to devote significant time to weaving, to the detriment of other tasks integral to the household economy. As a result, there was considerable resistance to the practice of the subdelegados, and given Bourbon hostility toward the repartimiento and similar institutions, the political environment was favorable for native challenges to the reincarnation of the outlawed system.

In the context of declining repartimiento production, the mining enterprise at Santa Gertrudis must have taken on added economic significance. Economic change had its political analog: decline in the repartimiento worked to unravel the interdependence of alcaldes mayores and native officials that had developed earlier in the century. With a decline in potential profits from the repartimiento, the alcaldes mayores and the subdelegados who succeeded them after 1790 may have had less incentive to "keep the Indians happy" by granting noble titles and respecting local custom in electoral matters. These economic and political shifts, combined with resistance to the labor regime by the Cajonos and Rincón pueblos who worked on the hacienda and in the mines of Santa Gertrudis, focused serious political pressure on the native officials responsible for delivering the labor. Many now faced the double burden—an intensified political coercion—of delivering laborers *and* mantas to the mine owners and the subdelegados respectively.

A 1788–89 lawsuit brought by Echarrí against the Rincón pueblos for not living up to the labor quotas made painfully apparent the diminished political space in which cabildo officers could mediate between the mine owner and the alcalde mayor, on the one hand, and their fellow villagers, on the other. On 8 April 1788, in response to complaints by Echarrí, Intendente Antonio Mora y Peysal ordered that the pueblos of the Rincón provide the labor to Echarrí's mines as mandated by law. The intendente made sure to emphasize that the elected officials were ultimately responsible for fulfilling this order. The alcalde mayor required all of the cabildo officers of the Rincón to sign the intendente's order, and all complied with the exception of the officials of Josaa.[67]

The officials' promise to comply with the labor draft proved difficult to uphold. Indeed, it was unclear to what degree their political legitimacy in the pueblo could withstand the labor demands of the mines, or to what degree they could live up to their pledge to the alcalde mayor. On 27 November 1788, with the ink barely dry on the intendente's order, the alcalde mayor insisted that the officials sign an order he had drafted. In addition to complying with the labor quotas, he demanded that the cabildo officers stop the practice of sending proxies in the place of principales or other well-off villagers who could afford to buy their way out of the labor draft. These proxies were known as *valientes*. Principales were not exempt from the labor quotas, and in order to avoid the burden, they paid the administrator of the mine five pesos for the right to send a valiente in their place.

According to Echarrí, his administrators, and the alcalde mayor, this system fell apart either when the administrator failed to receive the five pesos, or when the valientes failed to show up for work. Much of the remainder of the case represented a coordinated attempt by Echarrí, his lawyer Joseph Antonio Ledesma, and the alcalde mayor to end the practice of sending valientes.[68]

The officials of all of the Rincón pueblos signed the alcalde mayor's order prohibiting the practice of sending valientes, but the practice and its attendant problems continued nonetheless. Whether the cabildo officers actively resisted the orders, or whether they had no control over the situation remains an open question. Shortly after the pueblo officials had signed the alcalde mayor's order, Ledesma sent the magistrate a letter complaining that the pueblos of Yagavila, Yagila, Teotlasco, and Josaa had not sent their laborers. Writing from Talea in December, Ledesma again complained that none of the pueblos of the parish of Yagavila had obeyed either the intendente's or the alcalde mayor's orders despite having signed the documents. He identified the centers of resistance as the pueblos of Yagila, Teotlasco, Josaa, and Zoogochi, and complained that their disobedience set a bad example for the other pueblos.[69]

Echarrí continued the barrage of complaints, putting pressure on the alcalde mayor to in turn pressure the cabildo officers to comply with the labor draft. He hired another lawyer in Antequera, Ignacio José Villaseñor, to oversee the case. On 10 January 1789, on behalf of his client, Villaseñor wrote to the alcalde mayor and recommended that the most efficient way to solve the problem was to punish the officials of the pueblos who did not comply with the labor draft. He lamented the "haughtiness and obstinacy" with which these men had disobeyed the *Reales Ordenanzas de los Intendentes* and the alcalde mayor to the "detriment of the authority of both," and to the detriment of the "royal income, public goods, and the private assets of the mine owner." Such obstinacy was particularly harmful in one of the "principal commercial and economic sectors of this Kingdom." On 27 January, the alcalde mayor informed the cabildo officers that he would punish them if they failed to provide their quota of workers.[70]

The governors who mediated the labor draft continued to resist Echarrí's demands with tactics such as "dissimulation," "foot dragging," and "false deference."[71] On 7 February 1789, the alcalde mayor called the governors of Yagila and Josaa to the district court and asked them why they had not complied with his or the intendente's order. They replied that since their time as governors was coming to an end, the villagers ignored their orders concerning the labor draft and other matters. They claimed that this attitude toward outgoing officials was "customary," so they could not be held accountable. This "foot dragging" through recourse to "custom" represented an effort by the officials to pry open the vise that had closed around them during the suit. Regardless of the veracity of their answer, they appear to have convinced the alcalde mayor, who accepted this response and decided to wait until the new officials received their staffs of office before informing them that they would be punished for failing to comply with the order. He did so in March of the same year, but to no avail. It appears that the new crop of cabildo officers was as ineffective or as unwilling to comply with the labor draft as had been the outgoing officials in the twilight of their terms of office.[72]

"Foot dragging" on the part of the cabildo officials continued, but this time they blamed structural issues related to the work regime for their failure to meet Echarrí's labor demands. On 18 July 1789, Ledesma informed the alcalde mayor that the pueblos of Yagavila, Yagallo, and Lalopa still failed to comply with their quota of laborers. In response, the alcalde mayor ordered the officials of Yagavila, Yagallo, and Lalopa to appear in the district court to answer for their failures. The officials of all three pueblos protested that it was not their fault. They ordered foremen to assign Indians to the work gangs, and with these foremen, the laborers would leave the pueblos. But just outside the pueblo boundaries, they hid to avoid going to the mines. Meanwhile, the officials assumed that they had gone to Santa Gertrudis. Again, the alcalde mayor appears to have accepted this lack of accountability, responding that he would pardon them this time, but that the next time he would imprison them as the intendente had ordered.[73]

The magistrate's threats had little effect. On 24 October 1789, Echarrí complained that the pueblos of Yagallo, Yagavila, Lachichina, Teotlasco, Yaneri, Lahoya, and Tepanzacualco had failed to send their quota of laborers for over a week, resulting in a labor shortage at the mines. The alcalde mayor responded that he had talked with the officials himself, had sympathized with their plight, and had not imprisoned them as the intendente had ordered. But given their continued lack of compliance, he would recall them to answer Echarrí's complaints.[74]

After listening to the testimony of the cabildo officers, the alcalde mayor concluded that the root of the problem was indeed the practice of sending valientes: either they never arrived to do the work, or those who had bought out their service never paid the appropriate fee. On 6 November 1789, the alcalde mayor officially abolished the practice of sending valientes. He insisted that all villagers, regardless of wealth or status (with the exception of caciques), had to serve personally in the mines. He sent a copy of his order to Echarrí so that he would notify his foremen not to negotiate with the cabildos over the issue of sending proxies.[75] Here, this particular dispute ends, but the conflict between Echarrí and the Rinconeros continued until 1791, when the first subdelgado of Villa Alta, Bernardo Bonavia, reached a decision in a case brought by the officials and principales of Santiago Lalopa against Echarrí. The case began in 1788 when the officials of Lalopa made a plea on their own that due to the harsh working conditions, and in keeping with local custom, principales should be exempted from service in the mines. In June 1791, Bonavia maintained that in keeping with the orders of the Real Audiencia, all tributaries, including principales, were required by law to work in the mines and were prohibited from sending valientes in their place.[76]

The political coercion at work in the dispute between Echarrí and the Rincón pueblos points to marked shifts in the relationship between cabildo officers and the alcaldes mayores from the boom years of the repartimiento (1740–90) to the ascendance of the mines of Santa Gertrudis in the last decades of the eighteenth century. Whereas the repartimiento de efectos had provided an incentive for the alcalde mayor to allow principales with legal skills to litigate their way to cacique status and into high office, the labor regime in the mines established a political climate in which those same upstarts and principales could not buy their way out of their turn of service.

This shift was bound up in a qualitative difference between the repartimiento de efectos and mining as modes of production. As coercive and onerous as the repartimientos of cochinilla and cotton cloth were, they were home industries. As such, they were located in the native sphere, providing native producers and the native officials who mediated their functioning with some autonomy in matters of production and oversight.

Relatively speaking, cochineal production was much less disruptive of peasant life than other forms of colonial labor and production. While producing cochinilla, native villagers continued to live in their homes and produced staple crops for subsistence and local sale. *Nopaleros* (cactus groves) thrived just about anywhere, meaning that indigenous producers did not have to devote precious croplands to them. In fact, nopaleros were often located in the courtyards of indigenous homes, and women tended to them in the interstices of performing their household duties (as did children and the elderly), while men worked uninterrupted in the fields. The relative ease with which indigenous families could balance the needs of cochineal and subsistence production ensured the continued strength and vitality of indigenous pueblos in Oaxaca in comparison with other regions of colonial Spanish America where labor demands were more disruptive of communal structures.[77]

Spaniards overtly interfered in native cochineal and cotton mantle production only on occasion, when they appeared in the pueblos to distribute the raw materials and collect the finished goods. Even if the magistrates had wanted to exercise greater oversight in the production of *grana de cochinilla*, they could not have done so because the cultivation of the insect that produced the dye was a native art that the Spaniards had attempted to emulate in vain. For native intermediaries, mediating the repartimiento was a burden, but there was great potential for profit.

In contrast, in the case of mining, labor and production occurred outside the Indian pueblo and home, under watchful Spanish eyes, and, although this was illegal, under the crack of a foreman's whip. Cabildo officers had no oversight over labor and production; they were responsible only for providing bodies. Once the laborers left the pueblo, the officials could do little to mediate production or oversee native labor. In short, during the term of labor, cabildo officers lost their authority over the men they sent to the mines; they thus ceased to be intermediaries in the productive process and instead became ciphers for Indian labor. There were no profits to look forward to, only grief and complaints from their fellow villagers, the subdelegado, and the mining administrators.

We should note that the effects of mining on the district of Villa Alta were limited to the Cajonos and Rincón areas. In this regard, the effects of the Bourbon Reforms were variable not only from region to region, or district to district, but within a district itself. This may have been particularly true for Villa Alta since it was such an ecologically and topographically varied zone, in addition to being a diverse area ethnically, culturally, and linguistically. Differing effects in the realm of cultural and political reforms paralleled variations in the effects of economic reforms. Spanish language–only legislation may have gained some traction in the Zapotec Rincón, where most principales were ladinos, but the Mixe or Chinantec regions, where most principales were monolingual, presented the Bourbon reformers with a different politico-cultural landscape.

The changes in the political economy of the district of Villa Alta during the 1780s and 1790s worked in tandem with Bourbon mining initiatives and legislation on native language and "custom" to diminish the power of native intermediaries in the Nexitzo and Cajonos pueblos, the two ethno-linguistic zones that had experienced the most contact with Spaniards. Since the Spaniards' expectations of the economic role of native inter-mediaries had changed with the decline of the repartimiento, they also increasingly preferred cabildo officers who were accountable to Spanish needs and less rooted in native concepts of power and authority. The political influence of the alcalde mayor and later, subdelegado, in native elections and pueblo politics also changed. Whereas the electoral conflicts in San Juan Yatzona from the 1670s to the 1690s were largely resolved through the negotiation of native intermediaries from Yatzona with the Audiencia, in the case of electoral conflict in San Juan Tabaa one hundred years later, no such negotiation occurred. Rather, Bourbon legislation and, more broadly, a changed attitude on the part of Bourbon administrators toward the question of native autonomy, empowered the magistrate (and, later, subdelegado) to act as kingmaker and to determine a governor's suitability based on hispanization and Spanish criteria alone.

Native expectations of their elected officials also put greater pressure on cabildo officers. In particular, the unspoken mandate to pursue litigation could determine whether a native official enjoyed support or met resis-tance from his fellow villagers. A marked increase in legal conflicts and an expansion of legal culture in native pueblos during the second half of the eighteenth century, and particularly during the Bourbon Reforms, meant that much of the political and economic energy of the cabildo officers and native pueblos as a whole was directed toward litigation.

CONCLUSION: THE POLITICAL SPACE CLOSES

Bourbon cultural and economic programs tightened the political vise around native intermediaries in the late eighteenth century and eroded native autonomy in the Cajonos and Rincón regions of Villa Alta. Given their hostility toward intermediary figures of all origins and ethnicities, Bourbon reformers would have considered this political shift salutary. Bourbon jurists, legal theorists, and administrators might have been surprised however, by the way this shift took place. Where possible, local magistrates applied Bourbon Spanish-language requirements for native officeholding, selectively, in cases that had an impact on Spanish interests, such as the electoral dispute in San Juan Tabaa, a pueblo that provided labor for the favored industry of the Bourbon kings. Furthermore, in the case of Villa Alta, implementation of Bourbon legislation directed at overhauling local politics and culture was complicated by unanticipated developments in local political economy (such as the persistence of the repartimiento de mantas) and resistance from cabildo officers and native pueblos alike. We should therefore consider the Bourbon Reforms in their proper context, as part of a constellation of changes in political economy and political culture shaped by a synergy of local conditions, local agency, and royal mandate. As key figures in the implementation of and resistance to the Bourbon Reforms, native intermediaries shaped their effects at the ground level. They also were bellwethers of the negative effects of the Bourbon Reforms on native political and cultural autonomy on the eve of Mexican independence.

Chapter 6

From "Indian Conquerors" to Local "Indians"

In 1761, the municipal authorities of the barrio of Analco in the district of Villa Alta brought a case to the *alcalde mayor* complaining of bad treatment at the hands of the Spanish *vecinos* of the district seat.[1] Abusive treatment of indigenous people by Spaniards in eighteenth century Villa Alta was common, but what set this case apart was the identity of the plaintiffs. The residents of the barrio of Analco were descendants of the indigenous military auxiliaries from central Mexico who facilitated the conquest of the Sierra Norte.

Through their specialized role in the region's security, which continued well into the eighteenth century, the Indian conquerors of the Sierra Norte made possible the maintenance of Spanish colonial rule in the region. Whereas the previous chapters of this book have emphasized the political and symbolic work of native intermediaries in the construction and maintenance of the colonial order in Villa Alta, this chapter focuses on the double-edged role—coercive and political—of a separate caste of native intermediaries: the sierra's *indios conquistadores*. Their role as an occupying and coercive force throughout the colonial period addresses the persistent puzzle articulated in the opening pages of this book: How did Mexico's imperial overlords maintain colonial rule in the empire's hinterlands despite a notoriously underdeveloped provincial bureaucracy and the lack of a standing army? As important as were the interpenetration of native and Catholic rituals, native political lead-

ership and colonial bureaucracy, and the channeling of indigenous grievances through the legal system, so too was the persistence of systematic
coercion in the Spanish colonial system, particularly in the more remote
regions of New Spain. But the persistence of coercion has tended to be
deemphasized in recent historical scholarship in favor of an emphasis on
the hegemony produced by Catholicism and the legal system.[2] The example of the indigenous conquerors of the Sierra Norte reveals how the
cultural and political incorporation of the Spanish Empire's indigenous
allies not only coexisted with, but also ensured colonial military security
through the threat and exercise of violence.

In order to ensure their role as a coercive force—a powerful role—and
maintain the legal privileges granted them by the Spanish Crown in return
for their services in the conquest, the Indian conquerors had to engage
in significant symbolic work. Violence—specifically military conquest—
provided an important symbolic register for expressing interindigenous
ethnic conflict. Spaniards *and* the Zapotec, Mixe, and Chinantec peoples
of the sierra provided audiences for the Indian conquerors' deployment of
the discourse of conquest. In order to address multiple audiences, the
indigenous conquerors had to mediate between two systems of signification and identity: race and ethnicity. For example, despite their identity
as "Indians," they had to project distinction from Zapotecs, Mixes, and
Chinantecs who were indigenous to the region in order to convince their
Spanish allies of their continued importance. In order to do so, they turned
to the symbolic repertoire—characterized by the intersection of race and
gender—that characterized the region's colonial order. They cast themselves as "loyal vassals," "good Catholic Christians," "Tlaxcalans," and "Indian conquerors" in opposition to the "idolaters" and "rebels" who inhabited the district's native pueblos. At the same time, they had to maintain
the impression among the region's native inhabitants that they could wield
legitimate violence against them, and that they held a privileged position
over them. They achieved this through a range of intermediary roles and
public performance.

In this regard, this chapter brings full circle the discussion of the politics
of indigenous identity in which race (crosscut by gender), ethnicity, culture, and community were in constant play, deployed by both Spanish
officials and native intermediary figures in what John and Jean Comaroff
have called the "challenge and riposte" of colonialism.[3] Claims to Tlaxcalan

identity by residents of the barrio of Analco represented simultaneously a claim to ethnic identity, communal privileges, and cultural and military superiority over other "Indians."

But as I discussed in chapter 5, in the interest of economic efficiency and political control, the Bourbons worked to homogenize indigenous identity. In the district of Villa Alta during the Bourbon era, there was no official room for linguistic plurality, exemptions for indigenous *principales*, or privileges for "Indian conquerors." Thus, over the long term, the Indian conquerors failed to maintain their privileged position in colonial society. Their decision to ally themselves militarily with the Spanish conquerors, and in the centuries that followed, to align their identity and interests with a colonizing power that came to view all of its indigenous subjects with contempt, led to their eventual subjugation in the late eighteenth century by the same legal system that they had used to their advantage in the centuries before. By the end of the colonial period, in the eyes of their former Spanish allies, the emphasis in the Indian conquerors' collective identity came to rest on *Indian* rather than *conqueror*.

INDIAN CONQUERORS

The participation of a few hundred indigenous military auxiliaries proved indispensable to Spanish expansion into the Sierra Norte of Oaxaca. As I noted in the introduction, in the wide sweep of the Spanish conquest of Mexico, the military campaign against the Zapotecs of Oaxaca's remote and rugged northern sierra proved especially bloody and brutal. Local resistance and the difficult terrain made it necessary for the Spanish conquistadors to make at least three attempts to subdue the region's native peoples. Once they had pacified the region (at least temporarily) in 1527, the Spanish conquistadors Gaspar Pacheco and Diego de Figueroa established the Spanish seat of power at San Ildefonso de Villa Alta. A few hundred of the indigenous auxiliaries, all of whom were recognized as *naborías* (free Indians), set up camp adjacent to the small Spanish settlement.[4]

It is unclear whether only a few hundred indigenous auxiliaries participated in the conquest of the sierra, or whether more participated but only a few hundred actually settled there. In either case, the question remains of why the numbers are so small in comparison with the thousands of native auxiliaries who participated in the conquest and colonization of Guatemala. The most likely answer appears to be the gap in potential wealth and prestige for the native militaries. If the indigenous auxiliaries did in fact perceive the "conquest" as their own project of military expansion, then the Sierra Norte of Oaxaca would have appeared a rather meager feather in the cap of empire. The region was remote, mountainous, and little known to the people of central Mexico. In fact, it is unclear whether it was ever conquered by the Triple Alliance. Furthermore, in contrast with the well-known ethnic states that dotted the route between central Mexico and Guatemala, the sierra had little to offer in terms of material resources or tributary population.

Whatever the reasons for their small numbers, the few hundred indigenous auxiliaries who remained in the Sierra Norte built a garrison next to the Spanish settlement of Villa Alta and served as an occupying force on the Spaniards' behalf. The naboría settlement came to be known as the "barrio of Analco," and its inhabitants as the "natives of Analco." During the early colonial period, the natives of Analco and their descendants proved adept at cultural assimilation: they practiced Christianity, came to speak both Spanish and Zapotec (in addition to their native Nahuatl), and married local women.[5] Their identification with Spanish culture and language and their social relationships with the local population positioned them as cultural intermediaries and power brokers in the region. During much of the colonial period, they also maintained their role as military auxiliaries. They helped the Spaniards to suppress a rebellion in the Nextizo Zapotec community of Tiltepec in 1531, a general rebellion that shook the region in 1550, an uprising in Choapan in 1552, and a Mixe rebellion in 1570.[6]

The Lienzo of Analco

The conventional narrative of the conquest of the Sierra Norte relies on the interpretation of documents written by the Spanish conquerors, which provide little access to the perspective of the indigenous allies who participated in the conquest. The Lienzo of Analco, an indigenous-produced pictographic history of the conquest of the sierra and map of the region provides an indigenous counterpoint to the Spanish narrative (see fig. 4). The document is important in that it offers an indigenous view of the conquest, and does so through an indigenous medium of communication presumably targeted at an indigenous audience.[7]

Florine Asselbergs has situated the Lienzo of Analco in both the "lienzo"

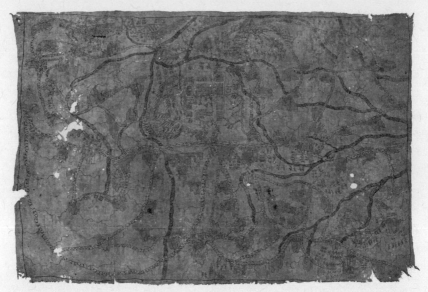

FIGURE 4 The Lienzo of Analco. Copyright, Biblioteca Nacional de Antropología e Historia (Mexico City).

and "cartographic history" genres of Mesoamerican narrative pictography. "Lienzo" refers to the medium: a large piece of linen or other cloth, and "cartographic history," to the content.[8] As a narrative of the conquest, the Lienzo of Analco belongs to a third genre, which Asselbergs identifies as "conquest pictorials." This subgenre includes two existing lienzos (the Lienzo of Tlaxcala and its copies, and the Lienzo of Quauhquechollan), and a missing lienzo, which belonged to a colony of central Mexican conquistadors who settled in Totonicapan, Guatemala. There are documentary references to this "ghost" lienzo, but no extant lienzo.[9]

The similarities among the extant conquest pictorials suggest that they were part of a broader tradition of indigenous pictographic narratives of the conquest, dating from the 1530s and 1540s,[10] and an extension of a preconquest tradition of conquest pictorials, which served to legitimize the status of a conquering group.[11] Taken together, the colonial-era conquest pictorials reflect the process of indigenous adaptation to colonialism and the ethnogenesis of the indigenous conquerors, whose story they told.[12]

Asselbergs argues that the Lienzo of Analco, like the other conquest pictorials, was produced by an indigenous artist (*tlacuiloque*) for an indigenous audience shortly after the conquest, most likely in the 1530s.[13] As was true of all Mesoamerican pictographic narratives, the Lienzo of Analco was meant to be seen and read, and also publicly performed by a storyteller, who interpreted scenes and provided details about the people and places portrayed in the conquest pictorial.[14] The performative nature of the conquest pictorials suggests that we have access to only part of the message that these documents were meant to communicate.[15] As a central part of a public ritual, the conquest pictorials served to "structure collective memory," thereby producing and reinforcing collective identity.[16] For Mesoamerica's Indian conquerors, all of whom left their communities of origin to conquer and settle new territory, the production and reinforcement of collective identity—in effect, a new, colonial identity—proved particularly important, and centered on participation in a successful campaign of conquest, commemorated in the conquest pictorials.

Although the conquest pictorials were produced for an indigenous audience, they took on an added purpose when they were directed toward Spaniards. Communities of Indian conquerors submitted conquest pictorials to Spanish courts along with alphabetic texts as evidence of their contributions to the Spanish conquest, and in support of claims to special privileges and exemptions. As evidence of this, the Lienzo of Analco was found in the barrio of Analco during the twentieth century with a bundle of colonial-era Nahuatl-language documents, which presumably elaborated on and supported the information communicated in the lienzo. That bundle of documents has since been lost.[17]

Viola König first identified the Lienzo of Analco as a map and pictorial narrative of the conquest of the Sierra Norte.[18] Mesoamerican narrative pictography often integrated representations of space, time, and people. Unlike European maps, which adopted a "chorographic" perspective (a bird's-eye view of space, reproducible by a mathematical grid), Mesoamerican cartographic pictography represented space in human terms, from a "communicentric" perspective.[19] People, places, and structures were portrayed at close range and were individualized, so that they could be associated visually with a particular community's identity. As Asselbergs puts it, in indigenous cartographic histories, "geography did not exist independently from history. It was the story that made the maps," and the audiences "lived" or "felt" the collective experiences that the documents communicated.[20]

The *tlacuiloque* who produced the Lienzo of Analco used stylistic conventions and narrative strategies similar to those found in the lienzos of Quauquechollan and Tlaxcala (the other extant conquest pictorials). For example, the tlacuiloque rendered the territory of the Sierra Norte and narrated the history of the conquest predominantly through a maze of roads marked by footprints. The foot-marked roads provide a sense of movement through time and space, and lead the "reader" through representations of mountains, rivers, and indigenous settlements (indicated by bell-shaped mountains). The Spanish settlement of Villa Alta occupies the rough center of the lienzo, and provides its orientation. Otherwise, there is no up or down, and it appears as though the tlacuiloque intended that the document be seen from above (it was probably meant to be laid on the ground) and viewed at any point around it.[21]

The Lienzo of Analco is crawling with people, most of whom are the indigenous conquerors. They are portrayed according to the different facets of military support that they provided to the Spaniards. They appear as guides and porters, leading Spaniards up and down the endless layers of mountains, gullies, and drainages, and carrying their persons, possessions, and equipment (see fig. 5). The tlacuiloque's rendering of the Spaniards perched on the backs of indigenous porters and on horseback, leading their indigenous allies into battle against Zapotec resistance, positions the Spanish as the commanders of the military operation (see fig. 6). But despite his clear signaling of Spanish leadership in the conquest, the tlacuiloque put the integral role of the indigenous conquerors into relief through sheer numbers: the lienzo is dense with the figures of Indian auxiliaries, and in many scenes, dozens of fierce-looking indigenous foot soldiers with pointed spears stand on the flanks or at the rear of the handful of Spanish commanders. This juxtaposition of a few Spaniards supported by large numbers of indigenous auxiliaries appears particularly poignant in the artist's rendering of what appears to be the battle of Tiltepec, portrayed in the upper-left quadrant of the lienzo (see fig. 7). The depiction of battle scenes shows war mastiffs (dogs) devouring the local population, the hanging of local leaders, and the dismemberment of local fighters (see figs. 8 and 9). In addition to representing the early battles of the conquest, the depiction of cruelty toward the local population might also have referenced the notorious misdeeds of the first alcalde mayor of Villa Alta, Luis de Berrio.[22]

The Lienzo of Analco effectively communicates a message that lay at the heart of later efforts on the part of the Indian conquerors of the barrio of Analco to project their collective identity. First, the conquest was a joint

FIGURE 5 Indian conquerors as porters, Lienzo of Analco. Copyright, Biblioteca Nacional de Antropología e Historia (Mexico City).

effort. The Indian conquerors were not conquered Indians but rather conquering allies of the Spaniards. Second, in the absence of the portrayal of a community of origin (an absence that I will discuss further in the section that follows), the Sierra Norte became the spatial focal point for the Indian conquerors' new colonial identity. Third, the Indian conquerors established their domination over the local population violently, and militarily, thereby privileging their identity over that of the local population. The narrative of the lienzo must have left both indigenous and Spanish audiences wondering how the conquest of the sierra would have been possible without the Spaniards' native allies.

"Tlaxcalans" or "Mexicanos"?

As we contemplate the perspective of the indigenous conquerors on their role in the conquest of the sierra, and their construction and projection of that role through the lienzo's narrative strategy, we are left to wonder who

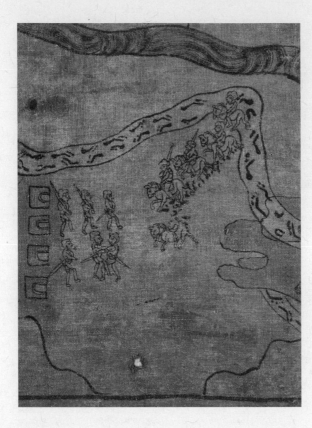

FIGURE 6 Spaniards on horseback, Lienzo of Analco. Copyright, Biblioteca Nacional de Antropología e Historia (Mexico City).

these people were and where they came from. In the cases of the lienzos of Tlaxcala and Quauquechollan, this question is immediately resolved by the inclusion of the community of origin (Tlaxcala and Quauquechollan, respectively) in the cartographic narrative.[23] In the case of the Lienzo of Analco, the community of origin is notably absent. It is unclear why, but scattered evidence on the ethnic identities of the Indian conquerors of the barrio of Analco suggests an answer: the ethnic heterogeneity of the indios conquistadores of the barrio of Analco may have precluded the portrayal of a single community of origin.

The central question—a political one—about the original identity of the indigenous conquerors of the sierra is to what degree they can be collectively categorized as "Tlaxcalans" or as "Mexicanos." "Mexicano," a term used by Spaniards to describe the language spoken by the natives they encountered, also referred to a variety of groups from Mexico's central valleys, the Valley of Oaxaca, and the Isthmus of Tehuantepec. But the term *Tlaxcalan* held special import because of the touted role of the Tlaxcalans as the most significant allies in Hernan Cortés's conquest of Tenochtitlán.

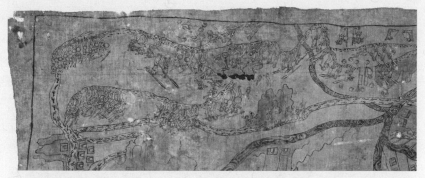

FIGURE 7 Battle scene, Lienzo of Analco. Copyright, Biblioteca Nacional de Antropología e Historia (Mexico City).

As has been well documented in the historiography of colonial Mexico, the Tlaxcalans, fierce enemies of the Aztecs, played a crucial role in the military conquest of Aztec territory, and in the "civilizing" and evangelizing projects of the Spanish colonizers. Through the skill of Cortés's interpreter Doña Marina, the Spaniards formed a long-standing alliance with the ethnic state of Tlaxcala.[24] Tlaxcalan rulers agreed to send tens of thousands of their best-trained men to serve as guides, interpreters, and foot soldiers for the small band of Spanish conquerors. First, Tlaxcalan auxiliaries and other long-standing enemies of the Aztecs made possible the conquest of the heart of the Aztec Empire. Afterward, they and military auxiliaries from other indigenous groups led the Spaniards through southern Mexico and Guatemala, subduing resistance and brokering alliances along the way.

Once the farthest reaches of the Aztec Empire had been conquered, the Spanish Crown reached a formal agreement with the rulers of Tlaxcala that guaranteed them special privileges as "Indian conquerors." In exchange for these privileges, the Tlaxcalan leadership sent hundreds of families to the frontiers of the new Spanish Empire. The Spaniards envisioned that the Tlaxcalans—sedentary agriculturists who were hispanized and evangelized—should provide a "civilizing" influence on indigenous groups in the north. These Tlaxcalan families formed model Christian communities and served as examples of "civilized Indians" in places as far-flung as the Chichimec frontier in the north of Mexico and the Philippine Islands. Other Tlaxcalans settled alongside their Spanish comrades-in-arms in the newly conquered regions. This role as conquering and "Christianizing" Indians was not unique to the Tlaxcalans; other ethnic groups from central

FIGURE 8 War mastiff, Lienzo of Analco. Copyright, Biblioteca Nacional de Antropología e Historia (Mexico City).

Mexico made similar agreements with the Spaniards and played similar roles, although the Tlaxcalans were the most famous (or notorious) participants in this imperial process.[25]

Chance identifies the indigenous conquerors of the Sierra Norte as "Nahuatl-speaking indios naborías from central Mexico, especially Tlaxcala."[26] Although he nods to the diverse ethnic affiliations of the indigenous conquerors through the general identification of "indios naborías from central Mexico," he emphasizes the Tlaxcalan aspect of their group identity by referring to the "Tlaxcalan heritage" of the barrio of Analco. He points out, however, that by the 1770s, the Tlaxcalan ethnic identity of the barrio's inhabitants had been significantly diluted by migration of locals to the barrio and by intermarriage.[27]

In the 1761 legal dispute I referred to at the beginning of this chapter, eight individuals from the barrio of Analco identified themselves as "descendants of the first Tlaxcalan auxiliaries of the first conquistadors of these provinces."[28] However, the temptation to assume a collective identity based on common origins is complicated by a 1555 legal dispute between two Spaniards over the rights to native labor and land in the sierra pueblos

FIGURE 9 The hanging of local caciques, Lienzo of Analco. Copyright, Biblioteca Nacional de Antropología e Historia (Mexico City).

of Yaci and Lobani. The court identified one of the witnesses in the dispute as Juan de Velasco, an Indian from Tehuantepec and an interpreter for the district. Velasco claimed that he had known one of the parties in the case for thirty-three years "since the time that he had accompanied the Spaniards who conquered this province."[29] In this statement, Velasco identified himself as one of the native auxiliaries who participated in the conquest of the Sierra Norte, but notably, he did not claim to be a Tlaxcalan, or a "Mexicano" (a native of central Mexico), but rather a "natural de Tehuantepec."

Furthermore, in a 1591 decree concerning the privileges and obligations of the indigenous conquerors of the sierra, the reference to Tlaxcala is nowhere to be found; instead, the Real Audiencia referred to the "naturales de Analco" as "yndios mexicanos que viven en el barrio de Analco" ("Mexicano Indians who live in the barrio of Analco").[30] In a royal decree (*real provision*) of 1683, the Audiencia referred to them as "naturales, naborías del barrio de Analco" ("free Indians of the barrio of Analco").[31] Francisco de Burgoa, the Dominican who chronicled the evangelization of Oaxaca, referred to them as "indios mexicanos muy leales" ("very loyal Mexicano Indians") and "mexicanos de Analco" ("Mexicanos of Analco").[32] In a 1683 case, the *cabildo* of Analco referred to the natives of their barrio as "conquistadores de estas provincias que adquirimos" ("conquistadors of these provinces which we acquired").[33]

Another kind of documentary reference to the ethnic identity of the Indian conquerors of the barrio of Analco can be inferred from the Lienzo of Analco. König and Asselbergs liken the style of the Lienzo of Analco to that of the Lienzo of Tlaxcala, hinting at a connection between the two places.[34] Might we consider the Tlaxacalan style of the lienzo to be part of the Indian conquerors' rhetorical strategy? By commissioning a lienzo in the Tlaxcalan style, or commissioning a Tlaxcalan artist, might the Indian conquerors of the sierra have attempted to communicate or project a Tlaxcalan identity? These questions are highly speculative, but it is noteworthy that although not all of the Indian conquerors of the Sierra Norte were Tlaxcalan, the Lienzo of Analco was rendered in a Tlaxcalan style.

These varying identifications make it difficult to determine whether the natives of Analco descended primarily from Tlaxcalan auxiliaries, or whether they were actually a more diverse group of indigenous conquerors from other regions. Given the Tlaxcalans' special place in the Spanish colonial project, and the privileges associated with Tlaxcalan identity, it would have been tempting for the natives of Analco to emphasize or claim Tlaxcalan heritage, even if their forefathers had more diverse ethnic roots. Perhaps, then, we should emphasize the utility of "Tlaxcalan" identification rather than attempting to categorize the indigenous conquerors of the sierra as Tlaxcalan or not.

Disillusionment: Services in Exchange for Privileges

Since we do not know the exact origins of the indigenous conquerors of the sierra, or the terms of their alliance with the Spaniards, we are left to wonder what they expected when they agreed to participate in the conquest of this notoriously fearsome, wild, and bellicose region. Did they expect to be awarded some of the spoils of conquest, or did they consider the military campaign against the Zapotecs as their own campaign of expansion? Asselbergs argues that the "city-state culture" of pre-Hispanic Mesoamerica, with its "continuously changing alliances, and shifts of power and status," provided the framework through which the Indian conquerors entered into alliance with the Spaniards. The Spaniards' indigenous allies likely assumed that they would become part of the new ruling system imposed by the conquering Spaniards, which would lead to increased wealth, status, and security.[35]

Whatever their objectives and expectations, the indigenous conquerors who accompanied the Spaniards as naborías must have been sorely disappointed when, following the conquest of the sierra, their Spanish allies drew little distinction between them and the recently conquered locals. As early as 1549, the indigenous conquerors complained to the viceroy of their treatment at the hands of Villa Alta's Spaniards. Recognizing their service to the Crown, Viceroy Antonio de Mendoza reinforced their status as naborías, insisting on their freedom from coerced labor and payment for their work.[36]

The viceroy's decree provided a foundation on which the Indian conquerors could negotiate a relationship with their former comrades in arms. This relationship, based largely on the logic of services in exchange for privileges, endured despite significant challenges through the first half of the colonial period. As Chance points out, in 1552 the cabildo of Villa Alta granted the indigenous conquerors land to the west of their town. In the 1560s, the settlement came to be known as Papalotipac, and soon thereafter as the barrio of Analco, the name it still bears today. In exchange for this land, the indigenous conquerors had to agree to the following conditions: its inhabitants were to remain part of the Spanish settlement of Villa Alta and subject to its political authorities; they could not take water illegally; they could not plant crops in the fields of the Spanish settlement; they could not crowd the roads entering and leaving the Spanish settlement; they had to provide messenger service to Antequera and Mexico City and repair the roofs of the church and Dominican convent when necessary; and they had to serve as firemen.[37] The population of the barrio of Analco, always larger than that of Villa Alta, fluctuated from about 175 to 270 between 1548 and 1703. Although the indigenous foot soldiers who inhabited Analco had outnumbered their Spanish allies from the start, migration of Zapotecs and other local indigenous groups to the barrio and intermarriage increased the barrio's population over the course of the colonial period.[38]

In the few decades that followed the establishment of the barrio of Analco, the "natives of Analco" won a series of royal decrees from the Real Audiencia in Mexico City, which recognized their status as "indios conquistadores," and secured for them a series of special privileges in recognition of their service to the Spanish Crown. In 1572, the Real Audiencia granted them exemption from tribute in exchange for voluntary services to Spanish residents of Villa Alta, a relationship that the Spaniards often abused.[39] In 1591, in response to Spanish abuses, the natives of Analco petitioned the Audiencia to reinforce their rights and privileges. The Audiencia issued a royal decree (*real provisión*) that prohibited the Spaniards of Villa Alta from forcing the natives of Analco to work against their will.[40] Other privileges recognized by the Audiencia included the right to be buried in the parochial church of Villa Alta, to be baptized in the baptismal font of the same church, and to carry the staff of office (*bara de justicia*) in Villa Alta. In exchange for these privileges, the indigenous conquerors were to provide special services to the local Spanish administration, which included the collection of tribute from the region's native population, and service as governors and municipal authorities in politically unstable or rebellious pueblos.[41]

In addition to these services, in the centuries that followed, the natives of Analco played an indispensable role in law enforcement and peacekeeping in the sierra, continuing to serve as a coercive occupation force under Spanish oversight and as midlevel legal and civil administrators. Their roles included deputy to the bailiff; transporters of prisoners from village jails to the prison in Villa Alta; messengers of orders and decrees to native cabildos; and interpreters, schoolmasters, prestigious witnesses, and spies.[42] Their conduct in these roles inspired a combination of respect, fear, and loathing among the local indigenous population, particularly since as spies and schoolmasters they were part of a larger colonial strategy of social control and eradication of native religious practices. These roles became especially important during the late seventeenth and early eighteenth centuries, when Spanish officials called on the natives of Analco to assist in squelching the uprisings in Villa Alta associated with the Tehuantepec rebellion of 1660, the Choapan uprising in 1684, and the Cajonos uprising in 1700.[43]

THE SWORD, THE PEN, AND PUBLIC PERFORMANCE: MAINTENANCE OF A PRIVILEGED IDENTITY

Legal vigilance, political instability, rebellion, and the Spanish campaign against idolatry in the Sierra Norte from the 1660s until the 1720s helped the Indian conquerors to maintain their privileged position. As I have discussed earlier in the book, the Church hierarchy and civil authorities were preoccupied to the point of obsession with idolatry in the district of Villa Alta. The indigenous conquerors of the barrio of Analco were keen readers of this situation and deployed a range of tactics in order to maintain their privileges, including public performance, coercion of local indigenous peoples, and, most important, recourse to the legal system. Throughout the late seventeenth and early eighteenth centuries, they turned to colonial courts and utilized Spanish discourses and legal rhetoric in order to play on Spanish fears of idolatry and rebellion, justify their continued role as keepers of regional peace and security, and distinguish themselves racially, ethnically, culturally, and politically from the local indigenous population.[44]

Ambivalent Conquest: The Fiesta of San Ildefonso

A late seventeenth-century conflict with the Zapotec pueblo of Lachirioag illustrates the legal and rhetorical efforts by the natives of Analco to define their collective identity against that of local indigenous pueblos. In January 1683, what appears at first glance to have been a turf war between the neighboring pueblos of Analco and Lachirioag eventually turned out to be a platform for the officials of Analco to distinguish themselves along the lines of ethnicity, culture, and power from the neighboring Zapotec pueblo. The case was provoked by the conduct of the Lachirioag natives during the fiesta of Villa Alta's patron saint, Ildefonso. Many of the pueblos of the district, including those of the Rincón region, Lachirioag, and Analco—participated in the fiesta of San Ildefonso in Villa Alta, which commemorated the conquest of the region. It was customary during the celebration for the natives of these pueblos to carry and play their drums and horns (*tambores y clarines*), musical instruments that were used in pre-Hispanic warfare. And although it was technically illegal for indigenous people of the sierra (with the exception of the natives of Analco) to carry firearms, the natives of Lachirioag appear to have broken this law in order to carry rifles in their procession to Villa Alta, and colonial officials appear to have looked the other way—at least until 1683.

The procession from Lachirioag to Villa Alta required passage through Analco to get to Villa Alta, and included men bearing arms and their staffs of office. The officials of Analco claimed that the presence of armed men among the natives of Lachirioag constituted an affront to the privilege of the indios conquistadores—exclusive among the region's Indians—to carry firearms. Furthermore, the officials of Analco interpreted the display of

Lachirioag's staffs of office in the confines of their territory as a challenge to the authority of Analco's officials to govern their own pueblo.[45] These complaints represented an effort by the officials of Analco to police not only their territory, but also the boundaries of their privileged collective identity. As a public celebration of the conquest, the fiesta of San Ildefonso was rife with symbolic meaning and provided an opportunity for the natives of Analco to reaffirm their status as Indian conquerors and reinforce the boundary that distinguished them from local Indians. Indeed, the actions of the natives of Lachirioag posed a symbolic threat to the Indian conquerors' privileged identity and to the region's established colonial order. As a celebration of the conquest, the procession of the feast day of San Ildefonso required the presence of a "vanquished opposite," a role that the natives of Lachirioag failed to perform by virtue of their public display of arms.[46]

For the natives of Analco, the procession provided an opportunity for the public performance of ethnic difference. It also lent ambivalence to the memory of the conquest itself. For Spaniards, the conquest of America represented military victory over "Indians." But the performance of the natives of Analco in the procession of San Ildefonso and their subsequent quarrel with the natives of Lachirioag made clear that the "Indian conquerors" did not view the world in terms of a simplistic opposition between "Indians" and "Spaniards." Rather, their performance reinforced an "indigenous perspective of ethnic heterogeneity," as the natives of Analco shared in the Spaniards' triumph and presented themselves as "ruler-subjects."[47]

In the course of their case against the pueblo of Lachirioag, the Indian conquerors defined themselves culturally against their indigenous neighbors and adversaries, whom they cast as frequent instigators of rebellion and unrest in the volatile Cajonos region. In their characterization of the natives of Lachirioag as rebellious, they made specific reference to Lachirioag's participation in the rebellion of 1660, thereby identifying the pueblo as a threat to regional peace. More important, however, they characterized the natives of Lachirioag as idolaters, pointing to the fact that many were currently jailed in the district prison on idolatry charges. Claims by the "Indian conquerors" that the natives of Lachirioag were known idolaters played on Spanish fears of the ambivalence of fiestas and processions performed by native peoples, specifically that they were a guise for idolatry.[48] Using the epithet of "idolater" in this context was a highly effective rhetorical strategy by the natives of Analco.

The rhetoric of idolatry and rebellion drew the boundary from the perspective of the colonizers between good and bad Indians, loyal vassals and the colonial "other." By contrast, the officials of Analco defined the residents of their barrio as "loyal vassals," "good Catholic Christians," and defenders of the Crown by virtue of their role in the military defense of Villa Alta during the 1660 uprising.[49] As I discussed in chapter 1, the gendered discourse of honor undergirded the distinction between "good" and "bad" Indians, rendering "good Indians" as masculine and (almost) Spanish, and "bad Indians" as feminine, childlike, and racially inferior.

Gender also infused the discourse of "conqueror" and "vanquished opposite." As Susan Kellogg and Pete Sigal have noted, pre-Columbian Mexica and Maya warriors (and more broadly, Mesoamerican warrior culture), like the Spanish conquistadors, "feminized" opponents in war, particularly opponents who were ultimately defeated.[50] By insisting on positioning the natives of Lachirioag as the "vanquished opposite," the natives of the barrio of Analco reinforced a highly masculine warrior identity for themselves, and a purportedly inferior, feminine identity for their neighbors. They also produced a gendered cleavage in indigenous identity: masculine "Indian conquerors" versus feminine "conquered Indians," who were also childlike "rebels" and "idolaters."

The rhetorical opposition between "loyalty to the Crown" versus "idolatry" and "rebellion" convinced the judge to decide in favor of the Indian conquerors and against the natives of Lachirioag. However, this decision did not ensure the privileges of the indigenous conquerors of Analco, nor did it represent a permanent recognition of their rights by the region's Spaniards. During the same year, the officials of Analco complained to the Audiencia of abuses visited on them by the Spaniards of Villa Alta. Their petition resulted in a royal decree issued in September 1683 that ordered those who had disregarded the special status of the Indian conquerors of Analco "to recognize the honors and privileges expressed in their legal titles, to cause them no further trouble, nor enter their barrio."[51]

Skillful use of the legal system thus afforded the natives of Analco a temporary victory in their power struggle with the district's Spaniards and other "Indians." These late seventeenth-century cases against the Zapotec pueblo of Lachirioag and the Spaniards of Villa Alta demonstrate that the Indian conquerors' privileged position resulted from constant legal and rhetorical work on two fronts, the first oriented toward halting Spanish challenges to their rights, and the second toward distinguishing themselves from the region's indigenous population.

Disciplining "Rebels" and "Idolaters"

The uprising in Choapan in 1684—one year after the legal disputes discussed above—justified the Spanish administration's maintenance of the privileges of the natives of Analco. Sixteen years later, the Cajonos region erupted in the most serious uprising that the district of Villa Alta had experienced since the conquest. The Cajonos uprising and the repression that followed proved a nightmare for the local indigenous population. As I discussed in chapter 2, it provided a political opportunity for the alcalde mayor and the secular Church hierarchy. Not surprisingly, it also was a boon for the privileged status of the natives of Analco. As was the case with the regional rebellion of 1660 and the Choapan uprising of 1684, the Spaniards of Villa Alta turned to their indigenous neighbors and allies in the barrio of Analco to help them restore law and order. In this regard, the Cajonos uprising contributed to the maintenance of the privileged collective identity of the natives of Analco, bolstering the military and legal work conducted during the previous decades. The violence and severity of the incident convinced the local Spaniards that they still needed the Indian conquerors for military defense and social control.

Following the Cajonos uprising, colonial civil and religious authorities deployed the natives of Analco to restore order in the region's pueblos de indios and participate in the extirpation campaign that followed. They stationed many as schoolmasters, following the logic that the Spanish language provided an important means of combating idolatry.[52] Andrés González, a *principal* from the barrio of Analco who spoke Spanish, taught the Spanish language and Christian doctrine in the Zapotec pueblo of Yatee in the years following the uprising. In addition to his duties as schoolmaster, he was also expected to report any suspicious or idolatrous conduct to Church officials in the Dominican convent in Villa Alta. The details of the case against him demonstrate the ways individual power brokers from Analco used the rhetoric of idolatry and the legal system to exercise political power, much as the officials of Analco had done in the service of collective power in the 1683 case against Lachirioag.[53] The case also demonstrates the hostility and tension that permeated the relationship between the Indian conquerors and the local indigenous population, and the persistence of the coercive role of the indigenous conquerors into the early eighteenth century.

The case begins with an accusation of idolatry by González against two men from Yatee who had been imprisoned in Villa Alta for idolatry following the Cajonos uprising. Because of their history as "idolaters," these men made easy targets. According to González, the two men entered the church when he and the community were praying and shouted, "First, there was the doctrine of the community [*Primero era la doctrina del común*]." The two men, backed by Yatee's village officials, denied the charges and countered with a case of their own. In their petition to the court, they presented a litany of abuses by González against their community, including adultery, corruption of children, abuse of power, extortion of money and services, interference in pueblo politics, desecration of municipal buildings, and theft of church property.[54]

In their complaints against him, the former "idolaters" from Yatee cast González as a "hispanized Indian [*indio ladino*]" who "knew how to write and talk to your majesty."[55] Their commentary betrayed a fear that González's linguistic skills and cross-cultural knowledge would win the Spanish magistrate's sympathy, thereby hurting the pueblo's case against the schoolmaster. But perhaps more important, they feared that González's literacy and acculturation would facilitate legal maneuvering by him that could be detrimental to their case.

The characterization of González as an indio ladino reveals the association of hispanized indigenous conquerors with colonial power, and highlights the fear and contempt that they inspired in the local population. The words also hint at the continued power that the Indian conquerors wielded in the region in the context of a perceived threat of idolatry and rebellion, and the considerable room for maneuver afforded them by the fears and insecurities of the Spanish ruling elite.

Proximity to "Spaniard" in Life and Death:
Burial in the Parochial Church of Villa Alta

Although the Cajonos Rebellion reminded the local Spanish administration of Villa Alta of the continued importance of the Indian conquerors, Bishop Angel Maldonado's antagonism toward the Dominican order in Villa Alta threatened to undermine the long-standing relationship between Spanish vecinos and the natives of Analco, based on services in exchange for privileges. In December 1703, Fray Bartolomé de Alcántara, official notary appointed by Bishop Maldonado in the *visita* (inspection) of the district of Villa Alta following the Cajonos Rebellion, compiled testimony and legal documents regarding a very special privilege reserved for the Indian conquerors of the barrio of Analco: burial in a designated nave of the parochial church of the Spanish district seat of Villa Alta. Alcántara's inquiry into this special privilege was part of a larger investigation ordered by Maldonado of Dominican administration of the district of Villa Alta.[56] As I discussed in chapter 2, Maldonado's curiosity was not disinterested; he was convinced of the misadministration of the district by the Dominicans, and he wanted to use the information produced during the investigation as evidence of Dominican negligence and wrongdoing, with an eye to replacing the sierra's Dominican priests with secular clergy.

The burial privileges reserved for the natives of Analco represented one of what Maldonado considered to be many irregularities in the Dominican administration of the sierra. According to the legal testimony compiled by Alcántara, the Dominican friars of Villa Alta had granted this privilege to the Indian conquerors and their descendants. Maldonado's investigation targeted the privilege for inquiry because it contradicted royal law concerning the legal distinction between the republic of Indians and the republic of Spaniards, and more specifically the separation among Spaniards, Indians, and castas in parish administration. Until the Bourbon Reforms, parishes and parish activities were separated officially by race, and the "principle of separation"[57] ideally extended from life into death. As a result, the natives of Analco had to produce the documentation that officially recognized their privilege, which Alcántara in turn recorded for Maldonado. What was remarkable about the compilation of documents was the apparent tenacity with which the natives of Analco defended this privilege against the Dominicans' tendency to ignore or forget it.

In 1638 and 1679 the Indian conquerors of the barrio of Analco complained to successive Dominican *visitadores* that the friars of Villa Alta had not respected the exclusive privilege of burial reserved for the natives of Analco in the parochial church. It appears that rather than denying burial in the church to the natives of Analco, in both instances, the friars had allowed unspecified "others" to be buried there, effectively diluting the exclusivity of the Indian conquerors' burial space. In both cases, the Dominican order mandated that on pain of a six-month suspension, the friars of Villa Alta should bury only the natives of Analco and their descendents "out of recognition and love for the brothers of the barrio of Analco."[58]

Christianity worked in tandem with the Iberian discourse of honor to produce a hegemonic code of conduct for native peoples in Spanish America. Christian burial represented a powerful symbol in this system of meaning. The privilege of burial in the Spanish parochial church of Villa Alta lent the Indian conquerors of Analco a degree of honor above that bestowed by Christian burial: proximity of their bodies to those of Spaniards, and a metaphorical identification of their community with that of their former comrades in arms. Their tenacious defense of this privilege was an effort to maintain the boundary that distinguished "conqueror" from "conquered," while blurring the line between "Spanish" and "Indian" conquistadors. Their petitions to the Dominican prelates represent claims to an identity somewhere in between Spanish racial categories: proximate to that of "Spaniard," and at significant distance from local "Indians."

The Threat of Administrative Change

The special status of the natives of Analco persisted through the early eighteenth century, thanks in part to the Cajonos uprising and the extirpation campaign that immediately followed, both of which justified their continued coercive role. But as demonstrated by Maldonado's inquiry into their privileged status, their utility as a coercive force was not sufficient to ensure their privileges. Military need had to be accompanied by legal vigilance in order to prevent the erosion of privilege.

This dynamic became clear once again in 1709 when the natives of Analco brought a case demanding that their privileges, especially their exemption from tribute, be respected by the colonial authorities of Villa Alta.[59] The petition they presented invoked their collective historical identity as Indian conquerors and their role as guarantors of regional security:

> We are descendents of the Mexican Indians [*indios mexicanos*] who joined the Spaniards to conquer these provinces and who settled in this barrio, and for these reasons were known as naborías of said Spaniards who reside in this Villa. In all of that time we have been continually attentive to the service of the King, our lord (may God keep him) that we have continued (and are ready to continue) to squelch the rebellions and uprisings that the pueblos of this district have committed, all at the

expense of our own meager wealth. We thus enjoy the right not to pay tribute as it declares in the royal decree . . . of 1589.[60]

In support of their claims, the natives of Analco presented a letter from Joseph Cardona, Dominican presbyter of the province of San Hipolito Martír de Oaxaca, and an official of the Inquisition. Cardona, who had spent "thirty years administering the holy sacraments in the district of Villa Alta," enumerated the privileges of the natives of Analco, which he claimed were widely recognized by the priests and friars of the region. Furthermore, he extolled the zealous participation of the natives of Analco in Bishop Maldonado's extirpation campaign following the Cajonos uprising. Finally, he noted the importance of the "naturales naborías del barrio de Analco," descendants of "indios mexicanos" in the maintenance of regional security post-Cajonos. If there was any sedition or rebelliousness in any pueblo of the region, claimed Cardona, a native of Analco was immediately appointed as governor of the troublesome pueblo.[61]

If they were so indispensable in matters of security, why did the Spaniards of Villa Alta attempt in 1709—nine short years after the Cajonos Rebellion—to ignore the widely recognized privileges of the descendants of the venerable Indian conquerors of the barrio of Analco and extract tribute from them? The character of Spanish administration in the district of Villa Alta was to blame. The year 1709 also happened to mark an administrative transition: a new alcalde mayor, Capitán Antonio de Miranda y Corona, took office in Villa Alta. As we saw in the introduction, the alcaldes mayores of Villa Alta were economic exploiters par excellence. During their four- or five-year terms, these men, who were appointed directly by the King, attempted to squeeze as much profit as possible from the lucrative trade in cochineal and textiles, the *repartimiento*, and Indian tribute.

Miranda y Corona replaced Diego de Rivera y Cotes, who had lent his considerable energies to Maldonado during the post-Cajonos extirpation campaign. As a result of the administrative turnover in 1709, the new alcalde mayor had little knowledge of local history or social relationships, and as a result may not have been aware of the long-standing privileges of the natives of Analco, or of their role in recent extirpation efforts. Or if he was aware of the historical role of the natives of Analco, he may have felt that he could get away with ignoring it. But given the importance of the participation of the natives of Analco in the post-Cajonos repression, once he was made aware through the testimony of Cardona and the presentation of the royal decrees that legitimized the Indian conquerors' claims, Miranda y Corona could do little other than to recognize the long-standing privileges of the natives of Analco and their recent contributions to regional security.[62] The descendants of the sierra's Indian conquerors thus warded off the diminution of their status threatened by change in local Spanish administration through an invocation of their coercive role and through the legal system.

DECLINE: BECOMING LOCAL INDIANS

During the middle and late eighteenth centuries, the status of the native conquerors of Analco eroded considerably. There were practical and political reasons for this. Increased political stability and a cooling of the war on idolatry during this period decreased their utility in matters of defense and social control. Further, their exemption from tribute impeded the push toward economic efficiency as the Bourbon kings attempted to squeeze as much revenue as possible out of the colonies during the second half of the eighteenth century.

Legal problems and sociocultural developments also contributed to the decline of the Indian conquerors. By the late eighteenth century, the natives of Analco appear to have lost the documents—the royal decrees—that secured their rights and privileges, a mishap that justified their mistreatment and exploitation by Villa Alta's Spaniards. But "lost" is probably a euphemism. It is highly likely that Spaniards stole the decrees, since throughout New Spain, Spaniards had the reputation for stealing and tampering with legal documents that belonged to indigenous individuals, groups, or pueblos, particularly when the documents contradicted their interests. Furthermore, migration of Indians from all over the district to Analco, and the intermarriage of these migrants with the Indian conquerors, diluted the ethnic identity on which their privileges were based.[63] Finally, a general hardening over time of Spanish racial attitudes toward indigenous groups and individuals, true for the colony as a whole, contributed to the demise of the Indian conquerors' special status. Their assertions of cultural superiority to the local Zapotecs no longer carried the weight that they had in the past.

Each of these factors appeared to play a role in two late attempts (in 1761 and 1774) by the Indian conquerors to defend their privileges in court. In the first case (with which we opened this chapter) the municipal authorities of Analco complained that local Spaniards had disrespectfully ignored the privileged status of the natives of Analco by attempting to collect tribute from them. They also complained that the Spanish magistrate no longer used them in the service of the administration of justice, preferring to use Spanish residents of Villa Alta instead.[64]

The authorities of Analco defended their privileges and exemption from tribute using a rhetoric of collective identity based on past deeds, particularly instances in which they had pacified the local population. In addition to the 1684 Choapan uprising and the 1700 Cajonos uprising, they referred to a number of other revolts in the pueblos of Lachixila, Yalalag, Guistepec, Yagavila, and Yojovi. "In all of these instances," they claimed, "we have conquered and remained victorious thanks to our Lord God and his saintly mother Mary who have favored us in so many valuable ways that we cannot enumerate them all in this petition because it would make it too long; so much has happened to us since the conquest of New Spain until the present."[65] In this nugget of legal testimony, the narrative of their history of military service folds into a wider performance of their Christian identity and a collective history guided by divine providence. The natives of Analco portray themselves as long suffering yet faithful, rewarded with conquest and victory through the intervention of Christ and Mary. How could the courts deny the special role of the natives of Analco, loyal allies of the glorious conquistadores, courageous warriors, and faithful Christians?

In an even more forceful attempt to prove Analco's continued loyalty and military utility and thereby defend the collective privileges of its residents, the cabildo of Analco submitted to the court a robust list of men from the community who would volunteer themselves and their sons "spontaneously as soldiers of your majesty without any motive except their honor."[66] In sum, their legal tactics and the emotive power of their rhetoric reveal a desperate attempt to hang on to privileges that were slipping through their fingers.

The Spanish magistrate responded to these grand claims of loyalty by demanding proof of their privileges and of the precise identities of the descendants of the Indian conquerors. He argued that since Indians from many local pueblos had migrated to Analco, they could therefore claim privileges to which they were not entitled. In the spirit of a good Bourbon-era administrator, he also argued that their exemption from tribute would hurt the royal coffers, and that he understood that the natives of Analco performed their services not in exchange for privileges, but voluntarily.[67] Perhaps the magistrate was suggesting that as loyal vassals and good Christians, the natives of Analco should not seek special privileges but should serve the Crown unconditionally.

Beyond the larger issue of exemption from tribute, the case also addressed the physical and racial boundaries that separated the Indian conquerors from their Spanish neighbors. The Spanish magistrate complained that the officials of Analco—in particular an alcalde named Juan Carpio—had chased the Villa Alta night patrol from their barrio. The alcalde argued that since the natives of Analco had always patrolled their own barrio, and the Villa Alta patrol had never before entered their jurisdiction, they had assumed that the Spanish patrol was a band of either thieves or vagabonds. The Spanish judge did not accept this explanation, claiming that the actions of the alcalde represented a contravention of royal justice.[68]

In yet another desperate attempt to hold on to the privileges afforded them as indigenous conquerors, eight men from the barrio of Analco singled themselves out from their community and claimed that they should be exempted from any erosion of their privileges given their direct descent from the indigenous conquerors of Tlaxcala. We never learn of the effect of their claim of particularity from their fellows and to Tlaxcalan identity, since the case ends with a mandate for further testimony on the matter.[69] However, in this context, the claim to Tlaxcalan identity hints at the persistent power of the category *Tlaxcalan*. The claim to Tlaxacalan identity may also have indicated the urgency felt by the residents of Analco to hold onto their privileges in the face of Spanish determination to forget or ignore them.

In a 1774 follow-up case regarding the privileges of the natives of Analco and the jurisdiction of the barrio's cabildo and civil patrol, the Spanish judge upheld the right of the natives of Analco to patrol their own community. But he rescinded the long-standing role of the Analco natives as night watchmen in Villa Alta. In stark contrast with the rhetoric of loyal vassalage and honor deployed by the natives of Analco, the prosecutor argued that the Spanish residents of Villa Alta could not have Indians patrolling their streets at night because of their "innate incapacities."[70]

Apparently, "race thinking" came to override the aspects of intimacy and interdependence that had in part characterized the long-term relationship of the Spaniards of Villa Alta to the Indian conquerors who lived in the barrio of Analco.[71] Although Spanish abuses of naborías had marred the relationship from the start, in practice, interdependence and the logic of services in exchange for privileges had mitigated the identity of the natives of Analco as Indians. At the very least, their coercive utility had served to distinguish them from the local population. Toward the end of the eighteenth century, the legal system that had upheld their privileges in the past recognized this distinction less frequently. Once the post-Cajonos extirpation campaign appeared to have more or less pacified and suppressed the "idolatrous" practices of the Zapotecs, Mixes, and Chinantecs of the Sierra Norte, the Spaniards of Villa Alta ceased to require the services that the natives of Analco had performed from the beginning of the colonial period, particularly in the realms of military defense and social control. As a result, the indios conquistadores' privileges—which had defined their power, status, and collective identity—disappeared. Without them, the indios conquistadores were nothing more than local Indians.

CONCLUSION

Notwithstanding these late colonial dynamics, for the better part of three centuries, the natives of Analco, alongside the descendants of their Spanish comrades in arms, formed part of the Sierra Norte's ruling elite. Rebellion, resistance, political autonomy, and illicit religious practices characterized the pueblos of the Sierra Norte well into the eighteenth century. In this context, the exigencies of regional security helped the Indian conquerors' role as military allies to evolve into one of guarantors of Spanish security. We must also acknowledge the skilled use of the colonial legal system on the part of the Analco natives as the other central factor in the maintenance of their privileges, given the Spanish tendency to abuse the relationship of services in exchange for privileges. Spanish reliance on coercion and indigenous recourse to the legal system therefore worked in tandem to maintain the privileged status of the sierra's indigenous conquerors and colonial control of the region. In this regard, the natives of Analco both inserted themselves and were co-opted into the sierra's colonial system. Unfortunately for them, once they had outlived their coercive role, the legal system no longer protected their privileged identity.

The decline of the status of the Indian conquerors of the sierra represents the confluence of political changes on the ground in the district of Villa Alta with Bourbon-era ideology concerning Spain's "Indian" subjects. Ilona Katzew situates the *casta* paintings of eighteenth-century New Spain, which articulated through visual and textual means a remarkable "taxonomy" of race mixture, in an Enlightenment culture of classification, categorization, difference, and hierarchy. Her analysis of the unpublished manuscript "Origen, costumbres, y estado presente de mexicanos y philipinos," written by the Spaniard Joaquín Antonio de Basarás y Garaygorta in 1763, points to a tendency among Bourbon-era Spanish elites to erase the ethnic and cultural distinctions among "Indians" in order to "underscore the difference between Indians and Spaniards."[72] Basarás and many of his contemporaries portrayed the native peoples of the Spanish Empire in a negative light, referring to their "customs" and "nature" in terms of "barbarism." As the boundaries among native ethnic groups dissolved and the distinction between Spaniards and Indians became starker in the ideology of the times, the middle ground occupied by native intermediary figures, both as groups (like the Indian conquerors) and as individuals, diminished. A colonial world without the mediating discourses of "indios ladinos," native "loyal vassals," "good and faithful Indians," "costumbre," and "Indian conquerors" could not persist in its old form. This symbolic order would be replaced through the crucible of violence by a new one at the center of which was the "nation."

Conclusion

This project began as a theoretical and historical examination of the role of native intermediaries in linking localities to colony-wide systems.[1] In the rewarding process of conducting historical research in Oaxaca, it became much more than that. The cultural and political landscape of Oaxaca foregrounded the intersection of state power, the politics of Indian identity, and forms of local rule. Through the tactics of cultural brokerage and the discourses of race, gender, ethnicity, community, and culture, native intermediaries negotiated an uneasy coexistence among indigenous semi-autonomy, an extractive and coercive economy, the evangelization project of the Catholic Church, and imperial politics.

Biculturalism and bifurcated legitimacy positioned native governors, priest's assistants, and legal agents at the porous boundary of two systems: a state system and a shadow system. Through the mediation of the *repartimiento* of cochinilla, service to the Church, and legal service to their pueblos, they acted as state makers. By preserving and, at times, renegotiating native forms of social and political organization, and defending local custom, native ritual, and electoral autonomy, they acted as gatekeepers. This double-edged role helps us to understand hegemony in terms of multi-layered hierarchies in which the state and native society constituted one framework, and hierarchies in native society itself—elites and commoners, caciques and *principales*, *cabeceras* and *sujetos*, and *parcialidades*—constituted others.

Through an ethnohistorical and interpretive methodology, this book has laid bare the "tactics" and rhetorical tools used by native intermediaries, parish priests, and Spanish magistrates in their struggles over forms of local rule. By looking outward from the realm of micropolitics to that of macropolitics, we can see "an ideological edifice under construction"[2] as native and Spanish brokers struggled over political power, economic resources, and souls. Native brokers often used the rhetorical framework provided by the colonizers to struggle for power in native society. By deploying the discourses of "sedition," "idolatry," criminality, "loyalty," "ladino," "cacique," and "Indian conqueror," they shaped, reproduced, and reinforced colonial categories, making clear the reciprocity of state-society relations. Their rhetorical work helps us to see political culture—the symbols, values, and norms that link individuals to wider political communities—in the making. Present-day struggles over *costumbre* and the beatification of the "martyrs of Cajonos" points to the salience of this political culture over the *longue durée*.[3]

But the durability of political culture in Oaxaca does not imply an absence of dynamism or of change over time. During the period under study, from 1660 to 1810, we see concentrated engagement and confrontation in the Sierra Norte between native and Spanish brokers, clashes born of state and Church projects of centralization and cultural homogenization, and of native resistance and accommodation. Following native uprisings in 1660 and 1684, the Spanish magistrates of Villa Alta sought to tighten their control of native politics and economic production by interfering in pueblo elections. During the same time, the Church intensified its war on idolatry. These tensions erupted in violence in 1700 in the Cajonos region.

The aftermath of the Cajonos Rebellion during the first half of the eighteenth century provided a political opening for a reinvigoration of Church and state efforts at centralization, most pointedly for the parish reform of Bishop Angel Maldonado. At the same time, a native population boom put new pressure on land, resources, and social and political structures. By fragmenting and recomposing *cacicazgo* and pueblo lands, native intermediaries in cabeceras and larger pueblos attempted to incorporate neighboring pueblos into their territory and political orbit, while native elites in sujetos and smaller settlements struggled to maintain or expand their land and independence. A near doubling of the number of parishes and parish priests points to the fruition of the Church's efforts and the success of the advocacy of native leadership in would-be cabeceras.

The imperial objective of cultural and ethnic homogenization complemented that of political centralization. Following the 1660 rebellion, the *alcalde mayor* imposed a dichotomy on the native elites of the sierra. They were either "loyal vassals" or "seditious subjects." Through the crucible of the war on idolatry and the Cajonos Rebellion, Church and civil authorities forced the Zapotec, Mixe, and Chinantec peoples of the sierra into the binary categories of "idolater" and "good and faithful Indian." During the late eighteenth century, Bourbon administrators sought to flatten the native social hierarchy that had exempted principales from labor in the silver mines of the Cajonos and Rincón regions. Bourbon attempts to homogenize the sierra's native population intensified as the alcaldes mayores, with the help of the Audiencia, increasingly disregarded the privileged identity of the sierra's "indios conquistadores" in favor of the category "Indian." Over the colonial period, and especially during the second half, through Church and state projects, the multiethnicity and social hierarchy of the sierra gave way to an officially imposed "Indian" identity. Michel Foucault has argued that state production of identities—at once totalizing and individuating—constitutes a central aspect of "governmentality": the process by which states become modern.[4] By making principales, Zapotecs, Chinantecs, Mixes, and Mexicano conquistadors into "Indians," the Bourbon state facilitated its efforts to extract resources from and restrict the political agency of its native subjects.

But turning a plurality of native peoples into Indians was fraught with ambivalence and contradictions, in large part because the colonial state— especially under the Bourbons—simultaneously sought to transform native peoples into pale imitations of Spaniards. The Bourbons reanimated long-standing efforts to hispanize native peoples through Christian education and the Spanish language. Yet their commitment to maintaining the hierarchy between Spaniards and Indians on which colonialism was based undercut efforts at acculturation, a contradiction that Carolyn Dean calls the "colonizer's quandary."[5]

These twin impulses—the reflex to see the world in terms of "Spaniard" and "Indian" and the "civilizing" mission to acculturate—made the Bourbons hostile on principle to the people who mediated between Spanish and Indian worlds. Bourbon efforts to close the space for cultural brokerage hampered Spain's ability to rule and to mitigate the effects of its extractive and absolutist political economy. The Bourbons sought to eliminate any obstacles to their squeeze on native pueblos. They did not anticipate that native pueblos and their leadership might bite back. In this regard, the "colonizer's quandary" turned out to be the Bourbon's "blind spot."

Despite Bourbon "race thinking,"[6] a heterogeneous indigenous identity did not go away in the district of Villa Alta. Parcialidad organization, native ritual, local custom, and monolingualism persisted as the framework of the region's shadow system. What was the nature of this system? Scholars of the Andes have argued that during the colonial period, native Andeans transformed the Spanish category of "Indian" into the foundation of an anticolonial ideology that cut across ethnic lines, thereby creating a sub-terranean "racial consciousness" that subverted the colonial system.[7] The political economy of the Andes shaped a different colonial society, how-ever, than that of the Sierra Norte. Labor drafts and migration loosed native Andeans from their local moorings and facilitated the creation of new identities that crosscut locality. By contrast, in the district of Villa Alta, linguistic and geographical divisions among Zapotec, Mixe, and Chi-nantec peoples trumped a "racial consciousness." That does not neces-sarily mean that native identities were constrained by the boundaries of the pueblo or subregion. In the 1688 campaign against the alcalde mayor led by Felipe de Santiago and Joseph de Celis, we see a range of shifting alliances at the elite level. Yet despite the regional solidarities that native intermedi-aries forged during the political struggle for electoral autonomy of the 1680s and 1690s, and during the Cajonos Rebellion, these movements were not expressly anticolonial: native elites and commoners directed their resistance toward local representatives of colonial authority rather than the colonial system writ large.

Rather than the expression of an "anticolonial ideology," the shadow system in the Sierra Norte of Oaxaca bears greater structural resemblance to the "unsanctioned domain" described by Laura Lewis in her analysis of power, witchcraft, and caste in colonial Mexico. Lewis identifies two trajec-tories of power in colonial Mexico, characterized by a "sanctioned domain" that was culturally Spanish and Christian, and expressed institutionally by the Church and the colonial legal system, and an "unsanctioned domain" that was Indian and characterized by witchcraft and healing. These two domains penetrated one another as Indians sought redress in court for grievances caused by Spaniards, and Spaniards sought healing from indigenous curers in an effort to escape the "magic" of Indians, Africans, and castas who poisoned or cursed them.[8] In my analysis of Villa Alta, like Lewis's "unsanctioned domain," the shadow system constituted a parallel set of social networks and cultural logics that coexisted with and interpenetrated the "sanctioned domain."

In the case of Villa Alta, the colonial state (and Church), on the one hand, and the shadow system, on the other, provided native intermediaries with two trajectories of power. Each constituted a resource for political and cultural struggle and for accommodation and resistance to colonialism. The two systems shaped one another, as magistrates took local custom into account in deciding pueblo conflicts, and native parcialidades used Spanish discourses to discredit their rivals. In many regards, both systems continue to provide a resource for native brokers in their negotiations with the Mexican state to the present day.

What kind of "late flowering" colonial society did native intermediaries, through recourse to the state and shadow system, coconstruct in the district of Villa Alta from 1660 to 1810? In short, they helped to build a society in which they were indispensable. What has made Villa Alta and indeed much of Oaxaca governable from the colonial period to the present has been a space for negotiation, a space produced and maintained by native intermediary figures. A remarkable plurality of indigenous municipalities, the most by far of any state in Mexico, is one of Oaxaca's most notable colonial legacies, and has produced a highly exaggerated localism. The only way that this decentralized political structure has been able to function has been through cultural brokerage and political negotiation. The work of native intermediary figures in Oaxaca's ethnolinguistic regions may help to explain the largely peaceful transition from colonialism to independence, political continuities in the shift from colonialism to "liberalism," and general political stability over time. Stability should not imply, however, that the people of Oaxaca have been "reactionary" and "passive" in the face of political crisis and change, as has been suggested by the "Black legend of Oaxaca."[9] Stability has been achieved through conflict and negotiation.

In her study of postindependence Oaxaca from 1812 to 1825, Karen Caplan argues that Oaxaca's new state government had to be flexible in order to maintain a governable population. Recognition of the heterogeneity of indigenous identities represented a key strategy in Oaxaca's hegemonic order. During the nineteenth century, the state of Oaxaca respected indigenous custom even though it was at odds with the liberal project of Mexican state makers. The patriarch of Mexican liberalism, Benito Juárez, himself Zapotec, claimed that the maintenance of custom in Oaxaca was both "ancient and beneficial." Official recognition of the diversity of native custom ensured that the legacy of liberalism in Oaxaca would be different from other parts of Mexico, as Oaxaca's indigenous communities through political negotiation maintained communal lands and local autonomy.[10]

Through local struggles in the colonial and national periods, native intermediaries have shaped a tension that remains at the heart of Mexican nationhood: multiethnicity versus *indigenismo*. Indeed, the "Indian question"—the identity of native peoples and whether or how to incorporate them into the body politic—has been central to colonial and modern state formation in Mexico and in much of Latin America.[11] The question emerged at the inception of the colonial period, as Spanish conquistadors and native elites tried to fit each other into their respective worldviews. After the early seventeenth century, Spaniards perceived and portrayed their native subjects—even the native nobility—in an increasingly pejorative light. In particular, the failures of the spiritual conquest and the abandoned efforts to create a mestizo nobility from the unions of Spanish conquerors and native noblewomen augured a shift in Spanish perceptions of native peoples from "civilized" to "barbaric." These changing perceptions shaped the form of Spanish rule, as evidenced by Bourbon measures to eradicate Indian custom and language.

The displacement of ethnic and status difference at the symbolic level by the category "Indian" over the course of the colonial period has had significant effects on postcolonial Mexico. The enduring struggle over the meaning of *Indian* has produced a symbolic framework with which native peoples have had to contend in their dealings with the Mexican state. At the dawn of Mexican independence, José María Morelos opened a forking path with his radical vision of agrarian reform and a raceless Mexico in which there would be no *indios*, *castas*, or *negros*, but only *americanos*. Morelos's vision died with him, and Mexican state makers have chosen to maintain the distinction between Indians and Mexicans at the level of state policy while incorporating Indians at the rhetorical level as the symbolic heart of the nation. Yet indigenismo has had unintended consequences. As in the colonial Andes, in the Mexico of the twentieth and twenty-first century, "Indian" identity has galvanized resistance to the state as much as it has allowed state makers to achieve hegemony. The mobilization and appropriation of the voice of "Indian" Mexico by the Zapatista National Liberation Army provides but one example of this strategic essentialism.[12]

The shadow cast by colonialism in Mexico's largely "peripheral" and indigenous regions has proven dark and enduring. The fact that the "martyrs" of Cajonos face possible canonization whereas the "rebels" of Cajonos remain fated to infamy and obscurity speaks to this powerful legacy. Can today's native intermediary figures shift the terms of debate and move "Indian" Mexico toward a democratic, economically redistributive, and multiethnic nationhood?

As this book goes to press, the people of Oaxaca are suffering through a period of intense civil turmoil. A popular uprising born of an alliance between the state teacher's union and the Popular Assembly of the Peoples of Oaxaca (Asamblea Popular de los Pueblos de Oaxaca, or APPO)—an alliance brokered with the help of the Zapatistas—in response to decades of political violence, state repression of popular initiatives, the exploitation of indigenous peoples and their cultures and lands, and state neglect of schools and other public services, has riveted the nation. The APPO, which virtually took over Oaxaca City during the summer of 2006, has taken its case to the nation's capital (Mexico City) and the United Nations, and has demanded the resignation of Oaxaca's governor, Ulises Ruíz, to no avail thus far. In October of 2006, President Vicente Fox sent federal forces to Oaxaca to restore order, and as a result, the conflict intensified. On 4 December, three days after he was inaugurated, Mexico's new president, Felipe Calderón, arrested the APPO leadership, who only days earlier had come to Mexico City to negotiate in good faith with the Fox government. Meanwhile, other APPO sympathizers, suspected sympathizers, and sometimes innocent bystanders continued to be detained, beaten, imprisoned, and tortured by state authorities. By mid-December, some observers, such as the internationally acclaimed Zapotec artist Francisco Toledo, warned that Oaxaca teetered on the brink of civil war. Although a veneer of calm has returned to the city, sporadic violence, detentions, and repression continue. Claims to "pluriethnicity" by the Mexican state ring hollow in the face of state repression of APPO's multiethnic grassroots mobilization.

In the midst of this conflict, a popular assembly that claimed to speak on behalf of the native communities of the Sierra Norte circulated a statement, which arrived in my e-mail account in Bozeman, Montana—in English. The "Declaration of Guelatao," penned by the Assembly of the Zapoteco, Mixe, and Chinanteco Peoples of the Sierra Juárez, Oaxaca, on 19 November 2006, demanded "a profound transformation of Oaxaca with the goal of resolving the unanswered needs, in which our peoples, marginalized and forgotten, find themselves." The assembly demanded "the departure of the federal forces from Oaxaca, the demilitarization of the communities of the Sierra Norte, the release of political prisoners, the return alive of the disappeared, the cancellation of arrest warrants, respect for the autonomy of the university and the cessation of all kinds of aggression toward the popular movement of Oaxaca." It remains to be seen how this assembly, and others like it, will work with their popular bases to mobilize indigenous identities and form multiethnic alliances in support of demands and political claims in the Sierra Norte and "Indian" Mexico of the Calderón era and beyond.

Notes

PREFACE

1. Simpson, *Many Mexicos*.
2. Díaz Couder, "Lenguas indígenas," 149.
3. See, e.g., the synthesis of indigenous relations with Latin American states from the colonial period to the present in Stavenhagen, *Derecho indígena y derechos humanos*.
4. Analyses of the cultural and political roles of caciques and gamonales can be found in Becker, *Setting the Virgin on Fire*; Lomnitz-Adler, *Exits from the Labyrinth*; and Poole, *Unruly Order*.
5. The relationship of indigenous communities to Latin American nation-states has been a central topic of debate among Latin America scholars. One argument is that the struggles between Indians and institutions of the nation-state have proven crucial to the definition of indigenous ethnic identity and the nation. See Smith, *Guatemalan Indians and the State*; and Urban and Sherzer, *Nation-States and Indians*. Another trend studies the relationship between local political cultures and state formation in Latin America, particularly in Mexico and Peru. In these studies, the focus is not on "Indians," but on "peasants" or "popular culture." See Mallon, *Peasant and Nation*; and Joseph and Nugent, *Everyday Forms of State Formation*.
6. Maybury-Lewis, *Politics of Ethnicity*.
7. Controversy has surrounded Rigoberta Menchú Tum since anthropologist David Stoll challenged the veracity of her widely read autobiography. Stoll's work, itself controversial, unleashed a torrent of academic and popular debate concerning the popular nature of the Guatémalan revolutionary movement, the politics of identity, storytelling, "truth" claims, and anthropological projects. See Burgos-Debray, *I Rigoberta Menchú*; Stoll, *Rigoberta Menchú*; Wilson, "Challenge to the Veracity"; and Grandin and Goldman, "Bitter Fruit." For an

insightful discussion of contemporary Bolivian politics and the contested nature of Evo Morales's "Indian" identity, see Guillermoprieto, "New Bolivia?"

8. I maintain the anonymity of the community in question in order to protect the identity of the primary actors since some critical issues in the dispute remain unresolved and others are bitterly contested.

9. Nandy, *Intimate Enemy*; Comaroff and Comaroff, *Ethnography and the Historical Imagination*; Comaroff and Comaroff, *Of Revelation and Revolution*, vols. 1 and 2; Bhabha, *Location of Culture*.

10. Spivak, "Can the Subaltern Speak?"

11. Stern, "Feudalism, Capitalism, and the World System."

12. Daniels and Kennedy, *Negotiated Empires*.

13. Notable books in this vein include Rubin, *Decentering the Regime*; Overmyer-Velázquez, *Visions of the Emerald City*; and Stephen, *Zapotec Women*.

INTRODUCTION

1. William Taylor ("Between Global Process and Local Knowledge") articulated this question and situated it as a central issue in the historiography of colonial Latin America. He suggested that intermediary figures might provide an answer and called on young historians to pursue them as a subject of study.

2. Taylor, *Drinking, Homicide and Rebellion*; Stern, *Rebellion, Resistance and Consciousness*; Gosner, *Soldiers of the Virgin*; Schroeder, *Native Resistance*; Patch, *Maya Revolt and Revolution*; Van Young, *Other Rebellion*.

3. One of the most influential of these works is Mignolo, *Darker Side of the Renaissance*.

4. For the case of Mexico, the seminal works include Gibson, *Aztecs under Spanish Rule*; Farriss, *Maya Society*; García Martínez, *Pueblos de la sierra*; Lockhart, *Nahuas after the Conquest*; Restall, *Maya World*; and Terraciano, *Mixtecs of Colonial Oaxaca*. For the case of the Andes, see Stern, *Peru's Indian Peoples*; Spalding, *Huarochirí*; Larson, *Cochabamba*, 1st ed.

5. Eric Wolf (*Sons of the Shaking Earth*, 233–56) characterizes the itinerant merchants, muleteers, and liminal people of Mesoamerica as the "power seekers" by virtue of their lack of rootedness in native communal structures or bonds of reciprocity; Steve Stern (*Peru's Indian Peoples*) and Karen Spalding (*Huarochirí*) argue that the intensity of the mining economy created a class society in which *kurakas* (native elites) used their intermediary position to exploit the labor and resources of their communities. Stern characterizes their position in terms of the "tragedy of success." Merrell (*Into the American Woods*) portrays Andrew Montour, a *métis* interpreter and go-between, as a tragic figure, destroyed by the contradictions of his bicultural identity. For a broader, more complex, perspective that marks a departure from earlier narratives about native intermediaries in colonial Latin America, see Ares Queija and Gruzinski, *Entre dos mundos*. See also Alida C. Metcalf's pathbreaking *Go-betweens and the Colonization of Brazil*.

6. Paz, *Labyrinth of Solitude*, 65–88.

7. Ibid., 79.

8. Ibid., 86.

9. Díaz, *Conquest of New Spain*, 85–87.

10. Restall, *Maya Conquistador*; Restall, *Seven Myths*.

11. Karttunen, *Between Worlds*, 1–23.

12. Restall, *Seven Myths*, 86.

13. Townsend, *Malintzin's Choices*, 55–84.

14. See Susan Kellogg's masterful synthesis of the precolonial and colonial history of indigenous women; Kellogg, *Weaving the Past*, 3–89.

15. For a narrative of the violent and conflict-ridden sixteenth century in Yucatan, see Clendinnen, *Ambivalent Conquests*.

16. My summary of Chi's career in the preceding paragraphs is based on the chapter that Frances Karttunen devotes to him in *Between Worlds* (84–114).

17. Ibid.

18. Richter, "Cultural Brokers," 40–67, 41.

19. Ibid., 41.

20. De Certeau, *Practice of Everyday Life*, xiv–xix, 30–40.

21. Richter, "Cultural Brokers," 41.

22. Ibid.

23. Adorno, "Indigenous Ethnographer"; Adorno, "Arms, Letters and the Native Historian"; Adorno, *Guáman Poma*.

24. In his *Maya Revolt and Revolution*, Robert Patch characterizes Spanish colonialism in Yucatan as a constellation of "colonial bargains" between the Maya and their colonial overlords.

25. MacLeod, "Some Thoughts on the Pax Colonial," 141, 138, 130.

26. See, e.g., Taylor, *Drinking, Homicide and Rebellion*; Stern, *Rebellion, Resistance and Consciousness*; Gosner, *Soldiers of the Virgin*; Patch, *Maya Revolt and Revolution*; Schroeder, *Native Resistance*; Van Young, *Other Rebellion*.

27. MacLeod, "Some Thoughts on the Pax Colonial," 139.

28. Borah, *Justice by Insurance*.

29. Lomnitz-Adler, *Exits from the Labyrinth*, 261–81; Lewis, *Hall of Mirrors*; Silverblatt, *Modern Inquisitions*.

30. Silverblatt (*Modern Inquisitions*, 17) borrows this term from Hannah Arendt in order to move us beyond the "narrow, nineteenth-century connotations" of "racism."

31. See R. Douglas Cope's discussion of the origins and history of the caste system and his synthesis of early scholarship on the matter; Cope, *Limits of Racial Domination*, 13–26.

32. For the case of colonial Mexico, Magnus Mörner (*Race Mixture*), and Robert McCaa, Stuart Schwartz, and Arturo Grubessich ("Race and Class in Colonial Latin America") presumed that the caste system mirrored the actual principles of social organization on the ground. John Chance and William Taylor

("Estate and Class") countered that the organizing principles of colonial society changed over time, and that class became more important than race by the end of the colonial period. In his study of Antequera, Chance (*Race and Class*) posited that there was a struggle between different principles of rank at any given historical moment. Rodney Anderson ("Race and Social Stratification") argues against an either race or class approach, and for consideration of a multiplicity of factors.

33. Patricia Seed helped to reframe the question of racial hierarchy by asking how racial categories were perceived, to what extent these perceptions were shared, whether the caste system was hegemonic or not, and how "social race" was constructed. See Seed and Rust, "Estate and Class"; Seed, "Social Dimensions of Race." In this vein, the following works argue that blacks, Indians, and castas did not internalize the *sistema de castas*, but rather intermarried and formed social networks that transcended racial categories: Palmer, *Slaves of the White God*; Carroll, *Blacks in Colonial Veracruz*; and Cope, *Limits of Racial Domination*.

34. Carmagnani, *Regreso de los dioses*; Bennett, *Africans in Colonial Mexico*.

35. Cahill, "Colour by Numbers."

36. Chance, *Conquest of the Sierra*, 125.

37. Lomnitz-Adler, *Exits from the Labyrinth*, 264.

38. Matthew and Oudijk, *Indian Conquistadors*; Weber, *Bárbaros*.

39. See, e.g., Warren and Jackson, *Indigenous Movements*.

40. Kellogg, "Back to the Future."

41. Immanuel Wallerstein (*Modern World System*) coined the terms *core* and *periphery* as part of his influential world systems theory. As Steve Stern has pointed out, Latin American dependency theorists had elaborated similar theories (of greater complexity) well prior to Wallerstein's formulation. For a thorough review of the *dependista* literature and a critique of Wallerstein, see Stern, "Feudalism, Capitalism, and the World System."

42. Altman, "Reconsidering the Center," 55.

43. The literature on the repartimiento in Spanish America is extensive. For a general study of New Spain, see Pastor, "Repartimiento de mercancías." For the case of Oaxaca, see Hamnett, *Politics and Trade*; Romero Frizzi, *Economía y vida de los españoles*; Baskes, "Coerced or Voluntary?"; Baskes, *Indians, Merchants, and Markets*; Romero Frizzi, *Sol y la cruz*; and Chance, *Conquest of the Sierra*.

44. Baskes, "Coerced or Voluntary?"; Baskes, *Indians, Merchants, and Markets*.

45. Hamnett, *Politics and Trade*, 16.

46. Amy Turner Bushnell ("Gates, Patterns, and Peripheries") characterizes the Sierra Norte of Oaxaca as an "internal periphery" in New Spain.

47. Romero Frizzi, *Sol y la cruz*, 61.

48. Romero Frizzi y Vásquez Vásquez, "Memoria y Escritura," 397; Oudijk, *Historiography of the Bénizáa*, 224–25. Oudijk draws these conclusions from his study of the *lienzos* of the Sierra Zapotec pueblos of Tiltepec and Tabaa.

49. Ibid., 10–11, 192–229.

50. Beals, *Ethnology of the Western Mixe*, 6–7.

51. Lipp, *Mixe of Oaxaca*.

52. Dalton, *Breve historia de Oaxaca*, 27.

53. Rendon, *Diversificación de las lenguas zapotecas*.

54. Chance, *Conquest of the Sierra*, 13–14, 16–20. Gerhard, *Guide to the Historical Geography of New Spain*, 367–73.

55. Gerhard (*Guide to the Historical Geography of New Spain*, 370) and Chance (*Conquest of the Sierra*, 62–63) both provide figures for the Spanish population of the district seat of Villa Alta.

56. Chance, *Conquest of the Sierra*, 62.

57. Ibid., 13–14.

58. Hamnett, *Politics and Trade*; Chance, *Conquest of the Sierra*.

59. Chance, *Conquest of the Sierra*, 159.

60. Lomnitz-Adler (*Exits from the Labyrinth*) coins the term *central place hierarchy* as one of his concepts for the study of regional culture. He argues that national and regional economic core-periphery designations were overlaid by local political, cultural, and economic spatial hierarchies, which combined to form a local "central place hierarchy."

61. Taylor, "Between Global Process and Local Knowledge." With regard to historical anthropology, my book owes a profound debt to the founders of that tradition. See Comaroff and Comaroff, *Ethnography and the Historical Imagination*.

62. For the case of the Andes, see Jacobsen and Aljovín de Losada, *Political Cultures in the Andes*. For an exemplary study for the case of Mexico, see Guardino, *Time of Liberty*. See also Cañeque, *The King's Living Image*.

63. Gramsci, *Selections from the Prison Notebooks*, 12.

64. Roseberry, "Hegemony and the Language of Contention."

65. Scott, *Weapons of the Weak*; Scott, *Domination and the Arts of Resistance*.

66. Lewis, *Hall of Mirrors*.

67. Espejo-Ponce Hunt and Restall, "Work, Marriage, and Status," 233.

68. Sousa, "Women and Crime in Colonial Oaxaca."

69. Chance, *Conquest of the Sierra*.

70. Dehouve, *Quand les banquiers étaient des saints*; García Martínez, *Pueblos de la sierra*.

71. Chance, *Conquest of the Sierra*, 62.

72. Romero Frizzi, *Sol y la cruz*, 195–206.

73. Díaz-Polanco, *Fuego de la inobediencia*.

74. Zeitlin, *Cultural Politics in Colonial Tehuantepec*, 198.

1. "LOYAL VASSAL," "SEDITIOUS SUBJECT"

1. Accounts of the rebellion of 1660 can be found in Díaz-Polanco, *Fuego de la inobediencia*; Romero Frizzi, *Sol y la cruz*, 195–206; and Zeitlin, *Cultural Politics in Colonial Tehuantepec*, 168–202.

2. See Zeitlin, *Cultural Politics in Colonial Tehuantepec*, 172–84; and the essays in Díaz-Polanco, *Fuego de la inobediencia*.

3. Díaz-Polanco and Burguete, "Sociedad colonial y rebelión indígena," 31–39.

4. Chance, *Conquest of the Sierra*, 110.

5. AGI México 600, fol. 109. Letter to the viceroy dated 29 October 1660 in which the bishop of Puebla, Palafox, argues that the practices of the alcaldes mayores offended divine law and imperiled the administration of the empire. This letter echoes three others that Bishop Palafox penned to the viceroy dated 24 June 1641, 25 July 1642, and 25 September 1642, in which he recommends abolition of the *alcaldías mayores*. AGI México 600, fols. 1–4v, fols. 11–11v, fol. 32.

6. Zeitlin, *Cultural Politics in Colonial Tehuantepec*, 172–84.

7. Chance, *Conquest of the Sierra*, 110.

8. AGI México 600, Copía del despacho hecho al Sr. Virey sobre el estado de las provincias de yndios del Obispado de Oaxaca, fols. 476–81.

9. Adorno, "Images of Indios Ladinos in Early Colonial Peru," 235.

10. For a discussion of the meanings of *ladino* in the Andean case, see ibid. For the Guatemalan case, see Matthew, "Náhuatl y identidad mexicana."

11. For petitions from Sierra Norte caciques, see AGN Indios, vol. 30, exp. 323, fols. 297–97v (1690); AGN Indios, vol. 12, part 1, exp. 250, fol. 158v (1635); AGN Indios, vol. 12, part 1, exp. 186, fol. 119 (1635); AGN Indios, vol. 27, exp. 26, fol. 11 (1680); AGN Indios, vol. 9, exp. 72, fols. 39–39v (1618); AGN Indios, vol. 9, exp. 73, fol. 39v (1618); AGN Indios, vol. 9, exp. 74, fols. 39v–40 (1618); AGN Indios, vol. 9, exp. 81, fol. 43 (1618); AGN Indios, vol. 14, exp. 21, fols. 21v–22; AGN Indios, vol. 30, exp. 387, fols. 355–55v (1690); AGN Indios, vol. 30, exp. 339, fols. 306v–7 (1690); AGN Indios vol. 7, exp. 270, fol. 134v (1618); AGN Indios, vol. 42, exp. 168, fols. 209v–10 (1719).

12. Tavárez, "Invisible Wars."

13. AVA Criminal, exp. 61 (1688), "Contra Joseph de Celis por agitar al pueblo."

14. Chance, *Conquest of the Sierra*, 98, 117, 136.

15. AGPEO, leg. 6, exp. 9 (1684), "Antequera: Autos y diligencias hechas sobre el socorro que se envió al alcalde mayor de la Villa Alta." This document outlines the events surrounding the Choapan uprising, the request on the part of the alcalde mayor of Villa Alta for military backup from the alcalde mayor of Antequera, and the actions taken by Antequera's civil authorities, which included the deployment of militias to the Sierra Norte.

16. Adorno, *Guáman Poma*; Adorno, "Indigenous Ethnographer"; Adorno, "Arms, Letters and the Native Historian"; Seed, " 'Failing to Marvel.' "

17. AGN Indios, vol. 28, exp. 205–6, fols. 172v–74 (1685), "Vuestra Excelencia manda continue por aora en el oficio de gobernador del pueblo de Santo Domingo Latani de la Jurisdicción de la Villa Alta Don Miguel de Zarate por ser de satisfacción del Alcalde Mayor de la jurisdicción."

18. AGN Indios, vol. 30, exp. 322, fols. 294–96v (1690), "Para que los gobernadores

alcaldes electores y principales de la jurisdicción de la Villa Alta prosedan a sus elecciones con livertad sinque el Alcalde mayor, sus thenientes ni otras personas se lo ympidan executando todo lo demas que por este despacho se manda."

19. For a detailed ethnohistorical study of the indigenous cabildo, see Haskett, *Indigenous Rulers*.

20. I have borrowed this very useful term ("shadow government") from Robert Stephen Haskett. See Haskett, "Indian Town Government."

21. Baskes, "Coerced or Voluntary?"; Romero Frizzi, *Sol y la cruz*; Chance, *Conquest of the Sierra*.

22. Chance, *Conquest of the Sierra*, 147.

23. AGN General de Parte, vol. 16, exp. 207, fols. 185v–86 (1688), "Se manda a la justicia mas cercana del partido de la Villa Alta de San Ildefonso notifique a Don Juan Manuel de Quiroz alcalde mayor de ella comparezca en esta corte dentro de veinte dias contados de la notificacion dexando persona que administre justicia debaxo de las penas que se expresan."

24. AVA Civil, exp. 27 (1690), "Real Provisión para que se le presten los servicios necesarios para desempeñar su función al alcalde mayor, Juan Manuel Quiroz." The title of this document is somewhat misleading. The document in the folder is a legal dispute brought by the municipal governments of Yatzona, Yahuio, and other pueblos near the town of Villa Alta against the alcalde mayor. Among the legal documents is a *real provisión* dated 20 December 1689 that orders the alcalde mayor, Quiroz, to compensate the plaintiffs for their goods and services.

25. AVA Civil, leg. 5, exp. 3 (1698), "Real Provisión para que Don Felipe de Santiago de San Juan Yatzona [?] reales provisiones pertenecientes [?]," fols. 2–3. The title page of this expediente is in marginal condition, with many holes and washed out ink. In this document, Santiago, Celis, Martín, and Martín are identified by native witnesses and Spanish officials as the organizers of this campaign against the intereference of Quiroz in village elections.

26. Lockhart, *Nahuas after the Conquest*; Restall, *Maya World*. Kevin Terraciano (*Mixtecs of Colonial Oaxaca*) presents a different picture of native identity in the Mixtec region of Oaxaca. In Mixtec-language documents, Mixtec people refer to themselves as *ñudzahui*, or "rain people," pointing to a sense of ethnic identity that transcended the individual village.

27. Taylor, *Drinking, Homicide and Rebellion*.

28. AVA Civil, exp. 27 (1690), "Real Provisión para que se le presten los servicios necesarios para desempeñar su función al alcalde mayor, Juan Manuel Quiroz." This document encompasses these three orders by the Audiencia.

29. AVA Civil, leg. 5, exp. 3 (1698), "Real Provisión para que Don Felipe de Santiago de San Juan Yatzona [?] reales provisiones pertenecientes [?]." This case, in which multiple villages dispute the possession of the three *reales provisiones*

issued by the Audiencia in 1690, contains copies and summaries of the three reales provisiones.

30. AVA Criminal, exp. 61 (1688), "Contra Joseph de Celis por agitar al pueblo."

31. AVA Criminal, exp. 65 (1688), "Contra Felipe de Santiago por el robo de unas mulas."

32. AVA Criminal, exp. 65 (1688), fol. 7v. In his statement to the court, Santiago testified that on this occasion he used mules to trade cochineal dye in the jurisdiction of Ixtepeji.

33. AVA Criminal, exp. 65 (1688), fol. 6v–7.

34. Chance, *Conquest of the Sierra*, 114.

35. AVA Criminal, exp. 3 (1650), "Contra Juan Gregorio y Juan Bautista por hurto de mulas. Betaza"; AVA Criminal, exp. 6 (1652), "Contra Juan Velasco y socios de Yatzona por robo de mulas" (in this case, the charges were brought against three men, Juan de Velasco and Gregorio de Vargas of San Juan Yatzona and Pablo de Velasco, governor of Reagui); AVA Criminal, exp. 82 (1695), "Contra Jacinto de Vargas por robo. Yatzona"; AVA Criminal, exp. 103 (1700), "Contra Pedro Mateo por robo de una mula. San Cristobal Lachirioag"; AVA Criminal, exp. 104 (1700), "Contra Francisco Chaves de La Olla por robo de una mula"; AVA Criminal, exp. 107A (1701), "Averiguaciones de la fuga hecha en la carcel de Analco por varios reos." (In this case, of the eleven prisoners who escaped, six had been accused of mule theft. In addition to Pedro Mateo and Francisco Chaves whose cases are listed above, the other accused mule thieves were Joseph Antonio of Tepanzacualco, Sebastian Osorio and Nicolas de Vargas of Totontepec, and Pedro Ignacio of Etla, Valle de Oaxaca.)

36. AVA Criminal, exp. 61 (1688), "Contra Joseph de Celis por agitar al pueblo." The year of Celis's conviction for this crime is uncertain. The court noted only that the alcalde mayor Cristóbal del Castillo Mondragón had issued the conviction. Mondragón served as alcalde mayor twice: in 1668 and from 1677 to 1683. It is most likely that the conviction occurred during Mondragón's second term.

37. Torre, "Politics Cloaked in Worship," 42–92, 86–89. Torre discusses the importance of the Baroque monstrance in the process of seventeenth-century parish formation in rural Italy.

38. Ibid., 86–89.

39. Alcina Franch, *Calendario y religión*.

40. Tavárez, "Invisible Wars."

41. Tavárez, "Letras clandestinas."

42. Alcina Franch, *Calendario y religión*, 93.

43. Chance, *Conquest of the Sierra*, 152–53.

44. AVA Criminal, exp. 61 (1688), "Contra Joseph de Celis por agitar al pueblo."

45. Scott, *Weapons of the Weak*, 184–85.

46. AVA Criminal, exp. 65 (1688), "Contra Felipe de Santiago por el robo de unas mulas."

47. AVA Criminal, exp. 61 (1688), "Contra Joseph de Celis por agitar al pueblo."

48. AVA Criminal, exp. 61 (1688). The Audiencia's order chastizing the alcalde mayor is included in this case.

49. AVA Civil, exp. 27 (1690), "Real Provisión para que se le presten los servicios necesarios para desempeñar su función al alcalde mayor, Juan Manuel Quiroz."

50. AVA Civil, leg. 5, exp. 3 (1698), "Real Provisión para que Don Felipe de Santiago de San Juan Yatzona [?] reales provisiones pertenecientes (?)," fols. 2–3. This expediente contains all of the legal documentation concerning the dispute over the possession of the three reales provisiones.

51. AVA Civil, leg. 5, exp. 3 (1698), fols. 3–4.

52. Ibid., fols. 4–9.

53. Ibid., fols. 9–10v.

54. Ibid., fols. 13–26v.

55. Ibid., fols. 25v–26v.

56. Ibid., fols. 26v–28v.

57. Van Young, "Conflict and Solidarity in Indian Village Life."

58. Romero Frizzi, *Sol y la cruz*, 182.

59. Rappaport, *Cumbe Reborn*, 7.

60. AVA Civil, exp. 44 (1694), "Juan Lopez contra Juan Marcos por un terreno, ambos de Tagui."

61. AVA Criminal, exp. 84 (1696), "Contra Miguel de Santiago por sedicioso."

62. AVA Civil, exp. 25 (1689), "Los principales y naturales del pueblo de Temascalapa contra Juan Bautista del pueblo de Yatzona por tierras"; AVA Civil, exp. 75 (1702), "Diligencias de posesión de tierras hechas a pedimento de Juan y Miguel Vargas y Juan Severino, naturales del pueblo de Temascalapa. Títulos de posesión y propiedad"; AVA Criminal, uncatalogued document (1696), "Contra el gobernador Diego Velasco por abusos."

63. AVA Criminal, exp. 100 (1699), "Contra Pablo de Vargas y socios de Yatzona por disponer del deudo para la construcción de la iglesia," fols. 6–7. This case, which forms part of the legal struggle among Pablo de Vargas, Felipe de Santiago, and Joseph de Celis for control over the cabildo of Yatzona, contains the real provision dated 26 January 1696 which forbids Santiago to act as interpreter or apoderado anywhere in the jurisdiction; AGN Civil, vol. 343, exp. 3, fols. 198–266 (1699): fols. 211–13v, "Don Felipe de Santiago de San Juan Yatzona pide despacho para que el dicho Don Joseph de Celis y los demas salgan a el destierro"; AGN Tierras, vol. 179, exp. 5 (1700): fols. 91–100, "Phelipe Robles Lopez y Nicolas de la Cruz contra Don Pablo de Bargas y demas caciques del pueblo de San Juan Yatzona sobre derramas." These three documents, related to electoral strife in San Juan Yatzona, contain testimony from the cabildos of Choapan and Yalahui alleging that Nicolas de la Cruz, interpreter general, and Santiago had abused their positions as interpreter and apoderado.

64. The following studies identify and analyze indigenous forms of social organiza-

tion that persisted in relationship to the colonial model of the "pueblo" and superceded it in social and political significance. For discussion of the "altepetl," see Lockhart, *Nahuas after the Conquest*; for discussion of the "cah," see Restall, *Maya World*; for discussion of the "ñu," see Terraciano, *Mixtecs of Colonial Oaxaca*. For discussion of the "chinamit," see Hill and Monaghan, *Continuities in Highland Maya Social Organization*. For discussion of the "noble house," see Chance, "Barrios of Tecali"; and Chance, "Noble House." For a discussion of present-day Mixtec social organization, see Monaghan, *Covenants of Earth and Rain*; and Monaghan, "Mesoamerican Community as 'Great House.'"

65. These cases include AVA Criminal, exp. 36 (1676), "Averiguación de la muerte de Luis Velasco alcalde (en un incendio)"; AVA Criminal, exp. 59 (1687), "Contra Don Pablo de Vargas por peculado y robo de la caja común"; AVA Criminal, exp. 72 (1692), "Contra Don Pablo de Vargas y Sebastian Ramos por sediciosos y alborotadores"; AVA Criminal, exp. 81 (1695), "Contra José Mendez y socios de Yatzona por sedicioso"; AVA Criminal, exp. 80 (1695), "Contra Don Francisco de Paz, Don Juan de Santiago y Pedro Jiménez, gobernador y alcaldes de Yatzona por derramas económicas, agravios y vexaciones"; AGN Indios, vol. 32, exp. 346, fols. 302–3 (1696), "Se confirma la elección que vino aprobado del Alcalde Mayor de la Villa Alta en que parece salió electo Governador del pueblo de San Juan Yatzona para este año de noventa y seis Don Pablo de Vargas y los demas oficiales de republica que se expresan, y manda a dicho Alcalde Mayor que de aqui adelante enbie las elecciones de los pueblos de su jurisdiccion al superior govierno para que se les de el despacho nesesario a los naturales"; AGN Civil, vol. 343, exp. 3, fols. 198–266 (1699), "Don Felipe de Santiago de San Juan Yatzona pide despacho para que el dicho Don Joseph de Celis y los demas salgan a el destierro"; AVA Criminal, exp. 100 (1699), "Contra Pablo de Vargas y socios de Yatzona por disponer del deudo para la construcción de la iglesia."

66. AVA Criminal, exp. 80 (1695), "Contra Don Francisco de Paz, Don Juan de Santiago y Pedro Jiménez, gobernador y alcaldes de Yatzona por derramas económicas, agravios y vexaciones."

67. Ibid.

68. Ibid.

69. Ibid.

70. Scott, *Weapons of the Weak*, 23.

71. AVA Criminal, exp. 59 (1687), "Contra Don Pablo de Vargas por peculado y robo de la caja común."

72. Chambers, *From Subjects to Citizens*, 4. For more on honor and social hierarchy, see Gutiérrez, *When Jesus Came, the Corn Mothers Went Away*, 176–270.

73. Dean, *Inka Bodies and the Body of Christ*, 47.

74. Scott, *Weapons of the Weak*, 23.

75. AGN Indios, vol. 32, exp. 346, fols. 302–3 (1696), "Se confirma la eleccion que

vino aprobado del Alcalde Mayor de la Villa Alta en que parece salió electo Governador del pueblo de San Juan Yatzona para este año de noventa y seis Don Pablo de Vargas y los demas oficiales de repulica que se expresan, y manda a dicho Alcalde Mayor que de aqui adelante enbie las elecciones de los pueblos de su jurisdiccion al superior govierno para que se les de el despacho nesesario a los naturales."

2. CAJONOS REBELLION AND AFTER

1. The friars' letters are reproduced in Gillow, *Apuntes históricos*. Eulogio Gillow served as bishop of Oaxaca, archbishop of Antequera (appointed by the pope in 1891), and was a committed church historian. Through his chronicle of Dominican evangelization in Oaxaca, he argued for the canonization of the "martyred" *fiscales* of San Francisco Cajonos. See ibid., 131–37, appendix 4, for a transcription of the friars' letters to the provincial. Gillow synthesizes and summarizes the testimony of the Spanish witnesses Don Antonio Pinelo, José de Valsalobre, Diego de Mora, Manuel Rodriguez, Diego Bohorquez, José de la Trinidad, Juan Tirado, Francisco Mejía, Sebastian de Rua, Manuel Martínez, and Juan de Chávez, in ibid., 103–16.

2. The documents related to the investigation of the rebellion and the criminal trial of the officials of San Francisco Cajonos and surrounding pueblos are compiled in AVA Criminal (uncatalogued) (1701), "Contra los naturales del pueblo de San Francisco Cajonos por sedición, sublevación e idolatría." At the time of my research in August 2001, the expediente concerning the Cajonos Rebellion was in possession of the Tribunal Superior de Oaxaca, rather than the Archivo del Poder Judicial. The expediente had been missing from the Archivo del Poder Judicial for an unspecified amount of time (at least a year). It was then recovered and turned over to the Tribunal Superior, where it remained during the beatification of Bautista and Angeles in 2001. The authorities at the Tribunal were kind enough to allow me to consult the expediente.

In addition, Gillow transcribed and reproduced most of the documents that appear in the expediente in his chapter "Diligencias judiciales," in *Apuntes históricos*, 117–224.

3. Taylor, *Magistrates of the Sacred*, 324. For further discussion of the role of fiscal, see also Haskett, *Indigenous Rulers*, 114–16, 200.

4. Taylor, *Magistrates of the Sacred*, 324–30.

5. Burgoa, *Geográfica descripción*, 148–49. Chance, *Conquest of the Sierra*, 155.

6. Chance, *Conquest of the Sierra*, 154.

7. Ibid., 156.

8. Taylor, *Magistrates of the Sacred*, 330.

9. Gillow, *Apuntes históricos*, 103.

10. Ibid., 104–5.

11. Ibid., 105.

12. Ibid., 105–6.

13. Ibid., 107–12. See also "Carta de los RR. PP. Fr. Alonso de Vargas y Fr. Gaspar de los Reyes al R.P. Provincial de Santo Domingo en Oaxaca," 15 September 1700; "Carta del P. Vicario de Caxonos al R.P. Provincial," 16 September 1700, in Gillow, *Apuntes históricos*, 131–33, appedix 4.

14. Ibid.

15. Tavárez, "Invisible Wars."

16. Tavárez, "Letras clandestinas," 78–80.

17. Griffiths, *Cross and the Serpent*; Mills, *Idolatry and Its Enemies*.

18. Robert Ricard's seminal *La Conquista espiritual de México* attributed the success of the Spanish conquest to the "Spiritual Conquest" of the indigenous population by the missionary orders, and in particular to the capacity of the missionary orders to remain flexible as to the persistence of folk religious ways among the natives. Missionary flexibility allowed for the development of a relatively syncretic Catholicism, and paved the way for the development of a distinctive national Catholicism in Mexico. This thesis has since been overturned by studies that have proven the limitations of the Catholic evangelical project in colonial Spanish America, such as open and clandestine resistance to Catholicism and the persistence of native ritual and belief in opposition to the teachings of the Catholic Church. See Farriss, *Maya Society*; Burkhart, *Holy Wednesday*; Burkhart, *Slippery Earth*; Alcina Franch, *Calendario y religión*; Tavárez, "Invisible Wars"; Griffiths, *Cross and the Serpent*; and Mills: *Idolatry and Its Enemies*.

19. Burkhart, *Holy Wednesday*; Burkhart, *Slippery Earth*; Griffiths, *Cross and the Serpent*; Mills, *Idolatry and Its Enemies*.

20. Farriss, *Maya Society*, 286–319.

21. Alcina Franch, *Calendario y religión*.

22. Tavárez, "Idolatría letrada"; Tavárez, "Letras clandestinas."

23. Tavárez, "Idolatry as an Ontological Question," 117, 137.

24. Gillow, *Apuntes históricos*, 113–14; See also "Carta de Don José Martínez de la Sierra al alcalde mayor de Villa Alta Don Juan Antonio Mier del Tojo, 16 septiembre 1700," in ibid., 117.

25. Gillow, *Apuntes históricos*, 114–16.

26. Ibid., 116. See also "Carta de los R.R. PP. Vargas y Reyes al R.P. Provincial," 17 September 1700, in Gillow, *Apuntes históricos*, 133–35, appendix 4; "Carta de Don José Martínez de la Sierra al alcalde mayor de Villa Alta Don Juan Antonio Mier del Tojo," 17 September 1700, in Gillow, "Diligencias judiciales," in *Apuntes históricos*, 118; "Acta del Alguacil Mayor Don José Martínez de la Sierra, San Francisco Cajonos," 17 September 1700, in ibid., 118–19.

27. "Carta de Don José Martínez de la Sierra al alcalde mayor de Villa Alta Don Juan Antonio Mier del Tojo," 17 September 1700, in Gillow, "Diligencias judiciales," in *Apuntes históricos*, 119.

28. "Carta de Don Juan Antonio Mier del Tojo alcalde mayor de Villa Alta a Don

José Martínez de la Sierra, alguacil mayor de Villa Alta," 17 September 1700, in Gillow, "Diligencias judiciales," in *Apuntes históricos*, 119; "Carta del Reverendísimo P. Provincial y de los Señores del muy Ilustre Cabildo de Oaxaca al Fr. Alonso de Vargas, R.R. P.P. de San Francisco Cajonos," in ibid., 120; "Auto de remision del expediente al Abogado de la Real Audiencia de México, residente en Oaxaca," 12 November 1700, in ibid., 139–41.

29. "Carta de Don Juan Antonio Mier del Tojo alcalde mayor de Villa Alta a Don José Martínez de la Sierra, alguacil mayor de Villa Alta," 17 September 1700, in Gillow, "Diligencias judiciales," in *Apuntes históricos*, 119.

30. "Auto del Alcalde Mayor remitiendo los autos originales al Virey," 21 September 1700, in Gillow, "Diligencias judiciales," in *Apuntes históricos*, 122.

31. "Consulta al Abogado Asesor residente en Oaxaca, y su contestación," 24 September 1700, in Gillow, "Diligencias judiciales," in *Apuntes históricos*, 122–23.

32. "Carta requisitoria de Don José Martínez de la Sierra a las autoridades de Teotitlán," 22 September 1700, in Gillow, "Diligencias judiciales," in *Apuntes históricos*, 123; "Contestación de la Justicia de Teotitlán," 22 September 1700, in ibid., 123; "Primera carta del Señor Don Antonio Mier del Tojo a la autoridad de Teotitlán," 21 September 1700, in ibid., 124; "Diligencias de las autoridades de Teotitlán y Tlacolula in ibid., 124; "Segunda carta del Señor Alcalde Mayor de Villa Alta a la autoridad de Teotitlán," 28 September 1700, in ibid., 124–26; "Carta del Señor Don Antonio Mier del Tojo a la Jurisdicción de Ixtepeji," 6 October 1700, in ibid., 126–27.

33. "Declaraciones de Nicolas Martín (Yasache), Lucía de los Santos del Rosario, Bernardo Martínez Salgado, Juan de la Sierra, Juan Martínez, Pablo Marcos, Raymundo de la Cruz, Sebastian de Rua, José de los Angeles, Pedro Flores, Jacinto de Vargas, José Vargas, Francisco de Vargas, and Felipe de Olivera," in Gillow, "Diligencias judiciales," in *Apuntes históricos*, 127–34.

34. AVA Criminal (uncatalogued) (1701), "Contra los naturales del pueblo de San Francisco Cajonos por sedición, sublevación e idolatría, Dictámen del Señor Fiscal del crímen, Dr. D. José de Espinoza, 22 diciembre 1700," fols. 1–4.

35. AVA Criminal (uncatalogued) (1701), "Contra los naturales del pueblo de San Francisco Cajonos por sedición, sublevación e idolatría: Don Joseph Patiño de las Casas por el gobernador, alcaldes, y oficiales de República y demás común del pueblo de San Francisco Cajonos de la jurisdicción de la Villa Alta, 10 marzo 1701."

36. Tavárez, "Letras clandestinas," 80.

37. AVA Criminal (uncatalogued) (1701), "Contra los naturales del pueblo de San Francisco Cajonos por sedición, sublevación e idolatría: Informe del Alcalde mayor de Villa Alta al Virey," 17 March 1701, fols. 5v–7v.

38. AVA Criminal (uncatalogued) (1701), "Contra los naturales del pueblo de San Francisco Cajonos por sedición, sublevación e idolatría: Informe del Alcalde mayor de Villa Alta al Virey," 17 March 1701, fols. 5v–7v.

39. AVA Criminal (uncatalogued) (1701), "Contra los naturales del pueblo de San Francisco Cajonos por sedición, sublevación e idolatría: Informe del Alcalde mayor de Villa Alta al Virey," 17 March 1701, fol. 7.

40. AVA Criminal (uncatalogued) (1701), "Contra los naturales del pueblo de San Francisco Cajonos por sedición, sublevación e idolatría," fols. 11–19. These pages consist of a claim to exemption from tribute brought on the part of a descendant of Jacinto de los Angeles to the alcalde mayor of Villa Alta from 1774 to 1775. This claim is embedded in the documents related to the investigation of the Cajonos Rebellion and the trial of the accused rebels.

41. "Contestación del Corregidor de Oaxaca al Virey," in Gillow, "Diligencias judiciales," in *Apuntes históricos*, 158–60.

42. AVA Criminal (uncatalogued) (1701), "Contra los naturales del pueblo de San Francisco Cajonos por sedición, sublevación e idolatría": testimony of the witnesses presented by the defense.

43. AVA Criminal (uncatalogued) (1701), "Contra los naturales del pueblo de San Francisco Cajonos por sedición, sublevación e idolatría": testimony of Juan Martín of San Miguel Cajonos and testimony of Francisco Luis of San Francisco Cajonos.

44. AVA Criminal (uncatalogued) (1701), "Contra los naturales del pueblo de San Francisco Cajonos por sedición, sublevación e idolatría": testimony of the witnesses presented by the defense.

45. AVA Civil, exp. 73 (1701), "Felipe Santiago cacique del pueblo de Yatzona y preso en la carcel publica otorga su poder cumplido y bastante a Miguel Martín."

46. AVA Criminal, exp. 100 (1699), "Contra Pablo de Vargas y socios de Yatzona por disponer del deudo para la construcción de la iglesia."

47. AGN Tierras, vol. 167, exp. 2, part 1, fols. 10–47 (1698), "Don Felipe de Santiago cacique y principal del pueblo de San Juan Yatzona de la jurisdicción de la Villa Alta contra Nicolas Martín y Nicolas Mendes sobre tierras y lo demás." AGN Civil, vol. 343, exp. 3, fols. 198–266 (1699), "Don Felipe de Santiago de San Juan Yatzona pide despacho para que el dicho Don Joseph de Celis y los demas salgan a el destierro." This case is a continuation of the dispute concerning Pablo de Vargas's head tax for church construction and Felipe de Santiago's alleged misappropriation of funds. In this case and in the land dispute cited above, the alcalde mayor, Santiago's political opponents in Yatzona, and disgruntled witnesses in other pueblos alleged that Santiago abused his role as apoderado.

48. AVA Civil, exp. 66 (1699), "Entre Don Felipe de Santiago y Nicolas Martín por tierras"; AGN Tierras, vol. 167, exp. 2, part 1, fols. 10–47, "Don Felipe de Santiago cacique y principal del pueblo de San Juan Yatzona de la jurisdicción de la Villa Alta contra Nicolas Martín y Nicolas Mendes sobre tierras y lo demas"; AVA Civil, exp. 60 (1697), "Testamento hecho por Marta de la Cruz del

pueblo de Yatzona en idioma Zapoteco y traducido en Español." The title of this document is somewhat misleading. The last will and testament of Marta de la Cruz was used as evidence in a land dispute between Santiago and Vargas, on the one hand, and Nicolas Martín and Gaspar Mendes, on the other, all from the pueblo of Yatzona. The testament is therefore a supporting document in the body of the case.

49. AGN Tierras, vol. 179, exp. 5 (1700), fol. 91, "Phelipe Robles Lopez y Nicolas de La Cruz contra Don Pablo de Vargas y demas caciques del pueblo de San Juan Yatzona sobre derramas." The Audiencia's description of the charges against Felipe de Santiago and the circumstances of his imprisonment are included in the order to release him, dated 20 September 1700. The Audiencia's decree is tacked onto the end of this case in which Vargas accuses Santiago of misusing the fees that the cabildo of Yatzona had paid him for serving as apoderado.

   AVA Criminal, exp. 100 (1699), "Contra Pablo de Vargas y socios de Yatzona por disponer del deudo para la construcción de la iglesia," fols. 19–25v. Buried in this case against Vargas are proceedings against Santiago for sedition.

50. AVA Civil, exp. 73 (1701), "Felipe de Santiago cacique del pueblo de Yatzona y preso en la cárcel publica otorga su poder cumplido y bastante a Miguel Martín." In addition to the authorization of Miguel Martín with Felipe de Santiago's power of attorney, this case includes Santiago's appeal to the Audiencia, the Audiencia's response, and the alcalde mayor's counterclaims and accusations.

51. AVA Criminal, exp. 100 (1699), "Contra Pablo de Vargas y socios de Yatzona por disponer del deudo para la construcción de la iglesia," 40v. Buried in this case against Pablo de Vargas are proceedings against Felipe de Santiago for sedition and troublemaking.

52. AGN Civil, vol. 343, exp. 3, fols. 198–266 (1699), "Don Felipe de Santiago de San Juan Yatzona pide despacho para que el dicho Don Joseph de Celis y los demas salgan a el destierro." This case details the legal proceedings against Felipe de Santiago; AVA Civil, exp. 73 (1701), "Felipe de Santiago cacique del pueblo de Yatzona y preso en la cárcel publica otorga su poder cumplido y bastante a Miguel Martín."

53. Alcina Franch, *Calendario y religión*, 72.

54. AVA Civil, exp. 75 (1702), "Diligencias de posesión de tierras hechas a pedimento de Juan y Miguel Vargas y Juan Severino, naturales del pueblo de Temascalapa." Santiago acts as apoderado in this case.

55. AVA Criminal (uncatalogued) (1701), "Contra los naturales del pueblo de San Francisco Cajonos por sedición, sublevación e idolatría: Ratificación de los reos." It is indicated in the proceedings that the prisoners were being turned on the rack as they "ratified" their confessions.

56. Tavárez, "Idolatry as an Ontological Question," 124–25.

57. Clendinnen, *Ambivalent Conquests*, 72–126.

58. Farriss, *Maya Society*, 341.

59. Tavárez, "Idolatría letrada," 241.

60. Gillow, *Apuntes históricos*, 90. In his discussion of the history of idolatry in the Cajonos region, Gillow cites Francisco de Burgoa, *Historia de la Provincia de Predicadores en Oaxaca*, chap. 64.

61. AVA Criminal (uncatalogued) (1701), "Contra los naturales del pueblo de San Francisco Cajonos por sedición, sublevación e idolatría: Ratificación de los reos."

62. Clendinnen, *Ambivalent Conquests*, 121.

63. Ginzburg, *Night Battles*.

64. AVA Criminal (uncatalogued) (1701), "Contra los naturales del pueblo de San Francisco Cajonos por sedición, sublevación e idolatría": Statement of the defense lawyer, Diego Bello de Aldana.

65. AVA Criminal (uncatalogued) (1701), "Contra los naturales del pueblo de San Francisco Cajonos por sedición, sublevación e idolatría: Sentencia."

66. AVA Criminal (uncatalogued) (1701), "Contra los naturales del pueblo de San Francisco Cajonos por sedición, sublevación e idolatría: Sentencia."

67. Foucault, *Discipline and Punish*, 23, 47.

68. Ibid., 49.

69. Ibid., 63.

70. Ibid., 9.

71. Silverblatt, *Modern Inquisitions*.

72. Foucault, *Discipline and Punish*, 55.

73. AVA Criminal (uncatalogued) (1701), "Contra los naturales del pueblo de San Francisco Cajonos por sedición, sublevación e idolatría: Sentencia."

74. Ibid.

75. Ibid.

76. AVA Criminal (uncatalogued) (1701), "Contra los naturales del pueblo de San Francisco Cajonos por sedición, sublevación e idolatría: Diligencia hecha en la ejecución de los reos," 14 January 1702.

77. "Alegato del defensor de los presos en Villa Alta, su representante en México," 7 July 1702, en Gillow, *Apuntes históricos*, "Diligencias judiciales," 184–85.

78. Tavárez, "Passion according to the Wooden Drum," 414.

79. Foucault, *Discipline and Punish*, 67.

80. De Certeau, *Practice of Everyday Life*, xiv–xix, 30–40.

81. AVA Criminal exp. 119 (1703), "Contral el pueblo de Tabaa por varios hechos." The title of this case is misleading. It is really a case against the alcaldes, regidores, and eleven principales of the pueblo for imprisoning their governor and his supporters and engaging in idolatry. The case opens with a petition on the part of the alcaldes, regidores, and principales of Tabaa in which they brought a complaint against their governor, Pascual Garcia.

82. AVA Criminal, exp. 119 (1703).

83. The voluminous documentation generated by Maldonado's wide-ranging in-

vestigation of Dominican administration of the indigenous pueblos of Oaxaca and the "idolatrous" practices of the pueblos of the district of Villa Alta can be found in the following legajos in the AGI: AGI México 879 (investigation of Dominican administration of indigenous pueblos in Oaxaca), AGI México 880 (legal conflict between Maldonado and the Dominican order regarding Maldonado's plan to overhaul Dominican administration by dividing Dominican *doctrinas* and appointing secular clergy), AGI México 881 (testimony concerning Dominican administration of the doctrinas of Villa Alta, and plans to divide the doctrinas and put them under secular administration), AGI México 882 (more documentation on reform of church administration in Villa Alta and the testimony of the cabildos of the district of Villa Alta regarding the "idolatrous" practices of their pueblos. This legajo also includes the ritual calendars confiscated from the pueblos of Villa Alta by Maldonado's chief extirpator, Licenciado Joseph de Aragón y Alcántara). Much of the information in this documentation has been synthesized by Chance, Alcina Franch, and Tavárez. See Chance, *Conquest of the Sierra*, 151–75; Alcina Franch, *Calendario y religión*; and Tavárez, "Invisible Wars."

84. Tavárez, "Invisible Wars," 239–44; Alcina Franch, *Calendario y religión*, 17–18.
85. Chance, *Conquest of the Sierra*, 156.
86. Ibid., 13.
87. Ibid., 157–58.
88. Alcina Franch, *Calendario y religión*, 19–25; Chance, *Conquest*, 156, 165–67.
89. Chance, *Conquest of the Sierra*, 167.
90. Tavárez, "Invisible Wars," 397–405.
91. Chance, *Conquest of the Sierra*, 167–70.
92. AVA Criminal, exp. 125 (1704), "Contra Juan de la Cruz y Agustín Hernández de Yalalag por varios hechos."
93. AVA uncatalogued (1703), "Contra Francisco de la Cruz y Joseph de la Cruz por idolatría." Misfiled at the back of AVA Civil, exp. 61 (1697), "Tierras en San Juan Yaée"; AVA, exp. 133 (1706), "Contra Juan Felipe y socios de Yalahui por perjuicios e idolatría"; AVA, exp. 184 (1718), "Contra el pueblo de Lachita por idolatría"; AVA, exp. 225 (1735), "Contra la república de Yalalag por idolatría"; AVA, exp. 227 (1736), "Contra el alcalde y naturales de Yalalag por idolatría"; AVA, uncatalogued (1753), "Contra Francisco Martín y Nicolas Vargas de Zoogoocho por idolatría."

3. REFORM, RESISTANCE, RHETORIC

1. Taylor, *Drinking, Homicide and Rebellion*, 23; Carmagnani, *Regreso de los dioses*; Pastor, *Campesinos y reformas*; Dehouve, *Quand les banquiers étaient des saints*; Dehouve, "Separaciones de pueblos en la región de Tlapa"; García Martínez, *Pueblos de la sierra*.
2. García Martínez, *Pueblos de la sierra*, 216–18.

3. Chance, *Conquest of the Sierra*, 62.
4. Carmagnani, *Regreso de los dioses.*
5. Chance, *Conquest of the Sierra*, 12–13.
6. García Martínez, *Pueblos de la sierra*; Torre, "Politics Cloaked in Worship."
7. The documentation for the almost century-long legal struggle over cabecera-sujeto relationships in the parish of San Juan Yae–San Juan Tanetze and a concomitant struggle in the parish of Santa Cruz Yagavila (both parishes were in the Rincón Zapoteco) is scattered in three archives: the Archivo del Juzgado de Villa Alta in the Archivo del Poder Judicial de Oaxaca, the Archivo General de la Nación in Mexico City, and the Rosenbach Museum and Library in Philadelphia (the documents in the Rosenbach's New Spain collection are original manuscripts collected by the Rosenbachs early in the twentieth century). The documentation in the AGN and at the Rosenbach includes copies of some of the litigation from the district court in Villa Alta as well as lengthy and repeated appeals to the Audiencia.
8. Chance, *Conquest of the Sierra*, 77–78; Gerhard, *Historical Geography*, 369.
9. AGN Tierras, vol. 2775, exp. 9 (1617), fols. 1–18v. Chance (*Conquest of the Sierra*, 77–78) discusses the history of Yae's parish status as well.
10. In a case brought to the alcalde mayor of Villa Alta by the cabildo of Santiago Lalopa, in which the pueblo claimed its own cabecera status independent of San Juan Yae, the cabildo of Yae offered three *reales provisiones*, dated 1695, 1702, and 1703, in which the Audiencia affirmed Yae's cabecera status. AVA Civil, exp. 102 (1709), "Los naturales del pueblo y común de Santiago Lalopa se oponen de ser subordinados del pueblo de San Juan Yaáe." See also Rosenbach Museum and Library New Spain 462/25, part 22, no. 6, 1736–69, 48v for an inventory of the Reales Provisiones and "instrumentos" submitted in the case, dated from 1695 to 1742.
11. Dehouve, *Quand les banquiers étaient des saints.*
12. For details about the cofradía, see the legal dispute over the jewels and ornaments: Rosenbach Museum and Library, Philadelphia, New Spain Collection, 462/25, part 21, no. 2 (1735–44); 462/25, part 21, no. 3 (1744); 462/25, part 25, no. 1 (1736–41).
13. Documents related to the suit (*pleito*) over the wealth of the cofradía are interspersed in the suit over cabecera-sujeto status. See Rosenbach Museum and Library, Philadelphia, New Spain Collection, 462/25, part 21, no. 2 (1735–44); 462/25, part 21, no. 3 (1744); 462/25, part 25, no. 1 (1736–41).
14. Chance (*Conquest of the Sierra*, 118–20) discusses this dispute over the markets in the Rincón.
15. AGN Indios, vol. 30, exp. 448 (1691), fols. 418v–20.
16. Testimony given to the Real Audiencia on 11 June 1735 by alcalde mayor of Villa Alta Don Joachin de Padilla y Estrada in a case concerning parish relationships in the partido of San Juan Yae–San Juan Tanetze. Rosenbach Museum

and Library, Philadelphia, New Spain Collection 462/25, part 21, no. 2 (1735–44), fols. 6v–8.

17. Carmagnani, "Local Governments and Ethnic Governments," 107–8, 111.

18. See the reales provisiones presented by the cabildo of San Juan Yaáe, dated 1695, 1702, and 1703, in which the Audiencia affirmed Yae's cabecera status: AVA Civil, exp. 102 (1709), "Los naturales del pueblo y común de Santiago Lalopa se oponen de ser subordinados del pueblo de San Juan Yae." See also the list of "instrumentos" or legal documents having to do with the cabecera-sujeto dispute catalogued by the Audiencia in its final decision in the case: Rosenbach Museum and Library New Spain 462/25, part 22, no. 6 (1736–69), fol. 48v.

19. AVA Civil, exp. 102 (1709). In this case, the autoridad of Lalopa refers to the reales provisiones, the first dated 1705, that exempted the pueblo from material obligations to Yae during religious celebrations.

20. AVA Civil, exp. 148 (1735), "Averiguación del porque no asisten a las fiestas de Semana Santa y otras los naturales de los pueblos de Yagallo, Lachichina y Yaviche."

21. Bauman, *Story, Performance, and Event*, 3.

22. Ibid., 4.

23. Ibid., 2. Here Bauman draws heavily on Roman Jakobson's sociolinguistic theories. See Jakobson, "Shifters, Verbal Categories, and the Russian Verb."

24. For a discussion of the complex relationships among Spanish vecinos and indigenous elites in the district of Villa Alta, see Yannakakis, "Indios Ladinos," 101–47.

25. Rosenbach Museum and Library, Philadelphia, New Spain Collection, 462/25, part 21, no. 2 (1735–44): fols. 34–34v.

26. Kroskrity, "Regimenting Languages," 8.

27. Rosenbach Museum and Library, Philadelphia, New Spain Collection, 462/25, part 21, no. 2 (1735–44): fols. 34–36.

28. This work was published in Mexico City by Francisco X. Sánchez in 1687. The imprint can be found at the John Carter Brown Library. I would like to thank David Tavárez for sharing with me this information about Pacheco de Silva's work on the Nexitzo Zapotec language.

29. AGI México 882 (December 1704), fols. 1253, 1310–12, 1318. The testimony of the Rincón cabildo officials constitutes part of the larger corpus of documentation (1,544 pages worth at the end of this legajo), produced by Maldonado's chief extirpator Licenciado Joseph de Aragón y Alcántara, curate of Ejutla, in his investigation of idolatry in the district of Villa Alta in 1704. In this instance, the cabildo officers responded to the question posed by Aragón y Alcántara concerning how frequently, when, and where their community engaged in "idolatry" collectively. In the cases of Yaviche, Lalopa, and Yae, the cabildo officials claimed that they had not as a community engaged in "idolatry" for 29

years, since the time of Pacheco de Silva. As the officials of Lalopa put it, "de veinte y nueve años a esta parte han cesado dichos sacrificios por que las diligencias que hicieron los Licenciados Don Diego Mendez Piñelo siendo Beneficiado y Don Francisco Pacheco su vicario de fulminar causas, quemar y destruir ídolos, poner cruces en los sacrificaderos y su continua predicación, destruyeron en el pueblo de estos declarantes dicha costumbre que entonces recojian las justicias para los sacrificios" (fol. 1255v).

30. *Recopilación de leyes de los reynos de las Indias*, 1:218, book 2, title 1, law 4, "Que se guarden las leyes que los indios tenían antiguamente para su gobierno, y las que se hicieren de nuevo." Emperor Carlos and Princess Juana, governor in Valladolid, 6 August 1555.

31. Ibid., 1:346, book 2, title 2, title 15, law 83, "Que las Audiencias tengan cuidado del buen tratamiento de los indios y brevedad de sus pleytos." Emperor Carlos in Law 20 of 1542. The Queen of Bohemia governor in Valladolid, 11 March 1550. Felipe II in Ordinance 70 of the Audiencias of 1563. And in Madrid, 3 July 1571. And in Ordinance 79 of the Audiencias, in Toledo, 25 May 1596.

32. Ibid., 2:120–21, book 5, title, 2, law 22, "Que los Gobernadores reconozcan la policía que los Indios tuvieren, y guarden sus usos en lo que no fueren con-trarios a nuestra Sagrada Religion, y hagan que cada uno exerza bien su oficio, y la tierra esté abastecida y limpia, y las obras públicas reparadas." Emperor Carlos and Emperess governor in Madrid, 12 July 1530.

33. Borah, *Justice by Insurance*, 8.

34. Benton, *Law and Colonial Cultures*, 43.

35. Borah, *Justice by Insurance*, 8.

36. Ibid., 8–9.

37. Lauren Benton (*Law and Colonial Cultures*, 11) has elaborated a series of heuristic terms for analysis of imperial legal regimes: multicentric legal orders, state-centered legal orders, and strong and weak legal pluralism.

38. Borah, *Justice by Insurance*, 35–45.

39. Cutter, *Legal Culture of Northern New Spain*, 37.

40. Anzoátegui, *Poder de la costumbre*, 309–40.

41. Cutter, *Legal Culture of Northern New Spain*, 34–39.

42. Benton, *Law and Colonial Cultures*, 11.

43. Borah, *Justice by Insurance*, 254.

44. Benton, *Law and Colonial Cultures*, 80–126. Benton coins the term *jurisdic-tional jockeying* in her discussion of jurisdictional tensions in Catholic and Islamic imperial legal traditions.

45. Borah, *Justice by Insurance*, 254.

46. Miceli, "Derecho consuetudinario en Castilla."

47. See Tanck de Estrada, *Pueblos de indios y educación*, 490–530, for a detailed examination of how pueblos de indios throughout New Spain managed com-munity finances and funded litigation.

48. For a discussion of the General Indian Court and the legal insurance of the Half Real, see Borah, *Justice by Insurance*.

49. Florescano, *Memoria indígena*, 257.

50. AVA Civil, leg. 11, exp. 26 (1744), "Protocolos de Instrumentos Públicos," document 26.04.

51. AVA Civil, leg. 11, exp. 26 (1744), document 26.05.

52. AVA Civil, leg. 11, exp. 26 (1744), document 26.08.

53. Rosenbach Museum and Library, New Spain 462/25, part 21, no. 3 (1735–44), fol. 1.

54. Anzoátegui, *Poder de la costumbre*, 318–36.

55. Ibid., 245.

56. Cutter, *Legal Culture of Northern New Spain*, 37.

57. Rosenbach Museum and Library, New Spain 462/25, part 21, no. 3 (1735–44), fol. 26–28.

58. Ibid., part 25, no. 1, fols. 22–24v.

59. Ibid., part 25, no. 1, fols. 26v–27.

60. Ibid., part 25, no. 1, fols. 21v–22v.

61. Ibid., part 25, no. 1, "Real Provisión," December 1743.

62. Ibid., part 21, no. 2, fol. 67v.

63. Anzoátegui, *Poder de la costumbre*, 328, cit. Solórzano, *Politica indiana*, 2.25, 9.

64. Ibid., 257, cit. Archivo General de la Nación, *Acuerdos del extinguido cabildo de Buenos Aires*, ser. 3, 4:606–9 (Buenos Aires, 1907–33).

65. Ibid., 257, cit. law 1, title 1, book 2 of the RI (Recopilación de Leyes de Indias), 408.

66. Ibid., 249–52.

67. Ibid., 250, cit. Juan Francisco de Castro, *Discursos críticos sobre las leyes y sus intérpretes en que se demuestra la necesidad de un nuevo y metódico cuerpo de Derecho para la recta administración de justicia* (Madrid, 1765; 2nd ed., Madrid, 1829), 1:118–99.

68. Anzoátegui, *Poder de la costumbre*, 252–53.

69. AGN Tierras, vol. 2771, exp. 10 (1744); Rosenbach Museum and Library, New Spain 462/25, part 21, no. 3 (1744); ibid., part 21, no. 2 (1735–44); ibid., part 29, no. 3 (1741–44).

70. AVA Civil, exp. 188 (1745), "El pueblo de San Juan Yae contra Santiago Yagallo y consortes sobre punto de cabecera"; AVA Civil, exp. 189 (1745), "El pueblo de San Juan Yae contra Santiago Yagallo sobre punto de cabecera."

71. AVA Civil, exp. 207 (1750), "Las justicias del pueblo de San Juan Yaee se quejan de las malas acciones que viene efectuando Francisco Mendoza contra la administración actual."

72. Rosenbach Museum and Library, New Spain 462/25, part 22, no. 6 (1736–69).

73. Taylor, *Magistrates of the Sacred*, 13.

74. Benton, *Law and Colonial Cultures*.

75. Charles Cutter (*Legal Culture of Northern New Spain*) elaborates the idea that in the absence of the legal professionals and many of the formal legal institutions that characterized the urban and central regions of New Spain, and through struggles over land and resources, Spanish officials and local residents of colonial New Mexico participated in the formation of a regional "legal culture."

4. CACIQUE AND CABILDO

1. AVA Civil, exp. 122 (1730), "Testamento de Miguel Fernández de Chaves."
2. Tiltepec's population increased from 352 in 1622 to 736 in 1703; Chance, *Conquest of the Sierra*, 52.
3. Oudijk, *Historiography of the Bénizáa*, 209–14; Chance, *Conquest of the Sierra*, 16, 22–23.
4. Chance, *Conquest of the Sierra*, 22–23.
5. AVA Civil, exp. 54 (1696), "Los naturales del pueblo de Tiltepec solicitan licencia para que se celebre un dia de tianguis a la semana en su pueblo."
6. Chance, *Conquest of the Sierra*, 46–69.
7. AVA Civil, exp. 54 (1696).
8. AGN Indios, vol. 32, exp. 365, fols. 317–17v (1696).
9. AVA Civil, exp. 101 (1709), "El pueblo de Yaviche y consortes piden que se celebre un día de tianguis en Yaviche"; AGN Civil, vol. 26, exp. 4, fols. 326–44v (1734), "Autos de pedimiento de los naturales de Santa Cruz Yagavila jurisdicción de Villa Alta sobre tianguis"; AGN Tierras, vol. 2771, exp. 10 (1744), fols. 0– 44v, "Autos que siguen los naturales de los pueblos de San Juan Taneche y otros de la Jurisdicción de la Villa Alta con el comun de los naturales de San Juan Yaee de la misma jurisdicción sobre la celebración de tianguis y mercado"; AGN Tierras, vol. 2771, exp. 8 (1743), 6 fols., "Expediente formado a pedimiento del comun y naturales del pueblo de San Juan Yaee de la jurisdicción de la Villa Alta sobre el tianguis que se hace en dicho pueblo."
10. Chance, *Conquest of the Sierra*, 114–16.
11. Ibid., 116–17.
12. AVA Civil, exp. 68 (1698–1700), "Los naturales del pueblo de San Francisco Yovego contra los de San Miguel Tiltepec por tierras," fols. 13–15.
13. Michel Oudijk, personal communication via e-mail, December 2005. I would like to thank Oudijk for his thoughtful commentary on this chapter.
14. Taylor, *Landlord and Peasant*; Pastor, *Campesinos y reformas*; Romero Frizzi, *Sol y la cruz*; Monaghan and Cohen, "Thirty Years of Oaxacan Ethnography."
15. Van Young, "Conflict and Solidarity in Indian Village Life."
16. AVA Civil, exp. 68, "Los naturales del pueblo de San Francisco Yovego contra los de San Miguel Tiltepec por tierras, 1698–1700," fols. 10–13.
17. AVA Civil, exp. 68, fols. 13–14v.
18. AVA Civil, exp. 68, fols. 15–17v.

19. Kellogg, *Law and the Transformation of Aztec Culture*, 51–52.

20. AVA Civil, exp. 68, fols. 16v–17.

21. Ibid., fols. 19–20v.

22. Ibid., fols. 25v–35.

23. Ibid., fols. 37–37v.

24. Ibid., fols. 38–38v.

25. Ibid., fols. 39–40.

26. Ibid., fols. 41–end; AVA Civil, exp. 68B (1700–1705), "Los naturales del pueblo de Yovego contra los de Tiltepec por tierras," part 2, fols. 1–27.

27. Chance, *Conquest of the Sierra*, 127–29; Guevara Hernández, *Lienzo de Tiltepec*; Oudijk, *Historiography of the Bénizáa*, 208–25.

28. Spores, *Mixtec Kings and Their People*, 116.

29. Chance, *Conquest of the Sierra*, 128.

30. Romero Frizzi, *Sol y la cruz*, 61; Guevara Hernández, *Lienzo de Tiltepec*, 15.

31. Chance, *Conquest of the Sierra*, 128.

32. Chance, "Noble House."

33. Ibid.; Chance, "Social Stratification."

34. Chance, *Conquest of the Sierra*, 128–30.

35. Ibid., 131; Romero Frizzi, *Sol y la cruz*, 218.

36. AVA Civil, exp. 68B (1700–1705), "Los naturales del pueblo de Yovego contra los de Tiltepec por tierras," part 2.

37. AVA Civil, exp. 68B (1700–1705), petition that begins on fol. 27v. See also Guevara Hernández, *Lienzo de Tiltepec*, 25.

38. Asselbergs, *Conquered Conquistadors*, 24.

39. Oudijk, *Historiography of the Bénizáa*, 185–225; Oudijk, "Espacio y escritura."

40. Oudijk, *Historiography of the Bénizáa*, 208–9.

41. For an overview of these transformations, see Kellogg, *Weaving the Past*. For seminal works, see Silverblatt, *Moon, Sun, and Witches*; Kellogg, *Law and the Transformation of Aztec Culture*; and Sigal, *From Moon Goddesses to Virgins*.

42. Monaghan, "Physiology, Production, and Gendered Difference," 287; cited in Kellogg, *Weaving the Past*, 7.

43. Kellogg, *Weaving the Past*, 7.

44. Sigal, *From Moon Goddesses to Virgins*.

45. Kellogg, *Weaving the Past*, 7, 19–30, 35–41.

46. Ibid., 24.

47. Kellogg, "From Parallel and Equivalent."

48. Kellogg, *Weaving the Past*, 71.

49. Spores, "Mixteca Cacicas"; Terraciano, *Mixtecs of Colonial Oaxaca*, 186–91.

50. Spores, "Mixteca Cacicas," 187.

51. Oudijk, *Historiography of the Bénizáa*, 215–16.

52. Ibid., 221–22.

53. AGN Indios, vol. 3, exp. 693 (1591), fols. 162–62v.

54. Oudijk, *Historiography of the Bénizáa*, 222–23.

55. AVA Civil, exp. 68B (1700–1705), "Los naturales del pueblo de Yovego contra los de Tiltepec por tierras," part 2.

56. AVA Civil, exp. 103 (1709), "Miguel Fernández de Chávez, cacique de San Miguel Tiltepec y Lachichina pide se le legalisen y extiendan títulos de propiedad de unas tierras que posee."

57. Ots Capdequí, *Manual de historia del derecho español*, 19–25; Ots Capdequí, *Estado español en las Indias*, 39–41.

58. Ouweneel, "From 'Tlahtocayotl' to 'Gobernadoryotl,'" 762.

59. AVA Civil, exp. 103 (1709), "Miguel Fernández de Chávez, cacique de San Miguel Tiltepec y Lachichina pide se le legalisen y extiendan títulos de propiedad de unas tierras que posee."

60. Taylor, *Landlord and Peasant*; Spores, *Mixtecs in Ancient and Colonial Times*; Pastor, *Campesinos y reformas*; Romero Frizzi, *Sol y la cruz*.

61. Taylor, *Landlord and Peasant*; Spores, *Mixtecs in Ancient and Colonial Times*; Pastor, *Campesinos y reformas*; Romero Frizzi, *Sol y la cruz*; Dehouve, *Quand les banquiers étaient des saints*; García Martínez, *Pueblos de la sierra*.

62. Farriss, *Maya Society*; Haskett, *Indigenous Rulers*; Ouweneel, "From 'Tlahtocayotl' to 'Gobernadoryotl.'"

63. Ouweneel, "From 'Tlahtocayotl' to 'Gobernadoryotl.'"

64. Terraciano, *Mixtecs of Colonial Oaxaca*, 230–31.

65. Zeitlin, *Cultural Politics in Colonial Tehuantepec*, 253.

66. Chance, "Caciques of Tecali"; Taylor, *Landlord and Peasant*, 35.

67. AVA Civil, exp. 121 (1729), "Protocolo de Instrumentos públicos." "Real Provisión sobre el caso de Miguel de Chavez casique del pueblo de Lachichina contra los oficiales de la Republica del pueblo de Tiltepec sobre deudos de diverso del arrendamiento de tierras"; "Don Miguel de Chaves casique del pueblo de Lachichina de esta jurisdicción contra los ofisiales de República del Pueblo de Tiltepeque Rincón sobre cuentas en orden a el suplemente que le havian echo de cantidad de 2028 para el litigio que el suso dicho con los de Yobego sobre las tierras de su cacicasgo (1727)."

68. AVA Civil, exp. 121 (1729), "Protocolo de Instrumentos públicos." "Don Miguel de Chaves casique del pueblo de Lachichina de esta jurisdicción contra los ofisiales de República del Pueblo de Tiltepeque Rincón sobre cuentas en orden a el suplemente que le havian echo de cantidad de 2028 para el litigio que el sus dicho con los de Yobego sobre las tierras de su cacicasgo (1727)," fols. 17v–31.

69. AVA Civil, exp. 122 (1730), "Testamento de Miguel Fernández de Chaves."

70. AVA Civil, exp. 122 (1730).

71. Ibid.

72. AVA Civil, exp. 127 (1730), "Testimonio del pago de dinero que hizo el cacique Miguel Fernández del pueblo de Lachichina a los principales del pueblo de San Francisco Yovego"; AVA Civil, exp. 129 (1730), "Testimonio de la donación de

tierras que hace el cacique de Lachichina Miguel de Chavez a los naturales del pueblo de Tiltepec"; AVA Civil, exp. 131 (1730), "Miguel Fernández de Chavez, cacique del pueblo de Santa Maria Lachichina reboca su testamento otorgado a favor del pueblo de Yovego y deja como unicos herederos de todos sus bienes y tierras a los naturales de Tiltepec."

73. Guevara Hernández, *Lienzo de Tiltepec*, 34.
74. Richter, "Cultural Brokers," 41.
75. Chance, *Conquest of the Sierra*, 137–46; Chance, "Caciques of Tecali."

5. BOURBON OFFICIALS

1. AVA Civil, leg. 27, exp. 4 (1789), "Sobre elecciones de nuevos funcionarios en Tabaa."
2. Chance, *Conquest of the Sierra*, 136–37.
3. Farriss, *Maya Society*, 355–75; Chance, *Conquest of the Sierra*, 173–74; Guardino, *Time of Liberty*, 105–6. See also Dorothy Tanck de Estrada's study of the fiscal history of the pueblos de indios during the Bourbon Reforms (*Pueblos de indios y educación*), and how the pueblos financed the rural schools established by the Bourbons.
4. Serulnikov, "Customs and Rules"; Walker, "Civilize or Control?"; Larson, *Cochabamba*, 2nd ed.; Beezley, Martin, and French, *Rituals of Rule*; Viqueira Albán, *Propriety and Permissiveness*; Estenssoro, *Música y sociedades coloniales*; Chambers, *From Subjects to Citizens*.
5. Brading, *Miners and Merchants*, 33–92.
6. Farriss, *Crown and Clergy*.
7. Farriss, *Maya Society*, 355–75.
8. Haskett, *Indigenous Rulers*, 199.
9. O'Phelan Godoy, *Rebellions and Revolts*.
10. Serulnikov, "Customs and Rules."
11. Guardino, *Time of Liberty*, 91–121.
12. Serulnikov, "Customs and Rules," 246.
13. Tanck de Estrada (*Pueblos de indios y educación*) has examined how the Spanish language education policy dovetailed with the Bourbon secularization program: transfer of the doctrinas of the missionary orders (most of whose members spoke indigenous languages) to secular parish priests (most of whom did not speak indigenous languages).
14. Walker, "Civilize or Control?," 82.
15. AVA Civil, leg. 25, exp. 11 (1784), "Varios principales de Tabaa anulan la elección de nuevos justicias en su pueblo."
16. Brading, *Miners and Merchants*, 159–68.
17. Guardino, *Time of Liberty*, 119.
18. Chance, *Conquest of the Sierra*, 94–96.
19. Guardino, *Time of Liberty*, 118.

20. Ibid., 114.

21. Chance, *Conquest of the Sierra*, 94–96.

22. Ibid., 96.

23. AVA Civil, leg. 26, exp. 16 (1788), "Sobre que los naturales trabajen en las minas de Sta. Gertrudis."

24. AVA Civil, leg. 25, exp. 01 (1783), "Real Provisión."

25. AVA Civil, leg. 27, exp. 11 (1789), "Real Provisión."

26. AVA Civil, leg. 25, exp. 11 (1784), "Varios principales de Tabaa anulan la elección de nuevas justicias en su pueblo," fols. 3–9v.

27. AVA Civil, leg. 25, exp. 01 (1783), "Los pueblos de Yojovi, Tabaa, y Solaga contra el Theniente Coronel Don Juan Francisco de Echarrí, dueño de minas en aquel partido sobre repartimiento por fandas de los yndios para su laborio, excesos, malos tratamientos, extorciones y agravios."

28. AVA Civil, leg. 25, exp. 8 (1784), "Sobre que las repúblicas de los pueblos se abstengan de imponer derramas a sus vecinos."

29. Guardino, *Time of Liberty*, 119.

30. AVA Civil, leg. 27, exp. 4 (1789), "Sobre elecciones de nuevos funcionarios en Tabaa."

31. AVA Civil, leg. 27, exp. 4 (1789), fols. 1–4.

32. Chance, *Conquest of the Sierra*, 137–46.

33. Ibid., 144, 147–48.

34. Cutter, *Legal Culture of Northern New Spain*, 34–35, 37–40, 93.

35. AVA Civil, leg. 27, exp. 4 (1789), fols. 1–4.

36. Ibid., fols. 6–6v.

37. AGI Indiferente, 1312 (1769–70), no. 3, 17 February–7 March 1770, fols. 4–10.

38. *Recopilación de las leyes*, law 18, title 1, book 6, "Que donde fuere posible se pongan escuelas de la lengua castellana, para que la aprendan los indios." Emperor Carlos and the Monarchs of Bohemia governing in Valladolid, 7 June 1550; law 5, title 13, book 1, "Que los curas dispongan a los Indios en la enseñanza de la lengua Española, y en ella la doctrina Christiana." Felipe IV in Madrid, 2 March 1634 and 4 November 1636.

39. AGI Indiferente, 1312 (1769–70), no. 3, Mexico City, 27 June 1769, fols. 1–4.

40. AGI Indiferente, 1312 (1769–70), no. 2, Puebla de los Angeles, 19 September 1769, fols. 1–12.

41. AGI Indiferente General, 1312 (1769–70), no. 1, Mexico City, 6 October 1769, fols. 1–2.

42. Ibid., fols. 2–5.

43. Ibid., fols. 8–9.

44. Ibid., fol. 9.

45. AGI Indiferente, 1312 (1769–70), no. 3, 17 February–7 March 1770, fols. 4–10.

46. AVA Civil, exp. 330 (1770), "Real Cédula para que se les enseñe la lengua española y la doctrina cristiana," fols. 1–5.

47. AVA Civil, exp. 330 (1770). The signatures appear on fols. 6–11v.

48. AVA Civil, leg. 24, exp. 15 (1781), "Varias cordilleras sobre elecciones de sus justicias," fols. 1–10.

49. Chance, *Conquest of the Sierra*, 124–25.

50. AVA Civil, leg. 27, exp. 4 (1789), "Sobre elecciones de nuevos funcionarios en Tabaa," fols. 7–7v; AVA Civil, leg. 26, exp. 13 (1788), "Diligencias contra el cura de Tabaa por cobrar tributos."

51. AVA Civil, leg. 27, exp. 4 (1789), fols. 7–7v.

52. AVA Civil, leg. 24, exp. 15 (1781), "Varias cordilleras sobre elecciones de sus justicias," fols. 1–2v.

53. Guardino, *Time of Liberty*, 102–4, 106; Taylor, *Magistrates of the Sacred*, 374; Serulnikov, "Customs and Rules," 247.

54. Chance, *Conquest of the Sierra*, 156.

55. AVA Civil, leg. 27, exp. 4 (1789), "Sobre elecciones de nuevos funcionarios en Tabaa," fols. 12–15; AVA Civil, leg. 26, exp. 13 (1788), "Diligencias contra el cura de Tabaa por cobrar tributos."

56. AVA Civil, leg. 27, exp. 4 (1789), fols. 12–15.

57. Ibid., fols. 15–16.

58. Ibid., fols. 17–18v.

59. Ibid., fols. 19v–end.

60. Ibid., "Real Provisión."

61. Sergio Serulnikov ("Customs and Rules," 8) documents the appointment of Hispanized native leaders (*kurakas*) in response to the refusal of others to conform to labor drafts and tributes.

62. Pastor, "Repartimiento de mercancías."

63. Chance, *Conquest of the Sierra*, 106–7; cit. Hamnett, *Politics and Trade*, 9, 32.

64. Chance, *Conquest of the Sierra*, 106–10.

65. Guardino, *Time of Liberty*, 99; Chance, *Conquest of the Sierra*, 110–11.

66. Guardino, *Time of Liberty*, 100.

67. AVA Civil, leg. 26, exp. 16 (1788), "Sobre que los naturales trabajen en las minas de Sta. Gertrudis," fols. 2–4v.

68. Ibid., fols. 4v–end.

69. Ibid., fols. 4v–9v.

70. Ibid., fols. 10–18.

71. Scott, *Weapons of the Weak*, xvi, 25.

72. AVA Civil, leg. 26, exp. 16 (1788), fols. 19–22.

73. Ibid., fols. 26–29.

74. Ibid., fols. 30–30v.

75. Ibid., fols. 30v–end.

76. AVA Civil, leg. 27, exp. 23 (1791), "Providencias a fin de que los de Lalopa concurrecer al trabajo de las minas de Talea."

77. Baskes, *Indians, Merchants, and Markets*, 18–20.

6. "CONQUERORS" TO "INDIANS"

1. AVA Civil, exp. 259 (1761), "Los naturales del barrio de Analco piden se les respete los privilegios que gozan como el de no pagar tributos."
2. Taylor, *Magistrates of the Sacred*; Kellogg, "Hegemony out of Conquest"; Kellogg, *Law and the Transformation of Aztec Culture*.
3. Comaroff and Comaroff, *Ethnography and the Historical Imagination*, 236.
4. Chance, *Conquest of the Sierra*, 46–88.
5. Ibid., 33–34, 42–43.
6. Ibid., 16–29.
7. Asselbergs, *Conquered Conquistadors*, 14.
8. Ibid., 20.
9. Ibid., 15.
10. Ibid., 215.
11. Ibid., 225.
12. Ibid., 215.
13. Ibid.
14. Ibid., 17.
15. Ibid., 197.
16. Leibsohn, "Primers for Memory," 161.
17. Asselbergs, *Conquered Conquistadors*, 216.
18. König, *Schlacht bei Sieben Blume*. I would like to thank Viola König for allowing me to reference her photos of the Lienzo of Analco, and I would also like to thank Michel Oudijk for sharing his slides of König's photos with me. See also Blom, "Lienzo de Analco." Franz Blom was the first to analyze and discuss the Lienzo of Analco.
19. Asselbergs, *Conquered Conquistadors*, 27.
20. Ibid., 29.
21. Ibid., 213.
22. Ibid., 215.
23. Ibid., 213.
24. Gibson, *Tlaxcala in the Sixteenth Century*; *Constructores de la nación*; Frye, *Indians into Mexicans*; Sego, *Aliados y adversarios*.
25. For discussion of the roles of Mesoamerican indigenous conquerors other than the Tlaxcalans, see Matthew, "Neither and Both"; Restall, *Maya Conquistador*; Asselbergs, *Conquered Conquistadors*; and Matthew and Oudijk, *Indian Conquistadors*.
26. Chance, *Conquest of the Sierra*, 33. Chance relies on the Papeles de Analco from the Archivo Parochial de Villa Alta for this particular categorization.
27. Ibid., 43.
28. AVA Civil, exp. 259 (1761), "Los naturales del barrio de Analco piden se les respete los privilegios que gozan como el de no pagar tributos."

29. AGI Justicia, 205, no. 5, Autos Fiscales México, 1558–64, "El fiscal contra Juan Antonio de Acevedo, vecino de Zapotecas, sobre el derecho a la mitad de los pueblos de Yaci y Lobani," 7 pieces.

30. AGN Indios, vol. 3, exp. 917, fols. 223v–24 (1591).

31. AGN Tierras, vol. 2968, exp. 121, fols. 296–99v (1683).

32. Burgoa, *Geográfica descripción*, 147.

33. AVA Ramo Civil, exp. 18 (1683), "Los naturales del barrio de Analco contra los del pueblo de Lachirioag para que respeten el contrato celebrado entre ambos con motivo de la festividad del patron del pueblo."

34. König, *Schlacht bei Sieben Blume*, 21–23. For a discussion of Tlaxcalan pictographic traditions, see Asselbergs, "Conquest in Images." See also Kranz, "Tlaxcalan Conquest Pictorials"; and Gillespie, "Saints and Warriors." For a discussion of the pictorial narratives of other Indian conquerors, see Asselbergs, *Conquered Conquistadors*.

35. Asselbergs, *Conquered Conquistadors*, 95.

36. Chance, *Conquest of the Sierra*, 33.

37. Ibid., 33.

38. Ibid., 62. According to his figures, the total population of Analco fluctuated as follows: in 1548, there were 200 inhabitants, in 1622, 177, in 1703, 271, in 1742, 135, and in 1781, 355.

39. Ibid., 34.

40. AGN Indios, vol. 3, exp. 917, fols. 223v–24 (1591).

41. AVA Ramo Civil, exp. 104 (1709), "Los naturales del barrio de Analco reclaman para que no se les quiten los privilegios otorgados por Real Provisión como el de no pagar tributos y otros." In this case, the cabildo of Analco petitioned the Real Audiencia to uphold the privileges granted to the indios conquistadores and their descendants after the conquest.

42. For examples of these roles, see the following cases: AVA Civil, exp. 16 (1677), "Los naturales de los pueblos de San Andres Yaa, San Francisco Yatee y Yohueche contra los de Betaza and Lachitaa por tierras"; AVA Criminal, exp. 200 (1725), "Contra Juan Martín gobernador y Nicolas Geronimo alcalde por ebrios consetudinarios"; AVA Criminal (uncatalogued) (1753), "Idolatría en Zoogocho"; Rosenbach Museum and Library, New Spain 462/25, part 25, no. 1 (22 December 1736–20 November 1741), fols. 24v–25; AGN Indios, vol. 62, exp. 57, fols. 77v–79 (1769); AVA Criminal, exp. 227 (1736), "Contra las Autoridades y el común del pueblo de Yalalag por idolatras"; AVA Civil, exp. 52 (1677), "Los naturales de los pueblos de San Andres Yaa, San Francisco Yatee y Yohueche contra los de Betaza y Lachitaa por tierras"; AGN Civil, vol. 1607, exp. 1, fols. 45–50 (1783).

43. AVA Civil, exp. 104 (1709), "Los naturales del barrio de Analco reclaman para que no se les quiten los privilegios otorgados por Real Provisión como el de no pagar tributos y otros." In this petition to the Real Audiencia for the preserva-

tion of their privileges, the cabildo of Analco cited the role of the descendants of the indios conquistadores in maintaining security during various uprisings and rebellions.

44. See, e.g., AGN Tierras, vol. 2968, exp. 121, fols. 296–99v (1683); AVA Civil, exp. 104 (1709), "Los naturales del barrio de Analco reclaman para que no se les quiten los privilegios otorgados por real provision como el de no pagar tributos y otros"; AVA Civil, exp. 259 (1761), "Los naturales del barrio de Analco piden se les respete los privilegios que gozan como el de no pagar tributos"; AVA Civil, exp. 366 (1774), "Los naturales del barrio de Analco piden se les respeten los privilegios de que gozan de imemorable año."

45. AVA Civil, exp. 18 (1683), "Los naturales del barrio de Analco contra los del pueblo de Lachirioag para que respeten el contrato celebrado entre ambos con motivo de la festividad del patron del pueblo."

46. Dean, *Inka Bodies and the Body of Christ*, 49. For an examination of fiestas as spaces for the performance of power and identity, see Curcio-Nagy, *The Great Festivals of Colonial Mexico City.*

47. Ibid., 178.

48. Ibid., 52.

49. AVA Civil, exp. 18 (1683).

50. Kellogg, *Weaving the Past*, 24; Sigal, *From Moon Goddesses to Virgins*, 42–53.

51. AGN Tierras, vol. 2968, exp. 121, fols. 296–99v (1683).

52. Alcina Franch, *Calendario y religión*, 20.

53. AVA Criminal (uncatalogued) (1706), "Idolatría en Yatee."

54. Ibid.

55. Ibid., fol. 27.

56. AGI México, 881, "Inquisición de la Visita de la Villa Alta: Consulta y testimonios del estado del obispado de Oaxaca, 27 de noviembre de 1704–23 julio de 1706": "Testimonio de aver donado los provinciales y difinitorio de esta provincia de padres dominicos de oaxaca la una nave de la parrochia de la villa alta a unos indios y señaladoles lugar de intierro en dicha parrochia contra el Rl Patronato y jurisdicción ordinaria," fols. 28–29v.

57. See Matthew O'Hara's discussion of the "principle of separation" governing the racial division of parishes in Mexico City and the tensions produced within and among parish-based communities by their racial integration during the Bourbon Reforms; O'Hara, "Stone, Mortar, and Memory."

58. AGI México, 881, "Inquisición de la Visita de la Villa Alta: Consulta y testimonios del estado del obispado de Oaxaca, 27 de noviembre de 1704–23 julio de 1706": "Testimonio de aver donado los provinciales y difinitorio de esta provincia de padres dominicos de oaxaca la una nave de la parrochia de la villa alta a unos indios y señaladoles lugar de intierro en dicha parrochia contra el Rl Patronato y jurisdicción ordinaria," fol. 29v.

59. AVA Civil, exp. 104 (1709), "Los naturales del barrio de Analco reclaman para

que no se les quiten los privilegios otorgados por Real Provisión como el de no pagar tributes y otros."

60. Ibid.

61. Ibid.

62. Ibid.

63. Chance, *Conquest of the Sierra*, 43.

64. AVA Civil, exp. 259 (1761), "Los naturales del barrio de Analco piden se les respete los privilegios que gozan como el de no pagar tributos."

65. Ibid.

66. Ibid.

67. Ibid.

68. Ibid.

69. Ibid.

70. AVA Civil, exp. 366 (1774), "Los naturales del barrio de Analco piden se les respeten los privilegios de que gozan de imemorable año."

71. An erosion of privileges and a closer approximation to the status of local Indians proved to be the trajectory for the Tlaxcalan settlers of the San Luis Potosí region as well. See Frye, *Indians into Mexicans*, 50, 53.

72. Katzew, *Casta Painting*.

CONCLUSION

1. Taylor, "Between Global Process and Local Knowledge."

2. Scott, *Weapons of the Weak*, 23.

3. Knight, "Is Political Culture Good to Think?," 28–29. In this essay, Alan Knight argues that the utility of "political culture" as an analytical frame depends on its *durability* and *salience*.

4. Foucault, "Governmentality."

5. Dean, *Inka Bodies and the Body of Christ*, 47.

6. Silverblatt, *Modern Inquisitions*, 17.

7. Stern et al. (*Rebellion, Resistance, and Consciousness*) initiated this discussion of "anti-colonial peasant consciousness" in the Andes. More recently, Silverblatt and Serulnikov have explored the dimensions of Indian identity and anticolonial ideology; Stern, *Rebellion, Resistance, and Consciousness*; Silverblatt, *Modern Inquisitions*; Serulnikov, *Subverting Colonial Authority*.

8. Lewis, *Hall of Mirrors*.

9. Chassen-Lopez, "Maderismo or Mixtec Empire?," 92.

10. Caplan, "Legal Revolution in Town Politics."

11. For a recent historiographical overview, see Otero, "'Indian Question.'"

12. Higgins, *Understanding the Chiapas Rebellion*.

Bibliography

ARCHIVAL SOURCES AND ABBREVIATIONS

AGI: Archivo General de las Indias (Seville)

AGN: Archivo General de la Nación (Mexico City)

AGPEO: Archivo General del Poder Ejecutivo de Oaxaca (Oaxaca City)

APJO, AVA: Archivo del Poder Judicial de Oaxaca, Archivo del Juzgado de Villa Alta (Oaxaca, Mexico) (The APJO recatalogued the AVA from 2001 to 2003 and imposed a new system of *legajos* and *expedientes*. My citations reflect both the pre-2001 and post-2003 systems. Where I include a legajo ["Leg."], I refer to the new system. Where a legajo designation is absent, I am using the old system. In all cases, I refer to the title of the document so that it can be more easily found.)

Archivo del Tribunal Superior de Oaxaca (Oaxaca City)

Rosenbach Museum and Library (Philadelphia)

PRINTED OR BOUND PRIMARY SOURCES

Burgoa, Francisco de. *Geográfica descripción: De la parte septentrional del polo ártico de la América y, Nueva Iglesia de las Indias Occidentales, y sitio astronómico de esta provincia de predicadores de Antequera, Valle de Oaxaca.* 2 vols. Mexico City: Juan Ruiz, 1674; reprint, Mexico City: Talleres Gráficos de la Nación, 1934; reprint, Mexico City: Porrúa, 1989.

Díaz del Castillo, Bernal. *Historia verdadera de la conquista de la Nueva España*, 2 vols. Mexico City: Porrua, 1955; English translation: Bernal Díaz, *The Conquest of New Spain*. New York: Penguin, 1963.

Gillow, Eulogio. *Apuntes históricos sobre la idolatría e introducción del cristianismo en Oaxaca.* Mexico City: Toledo, 1990 [1889].

Recopilación de leyes de los reynos de las Indias. Vols. 1–3. Facsimile edition copublished by the Centro de Estudios Políticos y Constitucionales and the

Boletín Oficial del Estado. Madrid: Imprenta Nacional del *Boletín Oficial del Estado,* 1998.

SECONDARY SOURCES

Adorno, Rolena. *Guáman Poma: Writing and Resistance in Colonial Peru.* Austin: University of Texas Press, 1986.

——. "Arms, Letters and the Native Historian in Early Colonial Mexico." In *1492– 1992: Re/Discovering Colonial Writing,* ed. René Jara and Nicholas Spadaccini, 201–24. Hispanic Issues 4. Minneapolis: Prisma Institute, 1989.

——. "Images of Indios Ladinos in Early Colonial Peru." In *Transatlantic Encounters: Europeans and Andeans in the Sixteenth Century,* ed. Rolena Adorno and Kenneth Andrien, 232–70. Berkeley: University of California Press, 1991.

——. "The Indigenous Ethnographer: The 'Indio Ladino' as Historian and Cultural Mediation." In *Implicit Understandings: Observing, Reporting, and Reflecting on Encounters between Europeans and Other Peoples in the Early Modern Era,* ed. Stuart B. Schwartz, 378–402. Cambridge: Cambridge University Press, 1994.

Alcina Franch, José. *Calendario y religión entre los zapotecos.* Mexico City: UNAM, 1993.

Altman, Ida. "Reconsidering the Center: Puebla and Mexico City: 1550–1650." In Daniels and Kennedy, *Negotiated Empires* (2002), 43–58.

Anderson, Rodney D. "Race and Social Stratification: A Comparison of Working-Class Spaniards, Indians, and Castas in Guadalajara, Mexico, in 1821." *Hispanic American Historical Review* 68 (1988): 209–43.

Anzoátegui, Victor Tau. *El poder de la costumbre: Estudios sobre el derecho consuetudinario en América hispana hasta la Emancipación.* Buenos Aires: Instituto de Investigaciones de Historia del Derecho, 2001.

Ares Queija, Berta, and Serge Gruzinski, coords. *Entre dos mundos: Fronteras culturales y agentes mediadores.* Sevilla: Publicaciones de la Escuela de Estudios Hispano-Americanos de Sevilla, 1997.

Asselbergs, Florine. *Conquered Conquistadors: The Lienzo of Quauhquechollan— A Nahua Vision of the Conquest of Mexico.* Leiden: CNWS, 2004.

——. "The Conquest in Images: Stories of Tlaxcalteca and Quahquecholteca Conquistadors." In Matthew and Oudijk, *Indian Conquistadors* (2007), 65–101.

Baskes, Jeremy. "Coerced or Voluntary? The Repartimiento and Market Participation of Peasants in Late Colonial Oaxaca." *Journal of Latin American Studies* 28 (1996): 1–28.

——. *Indians, Merchants, and Markets: A Reinterpretation of the Repartimiento and Spanish-Indian Economic Relations in Colonial Oaxaca, 1750–1821.* Stanford: Stanford University Press, 2000.

Bauman, Richard. *Story, Performance, and Event: Contextual Studies of Oral Narrative.* Cambridge: Cambridge University Press, 1986.

Beals, Ralph L. *Ethnology of the Western Mixe.* New York: Cooper Square, 1973 [1945].

Becker, Marjorie. *Setting the Virgin on Fire: Lázaro Cárdenas, Michoacán Peasants, and the Redemption of the Mexican Revolution.* Berkeley: University of California Press, 1995.

Beezley, William H., Cheryl E. Martin, and William E. French, eds. *Rituals of Rule, Rituals of Resistance: Public Celebrations and Popular Culture in Mexico.* Wilmington, Del.: SR, 1994.

Bennett, Herman Lee. *Africans in Colonial Mexico: Absolutism, Christianity, and Afro-Creole Consciousness, 1570–1640.* Bloomington: Indiana University Press, 2003.

Benton, Lauren. *Law and Colonial Cultures: Legal Regimes in World History, 1400– 1900.* Cambridge: Cambridge University Press, 2002.

Bhabha, Homi K. *The Location of Culture.* New York: Routledge, 1994.

Blom, Franz. "El Lienzo de Analco, Oaxaca." *Cuadernos americanos* 4 (1945): 125–36.

Borah, Woodrow. *Justice by Insurance: The General Indian Court of Colonial Mexico and the Legal Aides of the Half-Real.* Berkeley: University of California Press, 1983.

Brading, D. A. *Miners and Merchants in Bourbon Mexico, 1763–1810.* Cambridge: Cambridge University Press, 1971.

Burgos-Debray, Elizabeth, ed. *I Rigoberta Menchú: An Indian Woman in Guatemala.* Trans. Ann Wright. London: Verso, 1984.

Burkhart, Louise. *The Slippery Earth: Nahua-Christian Moral Dialogue in Sixteenth-Century Mexico.* Tucson: University of Arizona Press, 1989.

———. *Holy Wednesday: A Nahua Drama from Early Colonial Mexico.* Philadelphia: University of Pennsylvania Press, 1996.

Bushnell, Amy Turner. "Gates, Patterns, and Peripheries: The Field of Frontier Latin America." In Daniels and Kennedy, *Negotiated Empires* (2002), 15–28.

Cahill, David P. "Colour by Numbers: Racial and Ethnic Categories in the Viceroyalty of Peru, 1532–1824." *Journal of Latin American Studies* 26 (1994): 325–46.

Cañeque, Alejandro. *The King's Living Image: The Culture and Politics of Viceregal Power in Colonial Mexico.* New York: Routledge, 2004.

Caplan, Karen D. "The Legal Revolution in Town Politics: Oaxaca and Yucatán, 1812–1825." *Hispanic American Historical Review* 83 (2003): 255–93.

Carmagnani, Marcello. "Local Governments and Ethnic Governments in Oaxaca." In *Essays in the Political, Economic and Social History of Colonial Latin America,* ed., Karen Spalding, 107–24. Newark: University of Delaware Press, 1982.

———. *El regreso de los dioses: El proceso de reconstitución de la identidad étnica en Oaxaca, siglos XVII y XVIII.* Mexico City: Fondo de Cultura Económica, 1988.

Carroll, Patrick J. *Blacks in Colonial Veracruz: Race, Ethnicity, and Regional Development.* Austin: University of Texas Press, 1991.

Chambers, Sarah C. *From Subjects to Citizens: Honor, Gender, and Politics in Arequipa, Peru, 1780–1854.* University Park: Pennsylvania State University Press, 1999.

Chance, John K. *Race and Class in Colonial Oaxaca*. Stanford: Stanford University Press, 1978.

——."Social Stratification and the Civil Cargo System among the Rincón Zapotecs of Oaxaca: The Late Colonial Period." In *Iberian Colonies, New World Societies: Essays in Memory of Charles Gibson*, ed. Richard L. Garner and William B. Taylor. Unpublished proceedings, 1986.

——. *Conquest of the Sierra: Spaniards and Indians in Colonial Oaxaca*. Norman: University of Oklahoma Press, 1989.

——. "The Barrios of Tecali: Patronage, Kinship, and Territorial Relations in a Central Mexican Community." *Ethnology* 35.2 (1996): 107–40.

——. "The Caciques of Tecali: Class and Ethnic Identity in Late Colonial Mexico." *Hispanic American Historical Review* 76 (1996): 475–502.

——. "The Noble House in Colonial Puebla, Mexico: Descent, Inheritance, and the Nahua Tradition." *American Anthropologist* 102 (2000): 485–502.

Chance, John K., and William Taylor. "Estate and Class in a Colonial City: Oaxaca in 1792." *Comparative Studies in Society and History* 19 (1977): 454–87.

Chassen-Lopez, Francie R. "Maderismo or Mixtec Empire? Class and Ethnicity in the Mexican Revolution, Costa Chica of Oaxaca, 1911." *Americas*, July 1998.

Clendinnen, Inga. *Ambivalent Conquests: Maya and Spaniard in Yucatan, 1517–1570*. Cambridge: Cambridge University Press, 1987.

Comaroff, John, and Jean Comaroff. *Ethnography and the Historical Imagination*. Boulder: Westview, 1992.

——. *Of Revelation and Revolution*, vol. 1, *Christianity, Colonialism, and Consciousness in South Africa*. Chicago: University of Chicago Press, 1991.

——. *Of Revelation and Revolution*, vol. 2, *The Dialectics of Modernity on a South African Frontier*. Chicago: University of Chicago Press, 1997.

Constructores de la nación: La migración tlaxcalteca en el norte de la Nueva España. San Luis Potosí: Colegio de San Luis, 1999.

Cope, R. Douglas. *The Limits of Racial Domination: Plebeian Society in Colonial Mexico City, 1660–1720*. Madison: University of Wisconsin Press, 1994.

Curcio-Nagy, Linda. *The Great Festivals of Colonial Mexico City: Performing Power and Identity*. Albuquerque: University of New Mexico Press, 2004.

Cutter, Charles R. *The Legal Culture of Northern New Spain, 1700–1810*. Albuquerque: University of New Mexico Press, 1995.

Dalton, Margarita. *Breve historia de Oaxaca*. Mexico City: Colegio de México, Fideicomiso Historia de las Américas, Fondo de Cultura Económica, 2004.

Daniels, Christine, and Michael V. Kennedy, eds. *Negotiated Empires: Centers and Peripheries in the Americas, 1500–1821*. New York: Routledge, 2002.

Dean, Carolyn. *Inka Bodies and the Body of Christ: Corpus Christi in Colonial Cuzco, Peru*. Durham, N.C.: Duke University Press, 1999.

de Certeau, Michel. *The Practice of Everyday Life*. Berkeley: University of California Press, 1984.

Dehouve, Danièle. *Quand les banquiers étaient des saints*. Paris: Editions du Centre National de la Recherche Scientifique, 1990.

———. "Las separaciones de pueblos en la región de Tlapa (siglo XVIII)." In *Los pueblos de indios y las comunidades*, comp. Bernardo García Martínez, 99–124. Mexico City: Colegio de México, 1991.

Díaz Couder, E. "Lenguas indígenas." In *Los pueblos indígenas de Oaxaca: Atlas etnográfico*, ed. Alicia Mabel Barabas, Miguel Alberto Bartolomé, Benjamín Maldonado, 149–68. Mexico City and Oaxaca City: INAH, Fondo de Cultura Económica, and Gobierno del Estado de Oaxaca/Secretaría de Asuntos Indígenas, 2004.

Díaz-Polanco, Héctor, comp. *El fuego de la inobediencia: Autonomía y rebelión india en el obsipado de Oaxaca*. Mexico City: CIESAS, 1992.

Díaz-Polanco, Héctor, and Araceli Burguete. "Sociedad colonial y rebelión indígena en el Obispado de Oaxaca (1660)." In Díaz-Polanco, *Fuego de la inobediencia* (1992), 17–52.

Espejo-Ponce Hunt, Marta, and Matthew Restall. "Work, Marriage, and Status: Maya Women of Colonial Yucatan." In *Indian Women of Early Mexico*, ed. Susan Schroeder, Stephanie Wood, and Robert Haskett, 231–54. Norman: University of Oklahoma Press, 1997.

Estenssoro, Juan Carlos Fuchs. *Música y sociedades coloniales: Lima, 1680–1830*. Lima: Colmillo Blanco, 1989.

Farriss, Nancy M. *Crown and Clergy in Colonial Mexico, 1759–1821: The Crisis of Ecclesiastical Privilege*. London: Athlone, 1968.

———. *Maya Society under Colonial Rule: The Collective Enterprise of Survival*. Princeton: Princeton University Press, 1984.

Florescano, Enrique. *Memoria indígena*. Mexico City: Taurus, 1999.

Foucault, Michel. *Discipline and Punish: The Birth of the Prison*, 2nd ed. New York: Vintage, 1995 [1977].

———. "Governmentality." In *The Foucault Effect: Studies in Governmentality*, ed. Graham Burchell, Colin Gordon, and Peter Miller, 87–104. Chicago: University of Chicago Press, 1991.

Frye, David. *Indians into Mexicans: History and Identity in a Mexican Town*. Austin: University of Texas Press, 1996.

García Martínez, Bernardo. *Los pueblos de la sierra: El poder y el espacio entre los indios del norte de Puebla hasta 1700*. Mexico City: Colegio de México, 1987.

Gerhard, Peter. *A Guide to the Historical Geography of New Spain*. Rev. ed. Norman: University of Oklahoma Press, 1993.

Gibson, Charles. *The Aztecs under Spanish Rule: A History of the Indians of the Valley of Mexico, 1519–1810*. Stanford: Stanford University Press, 1964.

———. *Tlaxcala in the Sixteenth Century*. 2nd ed. Stanford: Stanford University Press, 1967 [1952].

Gillespie, Jeanne Lou. "Saints and Warriors: The Lienzo de Tlaxcala and the Conquest of Tenochtitlan." PhD diss., Arizona State University, 1994.

Ginzburg, Carlo. *The Night Battles: Witchcraft and Agrarian Cults in the Sixteenth and Seventeenth Centuries*. Baltimore: Johns Hopkins University Press, 1983.

Gosner, Kevin. *Soldiers of the Virgin: The Moral Economy of a Colonial Maya Rebellion*. Tucson: University of Arizona Press, 1992.

Gramsci, Antonio. *Selections from the Prison Notebooks*, ed. and trans. Quintin Hoare and Geoffrey Nowell Smith. New York: International, 1971.

Grandin, Greg, and Francisco Goldman. "Bitter Fruit for Rigoberta." *Nation*, 8 February 1999, 25–28.

Griffiths, Nicholas. *The Cross and the Serpent: Religious Repression and Resurgence in Colonial Peru*. Norman: University of Oklahoma Press, 1996.

Guardino, Peter F. *The Time of Liberty: Popular Political Culture in Oaxaca, 1750–1850*. Durham, N.C.: Duke University Press, 2005.

Guevara Hernández, Jorge. *El Lienzo de Tiltepec: Extinción de un señorio zapoteco*. Mexico City: Instituto Nacional de Antropología e Historia, 1991.

Guillermoprieto, Alma. "A New Bolivia?" *New York Review of Books*, 10 August 2006, 36–38.

Gutiérrez, Ramón A. *When Jesus Came, the Corn Mothers Went Away: Marriage, Sexuality, and Power in New Mexico, 1500–1846*. Stanford: Stanford University Press, 1991.

Hamnett, Brian. *Politics and Trade in Southern Mexico, 1750–1821*. Cambridge: Cambridge University Press, 1971.

Haskett, Robert Stephen. "Indian Town Government in Colonial Cuernavaca." *Hispanic American Historical Review* 67 (1987): 203–31.

——. *Indigenous Rulers: An Ethnohistory of Town Government in Colonial Cuernavaca*. Albuquerque: University of New Mexico Press, 1991.

Higgins, Nicholas P. *Understanding the Chiapas Rebellion: Modernist Visions and the Invisible Indian*. Austin: University of Texas Press, 2004.

Hill, Robert M., II, and John Monaghan. *Continuities in Highland Maya Social Organization: Ethnohistory in Sacapulas, Guatemala*. Philadelphia: University of Pennsylvania Press, 1987.

Jacobsen, Nils, and Cristóbal Aljovín de Losada, eds. *Political Cultures in the Andes, 1750–1950*. Durham, N.C.: Duke University Press, 2005.

Jakobson, Roman. "Shifters, Verbal Categories, and the Russian Verb." In *Roman Jakobson: Selected Writings*, vol. 2, 130–47. The Hague: Mouton, 1971.

Joseph, Gilbert M., and Daniel Nugent, eds. *Everyday Forms of State Formation: Revolution and the Negotiation of Rule in Modern Mexico*. Durham, N.C.: Duke University Press, 1994.

Karttunen, Frances. *Between Worlds: Interpreters, Guides and Survivors*. New Brunswick, N.J.: Rutgers University Press, 1994.

Katzew, Ilona. *Casta Painting: Images of Race in Eighteenth-Century Mexico*. New Haven, Conn.: Yale University Press, 2004.

Kellogg, Susan. "Hegemony out of Conquest: The First Two Centuries of Spanish Rule in Central Mexico." *Radical History Review* 53 (1992): 27–46.

———. *Law and the Transformation of Aztec Culture, 1500–1700.* Norman: University of Oklahoma Press, 1995.

———. "From Parallel and Equivalent to Separate but Unequal: Tenocha Mexica Women, 1500–1700." In *Indian Women of Early Mexico*, ed. Susan Schroeder, Stephanie Wood, and Robert Haskett, 123–44. Norman: University of Oklahoma Press, 1997.

———. *Weaving the Past: A History of Latin America's Indigenous Women from the Prehispanic Period to the Present.* Oxford: Oxford University Press, 2005.

———. "Back to the Future: Ethnohistory, Law, Politics, and Culture in Colonial Mexican Ethnohistorical Studies." In *Negotiation within Domination: Colonial New Spain's Indian Pueblos Confront the Spanish State*, ed. Ethelia Ruiz Medrano and Susan Kellogg. Boulder: University Press of Colorado, forthcoming.

Knight, Alan. "Is Political Culture Good to Think?" In Jacobsen and Aljovín de Losada, *Political Cultures in the Andes* (2005), 25–57.

König, Viola. *Die Schlacht bei Sieben Blume: Konquistadoren, Kaziken und Konflickte auf alten Landkarten der Indianer Südmexikos.* Bremen: Temmen, 1993.

Kranz, Travis Barton. "The Tlaxcalan Conquest Pictorials: The Role of Images in Influencing Colonial Policy in the Sixteenth Century." PhD diss., UCLA, 2001.

Kroskrity, Paul V. "Regimenting Languages: Language Ideological Perspectives." In *Regimes of Language: Ideologies, Polities, and Identities*, ed. Paul V. Kroskrity, 1–34. Santa Fe, N.M.: School of American Research Press, 2000.

Larson, Brooke. *Cochabamba, 1500–1900: Colonialism and Agrarian Transformation in Bolivia.* Princeton: Princeton University Press, 1988; 2nd ed. Durham, N.C.: Duke University Press, 1998.

Leibsohn, Dana. "Primers for Memory: Cartographic Histories and Nahua Identity." In *Writing without Words: Alternative Literacies in Mesoamerica and the Andes*, ed. Elizabeth Hill Boone and Walter D. Mignolo, 161–87. Durham, N.C.: Duke University Press, 1994.

Lewis, Laura A. *Hall of Mirrors: Power, Witchcraft, and Caste in Colonial Mexico.* Durham, N.C.: Duke University Press, 2003.

Lipp, Frank J. *The Mixe of Oaxaca: Religion, Ritual, and Healing.* Austin: University of Texas Press, 1991.

Lockhart, James. *The Nahuas after the Conquest: A Social and Cultural History of the Indians of Central Mexico, Sixteenth through Eighteenth Centuries.* Stanford: Stanford University Press, 1992.

Lomnitz-Adler, Claudio. *Exits from the Labyrinth: Culture and Ideology in the Mexican National Space.* Berkeley: University of California Press, 1992.

MacLeod, Murdo J. "Some Thoughts on the Pax Colonial, Colonial Violence, and Perceptions of Both." In *Native Resistance and the Pax Colonial in New Spain*, ed. Susan Schroeder, 129–42. Lincoln: University of Nebraska Press, 1998.

Mallon, Florencia E. *Peasant and Nation: The Making of Postcolonial Mexico and Peru*. Berkeley: University of California Press, 1995.

Matthew, Laura. "El náhuatl y la identidad mexicana en la Guatemala colonial." *Mesoamérica* 40 (2000): 41–68.

———. "Neither and Both: The Mexican Indian Conquistadors of Colonial Guatemala." PhD diss., University of Pennsylvania, 2004.

———, and Michel Oudijk, eds. *Indian Conquistadors: Native Allies in the Conquest of Mesoamerica*. Norman: University of Oklahoma Press, 2007.

Maybury-Lewis, David, ed. *The Politics of Ethnicity: Indigenous Peoples in Latin American States*. Cambridge: Harvard University Press, 2002.

McCaa, Robert, Stuart B. Schwartz, and Arturo Grubessich. "Race and Class in Colonial Latin America: A Critique." *Comparative Studies in Society and History* 21 (1979): 421–33.

Merrell, James. *Into the American Woods: Negotiators on the Pennsylvania Frontier*. New York: W. W. Norton, 1999.

Metcalf, Alida C. *Go-betweens and the Colonization of Brazil, 1500–1600*. Austin: University of Texas Press, 2005.

Miceli, Paola. "El derecho consuetudinario en Castilla: Una crítica a la matriz romántica de las interpretaciones sobre la costumbre." *Hispania* 63.1 (2002): 9–28.

Mignolo, Walter D. *The Darker Side of the Renaissance: Literacy, Territoriality, and Colonization*. Ann Arbor: University of Michigan Press, 1995.

Mills, Kenneth. *Idolatry and Its Enemies: Colonial Andean Religion and Extirpation, 1640–1750*. Princeton: Princeton University Press, 1997.

Monaghan, John. *The Covenants of Earth and Rain: Exchange, Sacrifice, and Revelation in Mixtec Sociality*. Norman: University of Oklahoma Press, 1995.

———. "The Mesoamerican Community as 'Great House.'" *Ethnology* 35.3 (1996): 181–94.

———. "Physiology, Production, and Gendered Difference: The Evidence from Mixtec and Other Mesoamerican Societies." In *Gender in Pre-Hispanic America: A Symposium at Dumbarton Oaks*, ed. Cecelia F. Klein, 285–304. Washington, D.C.: Dumbarton Oaks, 2001.

———, and Jeffrey H. Cohen. "Thirty Years of Oaxacan Ethnography." In *Handbook of Middle American Indians*, supplement 6, ed. John D. Monaghan, 150–78. Austin: University of Texas Press, 2000.

Mörner, Magnus. *Race Mixture in the History of Latin America*. Boston: Little, Brown, 1967.

Nandy, Ashis. *The Intimate Enemy: Loss and Recovery of Self under Colonialism*. Delhi: Oxford University Press, 1983.

O'Hara, Matthew D. "Stone, Mortar, and Memory: Church Construction and Communities in Late Colonial Mexico City." *Hispanic American Historical Review* 86 (2006): 647–80.

O'Phelan Godoy, Scarlett. *Rebellions and Revolts in Eighteenth Century Peru and Upper Peru.* Cologne: Böhlau, 1985.

Otero, Gerardo. "'The Indian Question' in Latin America: Class, State, and Ethnic Identity Construction." *Latin American Research Review* 38 (2003): 248–66.

Ots Capdequí, José María. *Manual de historia del derecho español en las Indias y del derecho propiamente indiano.* Vol. 2. Buenos Aires: Instituto de Historia del Derecho Argentino, 1943.

———. *El Estado español en las Indias.* 3rd ed. Buenos Aires: Fondo de Cultura Económica, 1957.

Oudijk, Michel. *Historiography of the Bénizáa: The Postclassic and Early Colonial Periods (1000–1600 AD).* Leiden: Research School of Asian, African, and Amerindian Studies, Leiden University, 2000.

———. "Espacio y escritura. El Lienzo de Tabáa I." In *Escritura zapoteca: 2500 años de historia,* coord. María de los Angeles Romero Frizzi, 341–91. Mexico City: CIESAS and INAH, 2003.

Ouweneel, Arij. "From 'Tlahtocayotl' to 'Gobernadoryotl': A Critical Examination of Indigenous Rule in Eighteenth-Century Central Mexico." *American Ethnologist* 22 (1995): 756–85.

Overmyer-Velázquez, Mark. *Visions of the Emerald City: Modernity, Tradition, and the Formation of Porfirian Oaxaca, Mexico.* Durham, N.C.: Duke University Press, 2006.

Palmer, Colin A. *Slaves of the White God: Blacks in Mexico, 1570–1650.* Cambridge, Mass.: Harvard University Press, 1976.

Pastor, Rodolfo. "El repartimiento de mercancías y los alcaldes mayores novohispanos: Un sistema de explotación, de sus orígenes a la crisis de 1810." In *El gobierno provincial en La Nueva España, 1570–1787,* coord. Woodrow Borah, 201–36. Mexico City: Universidad Nacional Autónoma de México, 1985.

———. *Campesinos y reformas: La Mixteca, 1700–1856.* Mexico City: Colegio de México, 1987.

Patch, Robert W. *Maya Revolt and Revolution in the Eighteenth Century.* Armonk, N.Y.: M. E. Sharpe, 2002.

Paz, Octavio. *Labyrinth of Solitude.* Trans. Lysander Kemp, Yara Milos, and Rachel Phillips Belash. New York: Grove, 1985 [1961].

Poole, Deborah. *Unruly Order: Violence, Power, and Cultural Identity in the High Provinces of Southern Peru.* Boulder: Westview, 1994.

Rappaport, Joanne. *Cumbe Reborn: An Andean Ethnography of History.* Chicago: University of Chicago Press, 1994.

Rendon, Juan José. *Diversificación de las lenguas zapotecas.* Mexico City: Instituto Oaxaqueño de las Culturas and CIESAS, 1995.

Restall, Matthew. *The Maya World: Yucatec Culture and Society, 1550–1850.* Stanford: Stanford University Press, 1997.

———. *Maya Conquistador.* Boston: Beacon, 1998.

——. *Seven Myths of the Spanish Conquest*. Oxford: Oxford University Press, 2003.

Ricard, Robert. *La Conquista espiritual de México*. Trans. Angel María Garibay. Mexico City: Jus, 1947.

Richter, Daniel K. "Cultural Brokers and Intercultural Politics: New York–Iroquois Relations, 1664–1701." *Journal of American History* 75 (1988): 40–67.

Romero Frizzi, María de los Angeles. *Economía y vida de los españoles en la Mixteca Alta, 1519–1720*. Mexico City: INAH, 1990.

——. *El sol y la cruz: Los pueblos indios de Oaxaca colonial*. Mexico City: CIESAS, 1996.

Romero Frizzi, María de los Angeles, coord. *Escritura zapoteca: 2500 años de historia*. Mexico City: CIESAS and INAH, 2003.

Romero Frizzi, María de los Angeles, and Juana Vásquez Vásquez. "Memoria y Escritura. La Memoria de Juquila." In Romero Frizzi, *Escritura Zapoteca* (2003), 393–448.

Roseberry, William. "Hegemony and the Language of Contention." In Joseph and Nugent, *Everyday Forms of State Formation* (1994), 355–66.

Rubin, Jeffrey W. *Decentering the Regime: History, Culture, and Radical Politics in Juchitán, Mexico*. Durham, N.C.: Duke University Press, 1997.

Scardaville, Michael. "(Hapsburg) Law and (Bourbon) Order: State Authority, Popular Unrest, and the Criminal Justice System in Bourbon Mexico City." *Americas* 50 (1994): 501–25.

Schroeder, Susan, ed. *Native Resistance and the Pax Colonial in New Spain*. Lincoln: University of Nebraska Press, 1998.

Scott, James C. *Weapons of the Weak: Everyday Forms of Peasant Resistance*. New Haven: Yale University Press, 1985.

——. *Domination and the Arts of Resistance: Hidden Transcripts*. New Haven: Yale University Press, 1990.

Seed, Patricia. "Social Dimensions of Race: Mexico City, 1753." *Hispanic American Historical Review* 62 (1982): 559–606.

——. " 'Failing to Marvel': Atahualpa's Encounter with the Word." *Latin American Research Review* 26 (1991): 7–32.

——, and Philip F. Rust. "Estate and Class in Colonial Oaxaca Revisited." *Comparative Studies in Society and History* 25 (1983): 703–10.

Sego, Eugene B. *Aliados y adversarios: Los colonos tlaxcaltecas en la frontera septentrional de Nueva España*. San Luis Potosí: Colegio de San Luis Gobierno del Estado de Tlaxcala Centro de Investigaciones Históricas de San Luis Potosí, 1998.

Serulnikov, Sergio. "Customs and Rules: Bourbon Rationalizing Projects and Social Conflicts in Northern Potosí during the 1770s." *Colonial Latin American Review* 8.2 (1999): 245–74.

——. *Subverting Colonial Authority: Challenges to Spanish Rule in Eighteenth-Century Southern Andes*. Durham, N.C.: Duke University Press, 2003.

Sigal, Pete. *From Moon Goddesses to Virgins: The Colonization of Yucatecan Maya Sexual Desire.* Austin: University of Texas Press, 2000.

Silverblatt, Irene. *Moon, Sun, and Witches: Gender Ideologies and Class in Inca and Colonial Peru.* Princeton: Princeton University Press, 1987.

——. *Modern Inquisitions: Peru and the Colonial Origins of the Civilized World.* Durham, N.C.: Duke University Press, 2004.

Simpson, Lesley Byrd. *Many Mexicos.* 4th ed. Berkeley: University of California Press, 1974.

Smith, Carol A., ed. *Guatemalan Indians and the State, 1540–1988.* Austin: University of Texas Press, 1990.

Sousa, Lisa Mary. "Women and Crime in Colonial Oaxaca: Evidence of Complementary Gender Roles in Mixtec and Zapotec Societies." In *Indian Women of Early Mexico,* ed. Susan Schroeder, Stephanie Wood, and Robert Haskett, 199–216. Norman: University of Oklahoma Press, 1997.

Spalding, Karen. *Huarochirí: An Andean Society under Inca and Spanish Rule.* Stanford: Stanford University Press, 1984.

Spivak, Gayatri Chakravorty. "Can the Subaltern Speak?" In *Marxism and the Interpretation of Culture,* ed. Cary Nelson and Lawrence Grossberg, 271–313. Urbana: University of Illinois Press, 1988.

Spores, Ronald. *The Mixtec Kings and Their People.* Norman: University of Oklahoma Press, 1967.

——. *The Mixtecs in Ancient and Colonial Times.* Norman: University of Oklahoma Press, 1984.

——. "Mixteca Cacicas: Status, Wealth, and the Political Accommodation of Native Elite Women in Early Colonial Oaxaca." In *Indian Women of Early Mexico.* Ed. Susan Schroeder, Stephanie Wood, and Robert Haskett, 185–98. Norman: University of Oklahoma Press, 1997.

Stavenhagen, Rodolfo. *Derecho indígena y derechos humanos en América Latina.* Mexico City: Colegio de México y Instituto Interamericano de Derechos Humanos, 1988.

Stephen, Lynn. *Zapotec Women: Gender, Class, and Ethnicity in Globalized Oaxaca.* 2nd ed. Durham, N.C.: Duke University Press, 2005.

Stern, Steve J. *Peru's Indian Peoples and the Challenge of Spanish Conquest: Huamanga to 1640.* Madison: University of Wisconsin Press, 1982.

——, ed. *Rebellion, Resistance and Consciousness in the Andean Peasant World: Eighteenth to Twentieth Centuries.* Madison: University of Wisconsin Press, 1987.

——. "Feudalism, Capitalism, and the World System in the Perspective of Latin America and the Caribbean." *American Historical Review* 93 (1988): 829–72.

Stoll, David. *Rigoberta Menchú and the Story of All Poor Guatemalans.* Boulder: Westview, 1999.

Tanck de Estrada, Dorothy. *Pueblos de indios y educación en el México colonial, 1750–1821*. Mexico City: Colegio de México, 1999.

Tavárez, David. "La idolatría letrada: Un análisis comparativo de textos clandestinos rituales y devocionales en comunidades nahuas y zapotecas, 1613–1654." *Historia mexicana* 49.2 (1999): 194, 197–252.

———. "Invisible Wars: Idolatry Extirpation Projects and Native Responses in Nahua and Zapotec Communities, 1536–1728." PhD diss., University of Chicago, 2000.

———. "Letras clandestinas, textos tolerados, colaboraciones lícitas: La producción textual de los intelectuales nahuas y zapotecos en el siglo XVII." In *Elites intelectuales y modelos colectivos*, ed. Mónica Quijada and Jesús Bustamente, 59–82. Madrid: Consejo Superior de Investigaciones Científicas, Instituto de Historia, Departamento de Historia de América, 2002.

———. "Idolatry as Ontological Question: Native Consciousness and Juridical Proof in Colonial Mexico." Journal of Early Modern History 6.2 (2002): 114–39.

———. "The Passion According to the Wooden Drum: The Doctrinal Appropriation of a Colonial Zapotec Ritual Genre." *Americas* 62.3 (2006): 413–44.

Taylor, William B. *Landlord and Peasant in Colonial Oaxaca*. Stanford: Stanford University Press, 1972.

———. *Drinking, Homicide and Rebellion in Colonial Mexican Villages*. Stanford: Stanford University Press, 1979.

———. "Between Global Process and Local Knowledge: An Inquiry into Early Latin American Social History." In *Reliving the Past: The Worlds of Social History*, ed. Olivier Zunz, 115–90. Chapel Hill: University of North Carolina Press, 1991.

———. *Magistrates of the Sacred: Priests and Parishioners in Eighteenth-Century Mexico*. Stanford: Stanford University Press, 1996.

Terraciano, Kevin. *The Mixtecs of Colonial Oaxaca: Ñudzahui History, Sixteenth through Eighteenth Centuries*. Stanford: Stanford University Press, 2001.

Torre, Angelo. "Politics Cloaked in Worship: State, Church, and Local Power in Piedmont, 1570–1770." *Past and Present*, no. 34 (1992): 42–92.

Townsend, Camilla. *Malintzin's Choices: An Indian Woman in the Conquest of Mexico*. Albuquerque: University of New Mexico Press, 2006.

Urban, Greg, and Joel Sherzer, eds. *Nation-States and Indians in Latin America*. Austin: University of Texas Press, 1991.

Van Young, Eric. "Conflict and Solidarity in Indian Village Life: The Guadalajara Region in the Late Colonial Period." *Hispanic American Historical Review* 64 (1984): 55–79.

———. *The Other Rebellion: Popular Violence, Ideology, and the Mexican Struggle for Independence, 1810–1821*. Stanford: Stanford University, 2001.

Viqueira Albán, Juan Pedro. *Propriety and Permissiveness in Bourbon Mexico*. Wilmington, Del.: SR, 1999.

Walker, Charles F. "Civilize or Control? The Lingering Impact of the Bourbon

Reforms." In Jacobsen and Aljovín de Losada, *Political Cultures in the Andes* (2005), 74–95.

Wallerstein, Immanuel. *The Modern World System: Capitalist Agriculture and the Origins of the European World-Economy in the Sixteenth Century.* New York: Academic, 1974.

Warren, Kay B., and Jean E. Jackson, eds. *Indigenous Movements, Self-Representation, and the State in Latin America.* Austin: University of Texas Press, 2002.

Weber, David J. *Bárbaros: Spaniards and Their Savages in the Age of Enlightenment.* New Haven: Yale University Press, 2005.

Wilson, Robin. "A Challenge to the Veracity of a Multicultural Icon." *Chronicle of Higher Education,* 15 January 1999, 4–6.

Wolf, Eric R. *Sons of the Shaking Earth.* Chicago: University of Chicago Press, 1959.

Yannakakis, Yanna P. "Indios Ladinos: Indigenous Intermediaries and the Negotiation of Local Rule in Colonial Oaxaca." PhD diss., University of Pennsylvania, 2003.

Zeitlin, Judith Francis. *Cultural Politics in Colonial Tehuantepec: Community and State among the Isthmus Zapotec, 1500–1750.* Stanford: Stanford University Press, 2005.

Index

acculturation. *See* cross-cultural competence

Adorno, Rolena, 11–12

Africans, 4, 14–15, 16, 66, 68, 225

agentes, 37–38, 120–21, 176–77

ahkin (chief priest, Yucatec Maya), 82

alcabala, 184

alcaldes mayores (Spanish magistrates), 20, 22–23, 37–38, 62–63; under Bourbon Reforms, 163, 214; conflicts of, with Catholic Church, 56, 234n5; extortion by, 46, 135, 214; interference in local elections by, 43–46, 161–62, 165, 168–72, 180–90, 221; judicial authority of, 110, 118; lieutenants of, 40; as targets of rebellion, 33–35; use of torture by, 79–81, 243n55

alcaldes (native magistrates), 43–44, 81; economic roles of, 170–71, 183; elections and appointments of, 181–82; hispanicization and Spanish-language skills of, 174, 181; labor conflicts and, 168; land and market disputes and, 134, 139–40, 149, 152; roles of, in uprisings, 84–85, 88–89

Alcántara, Fray Bartolomé de, 212

Alcina Franch, José, 70

Aldas, Antonio de, 122

Aldas, Francisco de, 110–16, 120

alguaciles mayores (Spanish bailiffs), 70

Altman, Ida, 19

Alvarado, Juan de, 39–43

Anahuác, 150

Analco, 192–219; Andrés González case and, 210–11; fiesta of San Ildefonso in, 207–10; Lienzo of, 133, 195–204, 256n18; population of, 205, 257n38. *See also* Indian conquerors

Anderson, Rodney, 231n32

Andes, Andean, 12, 69, 164, 179, 183, 223, 226

Angeles, Bartolomé de los, 86

Angeles, Jacinto de los, 1–2, 68–69, 71, 73–76

Angeles, Martín de los, 86

Antequera, 41, 51, 76, 89, 134. *See also* Oaxaca

Antonio, Nicolas, 86

Anzoátegui, Victor Tau, 124

apoderados, 37–38, 120–21, 176–77

Aquino, Ciprian de, 86

Cajonos Rebellion, 66, 75–76, 81; challenges of caciques by, 149–50, 152–56; economic roles of, 183–90; extortion by, 44, 183–84; mediation of repartimiento by, 44, 56, 170, 183–90; renegotiation of local rule by, 99, 131

cacicazgos (noble estates), 30, 136, 141–43, 155–56; cabildo-led challenges against, 149–50, 152–53; rents from, 149, 151, 152

caciques, cacicas (indigenous nobles), xi, 2, 26, 29–30; as apoderados, 121; cabildo-led challenges of, 149–50, 152–56; cross-culturalism of, 151–52; hereditary rights of, 143–48, 155; landholdings of, 30, 136, 141–43, 147–56; local government roles of, 43–44; Miguel Fernández de Chaves, 141–56; negotiation of cacique status by, 143–48, 152–54, 170; variable wealth and power of, 150–52, 155–56. See also indios ladinos

caciquismo, xi

cajas de comunidad, 120–21, 163–64

Cajonos Rebellion of 1700, 1–4, 29, 65–95, 206, 210–11, 223, 226; cabildo officers in, 66, 75–76, 81, 84–85; charges of idolatry in, 1, 68–70, 73–75, 78–79; confessions under torture in, 79–81, 84–87, 243n55; court documents of, 76, 239n2; fiscales in, 1–2, 66–69, 73–74, 81, 84; investigations and trials from, 70–76; Maldonado's parish reforms following, 89–95, 100–107, 179, 211–12, 221, 244n83; martyrs of Cajonos in, 1–2, 221, 226, 239n1; reconstructed political order following, 94–95, 100–107, 130, 132–33, 221; sentences for, 86–89; Span-

ish perceptions of danger in, 81–89; Spanish versions of, 66–70, 239n1

Cajonos Zapotec (language, region, ethnic group), 17, 21, 45, 208; mining in, 166–68, 185; political economy of, 188–91. See also rebellions and uprisings

Calderón, Felipe, 226–27

calendars of native rituals, 49, 70, 93

Caltepeque (Leahbichitoag) land parcel, 135–51, 153–54

Cañada, El Conde de la, 128

cantor. See maestros

Caplan, Karen, 224–25

Cardona, Fray Joseph de, 140, 214

cargo system, xii–xiii, 150

Carmagnani, Marcello, 102, 106

Carpio, Juan, 217

Carrera, Marcial, 154

cartographic pictography, 197

casta paintings, 219

castas (people of mixed race), 14

caste system, 4, 12, 14–16, 231n30, 231–32nn32–33

Castilblanque, Alonso Muños de, 58

Castillo Mondragón, Cristóbal del, 48–49

Castro, Juan Francisco de, 127–28

Catholic Church, 3; Baroque monstrances, 48–51; Bourbon Reforms of, 90, 92, 163–64, 253n13; cabecera-sujeto parish structure of, 29–30, 91, 95; campaigns against idolatry of, 1, 7–8, 49–50, 56, 65–85, 89–94, 221, 244n83, 247n29; choirmasters in, 82; disputes with civil authorities of, 56, 178–80, 234n5; education and schools of, 67, 92, 95, 100, 111, 146, 163, 172, 176–77; fears of syncretism by, 79–89, 208; fiscales (priests' assistants) of, 1–2, 66–69; fundraising and fees of,

Catholic Church (*cont.*)
66–69, 178–80, 184; Jesuit expulsion and, 163; Maldonado's extirpation campaign and, 89–94, 213–14; Maldonado's parish reforms of, 89–95, 100–107, 179, 211–12, 221, 244n83; martyrs of Cajonos and, 1–2, 221, 226, 239n1; mobile parish priests of, 106, 112–14; political involvement of, 49–50, 62–63, 91–92, 125, 168–69, 178–80; rituals of, 67, 93, 102–3; secular clergy of, 90, 92, 164, 212; on Spanish-only policies, 173–79; Spiritual Conquest and evangelism goals of, 69, 240n18; transformation of gender hierarchies by, 146

Celis, Joseph de (of San Francisco Cajonos), 68–69

Celis, Joseph de (of San Juan Yatzona), 38–64, 223; declarations of fealty by, 39–42, 56–57; electoral autonomy campaign of, 43–46, 63; rootedness in indigenous networks of, 57–62; standoff of, in pueblo of Lachirioag, 53–54, 63–64; trials and imprisonments of, 46–52, 63; use of indigenous parcialidades by, 59–62, 63

central place hierarchy, 23, 233n60

Cerda Benavente y Benavides, Bishop Bartolomé de la, 30

Certeau, Michel de, 10–11, 88

Chambers, Sarah, 61

Chance, John: on cabecera-sujeto structure, 91; on caciques, 150; on class hierarchies, 231n32; on Indian conquerors, 202, 205; on municipal offices, 44, 170; on native intermediaries, 48; on San Miguel Tiltepec, 133, 134

Charles III, king of Spain, 162

Chaves, Cristóbal de, 137, 147–48

Chaves, Francisco de, 135, 148

Chaves, Juan, 139

Chaves, Miguel Fernández de, 131–32, 141–56, 162

Chi, Gaspar Antonio, 7–9, 11

Chiapas, x, 71

Chinantec (language and ethnic identity), 17, 21, 40, 46

Chinantla, 40, 46

Choapan, 133–34; uprising in (1552), 22, 195; uprising in (1684), 40–43, 206, 210

choirmasters, 82

class contexts: caste system and, 4, 12, 14, 231n30, 231–32nn32–33; local government posts and, 43–45, 149–50; principales and, 17, 43–44, 100, 121, 185–88; stereotypes of Indians and, 76, 81–89, 111, 219, 225; vecinos and, 110, 121, 209–10, 216–18. *See also* caciques, cacicas; Indian conquerors; land ownership; repartimiento

Clendinnen, Inga, 80, 85

cochineal dye, 19–20, 44, 58, 135, 170, 183–84, 188–89

cofradía of the Virgin of Yabee, 104–5

cofradías, 104–5, 163–64

colonial context, xiii–xv, 2; caste system, 4, 12, 14, 231n30, 231–32nn32–33; centers of Spanish power, 18–19, 24; centrality of legal documents, 54–56; congregación (forced nucleation of settlement), 27, 92–93; decentralized power, 13; disease (the Great Dying), 22; gendered discourse of conquest, 27, 145–48, 209; gendered discourses of honor, 27, 60–61, 209, 221; Indian Conquerors, 17, 30, 192–206; invisibility of women, 7, 26–27;

order and rebellion, 1–4, 22, 28–29; use of torture, 79–81, 84–87. *See also* Catholic Church; local rule; rebellions and uprisings; tactics of native intermediaries

colonizer's quandary, 222–23

Comaroff, Jean, 193

Comaroff, John, 193

Comentarios reales de los Incas (Vega), 42

commoners (natives), 2, 14–24, 30, 34, 220–23. *See also* class contexts; land ownership; local rule; race contexts

communal landholdings, 135–41, 148–49

communication skills, 11; Bourbon Reforms' Spanish-language-only requirements and, 172–80; of *indios ladinos*, 111–12, 146; literacy, 111; oral performance, 108–10; relationship with audience, 110. *See also* rhetoric

community government. *See* local rule

Compendio histórico del reino de Texcoco (Ixtlilxochitl), 42

complementarity, 145–47

composiciones de tierras of 1709, 148–49, 157

congregación (forced nucleation of settlement), 27, 92–93

conquest, 5–7; gendered discourses of, 27, 145–48, 209; native intermediaries in, 4–7; pictorials of, 196–99; of Sierra Norte, 19–24, 27, 133–34, 192–209

consent, 25–26

contingency. *See* tactics of native intermediaries

Contreras, Ambrosio, 87–88

coquis, 136, 144

corregidores (Spanish governors), 42; of Mixapa, 138–39; of Oaxaca, 72, 75

Cortés, Hernán, 5–7, 30, 200–201

costumbre (custom), xiii, 17, 30, 224–25, 230n8; attacks on, by royal jurists, 127–28; Audiencia's interpretations of, 126–28, 169–72; under Bourbon Reforms, 168–80; codified status of, 115–20; as legal weapon, 108, 113–20; local administration of repartimiento and, 170; rhetoric of contingency, flexibility, and reciprocity and, 108, 112–25, 221, 225; romantic and primordial connotations of, 119, 124–25, 127

cotton cloth production, 19–20, 44, 58, 183–84, 188–89

Council of the Indies, 127, 169

courts. *See* legal system

criollos (creoles), 14

Croix, Viceroy Marqués de, 173

cross-cultural competence, xiii–xiv, 4–13, 151–52, 220; acculturation, xiv, 155, 172, 177, 211, 222; in communication and language skills, 11–13, 25; constructions of two-way bargains, 13, 231n24; participation in social networks, 9–10; promises, 11, 155–56; rhetoric of contingency, flexibility, and reciprocity in, 108, 112–25, 221, 225; survivor skills, 9; tactical sensibility, 10–11; use of Spanish narrative genres, 11–13

Cruz, Juan de la, 93–94

Cruz, Nicolas de la, 58, 77

Cruz, Pedro de la, 139

Cruz y Arriola, Martín de la, 153

Cuevas y Dávalos, Bishop Alonso de, 35–36, 61, 83, 177

cultural history, 25

cultural homogenization, 30, 163–64, 168–80, 222. *See also* cross-cultural competence

Cutter, Charles, 250n75

Dean, Carolyn, 61, 222

decentralized political structures. *See* local rule

"Declaration of Guelatao," 227

de las Casas, Joseph Patiño, 73–76

derramas, 120–21, 180

Díaz del Castillo, Bernal, 6, 133

Díaz-Polanco, Héctor, 28

Discursos críticos sobre las leyes y sus intérpretes (Castro), 127–28

disease and epidemics, 14, 22, 27, 138–39

Doctrina christiana en lengua zapoteca nexitza (Pacheco de Silva), 113, 247n28

doctrinas (church districts, parishes), 90

Dominican order, 23, 27, 179; extirpation campaigns of, 69–70; local schools of, 67; Maldonado's parish reforms and, 89–95, 100–107, 129, 211–12, 244n83; participation of, in legal disputes, 140

draft animals, 47–48

dye. *See* cochineal dye

Echarrí, Juan Francisco de, 165–69, 182–83, 185–90

education: under Bourbon reforms, 111, 163, 172, 176–77, 253n3; Dominican schools, 67; Indian conquerors as schoolmasters, 210–11; under Maldonado's parish reforms, 92, 95, 100. *See also* maestros

elections, x, 190, 221, 223; Bourbon Reforms and, 161–65; interference in, 38, 51, 168, 180–82; local autonomy in, 43–46, 63; San Juan Tabaa electoral conflicts, 165–80

encomenderos, 8, 22

encomiendas, 22–23

epidemics. *See* disease and epidemics

escriptas de convenio y obligación, 131

Espejo-Ponce Hunt, Marta, 26

Espinoza, José de, 73

ethnic districts, 106; ethnicity and, 16–17, 26, 193, 207, 220, 222, 225; groups and, ix, 20, 45, 201, 219; identity and, 16, 194, 199–204, 215; pluriethnicity and, xii, 226. *See also* race contexts

ethnohistory, 25

ethnonationalism, 45, 235n26

European intermediaries, 5

evangelical Protestantism, xii–xiii, 230n8

Fabian, Manuel, 182

Fabian y Fuero, Bishop Francisco, 173–75

Farriss, Nancy M., 82, 150, 164

fealty to Crown and Church, 39–42

Fernández, Tomás Manuel, 127

Fernández de Pantaleón, Manuel, 171, 178

Fernández de Villaroel y de la Cueva, Pedro, 35

fiestas, 100, 135; Bourbon Reform prohibitions of, 163; disputes over, in San Juan Yae, 112–13, 123, 125; roles of caciques in, 150; of San Ildefonso, 207–10

Figueroa, Diego de, 22, 194

fiscales (priests' assistants), 1–2, 66–69

Florentine Codex, 7

Flores, Christóbal, 128

Flores, Gabriel, 87–88

Flores, Joseph, 1–2, 68–69, 73–75, 87

Florescano, Enrique, 122

fluidity. *See* tactics of native intermediaries

Foucault, Michel, 10–11, 222; on torture, 86–87

Fox, Vicente, 226

Franciscan Inquisition of 1562, 7

Francisco, Geronimo, 86
Fuero Real, 116

Gálvez, José de, 164
gamonales (local strongmen), xi
gamonalismo, xi
García, Pascual, 88–89, 244n81
gender contexts: of cacique/cacica status, 144–48; of colonial discourses, 27, 61, 145–48, 209; of education, 146; invisibility of women and, 7, 26; of La Malinche, 6–7, 11; power of indigenous women and, 26–27; of pre-Columbian complementarity and parallelism, 145–47; of repartimiento system, 146; in Zapotec iconography, 27
genealogy, 143–48
General Indian Court, 14, 121
Gerónimo, Domingo, 181
Gillow, Eulogio, 239nn1–2
Ginzburg, Carlo, 85
gobernadores (native governors), 23, 29, 81, 95, 146; caciques as, 44, 150; economic activities of, 170; hispanicization and Spanish-language skills of, 174, 181–83, 190; interference of, in elections, 43–46, 77, 161–62, 171; in labor disputes, 181–83, 186–87; uprisings and resistance against, 28, 34, 88, 125. See also local rule
Godoy, Scarlett O'Phelan, 164
González, Andrés, 210–11
González, Francisco Manuel, 72
government. See local rule
Gramsci, Antonio, 25–26
Great Dying, the, 22
Great Maya Revolt of 1546, 7
Guardino, Peter, 164–65, 166, 168–69
Guelatao, 227
Guerrero, Fray Pedro de, 67

Guevara Hernández, Jorge, 154–55
Gutiérrez, María, 93–94

Hamnett, Brian, 184
Habsburg empire, 162, 163, 172–73
Haskett, Robert, 150, 164
hegemony, 25–26; consent and, 25–26
Hernandes, José, 181
Hernández, Ambrosio, 86
Hernández, Augustín, 93–94
Hernández, Francisco, 86
Hernández, Juan, 68–69
Hernández, Nicolas, 86
historical anthropology, 25, 233n61
historical background, x–xi; Aztec Empire, 6, 201; of legal custom, xiii, 17, 230n8; of Mixe and Chinantec peoples, 21; of native brokers, xi–xiii; of political autonomy, x–xi, 14, 17, 20–22, 229n5; of pre-Hispanic ethnic warfare, 21–22; Spanish conquest, 5–7, 21–24, 194–206; Zapotec migration to Sierra Norte, 20–21. See also colonial context
honor codes, 27, 60–61, 209, 221

idolatry: as alternative form of authority, 81–89; Catholic Church campaigns against, 1, 7–8, 49–50, 56, 65–81, 221, 244n83, 247n29; Catholic Church fears of syncretism and, 79–89, 208; Maldonado's extirpation campaign and, 89–94, 213–14; rhetoric of, 208–9
Inca Empire, 145
independence, 28–29, 224–27
Indian conquerors, 17, 30, 192–219, 222; burial rights of, 211–13; challenge to Spaniards of Villa Alta, 209–10, 216–18; civilizing and evangelizing roles of, 201–2; cultural assimilation of, 195, 208, 213;

Indian conquerors (*cont.*)
decline of status of, 215–18, 258n57, 259n71; ethnic identity of, 199–204; exemption of, from tribute, 213–17; fiesta of San Ildefonso and, 207–9; law enforcement roles of, 206–7, 210, 213–15, 218; legal/rhetorical roles of, 206–11, 218, 257n43; Lienzo of Analco and, 195–204; privileges and obligations of, 194, 203, 204–6, 213–15, 218–19; symbolic repertoire of, 193; tension of, with local Indians, 210–11

Indian identity, 14–18, 222–27; centrality of legal documents to, 54–56; ethnic identities and, 45, 235n26; under independence, 225–27; multiplicity of identities and, 17–18; officially imposed homogenization of, 215–18, 222–27, 258n57, 259n71, 259n7; political autonomy of, x–xi, 14, 17, 20–22, 229n5. *See also* costumbre

indigenismo, 5, 225–27
indios bárbaros, 17
indios ladinos, 18, 25, 30; Bourbon Reforms' Spanish-language-only requirements and, 172–80; creation of space by, 38–43; legal benefits of ladino performance and, 110–12; power of attorney (apoderado) roles and, 37–38, 120–21; Spanish ambivalence toward, 174; Spanish language and literacy skills of, 111–12; as targets of rebellion, 35–43

intendancy. *See* Bourbon Reforms
internal periphery, 20, 23–24
Isthmus of Tehuantepec. *See* Tehuantepec rebellion
Ixtepeji, 33, 34, 35, 47, 72
Ixtlán, 141, 151
Ixtlilxochitl, Fernando de Alva, 12, 42

Jesuit expulsion, 163
John Paul II, Pope, 2

Karttunen, Frances, 6–7, 9
Katzew, Ilona, 219
Kellogg, Susan, 138, 209
König, Viola, 197, 204, 256n18

labor: encomenderos, 8, 22; mining drafts, 165–69, 182–83, 185–90; tequio (communal labor), x, 150; valientes (labor proxies), 185–88. *See also* repartimiento
Labyrinth of Solitude, The (Paz), 5–6
Lachirioag (San Cristóbal Lachirioag), 52–56, 207–10. *See also* Celis, Joseph de (of San Juan Yatzona); Santiago, Felipe de
ladino term, 36–38
Lalopa. *See* Santiago Lalopa
Landa, Fray Diego de, 8, 79–80, 85
land ownership: cabildo-led revolts against caciques and, 149–50; cacicazgos (noble estates) and, 30, 136, 141–43, 147–56; communal landholdings and, 135–41, 148–49; composiciones de tierras of 1709 and, 148–49, 157; local disputes over, 135–52, 156–57; territorial expansion and, 132, 135–57
language skills. *See* communication skills
languages of Oaxaca, ix, x–xi
Leahbichitoag (Caltepeque) land parcel, 135–51, 153–54
Ledesma, Joseph Antonio, 186
legal resistance to cabecera-sujeto reforms, 99–130, 246n7; accusations of fraud in, 138; appeals to costumbre in, 108, 113–25; cabecera status and, 107, 120–25; cajas de comunidad and, 120–21; ladino

performances in, 110–12; oral testimonies in, 108–16; rhetoric of contingency, flexibility, and reciprocity
in, 108, 112–25; role of parish
priests in, 125, 140; sujeto status
and, 107–16; use of historical narrative in, 114–16, 139. *See also* San
Juan Yae–San Juan Tanetze conflict
legal system, 3, 29–30, 40, 61–62; costumbre in, xiii, 17, 30, 108, 113–20,
126–28, 169–80, 225, 230n8; court
officials of, 110, 250n75; escriptas
de convenio y obligación and, 131;
funding of, 120–21; legal documents in, 54–56, 215; legal representation in, 37–38, 120–24; local
role of, 38–46, 59, 61–62; native intermediaries in, 121–22; Ordenamiento de Alcalá and, 116–17;
Política indiana (Solórzano Peréira)
and, 117–18, 123–24, 126–27; preeminence of royal authority in,
116–20, 123, 127–28; *Reales Ordenanzas de los Intendentes* and,
124, 186; *Recopilación de las leyes
de las Indias* and, 115–17, 124; shift
in, toward rationalist legal theory,
127–30. *See also* Real Audiencia
Lewis, Laura, 223–24
Lienzo of Analco, 133, 195–204,
256n18; community of origin of,
199–204; as conquest pictorial,
196–99; discovery of, 197
Lienzo of Quauhquechollan, 196, 198,
200
Lienzo of Tabaa, 143–44
Lienzo of Tiltepec, 27, 143–48
Lienzo of Tlaxcala, 7, 196, 198, 200, 204
Lienzo of Totonicapan, 196
lienzos, 143, 195–96
lineage, 136
linguistic skills, 11

Lipp, Frank, 21
literacy (alphabetic), xiv, 11, 39, 50,
111, 120, 156, 211
local rule, x–xi, 18–24, 28–30, 224,
229n5; autonomy of local elections
and, 38, 43–46, 63, 73, 161–62, 165,
168–80, 221; cajas de comunidad
and, 120–21, 163–64; cargo system
and tequio, x, xii–xiii, 150; collection of clerical fees and, 178–80;
consensus practices of, x, 43–44;
core-periphery designations in, xiv–
xv, 18–20, 23–24, 27–28, 232n41,
233n60; costumbre in, xiii, 17, 30,
108, 113–20, 169–80, 225, 230n8;
extortion in, 44, 183–84; historical
context of, 20–22; mediation of
repartimiento in, 44, 56, 170, 183–
90; official posts in, 23, 43–45, 161;
parish priests' role in, 49–50, 62–
63, 91–92, 125, 168–69, 178–80;
republic of Indians and, 14–18; role
of cofradías in, 104–5; Spanish-
language-only policies in, 177–78.
See also alcaldes mayores; Bourbon
Reforms; cabecera-sujeto; cabildos;
renegotiations of local rule; shadow
system
Lomnitz-Adler, Claudio, 17, 233n60
Lopes, Francisco, 86
Lopes, Sebastian, 139
López, Clemente, 169
López, Juan, 182
López, Phelipe, 77
Lorenzana, Archbishop Francisco An-
tonio, 175
Lucas, Francisco, 86
Luis, Joseph, 86

MacLeod, Murdo, 13
maestros: de doctrina (native schoolmasters), 111; cantores (choirmas-

priests (Catholic). *See* Catholic Church; Dominican order; secular clergy

priests (native), 49–50, 82, 83

primordial titles (títulos primordiales), 136

principales (lower nobility), 17, 43, 100; as apoderados, 121; local government (cabildo) posts of, 44; participation of, in repartimiento, 185–88

Prison of Perpetual Idolatry, 69

Prison of San Juan de Ulua, 57

probanzas (testimonies), 12

procuradores, 121

promises as tactics, 11, 155–56

property rights, 135–41

Puebla, 18; bishop of, 35, 173–75; Sierra of, 28, 102, 142, 150, 156

pueblos de indios (definition), 17

Quiroz, Juan Manuel Bernardo de, 45–46, 52, 58, 62

race contexts, 4, 225–26; caste system, 4, 12, 14–16, 231n30, 231–32nn32–33; in contemporary Oaxaca, 225–27; of Indian conquerors, 193, 199–204, 215, 217–18; legal identity of Indians, 14–18, 222–23; of mestizos, 12, 14, 121; Morelos's raceless society, 225; of parish activities, 212; stereotypes of Indians, 76, 81–89, 110–11, 121, 209–10, 216–19, 225

Rangel, Rodrigo de, 21

Rappaport, Joanne, 55

Real Audiencia (royal court), 3, 11, 29–30; interpretations of costumbre by, 126–28, 169–72; ruling for Felipe de Santiago by, 78, 243nn49–52; rulings on Cajonos Rebellion by, 66, 72–76, 86–89; rulings on Indian conquerors by, 203, 257n43; rulings on mining labor drafts by, 167–68, 182–83; support of native autonomy by, 43–46, 51, 56–57, 77, 78

Real Ordenanza de los Intendentes of 1784, 124, 186

rebellions and uprisings, 3–5, 22, 208–9, 221–22, 226–27, 230n1; against alcades mayores, 33–35; Choapan uprising (1552), 22, 195; Choapan uprising (1684), 40–43, 206, 210; of 1550, 195; Indian conquerors' roles in, 206; against indios ladinos, 35–43; Mixe rebellion (1570), 22, 195; of 1660, 28–29, 33–36, 41, 208; Tehuantepec rebellion, 28, 33–36, 83, 177, 206; Tiltepec rebellion (1531), 22, 133, 195. *See also* Cajonos Rebellion of 1700

Recopilación de las leyes de las Indias of 1680, 115–17, 124

regidores (native councilmen), 44

relaciones de méritos y servicios (accounts of merit and service), 12

Relaciones Geográficas survey, 8–9

religious practices: Bourbon Reforms of, 90, 92, 178–80; cofradías, 104–5; native autonomy in, 28–29; native idolatry and syncretism, 1, 7–8, 49–50, 56, 65–89, 93–94, 208, 221, 240n18, 244n83, 247n29; nepantlism, 70; role of choirmasters in, 82; unsanctioned domain, 223–24; Virgin of Yabee and, 104–5. *See also* Catholic Church; native rituals

renegotiations of local rule, 99, 131–57; accusations of fraud and, 138; ascendance of Spanish-style authority in, 154–57; by Miguel Fernández de Chaves, 141–56; demographic changes and, 132–33; establishment of cacique status and, 143–48, 152–

Spalding, Karen, 230n5
Spanish colonialism. *See* colonial context
Spores, Ronald, 146–47
Stern, Steve, 230n5, 232n41, 259n7
Stoll, David, 229n7
subdelegados, 163, 184, 190
sujeto. *See* cabecera-sujeto
syncretism, 69–70, 79–89, 208, 240n18

Tabaa. *See* San Juan Tabaa
tactics of native intermediaries, 33–64, 121–25, 221, 224–25; accountability, 121–22; as alternative authority to colonial rule, 79–89; campaigns for electoral autonomy, 43–46, 63, 77, 223; centrality of legal documents in, 54–56; declarations of fealty to Crown and Church, 39–42, 56–57; discourse of honor in, 60–61, 209, 221; dual religious practices, 69–70, 82–83; establishment of alternative authority to colonial rule, 79, 81–89; ladino identity, 38–43; mastery of Spanish property law, 137; pressure from below on, 52–56, 63–64; rhetoric of flexibility and costumbre of, 108, 112–25, 221, 225; risks of criminal trials and punishment, 48–52, 57, 63, 76–79; rootedness in indigenous parcialidades, 57–62, 63; use of legal action, 38–46, 59, 61–62. *See also* shadow system
Tanck de Estrada, Dorothy, 253n3
Tanetze. *See* San Juan Yae–San Juan Tanetze conflict
Tavárez, David, 69–70, 73–74, 79–80, 82, 88
taxation, 120–21, 180, 184
Taylor, William, 24–25, 230n1, 231n32, 233n61; on caciques, 150; on

fiscales de iglesia, 67; on localized native identity, 45
Tehuantepec rebellion, 28, 33–36, 83, 177, 206
tenientes (lieutenants of the alcade mayor), 43–46, 47, 59, 62
tequio (communal labor), x, 150
Terraciano, Kevin, 146–47, 150, 235n26
textiles. *See* cotton cloth production
tianguis. *See* markets
Tiltepec. *See* San Miguel Tiltepec
tlacuiloque (indigenous artist), 196–97
Tlaxcala (language, region, ethnic group), 6–7, 30, 199–204, 259n71
Tojo, Juan Antonio Mier del, 52–54, 70–71, 72, 78–79, 139
Toledo, Francisco, 226
Toral, Bishop Francisco de, 8–9
torture, 79–81, 84–87, 243n55
Townsend, Camilla, 7
tribute, 3, 11, 22–23; exemptions from, 30, 137, 206, 213–17; gendered aspects of, 146; local collection of, 44, 46, 67; for maintenance of parish priests, 103; uprisings against, 41

unsanctioned domain, 223–24
uprisings. *See* rebellions and uprisings

valientes (labor proxies), 185–88
Vargas, Fray Alonso de, 66, 68–69
Vargas, Gaspar de, 77–78
Vargas, Pablo de, 58–62, 63, 77–78, 243n50
vecinos (local notables), 44, 110, 121, 209–10, 216–18
Vega, Garcilaso de la, 12, 42
Velasco, Juan de, 203
Veracruz, ix, 18, 57
viceroys, 9, 35, 73, 115, 118, 127
Villa Alta, 224; district archive of, 24;

Yanna Yannakakis is an assistant professor of history in the Department of History, Philosophy, and Religious Studies at Montana State University.

Library of Congress Cataloging-in-Publication Data
Yannakakis, Yanna, 1967–
The art of being in-between : native intermediaries and the politics of indigenous identity in colonial Oaxaca, 1660–1810 / Yanna Yannakakis.
p. cm.
Includes bibliographical references and index.
ISBN 978-0-8223-4142-0 (cloth : alk. paper)
ISBN 978-0-8223-4166-6 (pbk. : alk. paper)
1. Oaxaca (Mexico: State)—Politics and government. 2. Mediators (Persons)—Mexico. 3. Indians of Mexico—Mexico—Oaxaca (State)—Government relations. 4. Intercultural communication—Mexico. 5. Spain—Colonies—Administration. I. Title.
F1321.Y36 2008
972'.7402—dc22   2007045755